W9-CAI-577

The Sociological Adventure

A Holistic Perspective

Peter Roche de Coppens

East Stroudsburg University

KENDALL/HUNT PUBLISHING COMPANY
4050 Westmark Drive   Dubuque, Iowa 52002

This book and all the inspiration and work that went into it, as well as all encouragement and inspiration it can provide for others, is dedicated to my cherished mother, Alice de Coppens, who has ever been a shining example of unconditional love and trust in this world for me. Much of what I have been able to accomplish and achieve in this life, including this work which she has inspired me to write and to publish, is due to her! Her courage, sense of beauty and love of life, her social tact and sensitivity to others, and her undying faith and striving for excellence have been my best "Guardian Angels" and the "living model" that anyone who strives for excellence must find somewhere and somehow. I am just ever so grateful that I found it so close to home! And so the Flame of Love, Light and Life is passed on and continues. . . .

Other Books By the Author

Ideal Man in Classical Sociology, Pennsylvania State University Press, 1976.

Spiritual Man in the Modern World, University Press of America, 1976.

The Nature and Use of Ritual, University Press of America, 1977, 1979.

Spiritual Perspective, University Press of America, 1980.

Spiritual Perspective II: The Spiritual Dimension and Implications of Love, Sex, and Marriage, University Press of America, 1981.

The Nature and Use of Ritual for Spiritual Attainment, Llewellyn Publications, 1985.

The Invisible Temple, Llewellyn Publications, 1987.

Apocalypse Now, Llewellyn Publications, 1988.

The Art of Joyful Thinking, with Dr. Jacques Pezé, Element, 1991.

Divine Light and Fire, Element Books, 1992.

Divine Light and Love, Element Books, 1994.

La Voie Initiatique de l'An 2000, Louise Courteau, 1994.

Vivere Sani in un Mondo Malato, Eta dell'Acquario, 1994.

Forthcoming Book

Man—the Sky-scraper (Italian and French version with a later English version).

NOTE: Throughout this book, I have used the words, "Man" to mean, of course, both **men** and **women**. For the sake of brevity, I have used the pronouns, "his" and "him" implying also "her." In selected places, I have also used the form "he/she" and "him/her" to anchor and emphasize the former.

In dealing with the "Divine Spark," the "Lord," the "Holy Spirit" and various manifestations of the Divine, I have used the pronouns "He/Him" and "It/Its" implying also "She/Her." This I have done fully recognizing that the Divine Essence, or God, is Androgenous, above and implying all genders, masculine and feminine, personal and transpersonal, singular and plural.

In dealing with quotations, I have not always indicated the specific book, page, and publisher as the aim of the present book is to be a **practical teaching manual for students** and not a **research book for scholars.** But I have been careful to cite the author of the quote or citation to give him/her full credit for the ideas and concepts involved.

For the same reason, I have not included a bibliography at the end of this work.

Contents

Foreword to the Third Edition

A little more than three years have elapsed since the publication of the Second Edition of *The Sociological Adventure*. Since that time, many things have happened to the book, to myself, and to the world. More people than ever before are now using this book and I have received much feedback from both students, colleagues and friends. While many people still really do not "know and understand" what I am talking about when I speak of "adding the spiritual dimension" to the social sciences in general and to sociology in particular, more and more persons are agreeing upon and requesting a **holistic perspective** that looks at human nature, human behavior, and human consciousness, as well as social structures and processes, not as isolated parts but rather as **interrelated and interacting parts** that are connected with the whole of creation, being affected by it and affecting it. That is very gratifying to me because I am firmly convinced that the days of a "rationalistic, reductionistic, materialistic, and mechanistic and analytical perspective and model" are gone forever.

Whether we take a macroperspective and look at the society and at the world and its problems or whether we take a microperspective and look at the individual and at his problems, it becomes increasingly clear that only a **holistic** perspective that stressed **synthesis** rather than **analysis** and that looks at everything as being related to—and affected by—everything else, can effectively cope with our rapidly expanding and intensifying problems. This is true of the medical field, both physical and psychological, but it is also true of the economy, of politics, religion, education or the family. People and events are simply not isolated parts or systems working independently of other parts and systems. And this was the first, fundamental, distinctive contribution of this book that yet demands an ongoing "refinement" and "adaptation." The other was the inclusion of the "spiritual dimension." Again, to my great encouragement and gratification, I found more and more students, colleagues, and lay persons who are developing a genuine and mature interest in spirituality; who are beginning to suspect that "there are no more viable solutions on the horizontal dimension, only on the vertical dimension," and that without a "spiritual" or expanded level of consciousness, it is no longer possible to make sense of our human experiences and of the increasing complexification of life.

During the last year, I have been preparing the manuscript for a book that should first be published in Italian, then in French, but, ultimately, also in English and whose title is *Man the Sky-scraper: the "vertical axe of human consciousness" as the true key to human understanding*. In this work, I am arguing that the way in which we perceive reality, both inner and outer, and everything that is: knowledge, health, sickness, and healing, good and evil, life and death, love and hatred etc., is a *function of our level of consciousness and being*. In other words, that in changing our level of consciousness (which can be done in different ways and to different extents by everyone) we can *change our reality*. It is as if a human beings were a sky-scraper and that our consciousness can move "up and down" the 100 floors of that sky-scraper. Now, obviously, if we look out of the window on the 1st, the 10th, the 40th, or the 100th floor, we will not see the same thing. Our perception enlarges or restricts itself depending on whether we move "up" or "down" the floors. And that is exactly what happens to our consciousness and which explains why we have so many different and conflicting theories, explanations, and viewpoints on practically every subject imaginable.

While the *holistic perspective* can be utilized and experienced on *all levels of consciousness and being* though, obviously not in the same way or degree, genuine *spiritual consciousness* is meaningless to persons who have not awakened it and who function only on lower levels of consciousness, the sensory, emotional, or mental ones. In mathematics and geometry we now speak of multiple *dimensions of reality* which interpenetrate each other. A three-dimensional object will manifest in a two-dimensional world but will lose its distinctive 3-d characteristics and the same applies to the 4th, 5th, and other dimensions manifesting at a lower level. They would leave their "signatures" or "lower-dimensional impacts" but lose their distinctive characteristics. So it is with spiritual consciousness. On the lower dimensions of sensory, emotional, and mental consciousness, spiritual consciousness manifests itself in such a way as to bring a great deal of vitality and creative energy, courage and appreciation for what one is going through, and as a way to accept the unacceptable and to be able to do things which appear impossible. These are the so-called "miracles" which are attributed to spiritually awakened persons who seem to be able to accomplish things which should not be possible but which, in fact, are not "supernatural." What occurs, in fact, is that "laws and principles" and "energies," which are not known or operative on lower states of consciousness and being, are accessed and manifested.

More than ever, I believe that "the 21st century will be spiritual... or will *not be*" (a famous statement attributed to the well-known French thinker André Malraux). Without the unfoldment and operation of spiritual consciousness, life in the physical and sociocultural level will become more and more difficult and less and less meaningful. The cherished goals of the "Age of Enlightenment": the development of reason, through education and science, and its application through industrialization and technological development; the inevitability of progress through education and research, and the revolution of rising expectation with the "security net" established through the Welfare State, are crumbling world-wide leaving people in general, and the youth in particular, more and more insecure, confused, frustrated and bewildered. To live exclusively for material and social gratification seems less and less possible and more and more meaningless as life complexifies and becomes more and more difficult.

Thus, as economic, political, and educational/scientific rewards become less and less accessible and more and more meaningless, the perennial questions of human *identity, origins, destiny,* and *duty* are coming to the foreground of our individual and collective pre-occupations. Who am I? Where do I come from? Where am I going? And what have I come to do in this world? These are the questions that are becoming increasingly more important for and ever larger number of persons. And these "fundamental questions" cannot possibly be satisfactorily answered without the awakening an proper functioning of spiritual consciousness. . . for the simple reason that a human being is, in his/her essence, a *spiritual being*. This is one of the reasons why I feel that the "emergence of spiritual consciousness and its public recognition" is unavoidable in the long run and why "spiritually oriented books and perspectives" will come into greater and greater demand—because they alone can satisfy a truly central need and ideal of our time.

Our society and historical period, so important to understand our own personal experience, in that there is always a very strict correspondence between the microcosm (the human personality and its consciousness) and the macrocosm (the sociocultural environment with its basic trends and dominant themes) is a very particular one. It is characterized by the "explosion of all the latent contradictions," by the emergence of all the opposites, which must, in one way or another, be reconciled, and thus by **fundamental paradoxes.** These paradoxes make it such that the very best and the very worst, life and death, heaven and hell, good and evil, become ever more accessible to an ever-increasing number of persons. We are all confronted with incredible **dangers** and **opportunities,** by great **risks** but also by great **rewards** which depend upon the *personal choices we make* by the proper functioning of our **discernment** and **intuition** which, in turn, depend on our **moral sense** and on the functioning of our **spiritual consciousness.**

The **Zeitgeist,** or "spirit of our times, is rooted upon by basic processes which determine much of the personal functioning of an individual as well as the proper functioning of society. These processes are, essentially five: **polarization** (one must take a position and become committed to something for even "doing nothing" is making a choice that will have objective and subjective consequences); **intentification** (everything is becoming more intense and powerful, for good or for evil); **acceleration** (what used to take months, weeks or days is now taking hours, minutes, seconds and even microseconds); the **"psychologization of reality"** (what we consider "our reality" is more and more a psychosocial construction and less and less a "material reality"); and, the **expansion of consciousness** (human consciousness, like the universe are **expanding,** changing, and transforming themselves before our very eyes).

These are the reasons why a classical and traditional sociology, psychology, or anthropology, based on a **homo duplex** conception of human nature and human behavior, where the material, or biopsychic, and the human, or sociocultural, dimensions are no longer an adequate framework to explain the dynamics of society or the personal vicissitudes of an individual. Something "more," another "perspective," set of variables, or framework, is now becoming an absolute necessity. For, without this, we can no longer either explain causally or understand humanly the structures and processes of society or the psychosocial dynamics of an individual and of his personal experiences. To my mind, what is "missing" and what this book provides is the old/new framework and emerging perspective of the **holistic approach** and of the **spiritual dimension.** Armed with these new "variables," it becomes, once again possible to make rational sense of what we are all living, both as spectators and as actors. Human nature, human behavior, human consciousness as well as sociocultural structures, processes, and dynamics become, once again, transparent and meaningful. We can relate to them, understand our nature and our role, and our specific "vocation" or "duty" in the world and in the society in which we live.

Through this "new" way of "looking at things" and of "perceiving and interpreting reality," we can regain what we had lost along the way; namely, **hope, courage,** the **desire to live,** and the appreciation for the manyfold vicissitudes, trials and tests, of the human condition. Our minds, our hearts, and our wills are, thereby, nourished, vitalized, and vivified so that we can, once again, **long**

for the human adventure sustained by a new and growing consciousness that enables us to say a big "YES" to Life and to welcome all of its challenges, dangers and opportunities, and to unfold and manifest what the French aptly call "la joie de vivre" and which is the "signature" of true maturity and wisdom.

This is why I enthusiastically contributed to and welcome the "birthing" of the third edition of this work. Much has remained the same as in the previous editions but, together with some necessary corrections, I have added the present "preface" together with three more "appendices" consisting of the texts of lectures, which I have presented to diverse audiences in different countries and where both the "holistic approach" and the "spiritual dimension" are emphasized and given priority. I welcome the comments, criticism, and contributions of colleagues, students, and interested persons alike who are welcome to contact me through the publisher or through the organizers of the conferences and symposia in which I participate. Get in touch and let us know, this is only the "beginning," the first tentative "model," and some important "fragments" of a new and exciting adventure, the great adventure of human life and the unfoldment of human consciousness to ever greater heights and deeper depths, leading to new horizons and new creations. In this "new creation" we are all both "creators" and "creatures" for we co-create both ourselves and the world in which we live with God, our father, Nature our mother, and society/culture our offsprings.

Peter Roche de Coppens
East Stroudsburg, PA. USA
October 1995

Preface

Roche de Coppens is a pioneer—a pioneer on three counts: the first because he proposes a holistic approach to the study of sociology; the second because he does so in an introductory text; the third because he has the expectation that exposure to this holistic approach will go beyond mere understanding and appreciation of a cognitive model. The text will actually have an impact on the "personal lives" of those who read it.

This treatise then breaks new ground, not only for sociology, but for all the social sciences and perhaps for all those dedicated to the liberation of human potential. Indebted to the theoretical and methodological contributions of Henri Bergson, Pitirim Sorokin, Mircea Eliade, and Roberto Assagioli, Roche de Coppens has made an original contribution to the field. Further, he has made that contribution in a language and style that can be readily understood and utilized by the uninitiated inquirer.

Being a pioneer, he will undoubtedly have to "circle the wagons," fight off the "hostiles," and go where "few have ever gone before." His ability to do just that has been well-documented by his prior publications and his professional life. What makes this instance just a bit different is that Roche de Coppens has chosen to expose the mind and spirit of those yet uninitiated to the field of the scientific study of psychosocial interaction. It promises to be an exhilarating experience for both author and reader: for the author, because this is the beginning of a long and arduous journey involving the development and fine tuning of a conceptual system for an intellectual discipline; for the reader, because this could be the first step of a journey into something more than cognitive discourse with fellow students and/or intellectual mentors.

Roche de Coppens speaks of his world of sociology much like Dr. Richard Feynman (*The Feynman Lectures on Physics, 1963*) speaks of his world of physics.

"We can imagine that this complicated array of moving things which constitutes 'the world' is something like a great chess game being played by the gods, and we are observers of the game. We do not know what the rules of the game are; all we are allowed to do is to watch the playing. Of course, if we watch long enough, we may eventually catch on to a few of the rules. The rules of the game are what we mean by fundamental physics."

Dr. Roche de Coppens, in his holistic approach to sociology, would agree with Feynman that knowing the rules of the game would constitute perhaps fundamental sociology. That the world is like a chess game, and that by observation we are able to identify and put together a set of rules concerning how the game is being played, represents a succinct way of stating our personal level of sophistication in such an intellectual enterprise. I am not convinced that he would agree totally with Feynman's next statement however.

"Even if we know every rule, . . . what we really can explain in terms of those rules is very limited, because almost all situations are so enormously complicated that we cannot follow the plays of the game using the rules, much less tell what is going to happen next. We must, therefore, limit ourselves to the more basic question of the rules of the game. If we know the rules, we consider that we 'understand' the world."

Roche de Coppens would say, as I am sure Feynman would, that we can go just a bit further than merely understanding the world. There arise occasions in which we can, if we are willing to take the risk, enter into this cosmic chess game. We are able to make tentative moves using what rules we have observed. We are able to experience the thrill of playing the game regardless of how inconsequential or insignificant our involvement might be. The rewards, he would say, are worth the risk; for in making that move, in utilizing that rule, we expose ourselves to even greater insight and understanding of the great game all of us need to play.

Roche de Coppens wishes to go beyond rules identification and "understanding." He feels it is absolutely essential to expand human consciousness in order to achieve personal growth and self-actualization. In Roche de Coppens' own words the thrust of this work is "to enable students to better respond to the two fundamental classical injunctions: 'man know thyself' and 'man realize thyself' . . . leading students to know themselves and perfect themselves."

This objective is not unusual for mentors to specify for their students; what is unusual is for an author to have such exalted goals for an introductory monograph and to provide the opportunity for the professoriate to do the same. This is made possible by the utilization of this work in an environment conducive to the development of the capacities of human consciousness. The degree of success of both student and professor will be measured in the changed lives of the students and not in terms of scores on tests nor the content of term papers.

The holistic perspective of Roche de Coppens takes as a core concept "human nature" in a socio-cultural world and its manifestation in the integration of three interrelated systems: the biophysic which is a shared study of biology and psychology; the psychosocial studied by sociology, anthropology and other social sciences; and the spiritual which is the focus of transpersonal psychology and psychosynthesis. It is a developing discipline recognizing the application of the "scientific method" to this aspect of human nature; heretofore, the province of religion and parapsychology. It is this aspect of human consciousness that Roche de Coppens would say has been ignored in the investigation of sociology from the perspective of a holistic science.

In a word, Roche de Coppens is hypothesizing more rules that should increase our understanding of the "great" game. Beyond that, he is providing opportunities to use these rules and actually try our hand at playing the game. The extent to which we wish to commit ourselves to that endeavor is a function of the success we have already had at integrating our biophysic, psychosocial, and spiritual human nature and our willingness to take some risks.

Sociology studies the nature, genesis, and dynamics of the interaction of human beings. The "what" of that interaction is human consciousness, a preexistent condition of being human and a quality to be developed by the nature of the world and universe in which we find ourselves. Human consciousness then has three dimensions: cognitive, affective, and conative. The author then must somehow integrate the dimensions of "human nature," previously discussed, and "human consciousness" in a manner that recognizes the parameters of the discipline of sociology. Further, this task must be accomplished in a manner that, on the one hand is pragmatic for the academic community and, on the other challenging and dynamic for the student.

"Enlightenment is any experience of expanding our consciousness beyond its present limits. We could also say that perfect enlightenment is realizing that we have no limits at all, and that the entire universe is alive," so said Thaddeus Golas in *The Lazy Man's Guide to Enlightenment*. Certainly, Roche de Coppens, by this definition, will enlighten all who read this book. It represents a step toward that perfect enlightenment that will convince us that human consciousness has few limitations and that we are part and parcel members all of a universe alive.

James E. Gilbert, Ph.D., President

Chapter 1

Introduction

From time immemorial, it has rightly been claimed by all the great Traditions and their various intellectual perspectives—spiritual, philosophical, and scientific, and even literary—that the ultimate end of fruitful intellectual inquiry and endeavor is to KNOW MAN SO AS TO IMPROVE AND PERFECT HIM. If, therefore, the ultimate goal of cognitive explorations and developments is **self-knowledge, self-mastery,** and **self-integration**—the knowledge and improvement of human nature, consciousness, and behavior, then any academic discipline, if it is to be worthy of its calling and, more important, *if it is to perform a vital, significant, and humanly enriching service to its students,* must, in its own domain and ways, further these two great ends. Specifically, it must accomplish two fundamental tasks on two distinct levels, that is:

A. At the academic, formal, level, it must:
   a. Provide an integrated theoretical framework that will significantly add to man's overall cognitive universe; i.e., to his general body of knowledge.
   b. Provide specific and practical **paradigms** (i.e., sets of principles, "tools," and guidelines) which can profitably be integrated in a person's daily life so as to enrich it by better understanding and being able to deal with its specific domain and set of questions.

B. At the personal, existential, level, it must:
   a. Be directly related, or, at least, capable of being concretely related, to its students' **personal self** so as to increase their self-knowledge and self-mastery.
   b. Be directly connected or, at least, capable of being connected in practical ways, to its students' **personal lives** in their sociocultural environments, so as to lead them to fuller, richer, more creative and happy lives.

In fulfilling these fundamental tasks, any academic discipline—be it sociology, psychology, religion, history, or philosophy—will then contribute to what I consider to be absolutely essential for our times, namely to the **expansion of human consciousness** and to **personal growth and self-actualization.** In other words, it will lead to the **conscious actualization of human potentialities and faculties**—which are the true goal of a life well-lived. And it will move its students in the direction of being better able to answer the two fundamental classical injunctions: "Man, know thyself" and "Man, realize thyself." And thus justify its existence by leading its students to "know themselves" so as to "perfect themselves."

Different disciplines have different contributions to make to self-knowledge and self-realization, at different points of human evolution, but they must all make some significant, lasting, and distinctive contribution to justify their existence and the time, energies, and resources involved in them. This was the strong feeling of Lester Ward, the "American Aristotle," and one of the founding fathers of American sociology, and they are also mine.

At a time when human beings were primarily interested in their origin and in the metaphysical essence of their being and of the world, it was **theology** which was the "Queen of the Sciences" and the field that enjoyed the greatest prestige and attention. When human beings became more interested in relating and integrating their growing knowledge in a coherent and meaningful system, it was **philosophy** which emerged as the central discipline. Then, when human beings became more concerned with knowing the world so as to harness its raw materials and energies to improve their standard of living, it was the **natural sciences** that came into the foreground—as the greatest of all of man's creations and as the only "valid' avenue" by which to gather objective and useful knowledge. Today, however, as our value system and major concerns are, again, going through a major "paradigm shift" or qualitative transformation—from the physical world to human nature, human consciousness, and human relations, it might well be **sociology** that will emerge as one of the key disciplines of the near-future.

Sociology, however, one looks at it as profound and very practical contributions to make modern man in his quest for self-knowledge, for understanding the world in which he lives, and achieving self-realization therein. It is some of the most basic theoretical and practical contributions of sociology that we shall consider and analyze in this work. Please bear in mind that though sociology is a relatively young science and art, which is still in the process of laying down its foundations and articulating its basic insights and principles, it is, nevertheless, a highly intricate and complex discipline and that, as such, it requires years of study and practice to be properly understood and assimilated.

2

What is Sociology?

One can find perhaps as many definitions, conceptions, and explanations of what sociology is and does as there are great sociologists. Sociology, like the other social sciences and the humanities, is a field in which different definitions of the **same concept** and different interpretations of the **same phenomena** abound. This is due not so much to the fact that social scientists are "individualistic" or "fuzzy" thinkers," as to the fact that any discipline focusing upon human nature and human behavior can approach its area of investigation from many different existential viewpoints, value orientations, levels of human consciousness, and, therefore, **intellectual perspectives.** Thus, a certain flexibility of thinking, a creative and imaginative mindset and, yes, **humility,** are vital requisites for any serious student of the social sciences.

While there is plenty of diversity of personal opinion and of **contradictions** in our discipline, there is also a growing consensus as to what sociology **is** and **does.** My aim, in this work, is to lead you to understand what the essence of sociology is, seen from my particular frame of reference or **perspective.** Sociology has been variously defined as:

a. The Science of Man and Society
b. The systematic study of social institutions and social processes.
c. The scientific study of human interaction.

I would briefly define sociology as: "The intellectual adventure which explores the nature, causes, and consequences of human interaction;" or, even more simply put: "The adventure of becoming aware of what happens when one human being meets other human beings." The world of sociology, therefore, comes into being whenever human beings encounter each other . . . or the fruits of human interaction. . . . And, a little reflection will readily show us how, knowingly or not, all of us live in the world of sociology from the cradle to the grave and from the time we wake up in the morning to the time we fall asleep at night.

Sociology studies man meeting man and doing that with man, that is, the nature, causes and consequences of human interaction. As such, it has three fundamental objects:

a. First man himself or, rather, a specific part of human nature.
b. Then, the relationship of one human being to other human beings.
c. Finally, the fruits or creations of man's relationship with other human beings.

To be sure, sociology does not study the **whole man,** but only a **part** of man, what we call man's psychosocial nature—its nature, origin, unfoldment, expression, and completion. Thus sociology does not study man's *physical,* or animal *nature; it* does not study, directly, man's *spiritual,* or divine, *nature.* What it studies is man's *human or psychosocial nature*—how this nature was "born," how it is fed or maintained, and how it can further develop and realize itself. Sociology also studies what **part** of man interacts with what **part** when two or more human beings meet, and what "results," or is "being created," from this "coming together" of human beings. As you will see later, what sociology focuses on is not the interaction between **bodies** or the interaction between **spirits** but, rather, the interaction between **two or more human natures**—which is something quite different!

Finally, sociology studies the fruits or "creations" of man's relationship with other human beings—what we call the *sociocultural environment* in which men live which is different from the **physical** or the **spiritual** environment. Moreover, sociology studies human interaction as related to man's psychosocial nature and sociocultural environment in terms of its *objective and subjective consequences,* namely: of its consequences in the world and in man, of what happens to a person and of how that person interprets what has happened. In technical language, sociology studies the interrelationships between the **social system,** the **personality system,** and **the cultural system.**

Sociology explores the nature, genesis, and dynamics of human interaction. Fine, but when man meets man, **what interacts with what?** Earlier we stated that it was a person's **human nature** that interacted with the **human or psychosocial nature** of other persons. Now we can ask specifically, what precisely is **human nature?** And what are its key dimensions and characteristics? Briefly put, the **human** or **psychosocial nature** of a person is his **human consciousness**—what he came on earth to express, unfold, and realize. Human consciousness, for sociology, has three major dimensions: *thinking, feeling and willing*—what we call the "cognitive," "affective," and "conative" processes of the psyche. Human consciousness, moreover, embodies, at the existential level, the very essence of man—what the Holy Trinity is at the ontological level (The Father: Divine Knowledge, the Son: Divine Love, and the Holy Spirit: Divine Creative Energy or Life). A person is, indeed what he/she knows, loves, wills, and can do, and not what he/she looks like or owns! The physiological and morphological differences between an idiot and a genius are very small, indeed, and bank accounts can go up and down rapidly without changing the person in his essence. But what a person knows, loves, and can create are

4

truly his unique and distinctive features which will remain with him and characterize him for a long time—even though they, too, undergo an evolution and a growth process.

In studying the nature, genesis, and unfoldment of human interaction, therefore, sociology is studying the basic processes by which human consciousness—thinking, feeling and willing—are born, expressed, and expanded. When human beings meet and do things with each other it is, therefore, their *thoughts,* their *feelings,* and their *wills* that interact with each other and not their bodies or their possessions. Emile Durkheim went as far as claiming that when human beings interact with each other, an "effervescent milieu" is created from the process of social interaction where a "creative psychic synthesis" is brought about . . . which is the new reality sui generis which he called "society." Thoughts mixing with thoughts generate new thoughts in a chain reaction; feelings meeting feelings engender new feelings, and wills facing wills liberate new energies. Thus is man's human or psychosocial nature engendered, nurtured, expanded, and realized—through the creative psychic synthesis resulting from human interaction.

The **existential** essence of man—what he knows, what he loves, and what he does, and his **capacity** for knowing, loving, and creating and acting—is elicited and structured by his *network of human relationships.* As the Greeks used to say in a brilliant sociological insight before modern times, "Man (at the *human* level) is a "zoon politikon," a "social being," and "intelligence is the daughter of the city;" i.e., the product of social life. For a long time, Europeans used to say that a **civilized person** was a person who had a rich and diversified network of social relations and social life, while a **primitive person** was one who lived in relative isolation with few human relations to fashion his or her psychosocial nature. Finally, Durkheim went as far as claiming that **self-control**—one of the distinguishing features of human beings—is the product of social discipline and that all of man's great ideals, values, customs, laws, and ideas—and, consequently, all of his social institutions are born and maintained by the creative psychic synthesis springing from varied and intensified social interactions.

An important point to note, however, is that **human interaction** does not *create,* or bring about *ex nihilo,* human consciousness but rather translates it from **potentiality into actuality.** It is true that infants or human beings who had lived in complete or semi-complete isolation were human only in their **appearances,** but not in their behavior; that is, they could not speak, think, feel, will, and act in a humanly meaningful fashion. Yet, they had the inherent potential for human consciousness that animals or machines will never be able to acquire in their entirety. From my

5

standpoint, therefore, I would contend that the potentialities and the latent structures of human consciousness, of the psychosocial nature of man, are **spiritual** in nature and origin, rather than being social; that social life and human interaction do not **create** human consciousness, rather that they **elicit, bring out, and actualize,** concretely and specifically, the **spiritual potentialities and structures** of man's human nature—in short, that they *translate preexistent* **potentialities** *into concrete* **actualities.**

My conclusion, therefore, just as that of contemporary sociology, is that man's distinctive trait, his **human consciousness**—what he knows, loves, and does—is engendered, nurtured, and expanded by his patterns of human interaction; that it is his **social life** that is the primary humanizing agent to enable him to become more and more of what he is potentially. Sociology, therefore, is the discipline which, in studying the nature, causes, and consequences of human interaction, is studying the origin, expression, and unfoldment of what is distinctively human in man and his greatest achievement—**human consciousness.** Contemporary sociology examines this process through the interrelationship of what it terms the **personality system** (the psychic structures wherewith man thinks, feels, wills, speaks, and acts—the **Psyche**), the **cultural system** (the great values, ideals, ideas, norms, and beliefs institutionalized by society), and the **social system** (the specific network of interacting human beings). Briefly put, it claims that the personality system internalizes specific and partial aspects of the cultural system through the agency of the social system.

One of the central aims of one of the major contemporary sociological perspectives, structural-functionalism, is to develop and to articulate a theory of **social action,** that is, to describe, analyze, and explain the conscious and meaningful aspects of human behavior—what people do in society. It does so by beginning to observe people's behavior or collective endeavors. Then, it works its way back to the **consciousness that structured this action pattern. Human Consciousness** Is subdivided into two basic categories: the actors' **intentions** and the actors' **motivation.** The first is the actors' conscious and rational motives for acting the way they do, while the second is the **subconscious** level of forces, both biopsychic and psychosocial, which drive them to do what they are doing. The key to unlock social behavior and to explain why a person acts the way he or she does resides in his or her **human** consciousness, in his or her ways of thinking, feeling, and willing; for it is the **will,** structured and directed by **thought** and activated and dynamized by **desire,** which guides and fashions a person's actions. In order to understand the motivational structures of the actor's ways of thinking, feeling, and willing, this approach utilizes the twin perspectives of a **psychodynamic** approach—knowledge of the workings of man's personality—and of a **sociocultural** approach—knowledge of the structures, values, ideals, ideas, norms, and beliefs operating in the society in which the actors live, move, and have their being. Modern sociology, in other words, seeks to expand, deepen, and heighten our awareness, knowledge, and understanding of ourselves, as **psychosocial beings,** and of the world in which we live at the **sociocultural level.**

Why does modern sociology seek to give a human being a greater knowledge of a central part of himself and of a key dimension of the world in which he lives? Why does sociology aim at expanding human consciousness? Simply because, as religion and other disciplines, its highest objective is to enable beings to live more full, conscious, and useful lives by becoming more "fully human," by actualizing the potentialities and faculties of their human nature—which is their ultimate purpose while here on earth and the fundamental reason why they have incarnated in this world! In helping man to gain systematic and precise knowledge and understanding of what he is (at the **psychosocial** level), of how he became what he is, and of what he might yet **become,** as well as of the nature, origins, and dynamics of the **sociocultural** environment in which man lives—in leading man to expand and actualize his human consciousness so as to lead a more full, conscious, and creative life, sociology is fully rooted in the great humanistic tradition whose central core has always been described by the ancient injunction: "O Man, know thyself, realize thyself, become thy Higher Self!"

While sociology has made **human interaction** and the twin products of the **creative psychic synthesis** it brings about— **human consciousness** in the person and **culture** in society—its specific domain and object of investigation, it must also unfold a larger and more synthetic connection and integration with what lies **below** and **above** its specific province. In other words, if its direct concern and areas of investigation is the **human** world, it must also have some basic notions of the "subhuman," or biological world, and of the "superhuman" or spiritual world. This not because it must encroach upon other territories or abandon the scientific method, but simply because it must be **holistic,** because physical and spiritual forces and agents do have an impact upon and influence human forces. As for the first, early sociology gave a great deal of time and attention to the connections of the emerging sociology with physics and biology which became its main "points of reference" and models. Then, it emancipated itself from them to fully articulate and unfold itself but, in so doing, it narrowed its basic perspective and vision and cut itself off from the infinite

7

forces and agents of reality both **below** and **above** itself that exist in the cosmos.

It is now my plea that modern sociology develop a **holistic** approach and that it integrate the emerging **spiritual dimension** of both Man and the World. As we well know, man is not a finished product, but an unfinished product undergoing an evolution, a self-actualizing product, and human consciousness is a dynamic entity still unfolding and expanding. One of the distinctive features of our age is the reemergence and rediscovered importance of **spirituality** and **spiritual consciousness** (a topic that I have more fully investigated in my last 7 books (*Spiritual Man in the Modern World, The Nature and Use of Ritual, Spiritual Perspective I, Spiritual Perspective II, The Nature* and *Use of Ritual for Spiritual Attainment, The Invisible Temple,* and *Apocalypse Now.*) What I see as happening, at the end of the 20th Century and at the beginning of the 21st Century is the birth and unfoldment of a **Spiritual Science** as well as a shift in emphasis from **Analysis** to **Synthesis**—from studying more and more about less and less to seeking to establish relationships wider and wider in the microcosm and macrocosm as well as at **qualitatively** different levels of consciousness and reality. If this assumption is correct, then sociology will have to recognize, integrate, and articulate the aspects and implications that follow from these. I see this connection and integration between an emerging **spiritual science** and a growing and maturing **sociology** in the following terms: Spiritual Science investigates three fundamental objects: God, Humanity, and Nature in the World, and the Spirit, Psyche, and Body, in Man; and three basic sets of relationships, or interactions: that of Man with God, of Man with Man, and of Man with Nature; and finally, that of the conscious self with the Superconscious, with the Conscious, and with the Unconscious. It works basically from **above below,** from Vision and Revelation to reason and observation, bringing greater Light, which is also Life, to the Field of Consciousness so as to expand it and amplify it.

Sociology, on the other hand, investigates basically two objects: Human Nature or, specifically, one dimension of Man—his psychosocial nature—and the World or, specifically, one dimension of the World—the sociocultural environment. It investigates, describes, analyzes, and explains the birth, growth, and expressions of **human consciousness** and its externalizations, concretizations, and consequences. It also examines the relation of Man to Man, the interaction between different human consciousnesses and their creative psychic syntheses. And it does this in a disciplined fashion by utilizing the "tools" of observation, reason, and experience at the conscious level. Moreover, it works, essentially, from **below**

8

upwards, from observation and reason to intuition, ever seeking to expand the sphere of the Consciousness into the vast, unexplored areas of the personal and collective Subconscious and Unconscious. This then might perhaps be the point at which maturing and unfolding sociology might meet an emerging spiritual science that brings the Superconscious into the Conscious: the attempt to expand and actualize human consciousness and its faculties so as to enable Man to lead a fuller, more conscious, creative, and happy life—to empower human beings to know and understand their whole **selves** and the **whole** world, in which they live, so as to realize that Higher Self in the world and to actualize **all** its faculties and potentialities. This "holistic approach" and added "spiritual dimension" should make sociology one of the most fascinating and, intellectually rewarding, adventures that any student and scholar can ever get into. It is my hope that it will prove to be such for many of you who are reading this book and who are taking my sociology courses. This work and the courses I teach are but steps on a long journey of many miles, but was it not said a long time ago by the ancient Chinese that the "journey of a thousand miles begins with the first step?"

Chapter 2

Sociological Perspectives

Sociology, as we have seen in the previous chapter, is the *disciplined study of human interaction, of its nature, causes, and consequences.* Human interaction brings about a "creative psychic synthesis" that unfolds and manifests a new dimension of reality, **the human dimension,** and it translates the potentialities of our human consciousness into actuality. Thus, in the individual, it unfolds **human consciousness** while in society, it generates **culture.** As such, it entails the systematic study of **human consciousness** as it arises out of human interaction and manifests in human interaction, and of **culture** as it is externalized and objectified by human consciousness and internalized by society. Human interaction, or relationships, involve the interaction between relatives, friends, coworkers, etc. and can take place in small groups, large organizations, or even entire societies. Sociology focuses on the different patterns of social behavior within these contexts and on the way a given social milieu and personal background influence people's actions.

Sociologists begin their work by looking at the social world and by choosing a given topic, issue or problem, they want to describe, analyze, and explain. Thus, they collect data that will help them understand the social phenomenon or process they are interested in, be it suicide, unemployment, the changing size and structure of the family, or population shifts. They also study systematically the behavior of both **individuals** (the microperspective) and of **groups** (the macroperspective). And they do this through different **explanatory perspectives,** or theoretical frameworks, the most important of which are today the *Structural-Functional,* or "Consensus" approach, the *Conflict,* or "Marxist" approach, and the *Interactionism* approach. To these, some authors have added the *social exchange theory, ethnomethodology,* and the *dramaturgical* approach—which are not quite as important and diffused as the former. Finally, one could add, as it is my intention, the one that I am proposing—a *holistic,* or "Integral" approach which seeks to combine and integrate all of the foregoing at a higher level of

11

abstraction, adding and emphasizing the *spiritual dimension of human nature and the universe.*

Most of the theoretical perspectives, or approaches, mentioned above (but with the exception of the *holistic* approach I am suggesting) take a **psychosocial** view of human nature. That is, they look at a human being as a **homo duplex**, as having two essential natures: the **biopsychic nature**, the body or biological organism, originating in and being shaped by Nature, or the material world, and the **psychosocial nature**, the "Mind" or human consciousness, originating in and being shaped by Society. The "Conflict," or Marxist, approach, however, in its original formulation and roots, takes a **biopsychic** approach to human nature. That is, it looks at a human being as having **one** essential nature, the physical or biopsychic one. Here, Man is essentially his body, human consciousness being but a **byproduct**, or an "efflorescence" of physical and biochemical processes. Interactionism, on the other hand, while still taking an essentially **psychosocial** view of human nature, is open to or "thrusting towards" a **bio-psycho-spiritual** view of human nature which includes and integrates the *spiritual dimension* of human nature and of the universe in its perspective.

As human evolution continues and as human consciousness unfolds and actualizes its manifold potentials and faculties, as Life and human societies and cultures complexify and differentiate further, we have now reached a crucial **transition point.** A point in which spiritual consciousness is now unfolding and manifesting in the psyche and lives of many people, bringing with it new, emergent **needs** and **aspirations** that must be listened to and answered. Whence the need for a major "paradigm shift" and a "qualitative" addition to the house of science in general—**Spiritual Science**—and to sociology in particular—**the spiritual dimension.**

Sciences differ from one another, and different "schools" within each science, in the **perspective** they adopt to analyze and explain the phenomena at hand. Thus, biologists tend to look for explanations in terms of genetic factors and economists in terms of market factors. Political scientists tend to pose and answer questions in terms of the characteristics and processes of political systems; psychologists of individual, psychic processes, and sociologists of human interaction and social system attributes. Thus, it is not so much **where** the disciplines or "schools" want to go that differentiates them, nor is it the manner in which they proceed; rather, it is **where they are coming from**—it is in the *choice of key explanatory variables that characterize the "perspective" of the discipline.* Sociology has two major classes of **perspectives:** the macrostructural perspective, emphasizing explanatory variables that are social-structural in nature, and the micro-interpretative perspective, emphasizing social-psychological explanations. From the macro-structural perspective, the cause of variation in human behavior lies in the *structure of the social system*. Here, people's actions are explained in terms of the forces that impinge upon the *social positions they occupy in the social system*. From the micro-interpretative perspective, the cause of variation of human behavior stems from their perceptions and definitions of their situations. The basic idea here being simply that *people act as they do because there are basic norms, or rules, telling them how to act,* and because people usually **know** and **obey** the rules. It follows logically, from this viewpoint, that it is possible to explain people's actions, *if we know the rules that govern the relevant situation they face in their society.* These rules, expectations, or "norms," constitute the **normative structure of society.** Moreover, here sociologists must discover whether the actor **knows** the rules, how important they are to him, and how he perceives them to apply to a concrete, specific situation.

The macro-structural perspective is, basically, external to the actors while the micro-interpretative is internal. The first concentrates on action that is chosen, intentional, and conscious. The other focuses on factors that mold our behavior often without our awareness, consciousness, or choice. One is collectivistic, the other individualistic. One begins with the premise that reality is a "hard" social fact (from the position of Emile Durkheim) with which we must learn to cope. The other arises from the assumption that reality is a "fragile construction" (from the position of Max Weber and Peter Berger) depending on consensus and always subject to change. Both perspectives are valid and complement each other. The Structural-Functional and the Conflict perspectives fall in the macro-structural approaches while Interactionism falls within the micro-interpretative approaches.

Today, the most important and influential "perspectives," "approaches," or "theoretical paradigms" are **Structural-Functionalism, Conflict Theory,** and **Interactionism.** A "perspective," "approach," or "theoretical paradigm" is a general approach to the study of reality, and a set of assumptions and interrelated core concepts that provide an essential way of seeing the world. It is also a fundamental image of society that suggests the basic questions that should be asked and how the answers, provided by research, should be interpreted. Let us now look in turn and analyze each of these major "perspectives."

Structural-Functionalism

Early sociologists noticed the similarities that existed between biological organisms and human societies. Biological organisms, they noted, of which the human body is the most complex example, are composed of a variety of "structures," or organs, that serve different functions for the whole organism. These organs, such as the brain, the heart, and the stomach, are related in complex ways that enable the whole organism to function properly in maintaining **equilibrium.** Human societies also have a variety of "structures," or social institutions, that serve various interrelated functions necessary for maintaining a properly functioning, or balanced society. The essence of the Structural-Functional approach is that *each structure serves a basic function for society.* Moreover, the function of a social institution is not the conscious purpose for which the institution was designed but, rather, the *consequences,* or effects, *that the social institution has on the rest of society.*

The Beginnings of Structural-Functionalism

Comte and Spencer

The analogy between biological organisms and human societies was first suggested by Auguste Comte and by Herbert Spencer. Then, this analogy was revived by American sociologists in the 1930's.

Spencer claimed that human societies evolve from simple to complex forms pretty much as the biological organisms of the species evolved. And Spencer's work and conclusions became the foundation for the philosophy of social Darwinism. Its basic premise being that without government interference, a society would either prosper or die and that the process of the "survival of the fittest" was very desirable as it would enable the "best" individuals and societies to survive and to improve themselves.

Emile Durkheim

By far the most important analysis of the social order, from an objective viewpoint, came from Durkheim who investigated many social phenomena and processes including religion, education, suicide, and the law. He suggested that one of the main differences between primitive, traditional, and modern societies was to be found in the kind of "social cement," social solidarity or social cohesion they unfolded and which became the basis of their social order. In primitive and traditional societies, social solidarity and order were derived from **shared values and beliefs, that is, social cohesion was ensured by similarities.** In modern industrial societies, on the other hand, social cohesion was based on "functional interdependence" which made "individualism" and ideological differences both possible and tolerated.

Contemporary Structural-Functionalism

Parsons and Merton

Talcott Parsons, whose voluminous theoretical writings were influenced by Durkheim (as well as by Max Weber), suggested that human societies develop social institutions, or "structures," to serve certain functions that are essential to the survival of society. Thus, economic institutions serve society by producing and distributing goods and services required and demanded by the members of society. Political institutions establish common goals and develop policies to achieve these goals. Religious institutions function to minimize the disruption of society by human frailties and contingencies and reinforce societal values and norms. The legal and educational institutions serve to hold societies together and to integrate individuals and groups into functioning units. Each institution has important consequences, or functions to perform, for society and all these functions are interrelated mutually influencing each other.

Robert Merton, who was influenced by Parsons, pointed out that the actions of social institutions and of individuals can be **functional** or **dysfunctional** for society. Social institutions, sometimes, have **dysfunctions,** that is, consequences that fail to serve the well being of society and that may even disrupt it. These institutions will act in such ways as to threaten societal equilibrium.

Merton also pointed out that while some of the consequences of the actions of social institutions or individuals are *obvious and intended,* other consequences are *hidden and unintended.* These are called **manifest functions** and **latent functions.** One of the latent functions of American schools, for example, is to act as a "marriage clearing house" where potential marital partners can meet.

Structural-functionalists are essentially concerned with the problem of **social order,** and with the Hobbsian question: *How can society exist? How does it manage to endure over time?* They regard **shared norms, values, beliefs,** and **symbols** as the fundamental basis of the social order, or the "social cement," and examine the various ways in which members of society come to acquire and internalize them. They also focus upon the rewards and benefits people gain from conforming to the expectations of society and their losses if they do not.

Critiques of Structural-Functionalism

Structural-Functionalism has been criticized for tending to support the existing social system, or the status quo. This view suggests that structural-functionalists are often conservative, that their perspective implicitly holds that social institutions contributing to social harmony are good for society (they say YES to society and to the existing establishment). But this view fails to take into account the concept of **dysfunction** which suggests that certain institutions, may, in fact, be **harmful** for society, or at least for some of its members.

Another problem here deals with the method of Structural-Functionalism. Whether an institution or the action of an individual is called **functional** or **dysfunctional** depends on the sociologist's values and point of reference. For example, a conservative sociologist might see high corporate profits as being functional for society in that they provide resources for reinvestment and economic growth, while a liberal sociologist might see these same high profits as dysfunctional in that they are acquired by "underpaying" workers. Yet, both interpretations would be consistent with a structural-functional perspective.

A final criticism of this perspective is that it overemphasizes **societal harmony** and, thereby, minimizes the importance of **conflict** and **change.** Structural-Functionalism sometimes implies that there is a great deal of consensus on societal norms, values, beliefs when, in fact, even the most harmonious of societies include groups that differ in some of their norms, values, and beliefs. Some structural-functionalists attempted to develop theories of conflict and change (Parsons Shils, and Bales) but their efforts have been less satisfactory than those of conflict theorists.

Applications of Structural-Functionalism: The Family

A structural-functionalist would investigate the consequences of the family for its members and for the rest of society in the following terms: The family

1. provides companionship and intimacy with sexual expressions.
2. reproduces new members of society.
3. trains, educates, and socializes children.

As the primary agent of reproduction and socialization, the family enables a society to endure through time. Early childhood training by family lays the foundation for the educational system to continue this work by making sure that children have internalized certain norms, values, beliefs, and symbols. Structural-functionalists would also investigate the division of labor within the family.

Conflict Theory

The conflict perspective encompasses several approaches to the study of society. All of these have certain basic foci, the most important of which are stress on **conflict** and **competition** for scarce resources such as **wealth, power,** and **prestige.** This perspective sees society as in a state of continual flux and change, emphasizing the sources of change, rather than the bases of order, in all societies. Conflict theory also looks at how some groups acquire power and maintain dominance over other groups, asking questions such as: **who gains** and **who loses** from the way that society is organized. And it suggests that groups will act on the basis of self-interest and may even resort to violence to achieve their important goals.

The Marxist Perspective

Karl Marx, the most influential of the early conflict theorists, claimed that the **economic system is the ultimate source of social behavior and social institutions.** Marx was concerned with conflict among groups that had different relationships to the "means of production," i.e., the resources, technology, factories, and labor used to produce goods and services. Marx observed that control over the means of production led some groups to oppress and exploit others. With the goal of eliminating social injustice, Marx developed a theory outlining a sequence of stages that all societies would go through until the private ownership of the means of production disappeared in the final stage—**communism.**

Marx also analyzed in great detail the origins of the capitalist system that prevailed in Western Europe and North American societies in the 19th century. His central argument was that a capitalist class, the **bourgeoisie,** owned the productive resources and exploited the working class, or **proletariat,** which supplied the labor to produce goods and services. He predicted that when the oppressed working class became aware of its collective predicament, it would unite and, in a violent revolution, destroy the capitalist system. Then, it would take control of the means of production and establish a socialist economy.

Marx contributed to contemporary sociology—specially to modern conflict theories—in many ways. His use of historical evidence to understand contemporary societies is quite important. He also drew attention to the question of **who gains** from existing social arrangements, and **who loses,** leading him to look for the hidden consequences of these arrangements. Marx's emphasis on **class** has influenced modern sociology, and, today, social class is one of the primary dimensions of social life studied by sociologists. But the concept of social class has been extended beyond Marx's original notion, for, today, social scientists regard class not just as position in the economic system of production, but have expanded this concept to include factors such as income, accumulated wealth, occupational prestige, education, and life style.

The Weberian Approach

Another German scholar who has had a profound influence on the development of conflict theory is Max Weber. For Weber, the social world was not a single, unified entity but, rather, a "mixture of contending parts." His views of class struggle were more complex than that of Marx. Whereas Marx saw class conflict as based on the ownership or nonownership of the means of production, Weber focused on the struggle to control various markets, such as money and credit, land, industry, and skills. Those who gain control of a lucrative market become the dominant class.

Unlike Marx who treated class conflict in the economic sphere as all important, Weber examined conflict in the cultural and political spheres as well. He pointed out that ethnic, racial, and religious groups often engage in conflict generated by differences **in life styles and world views.** Weber saw struggles among factions for control of the state or for control of a political party as a form of conflict that could be analyzed independently of both economic and cultural conflict, even though class interests and cultural differences were sometimes a basis of contention among political groups.

Modern Conflict Perspectives

These deal with conflict among groups that are defined by class, race, ethnicity, religious beliefs, political alliances, sex, age, and life style.

Ralf Dahrendorf: One important modern conflict theorist, Dahrendorf, sees conflict as intrinsic to any social organization in which there is an accepted difference in authority between groups. This conflict over authority involves Marx's notion of class conflict, but it also includes conflict between groups that are not defined by whether they own productive resources (e.g., there may be conflict between professors and their secretaries even though neither group owns any means of production). Dahrendorf's approach can also be used to analyze conflict in noneconomic organizations such as between parents and children in a family or between teachers and students in a school.

Lewis Coser: Another important conflict perspective is that of Coser, who expanded on early essays by the German sociologist

Georg Simmel. Coser's theory incorporates elements of both structural-functional and conflict theory, as is evident from the title of one of his most important books, *The Functions of Social Conflict* (1956). Coser treats conflict as a pervasive aspect of life in *all societies,* and he examines both the functions and the dysfunctions of conflict for society. He shows how conflict between two groups can increase the internal cohesion of each group. Conflict and competition also connect the opposing parties to each other, because conflict itself is a form of social interaction. Sometimes conflict increases social cohesion by leading groups to form coalitions against a common enemy; for instance, two juvenile gangs that had previously engaged in conflict might unite in the face of a common enemy. Conflict can also alert those in positions of power to the need for reform.

Critiques of Conflict Theory

Structural-Functionalists have criticized conflict theorists for paying too little attention to the question of **what** holds societies together, and too much attention to **conflict** and to **change.** Other critics claim that, at least until recently, conflict theorists have made little use of modern research methods such as statistical evidence and computer analysis. Conflict theorists respond that an analysis of the complexities of social life cannot be reduced to statistics and that doing so has caused some sociologists to lose compassion for their subjects.

Applications of Conflict Theory: The Family

The conflict perspective focuses on the way that the family is influenced by the economic system. In simple economic systems, it may be practical for women to perform chores associated with the home, because they are often pregnant or nursing. Men, being physically stronger, often perform tasks that require physical strength such as hunting or agriculture. Conflict theorists, however, note that women continue to be dominated by men in modern societies. These theorists claim that inequality persists between the sexes not because of biological differences but because it serves the needs of a capitalist economy. Conflict theorists regard the modern family as serving the economic interests of the ruling elite and of the needs of men who dominate it. Paying women less than men for comparable work serves the economic interests of the groups that dominate the economy by making low-paid jobs available.

Interactionism

Interactionism is a theoretical perspective that focuses on the ways that individuals direct and mold their interactions with others. This perspective does not examine entire societies or even large institutions but, instead, concentrates on the behavior and perceptions of individuals within small groups. The interactionism perspective draws on Max Weber request for an **understanding** of the **meaning** that behavior has to people as they interact with each other.

Symbolic Interactionism: is a theoretical perspective that examines the way in which participants in social interaction choose and agree on the **meaning of symbols.** Symbols are things that stand for something else, which has a socially standardized meaning attached to it, or that has deeper multidimensional meanings beyond the literal one. The meaning of symbols is assigned by the agreement of members of a group. Children learn to distinguish a police officer from a bus driver and a soldier from a football player by the uniforms they wear. **Language** and **number systems** (mathematics) are the most important set of symbols for social interaction. Words or numbers do not have intrinsic meanings, as you know if you ever tried to understand someone speaking a foreign language. Words mean only what people say they mean. Communication through language and numbers are two kinds of symbolic interactions.

Charles H. Cooley and **George H. Mead** were the pioneers of symbolic interactionism in the U.S. Both examined society as the product of the interactions of people who learned to interpret a variety of symbols. Both studied the process by which people develop images of themselves, or self-concepts, through their interaction with others; both concluded that a person's self-concept was the product of the way in which that person was treated by other people, and how that person interpreted the treatment by others. Thus a boy who is treated as a troublemaker by his parents, teachers, and friends is likely to see himself as such and might become a juvenile delinquent. **Herbert Blumer** is one of the major contemporary symbolic interactionists. Blumer views society as a *product of social interaction that people create in an ongoing, continuous way—meaning that people continually* **redefine** the social situation through their interactions with one another. Blumer has applied the symbolic interactionist approach to the study of the forms of collective behavior, such as crowds or social protest. He argued that social problems are most accurately seen as the product of collective definition that occurs through social interaction, rather than as the inevitable result of objective conditions such as poverty or drunken driving (1971).

The Dramaturgical Approach

Another interactionist perspective is Erving Goffman's **dramaturgical** approach, which analyses behavior much the same way that one would analyze the presentation of a play to an audience. According to Goffman, people present certain aspects of themselves to others, and the way the self is presented depends on the **social context.** You act quite differently in an interview for a job than you do at a party with your friends!

Critiques of Interactionism

Interactionists have been criticized for paying too little attention to entire societies and large institutions. Their response is that societies and institutions are made up of individuals who interact with each other and do not exist apart from those members (Homans, 1964). They claim that an understanding of the process of social interaction illuminates the nature of these large social structures. However, interactionists have not, in fact, contributed much to the study of societies and social institutions, and to the understanding of the process of social change as have structural-functionalists and conflict theorists. Nonetheless, interactionism complements structural-functionalism and conflict theory in important ways by examining the actual ways in which people interact.

Applications of Interactionism: The Family

Interactionists study the family in terms of how the husband and wife, parents and children, relate to one another and to the world at large (Reiss, 1981; Motz, 1985). They examine the process by which the members of a family learn from their parents and friends how to behave towards the other members of the family. They also look at how the members of a family develop common understanding of one another's actions through both verbal and nonverbal communication and how this communication reflects differences among family members in wealth, power, and prestige.

Interactionists note that parents begin more conversations, and speak and interrupt more often than do their children. They might observe that husbands do all of these things more often than wives. Because research shows that people who speak more, begin more conversations, and interrupt more often tend to have the most influence in making group decisions, an interactionist might conclude that, within the family, parents have more influence than children, and husbands have more influence than wives. An interactionist would also look for other indications of power differences within the family. One piece of evidence might be the seating patterns at mealtime. The seating of the husband and father of the family at the head of the table might symbolize his dominance over other members of the family. Another symbol of dominance might be that the man, and not his wife, drives the car when the whole family goes somewhere.

Using These Three Perspectives

Although many sociologists express a preference for one of the three theoretical perspectives, one is not forced to choose between them. Each clearly has advantages and disadvantages, and many social phenomena are best understood by examining them from one or more perspectives—as seen in the example of the family. Structural-functionalism and conflict theory would underemphasize the interaction among family members while interactionists would not stress the relationship of the family to the economic system or the functions that the family serves for other social institutions. Yet, all of these questions must be examined in order to truly understand the institution of the family. At some point in the future, "someone might try to integrate these three perspectives into a **single sociological perspective** but, until then, the best solution is "to use each perspective as a different lens for examining social phenomena," wrote John E. Conklin. This, in fact, is precisely what I am striving to do in working towards unfolding a "holistic perspective" which includes the "spiritual dimension" and of which this work is the first formal attempt, at least in terms of some important "fragments."

The Holistic, "Integral", or "Synthetic" Perspective

This is the perspective which I now see emerging and which I am seeking to further and establish in various areas including sociology, psychology, and anthropology. The two fundamental assumptions, or core ideas, of this approach are simply that:

1. all perspectives, "schools," and theoretical frameworks have **some truth to them,** some anchorage in reality and, therefore, some basic *usefulness,* but that none has the **entire truth** and "final word" on social reality; and,
2. at this point in human evolution and the unfoldment of human consciousness, the **spiritual dimension** must be included and recognized as an emerging, qualitatively different "reality" than the well-recognized **human** or **psychosocial dimension** and the **physical or biopsychic dimension,** which is capable

of bringing about empirical **changes** and **measurable consequences** in the social and natural worlds.

If one accepts these assumptions, which are really "self-evident truths" to be ascertained in one's own personal experience, then the need for, and the feasibility of, a "holistic perspective" in the social sciences becomes manifest.

The pioneers and major theoreticians of this approach, which is both the "oldest" and the "newest," would include such people as the Saints, Sages, and Seers of all the great religions and spiritual traditions that have always existed and will always exist, the entire world over. It would include such well known thinkers and writers as Henri Bergson, Lecomte du Nouy, Pierre Teilhard de Chardin, Sri Aurobindo, Pitirim Sorokin, Mircea Eliade, Roberto Assagioli, and many more too numerous to mention.

The Holistic Perspective: Its Essence

This approach involves a radical "paradigm shift," or qualitative change, from what Pascal called the "Esprit de Géometric," the intellectual approach of the "Head" which is grounded in **analysis**, to the "Esprit de Finesse," the intuitive approach of the "Heart" which is grounded in **synthesis**. General Systems theory has already taken this position but, in my opinion, it has not gone far enough, failing to unfold the **spiritual dimension** around which to construct the growing synthesis. In other words, what this means is that the real "need for our time" is now for establishing greater and better **relationships** between various "parts" and even larger "wholes," both at the quantitative and at the qualitative levels. And it involves recognizing that, beyond the three basic levels of consciousness of the personality—the sensory, emotional, and mental lie other, higher and qualitatively different levels of consciousness which, for the lack of a better word, I would call **spiritual**. It is only when one has unfolded and activated this higher, "spiritual" state of consciousness that one can truly understand and know **oneself, life, the world, God, "Good and Evil"**, and the true meaning and purpose of what one is living and why one is living what one is living. The purpose of life on earth is not to "come from nothing to return to nothing" and neither is it "seek pleasure and avoid pain," or to "build up one's human ego" so as to have what the ego wants when it wants it. Rather, it is to **grow, to actualize and unfold potentialities and new faculties**—to *become more than what one was when one "arrived" on earth; to become a temple and channel through which Life, Love, and Consciousness can manifest evermore consciously and fully!*

The fundamental questions that this approach would ask are these: What is the meaning and purpose of this experience? What am I to learn from it? What lesson does it have for me and others? What can I realistically **do** and **change,** and what must I accept and live with discovering and abstracting some "good" from it?

Applications of the Holistic Perspective: The Family

In addition to looking at the family through the "lenses" of the Structural-Functional, Conflict, and Interactionism Approaches and asking their particular relevant types of questions, the Holistic Perspective would also ask:

1. What are the basic "assets and liabilities" of the family, for each of its members and collectively? What services and contributions can it best perform for the community and nation in which it lives?
2. What are the basic "lessons" and "trials" that each of its members has come to learn?
3. What is the meaning and purpose of what the various members of the family have to live at this point in time?
4. What situations must be "accepted" and "borne" as they are and what situations can, in fact, be changed and improved, and how can that best be done.
5. What does each member of the family need from the other family members and what do the other family members need from that person?
6. How can "right relationships" be developed between the members of that family, the larger extended family, their friends and associates, the community, nation, and the world?

In summary, it can be said that each "theoretical paradigm" has a basic *orientation,* a *distinctive image of society,* and certain "core questions" that it asks. Thus, let us see, concretely and practically what these would be for each perspective.

Structural-Functional Approach

Orientation: Macro-level of society

Image of society: Organic analogy where society is a system of interrelated parts that is relatively stable and where each part has functional consequences for the operation of society as a whole.

Core questions: How is society integrated? What are the major structural parts of society? What are their basic functions/dysfunctions? What are their manifest and latent consequences for the operation of society?

Conflict Theory

Orientation: Macro-level

Image of society: An ongoing process characterized by basic inequalities where any part of society benefits some categories of people more than others and where conflict-based social inequality promotes social change.

Core questions: How is society divided? What are the major patterns of social inequality? How do some categories of people attempt to protect their privileges? How do other categories of people attempt to improve their social positions? And what kinds of conflict ensue from this?

Interactionism

Orientation: Micro-level

Image of society: An ongoing process of social interaction in specific settings based on symbolic communication and where individual perceptions of reality are variable and changing.

Core questions: How is society experienced? How do interacting human beings sustain and change social patterns? How do individuals attempt to shape the reality perceived by others? How does individual behavior change from one situation to another?

Holistic Perspective

Orientation: Macro and Micro with a Spiritual Thrust

Image of society: A bio-psycho-spiritual laboratory of growth, crucible of experience, and school of life and becoming.

Core questions: Who am I? Where do I go from here? Where am I going? What is the meaning and purpose of this life and what am I to learn from it and to give to it? What specific lessons am I to learn from this situation? How can I find some "good" from this situation, recognize it, and integrate it in my consciousness and my being? What can I realistically change in my situation and what must I accept and reframe? And how can I go about changing or reframing my situation? What help can I get from others and what help can I give to them?

If a theoretical paradigm, a perspective, or a basic approach is really unfolding a basic image of society that suggests what are the vital questions that should be asked and how the answers given by research can be interpreted, then we can conclude that:

1. the **structural-functional** perspective is an approach based on the view that society is a system with many different parts all of which work together to generate stability and predictability in society;
2. the **conflict** perspective is an approach based on the view that society is a system characterized by social inequality, which generates social conflict, that brings about social change;
3. the **interactionist** perspective is an approach based on the view that society is the product of ongoing interaction among individuals in various settings; and,
4. the **holistic** perspective is an approach based on the view that society is the basic laboratory and crucible for the expansion of human consciousness and the actualization of human potential and faculties; that human nature is biopsychic, psychosocial and spiritual; and that all human experiences contain valuable lessons and opportunities for one's self-realization.

Chapter 3

The World of Sociology

Sociology, perhaps more so than other academic disciplines, deals with a whole "world," a world in which every human being lives, moves, and has his or her being. This is the WORLD OF HUMAN INTERACTION, which brings into being, or translates from potentiality inte actuality, "creates," the greatest of all human creations: HUMAN CONSCIOUSNESS in the individual, the microcosm, and HUMAN CULTURE, in society, the macrocosm. Like the fish in the ocean, but with the additional option of becoming conscious of this fact, we all live and move, and have our being in this world from the cradle to the grave. Perhaps the greatest human challenge of all times and THE great challenge of our present time is TO CRE-ATE A PSYCHOLOGICAL COSMOS OUT OF CHAOS, TO CRE-ATE, FORGE AND FASHION OUR VERY BEING AS WE CREATE, FORGE AND FASHION THE SOCIOCULTURAL ENVI-RONMENT IN WHICH WE LIVE. For, as we develop a culture, society, and civilization so we also, concomitantly, unfold our human consciousness and our being. The human adventure of GROWTH and BECOMING involves a double activity and crea-tion—an EXTROVERTED fashioning of our external sociocultural world and an INTROVERTED fashioning of our internal biopsy-chospiritual work. For it is in ACTION that we find and become our Self as it is in relationships with others that we discover and become able to express our Self; for the Psyche is, indeed, an organ of interaction as, ultimately, we are ALL ONE, or part of one great Life and Consciousness. In our earthly pilgrimage we move progres-sively through various great stages of development and personal ex-pression; first, the *biopsychic,* or the full development of our animal nature and adaptation to our physical environment through the in-stincts, then the *psychosocial,* of the full development of our human nature and adjustment to our sociocultural environment through human consciousness and culture, and finally the *psycho-spiritual,* or the full development of our spiritual being and the ful-fillment of our destiny through intuition and spiritual consciousness. Today, we are all living in, as both *spectators* and

27

actors, and are participating in a period of massive change and general TRANSFORMATION: biopsychospiritual and sociocultural TRANSITION from the human to the spiritual world, from the psychosocial to the psychospiritual, from reason to intuition, which will finally link the conscious with the superconscious and the human ego with the spiritual Self. This is truly a great and glorious adventure, the very meaning and purpose of our incarnation in the physical world!

Sociology, the Discipline

Here a basic distinction must be made between the *world of living and substantial sociology* and the world of *formal, academic, and scientific sociology.* In the first world, that of living and substantial sociology, you have been living from the time you were born on this earth and you will be living in it for as long as you will be here, for this is the world of HUMAN INTERACTION AND OF SOCIAL LIFE. The fundamental teaching of sociology is precisely that HUMAN BEINGS ARE SOCIAL BEINGS, INTERACTING BEINGS, and that the Psyche, the organ of human consciousness, is AN ORGAN OF INTERACTION which grows, feeds itself, unfolds and expresses itself through HUMAN RELATIONSHIPS. Thus, the family, the school, the church, the store or factory, the bus or subway, the playground, the library or wherever human beings get together and do something with each other is its LIVING LABORATORY. The world of formal, academic, and scientific sociology which you are about to enter is made up of various theories, theoretical frameworks, scientific concepts, methodologies, research procedures, and rules of validity and reliability which you will learn and master, together with the ability to observe yourself and others and to analyze and synthesize with the processes of induction and deduction.

Why should you enter this new world and learn all of these intellectual, cognitive, or academic "tools?" So as to create a MAGNIFYING GLASS THAT YOU CAN THEN TURN TO AND APPLY TO SEE MORE, KNOW MORE, AND UNDERSTAND MORE ABOUT WHAT GOES ON IN THE WORLD OF LIVING AND SUBSTANTIAL SOCIOLOGY. The two worlds are obviously the same. What changes is our approach, perception, definition, and response to this same world.

Briefly put, the central aim of formal sociology is to extend our *awareness* and increase our *knowledge* and *understanding* of the social world as we know it in a precise and progressive way far beyond those of the layman. Thus, modern contemporary formal sociology transforms our *awareness* (what we perceive), our *knowledge* (our intellectual labeling and categorizing), and our *understanding* (our experience) of our *psychosocial nature* and of the *sociocultural environment* in which we live but it does not yield WISDOM (the synthesis of awareness, knowledge, and understanding with practical applications which have *moral* implications). This we must acquire for ourselves with the guidance of other traditions and with the fusion in our own being of Knowledge, Love, and Will.

Modern contemporary sociology is the DISCIPLINED STUDY OF HUMAN INTERACTION, ITS NATURE, CAUSES, AND CONSEQUENCES (a simple and practical definition of sociology). Why does sociology study human interaction? So as to provide us with a greater knowledge and understanding, and thus mastery, of *one aspect* of our being and of one aspect of the world in which we live. Sociology does not study the entire range of human nature (our biopsychic, psychosocial, and spiritual nature) nor does it study the entire spectrum of the world in which we live (physical, sociocultural, and spiritual environment); it focuses essentially, as its own domain and province, upon our *psychosocial nature* and the *sociocultural* milieu in which we live (meaning our *consciousness* as it arises out of *human interaction* and manifests in *human interaction,* and *people* and their *ideas*) so as to expand our awareness of ourselves, as sentient and social beings, and of the social world in which we live; to increase our knowledge and understanding of our own nature, limits and potentialities on its focused dimension. As Peter Berger incisively put it, (INVITATION TO SOCIOLOGY, Doubleday Anchor, 1963, pp. 21–22), but in different words:

"(Sociology) is not the excitement of coming upon the totally unfamiliar, but rather the excitement of finding the familiar becoming transformed in its meaning. The fascination of sociology lies in the fact that its perspective makes us see in a new light the very world which we have lived all our lives. This also constitutes a *transformation of consciousness.* Moreover, this transformation is more relevant existentially than that of many other intellectual disciplines, because it is more difficult to segregate in some special compartment of the mind. . . . The sociologist lives in society, on the job and off it. His own life, inevitably, is part of his subject matter. The sociologist moves in the common world of men, close to what most of them would call real. The categories he employs in his analyses are only refinements of the categories by which other men live—power, class, status, race, ethnicity. As a result there is a deceptive simplicity and obviousness about some sociological investigations.

The Sociologist, His Daemon or Self Image

In seeking to understand the true nature and motivation of the sociological quest, it might be useful to turn, for a moment, to the various partial and inadequate images of the sociologist that have emerged upon the screen of popular belief in the last century and a half. Peter Berger distinguishes five major such images: The Sociologist as a Social Worker, the Sociologist as a Disciple of the Theory of Reason and Progress, the Sociologist as the Gatherer of Statistics, or Statistician, the Sociologist as the Methodologist, and the Sociologist as the cold and sardonic Manipulator of Men. None of these truly incapsulates the heart of the sociological quest or of the sociologist's true self-image, yet each does contain some partial truths which are worth examining.

The Sociologist as the Social Worker

The sociologist and the social worker share two basic interests in common: a cognitive interest in the study of human nature and human behavior and a practical interest in helping people have more conscious, creative, and responsible lives. But they also have many differences: the sociologist has more formal education and is more theoretically oriented; he is interested in understanding and studying all the different types of human beings that exist, those that are successful and "make it" in society as well as those who are not successful and do not "make it" in society; politically, he is, generally, less actively involved and more towards the center of the political spectrum; and he views his central contribution to his field and to the human community as being that of providing greater *knowledge* and *understanding* of the psychosocial nature of Man and of the sociocultural environment. The social worker, on the other hand, has less formal education and is more practically oriented; he is clearly oriented in helping those who are maladjusted, who are "unsuccessful," and who "do not make it" in society; politically, he is, generally, more actively involved and tends towards the left end of the political spectrum; and he views his central contribution to his field and to the human community as being that of providing greater knowledge and understanding of those personality types and social conditions that lead a person to become marginal in society so as to help that individual to become reinserted in the main stream of society and to cope more adequately with the myriad of human problems that face marginal people in a complex and fast changing society. Thus, clearly, the sociologist, though he shares certain basic interests and concerns with the social worker is not a social worker.

The Sociologist as the Disciple of the
Theory of Reason and Progress

To properly appreciate this image of the sociologist, one has to go back to the origins of sociology, to the time when Auguste Comte was finally formulating a "science of Man and Society." Sociology was born as the "offspring" and in the wake of the Age of Reason, the 18th century, which deified reason and believed implicitly in progress, in the "infinite perfectability of Man and Society." The brightest minds of the time felt that if one could only turn and apply reason to the study of Man and Society, the same progress that was made when the natural sciences used reason for the study of nature, and the harnessing of its raw materials and energies to raise human standards, would be now accomplished by the social sciences in the human realm. Thus early sociologists and social scientists were, to a certain extent, the "disciples of the theory of reason and progress." But, we have come a long way since then and the present century has witnessed and is still experiencing a tremendous "scientific explosion" and development but not accompanied by truly better human and social conditions as evidenced by the Great Wars, the social unrest, the arms race, and the ecological pollution problems. Thus, a progressive disenchantment with reason, progress, and science as being the key to solve all human problems has ensued. Today, the sociologist can no longer be viewed as a "disciple of the theory of reason and progress" even though he may have been that during the last century.

The Sociologist as the Gatherer of Statistics or Statistician

American sociology, when it finally established itself and acquired academic recognition at the turn of the century and in the first decades of the 20th century, reacted sharply to European sociology which was perceived as being too theoretical and academic, as being social philosophy rather than a truly empirical science. Thus, it focused primarily upon the "gathering of empirical data," or "facts" and became, for a while, closely allied with statistics and various kinds of "surveys." Statistics is a very important sociological *tool* and should be used as such, but it is not sociology proper. It is a means to an end, which is sociological knowledge derived from the analysis and interpretation of data and facts in the light of various theoretical frameworks.

The Sociologist as the Methodologist

The fourth image of the sociologist, like the preceding one, emerges from giving too much importance to *one aspect* of the sociological enterprise to the detriment of the other aspects and of turning a legitimate *means* into an illegitimate *end*. Methodology, or the procedures and instruments one utilizes to obtain one's facts and data, is a very important aspect of all sciences, and certainly, of the social sciences. The assumptions one makes, the categories one utilizes, and the procedures and instruments one works with have a great structuring impact upon the aspects of Reality and the "facts" one will uncover. Thus methodology is important and should be explicitly articulated but it remains a *means* to the end, which is sociological knowledge and should never be turned into the end itself. Poincaré once stated, "When I go to conventions of natural scientists, I hear them discuss their results but, when I go to meetings of social scientists, all I hear is about the methods they are going to use to get their results!" Sociologists should develop and use a specific methodology that is congruent with their theories, but they are not methodologists.

The Sociologist as the Cold and Sardonic Manipulator of Men

This image arises from the common myth that scientists can be very intelligent and powerful but that they have little love and care for others in their hearts. While it is true that knowledge leads to power (Comte himself stated, "voit pour savoir, savoir, pour prévoir, et prévoir pour pouvoir," "to see in order to know to know in order to predict, and to predict in order to have power"), the heart of the sociological concern lies with *understanding* human beings and not *controlling* them. The sociologist is not the "master-puppeteer" pulling the strings that make people dance to his tune. Social science knowledge can, and indeed, has been used for that end: to manipulate people into buying or doing what their clients want, but this is an abuse, a prostitution, of the true purpose and calling of this discipline. Moreover, immature and unselfactualized human beings can be manipulated and controlled by "pulling the right strings" and "pushing the right buttons" of their consciousness but, as soon as they develop themselves, actualize their potentialities, and "find themselves," they can always say "no" and assume control over their being and their lives, rejecting the "subtle persuasion" of advertisement, high pressure salesmanship, and political or financial manipulation: from *social objects,* they can become *social beings*. This entails "redefining" their values and their being from *possessing things* to *being* and *creating*. This is a long process but it can be accomplished and is part of the main purpose of earthly and social existence. Thus, the sociologist is not, truly, a "cold and diabolic manipulator of men."

To these partial images of the sociologist, Peter Berger goes on to add his own perceptions and understanding which he considers to be more precise and comprehensive. Hence, he tells us (Ibid, p. 16):

"The sociologist is someone concerned with understanding society in a disciplined way. The nature of this discipline is scientific. This means that what the sociologist finds and says about the social phenomena he studies occurs within a rather strictly defined frame of reference. One of the main characteristics of this scientific frame of reference is that operations are bound by certain rules of evidence. As a scientist, the sociologist tries to be objective, to control his personal preferences and prejudices, to perceive clearly rather than to judge normatively. This restraint, of course, does not embrace the totality of the sociologist's existence as a human being, but is limited to his operations *qua* sociologist."

And he goes on to describe the daemon of the sociologist and to formulate an "ideal type" of what truly motivates and concerns a good sociologist in the following words (Ibid, pp. 18–19):

"We would say then that the sociologist (that is, the one we would really like to invite to our game) is a person intensively, endlessly, shamelessly interested in the doings of men. His natural habitat is all the human gathering places of the world, wherever men come together. The sociologist may be interested in many other things. But his consuming interest remains in the world of men, their institutions, their history, their passions. And since he is interested in men, nothing that men do can be altogether tedious for him. He will naturally be interested in the events that engage men's ultimate beliefs, their moments of tragedy and grandeur and ecstasy. But he will also be fascinated by the commonplace, the everyday. He will know reverence, but this reverence will not prevent him from wanting to see and to understand. He may sometimes feel revulsion or contempt. But this also will not deter him from wanting to have his questions answered. The sociologist, in his quest for understanding, moves through the world of men without respect for the usual lines of demarcation. Nobility and degradation, power and obscurity, intelligence and folly—these are equally *interesting* to him, however unequal they may be in his personal values or tastes. Thus his questions may lead him to all possible levels of society, the best and the least known places, the most respected and the most despised. And, if he is a good sociologist, he will find himself in all these places, because his own questions have so taken possession of him that he has little choice but to seek for answers. It would be possible to say the same things in a lower key. We would say that the sociologist, but for the grace of his academic title, is the man who must listen to gossip despite himself, who is tempted to look through keyholes, to read other people's mail, to open closed cabinets. Before some otherwise unoccupied psychologist sets out to construct an aptitude test for sociologists on the basis of sublimated voyeurism, let us quickly say that we are speaking merely by way of analogy. Perhaps some little boys consumed with curiosity to watch their maiden aunts in the bathroom later become inveterate sociologists. This is quite uninteresting. What interests us is the curiosity that grips any sociologist in front of a closed door behind which there are human voices. If he is a good sociologist, he will want to open that door, to understand these voices. Behind each closed door he will anticipate some new facet of human life not yet perceived and understood.

The sociologist will occupy himself with matters that others regard as too sacred or as too distasteful for dispassionate investigation. He will find rewarding the company of priests or of prostitutes, depending not on his personal preferences but on the questions he happens to be asking at that moment. He will also concern himself with matters that others may find much too boring. He will be interested in the human interaction that goes with warfare or with great intellectual discoveries, but also in the relations between people employed in a restaurant or between a group of little girls playing with their dolls. His main focus of attention is not the ultimate significance of what men do, but the action in itself, as another example of the infinite richness of human conduct. So much for the image of our playmate."

I would summarize the essence of the foregoing by citing two ancient and well-known aphorisms which get right to the very heart of what characterizes a good sociologist. The first comes from St. Augustine who stated, "Man ponders over the infinity of the skies, man wonders over the restless seas, yet man forgets that, of all wonders, he is, himself, the most wonderful and that, of all treasures, he is, himself, the most precious." The second has been used by many people but could be traced to Lactantius who declared "Nihil Humanum Alienum a me puto" or "nothing that is human will be foreign or uninteresting to me." These then, are the distinguishing features, or the daemon, of the sociologist: TO SEE MAN AS THE GREATEST WONDER IN THE WORLD AND TO BE PASSIONATELY INTERESTED IN STUDYING AND UNDERSTANDING THE FULL RANGE OF HUMAN NATURE AND THE ENTIRE SPECTRUM OF HUMAN BEHAVIOR.

The Sociologist Perspective

The sociological perspective, or the "fruits" of doing sociology, rests upon three basic pillars: *The 4 Fundamental Questions, the 3 Motifs,* and the *Sociological Perspective proper.*

The 4 Fundamental Questions: All of the established academic disciplines rest upon certain "fundamental questions" which must be raised by the theoreticians of each discipline and the answer to which constitutes their "intellectual system." Thus, for example, philosophy rests upon 4 "fundamental questions" the answer to which is the "philosophical system" of a given writer. These are:

1. What can men know—Ontology.
2. How do men know what constitutes valid knowledge—Epistemology.
3. How should men live, what should be the "guiding principles" of one's life—Ethics.
4. What can man hope for—Eschatology.

Sociology, too, rests upon 4 "fundamental questions," the answers to which constitute the essence of the "sociological system" of a given writer. These are:

1. What are people doing here with each other?
2. What is their relationship to each other?
3. How are these relationships organized into and regulated by social institutions?
4. What are the collective ideas that move both men and social institutions: their nature, causes, and consequences?

The first question provides the starting point of the sociological enterprise, for sociology begins with the observation and study of human interaction, two or more people doing something with each other. The most essential and basic sociological assumption and principle is that HUMAN BEINGS ARE SOCIAL BEINGS, INTER-ACTING BEINGS. Human beings can choose and decide with whom, when, and how to interact with others but not WHETHER they should interact, for without human interaction a human being cannot become and remain *human*—his psychosocial or human nature is truly a social product. His human consciousness is translated from potentiality into actuality by his network of daily human relationships.

The second question deals with how human beings relate to each other, and how sociologists can study these relationships in a disciplined fashion. To this end, sociologists have developed what is known as a SOCIOGRAM. The sociogram is composed of 5 basic dimensions:

1. *Frequency:* how often do people in a certain group interact with each other over a certain period of time.
2. *Directionality:* When two or more people interact with each other, who initiates the interaction?
3. *Affectivity:* When people interact with each other do they express their emotions or not? What does their sociocultural system expect of them, to express or not to express their emotions in the given role-relationship? And what happens when people go counter to their cultural dictates: when they express emotions but are not expected to do so, or when they do not express their emotions but are expected to do so?

4. *Specificity:* Do people relate to each other in a specific or in a diffuse way? That is, is their relationship unistranded or multistranded and what happens when there is role-conflict between one strand of the relationship and another strand?
5. *Subordination/Superordination:* Do people relate to each other as equals, inferiors or superiors, and with what consequences for themselves and for the social system in which they operate?

The third question deals with social institutions which, technically defined, are composed not of a group of people or an aggregate of buildings but, rather, of a SET OF NORMS, VALUES, BELIEFS, AND SYMBOLS, which are ideas and of which Norms are the most important ones. Sociologically speaking, Norms are defined as RULES PRESCRIBING ADEQUATE AND INADEQUATE BEHAVIOR, WHICH TELL PEOPLE WHO THEY ARE AND WHO OTHER PEOPLE ARE, AND WHAT THEY CAN MUTUALLY EXPECT OF EACH OTHER IN THEIR VARIOUS ROLE RELATIONSHIPS. Norms are absolutely essential for human beings, for society, and for the unfoldment of human consciousness, or the emergence of what sociologists call *"human* nature." For, without norms there could be no human society; and without a human society there could be neither an emerging human consciousness, or psychosocial nature, nor . . . a discipline of sociology!

To illustrate the tremendous importance of norms and the functions they perform for individuals and social systems, let me tell you the following stories:

Suppose that you are driving on the only paved highway of Patagonia, along the coast, towards its southern most tip, which is one of the coldest and most desolate places you can find in Argentina. As you drive, way in the distance, you see a patagonese jalopy coming in front of you. Now, you are a cosmopolitan and sophisticated person and know that in America people drive on the right hand side of the road and overpass on the left; that in England, they drive on the left and pass on the right; and that in Italy . . . they drive in the middle of the road! But you have no idea as to where the Patagonese are supposed to drive. The Patagonese coming opposite you is also a fairly sophisticated person and knows that Americans drive on the right, British on the left, and Italians in the middle, but . . . as you are driving a Toyota, he has no idea as to who you are and what he can expect from your driving! In other words, there are no formal or informal norms at work here and thus both parties fall in a double bind which prevents meaningful interaction to occur. To come out of that impasse, there are two basic solutions: an irrational one whereby you would look at where the Patagonese car is and where you are and continue driving in that way, hoping that the other car would not change course at the last moment! The other solution, the rational one, is for both of you to stop in front of each other and to say, "Me here and you there," whatever that means, thereby establishing an informal norm that will tell both of you what you can *mutually expect from each other* and, thereby, establish a meaningful form of human interaction.

When I first came to the U.S., I went to the University of Denver and joined a fraternity to learn American social ways. My fraternity brothers told me about "blind dates" and got me one. The day I was supposed to go out for dinner and then dancing with my American date, a European girl I knew from back home (who was not a girl-friend) happened to be coming through Denver and that evening was the only chance we had to spend some time together. Thus, I took her along on my "date" (as this was perfectly acceptable in a European context but, apparently, not in the U.S.). I will never forget the look on the face of the America girl as we showed up or how tense the atmosphere was for the first hour we spent together! What had happened is simply that we used a different set of "norms" or expectations and thus did not communicate.

Another experience that I had was that I went out *three times* with a girl, whom I did like. The next time I called her, she told me that she was not feeling well and could not go out with me, and she did not suggest another time. Then, the second time I called her she told me that she had to go to Chicago to see her grandmother, and the third time she had to prepare exams, never suggesting alternate days and times. I naturally came to the conclusion that she did not like me, and "wrote her off." Several weeks later, as I was having lunch with a mutual friend, I casually remarked that it was "too bad this girl had not liked me," but my friend looked surprised and told me that he had been told that she did like me but that it was I who did not like her! We got into an argument about this and I tried to make him see my point of view and he told me he would inquire further. The next time we met, he told me, with a big grin on his face, that we had gotten "our wires crossed" because of different cultural backgrounds. When I asked him to explain, he told me that I had taken her back to her dorm after each date we had had, that I had shaken her hand and said "Goodnight," which was exactly what had happened! He then proceeded to tell me that she was looking for a boyfriend and, as I had not attempted to kiss her or to make advances to her, I must not be interested in her as a potential "girl-friend." She had thus not wanted to spend more time with me.

These are some of the things that can happen when norms are ambiguous, ill-defined, contradictory, or coming from different value and normative systems. It, inevitably, leads to confusion, frustration, and anomie. Anomie, moreover, has three basic dimensions:

a. a *sociological* dimension, *normlessness;*
b. a *psychological* dimension, *rootlessness,* the absence of belonging; and
c. a *cultural* dimension; a *gap,* for certain groups of society and their members, between the *goals* that society gives out to its members and the *means* that these groups and their members have to realize them through legitimate means.

The fourth question deals with VALUES for it is values that are the "collective ideas that move both men and social institutions." Sociologically defined, values are CRITERIA FOR WHAT IS REAL, IMPORTANT, AND DESIRABLE, or what I call INDICATORS FOR WHAT ONE LOVES, for whatever one loves is, indeed, real important, and desirable for that person. Values are also of great importance to sociology for modern sociology sees the very essence of personality, society, and culture to be defined in terms of basic values that make up their very core. Thus, in any form of human interaction, sociologists must identify, render explicit, and understand the nature, causes, and consequences of the norms and of the values that are regulating the human interactions they study and seek to understand in a sociological perspective.

The 3 Motifs: According to Peter Berger, there are 3 basic "motifs" or central themes that all sociologists must understand and use in their practice and which thus constitute one of the central "pillars" of the "sociological perspective." These are *Debunking, Unrespectability,* and *Relativizing.*

1. *Debunking.* This motif has emerged as a consequence of the discovery of the Unconscious at the end of the 19th century through the work and discoveries made by physicians, neurologists, and psychiatrists such as Joseph Breuer, Jean-Paul Charcot, and Sigmund Freud. Its basic meaning is that *human behavior is largely unconsciously motivated.* If this is so, then most people DO NOT REALLY KNOW WHY THEY BEHAVE THE WAY THEY DO, not because they are inveterate liars or want to deceive others, but because they, themselves, do not understand the true motivation of their actions which lies below the threshold of their consciousness. Hence, sociologists must become "detectives" and go from the surface to the core, from the symptoms to the cause, and from human explanations and rationalizations to the true motivation for their actions. They must not take literally, and at their face value,

what people tell them and how they explain their behavior, but evaluate what the actors say about themselves in the light of what other people say and what the sociologists can observe for themselves.

2. *Unrespectability:* All human societies have a social stratification system which means that they all have "top dogs" and "underdogs," people who have more or less power, prestige, and money. People who are integrated in the main stream of society, who have a good education, a steady and respectable occupation, who abide by the mores and folkways of their society, and who are actively participating in the social affairs of their community are called "respectable people." Whereas people who have little education, temporary jobs, who may have physical or psychological handicaps, and, especially those who are deviants and who do not conform to the laws, mores, and folkways of their society are called "unrespectable people." Peter Berger correctly observes that society and people listen much more to what "respectable people" say, to the versions and explanations they give of social events and of their actions, than they do to "unrespectable people." What "unrespectable people" say is, generally, not listened to or given little weight, and this is *bad sociology.* To be a good sociologist, one must listen and take into account what all the actors say, regardless as to whether they are labeled "respectable" or "unrespectable." This is what "unrespectability" means and it implies going against the natural tendency of society to listen more to what their "respectable" members say and less to what their "unrespectable" members say.

3. *Relativizing:* In their researches and studies, sociologists will come across people who come from all kinds of cultures, subcultures, and contracultures. They will note the universal tendency of societies and people to absolutize their religious, moral, political, economic, and social ideas and rules. But these systems which claim to be absolute and valid for all people of all times actually contradict each other and change, not only in place but also in time. Thus, sociologists have come to the conclusion that all human ideas, irrespective of the claims made by various societies and their members, are RELATIVE, relative to their history, traditions, collective and personal experiences, and to their level of consciousness and personal maturity. And thus sociology "relativizes" all ideas-systems by "tearing down" and "demystifying" the norms, values, beliefs, and traditions that were, hitherto, perceived and defined as "absolute." Relativizing has a double psychosocial impact. On the one hand, it makes people more tolerant, flexible, and less

judgmental of other ways of thinking, feeling, willing, speaking, and acting than their own and it promotes *humility*. On the other hand, however, it also makes deviance and non-conformity to accepted beliefs and norms far more easy—which is precisely what has happened amongst Western educated persons. And it tends to undermine the traditional authority of the Church, the State, and the School and thus also of the Family.

The Sociological Perspective Proper: The impact of "doing sociology" in a serious and professional manner, over a long period of time, or the "psychosocial fruits" of being involved with sociology upon one's Weltanschauung, self-image, and cognitive system, are to *develop a cosmopolitan and pluralistic outlook towards life, people, and ideas in an individual so that he can move easily, both mentally and emotionally, to different view-points, world views and systems of meaning.* That is, being a sociologist and practicing sociology will make a person more flexible, tolerant, and less judgmental of viewpoints, rules, aspirations, and lifestyles that differ from his own; it will make that person less egocentric, ethnocentric, and chauvinistic and thus more humble and less threatened by "foreign ways." This will enable him or her to be more at ease and make others feel more at ease in various social situations and thus to *be able to interact meaningfully with more and more people and wider and wider groups* thereby considerably enriching his or her social life and personal growth.

In conclusion, sociology does not, necessarily, make its practitioners more wise and loving, for its fundamental objective is to increase one's knowledge and understanding, and to expand one's consciousness. But it does make substantial and very important contributions to the process of acquiring systematic and objective self-knowledge, knowledge of the sociocultural milieu in which one lives, and knowledge of intrapersonal, interpersonal, and transpersonal relationships with the final aim of ESTABLISHING RIGHT HUMAN RELATIONSHIPS. As such, it is a very timely and important discipline which is worthy of personal study and applications, which has universal and timeless applications, and which can make distinctive and substantial contributions towards the development of an INTEGRAL PHILOSOPHY AND ART OF LIVING; THE GREAT HUMAN WORK OF OUR TIMES.

Chapter 4

Interaction: The Law of Life, Love, and Growth

In the previous chapter, we have discussed the fact that modern sociology is the *disciplined study of human interaction, its nature, causes, and consequences,* that the most fundamental axiom of sociology is that human beings are *social* or *interacting beings, and* that to truly know oneself one must know and understand not only the *biological* but also the *psychosocial* part of one's being which is forged and fashioned by the *sociocultural milieu* in which one lives. In this chapter, we are going to examine the nature, dimensions, dynamics, and consequences of *human interaction* by looking at it from the larger framework of interaction theory and then by analyzing it in terms of its own inner dynamics and details. The fundamental theme of this chapter is simply that: WHAT PHYSICAL NOURISHMENT, OR FOOD, IS TO THE BODY, PRAYER IS TO THE SOUL AND TO SPIRITUAL CONSCIOUSNESS; HUMAN INTERACTION IS TO THE PSYCHE AND TO HUMAN CONSCIOUSNESS: EXCHANGES OR "FEEDING" ARE VITAL FOR THEIR RESPECTIVE SURVIVAL AND PROPER FUNCTIONING.

To understand human interaction within the perspective of interaction theory, we must first briefly discuss what *human nature* is in terms of our basic assumptions concerning an integral theory of human nature, or what makes up a human being. Then, we shall discuss systematically and in technical language what are the two great "products" or "creations" of human interaction; *human consciousness* in the intrapsychic microcosm and *human culture* in the interpsychic macrocosm. Let us begin by looking for definitions of human nature that contain and highlight our basic assumptions.

Man has been seen and defined in many ways by different intellectual traditions and perspectives. Thus, for example, Man has been called "the King of the Beasts," and "the Glory of Creation," "the thinking reed" and "the image of God" as well as "the knower, the creater, and the destroyer." The humanistic and the spiritual traditions, like other traditions and perspectives, at their very core, have described Man in three basic ways, namely as: MAN, THE MICROCOSM OF THE MACROCOSM; MAN, THE

LINK BETWEEN GOD AND NATURE, BETWEEN SPIRIT AND MATTER; and MAN, THE INTERACTING BEING.

To these, the Western Spiritual Tradition has added three fundamental injunctions which one can find, explicitly stated, in Greek classical philosophy which aimed at Wisdom, or SOPHIA, as its final goal rather than merely at Knowledge which yields Power. These are: O MAN, KNOW THYSELF . . . if you wish to know the universe for your Psyche is the Key to understanding the universe; BE THE MASTER OF THY SELF . . . if you wish to be in control of the external elemental forces, and to gain personal autonomy and integrity; FIND THY HIGHER SELF . . . if you wish to be true to your Self and to become a full Human Being.

Man, the microcosm of the macrocosm is the Greek equivalent of the Judeo-Christian view of Man as being "made in the image of God." It implies that Man is a small replica of all there is, being a small cosmos mirroring the larger cosmos. In man, therefore, all dimensions as aspects of Reality are present and synthesized. As Reality is a trinity so is Man a trinity for in him we find a part of Nature, his biological organism; a part of humanity, his psyche or human consciousness; and a part of God, his Divine Spark. But, these various aspects are still, for the most part, latent and asleep, and must be gradually brought out and activated or translated from potentiality into actuality. To "know oneself," therefore, is most important as it is the key to really knowing anything else objectively. It is because of this basic assumption that the Greeks used to say that, in every human being, there sleeps a Beast, a Man, and a God who can be awakened and brought into expression according to what one loves (one's basic values), how one lives (one's lifestyle), and, especially, according to how one treats other human beings (the quality of one's human relationships).

Man, through his biological organism, is a material being while, through his Divine Spark and his Soul, he is a spiritual being, and through his psyche and his human consciousness he becomes the link or bridge between Spirit and Matter. It is through Man (or Humanity) that Nature becomes conscious of itself and acquires self-consciousness by a long evolutionary process. And it is also through Man (or Humanity) that the Spirit becomes conscious of Itself and becomes able to express Its attributes in Creation. Thus it is in human nature that Creation reaches its fulfillment and perfection and that God acquires a complex instrument of expression to manifest in Creation.

As far as modern sociology is concerned, however, it is the third definition and basic assumption, "Man, the interacting being", that is truly crucial and upon which we shall focus our present analysis. What it implies, essentially, is that it is through interaction with

Nature, with Humanity, and with God that Man is born, that he can "feed and nourish" various parts of his complex nature to survive, and that Man can grow and actualize his enormous potential and his various faculties—that, without interaction, a human being could neither be born, survive, nor reach self-actualization and self-realization. And this law is just as true on the physical plane as it is on the human and the spiritual ones. Thus, without sexual interaction on the part of his parents, without eating, breathing, and drinking a human being could not be born, survive biologically, nor reach biological maturity. Without human interaction, which is the analytical unit and focus of modern sociology, Man could not become and remain human; i.e., develop and expand his consciousness. Finally, without spiritual interaction, the Light and Energy exchange between the human and the spiritual Self, and the exchanges between the conscious and the superconscious, spiritual consciousness could not be born or unfold.

If we now put "Man, the interacting being" under our magnifying glass, or microscope, here is what our analysis reveals.

Beginning with the most tangible and visible part of Man, with his physical body, we can readily recognize, after a little investigation and appropriate reflection, that his birth, growth, and full development are fully dependent upon a process of interaction with the physical world or Nature. A popular saying claims that "Man is what he eats and drinks." Actually, a human being is far more than what he "eats and drinks" as his real self is not his biological organism that it fashions and utilizes as a vehicle of expression, but his physical organism is, indeed, largely the product of what he eats and drinks. The food and water Man draws from his natural environment is absorbed by his biological organism, broken down into various proteins, carbohydrates, and fats, and incorporated into his physical make up as "building materials" and energy. Through the processes of ingestion and excretion, of anabolism, metabolism, and catabolism, Man's biological organism is in constant interaction with Nature, drawing from her and returning to her, transformed, various chemical compounds. Hence, Man's physical body is, indeed, composed of the raw materials of nature—mineral, vegetal, and animal substances—which it assimilates and returns to nature transformed.

It is also a well-known biological fact that, approximately every seven years, all the cells of Man's biological organism are changed and renewed by the process of *catabolism,* which breaks down his cells and organs, by the process of *anabolism,* which generates new cells and organs, and by the process of *metabolism,* which regulates the energy flow and the other two processes. Consequently, even at the most material level, Man is in a process of constant interaction, of give and take, with nature from which he draws his physical sustenance and without which his physical existence would come to an end. A long cycle is thus formed, moreover, whereby every so many years Man's entire biological organism has to be renewed and rebuilt with fresh raw materials and energies taken from nature.

Then, consider the process of *breathing*. A human being is in constant interaction with the atmosphere of the place where he lives and acts in a much more rapid cycle of inhaling and exhaling. With each breath, Man draws into himself and incorporates into his organism all of the many gases and particles which enter his lungs. Thus, "pollute the air, and you will also pollute Man's lungs and body." Hence it is not only "what Man does unto other Men that he does unto himself" but also what he does to nature, to his environment that he does unto himself. This is the great "discovery" or "realization" of the ecologists of the last 20 years which gives us much food for thought . . . and then also for *action*.

Finally, it is easy to see from the foregoing analysis how dependent Man is on his physical environment for his own physical well-being and for his very existence. Without a constant process of physical interaction, of give and take, with nature, Man's biological organism could neither have been formed nor could it continue to exist or to grow into full maturity. To be alive and to function properly at the physical level Man must interact regularly and establish "right relationships" with nature.

At the next level, that of Man's *human*, or psychosocial, *nature*, the same basic principle is at work for the Laws of God and Nature are ever and inexorably working on all planes of Creation. As the ancient Hermetic Sages put it: "As Above, so Below; as Below, so Above!" Man's *human* consciousness, which defines what he is, (his ability to think, to feel, to will, to speak and to act in particular) is strictly dependent upon his *network of human relationships*. Thus the great insight of the Ancients—that Man is a "zoon politikon," that intelligence and morality are the daughters of the City, that men need each other and cannot realize their destiny and perfection without each other; in short, as modern sociology puts it THAT MAN IS A SOCIAL BEING—has now been fully and systematically corroborated by the social sciences which claim that Man's *human consciousness* is a *social product;* that *human consciousness* is born, sustained, and actualized through *human interaction*. It is from this central realization that comes the tremendous importance and the vital need to establish and LIVE RIGHT HUMAN RELATIONSHIPS . . . for they are, indeed, the crucible, the laboratory, or the cradle of human consciousness and, therefore, of Man's distinctively *human* nature. (For a precise and technical analysis of the nature, structure and functions of human consciousness, or the Psyche, see the next chapter.)

The early and classical sociologists of the 19th century, in their enthusiasm for the discovery of the "social and cultural dimension" went too far in ascribing the creation of human consciousness to human interaction. In the 20th century less philosophically inclined and more analytical sociologists recognized that human interaction and social life do not create human consciousness but, rather, *translate into actuality its inherent potentials*. Thus, for example, all normal human beings have the potential to learn and speak any given human language but it is being born and living in a given concrete society which will translate that potential into English, French, or Japanese.

Two basic sets of observations and case histories have led first to the former position and then to the latter position. These are:

Case histories such as those of Anna and Isabella, of the Wild Child of Paris, and, finally, of the Wild Man of Kenya led to the conclusion that a human being who has been socially abandoned or deprived of human interaction from birth, but kept biologically alive, is not *actually* but only *potentially* a *human* being. That is, this creature cannot think, feel, will, speak, and act, and therefore, *communicate* in a humanly meaningful fashion and thus remains practically at the animal or instinctual level.

The Case of the Wild Child Paris

Around the 1800's a young French doctor went horseback riding in the Forest of Fontainebleau, near Paris. As he was riding he saw in the bushes a strange creature scurrying about. Pursuing and getting close to that creature, he noticed to his amazement that it was not an animal but, rather, a human boy walking on all fours. Touched by his tragic situation he took this little wild boy with him to his house. At first, he came to the conclusion that the little boy was dumb, deaf, and feeble-minded as he appeared incapable of speaking, hearing, and thinking. Later, however, he was even more astonished when the little boy showed that he could, indeed, hear, speak and think and thus that his former diagnosis had been erroneous. What had happened was that the little boy had been abandoned by his parents for reasons that were never discovered as he died shortly thereafter and thus he had not been "socialized" and had, therefore, not developed a human consciousness for which he had all the innate potentials.

The Case of the Wild Man of Kenya

In the Pocono Record of Stroudsburg, Pennsylvania, on May 6, 1982, the following story was reported: "A wild man who acts like a monkey but looks like a human has been found on the shores of

Lake Victoria, the Homa Bay district health officer, Dr. Paul Maundu said Wednesday. Maundu told UPI in a telephone interview the being was almost certainly human but his behavior was not. "His behavior is just like that of a monkey even the way he eats bananas," Maundu said. "He eats them whole, skin and all, just like a monkey," The being, who has been nicknamed "John" by hospital staff at Homa Bay, was found two months ago by charcoal and wood gatherers in the rugged Lambwe Valley Forest. John was then brought to the hospital where he has been held *pending positive identification of his species.* Maundu said John does not sleep in a bed but prefers to squat like a monkey. He has "nibbling silly behavior with fast movements" similar to that of a monkey. The man cannot speak any known language but uses one "word" utterances to ask for food and water. The man eats raw bone meat and shuns vegetables and spends much of his time in the hospital yard collecting pieces of wood and leaves from a hedge. Doctors have estimated his age at about 27 years. A search has been launched in the rugged forest for villagers who may know the origins of the *primate.* Maundu said it was unlikely but not impossible that John had been raised by monkeys."

The major sociological principle and conclusion drawn from the foregoing is that a human being who has been abandoned or deprived of human interaction from birth is not *actually* but only *potentially a human* being. That is, this "creature" cannot think, feel, will, speak, act or relate to other human beings in a *humanly* meaningful and organized fashion. It cannot know itself or the world or communicate or relate meaningfully to other beings. Thus, for all practical purposes, this "creature" remains an *animal* functioning only at the biopsychic, instinctual level.

In the 20th century, other sociologists became suspicious of this simplistic conception of 19th century sociologists and conducted further experiments and observations to get at the bottom of this question, arguing that it is not possible that human interaction alone, without innate human potentials, could *create human consciousness.* Thus, one American sociologist (George Hallowell) decided to test this basic principle of early sociology by carrying out the following experiment. Having a human daughter about 2 months' old, he went looking in zoological gardens for a monkey about the same age. When he finally found one, he bought the monkey and brought it home with him to treat it in exactly the same fashion as he did his daughter to see what would be the *impact of human interaction* on the growth and developmental stages of that creature. At first, lo and behold, the monkey learned physical behavior and motor coordination *faster* than his human infant. But, in time, the latter continued growing and developing while the former remained "blocked" and was unable to unfold and manifest human behavior in terms of human consciousness, language, and communication processes. This showed conclusively what had already been "sensed" by normal "common sense," namely, that no amount of human interaction could develop an *authentic human consciousness* in a being that lacked the innate human potentials and faculties to do so. A human being is a far more complex, multidimensional being with other "bodies" or vehicles of consciousness, faculties, and potentialities, than is an animal or a machine!

The central point and basic conclusion is that should an average human being be deprived of or cut off from human interaction over a long period of time, that being will starve at the human level as it would starve at the physical level if deprived of food. That being will, become "psychologically, socially, and culturally deprived" with its human consciousness: mind, feelings, and will, as expressing in its speech and behavior, beginning a degenerative, "shrinking" and "narrowing" process. The integration of the psyche of that being and its psychological and social processes would begin to dissociate, to break down, becoming weaker, more confused, and ill-defined. That being would, in other words, begin to lose its sense of self-knowledge, self-mastery, and self-organization, and ability to cope in the human world.

In short, JUST AS MAN'S PHYSICAL NATURE CAN STARVE FROM LACK OF HUMAN NOURISHMENT, SO CAN MAN'S HUMAN NATURE STARVE FROM LACK OF PROPER HUMAN NOURISHMENT (which I have called "Love Vitamins") OBTAINED THROUGH VARIED AND MEANINGFUL *HUMAN INTERACTION*. Emile Durkheim, the great French Sociologist of the turn of the century, moreover, went as far as claiming that human deprivation, being cut off from a meaningful network of interpersonal relationships (see "network therapy" and right relationships within one's psychosocial network) would greatly increase the likelihood of a person *committing suicide*. This would indicate that the lack of regular and meaningful human interaction endangers not only the psychosocial nature and functioning of a person but also his very physical survival! Hence, we can conclude that Man, in order to realize himself and actualize his human potential, to expand, deepen, and heighten his human consciousness and actualize his human faculties and potentialities, NEEDS A MEANINGFUL AND VARIED SET OF HUMAN RELATIONSHIPS WITH DIFFERENT TYPES OF PEOPLE IN DIFFERENT TYPES OF ROLE RELATIONSHIPS. In short, that just as an unvaried diet, always eating the same types of food, can impoverish Man's physical organism, so the lack of varied and diversified HUMAN RELATIONSHIPS CAN IMPOVERISH MAN'S *HUMAN NATURE* AND FAIL

TO ACTIVATE NEW LAYERS AND NEW POWERS IN HIS
HUMAN CONSCIOUSNESS.

In my own personal experience, I have noted, time and again,
that I could crave human company far more subtly and yet acutely
than physical nourishment; that the right kind of human relationship, at the right moment, could do more for me to make me "come
alive," truly "be myself," and be able to "express myself" in a creative and joyous fashion than all the food I could eat, all the sleep I
could get, and even all the vitamins and tonics I could take! I have
also noted that no human being, however wise, interesting, or be-
loved could ever fill all of my needs and respond to all my aspirations. Thus it is that I realized that, in order to be at "my best" and
to continue growing and maturing, I needed to interact meaningfully with different kinds of people in different types of relationships. Finally, I also noticed, that, many times, when I met a new
person I also came face to face, or brought into consciousness, another latent and hitherto unknown part of my psyche.

Several years ago, I lived through a very interesting kind of
"sociological situation" that taught me more about the fundamental
need that human beings have for human interaction and what happens when one suddenly finds oneself deprived of it than all the
sociological courses I had taken and the various books and articles
I had read on this subject. This story is the following. At the time,
I was spending a vacation in Milan, Italy, and I was very interested in writing an important chapter of a book I was putting together. My social life in Milan, however, was such that it was
impossible for me to find the necessary time I needed to do the
thinking, reading, and writing that necessarily go with the production of a book. I would wake up around 9:30–10:00 A.M, get my
breakfast in bed with the daily newspaper which I would read.
Then, I would get up and go for a walk to wake up my still sleeping
body and psyche and return home to attempt some work. But the
telephone would ring or someone would drop by to invite me, or
invite themselves, for lunch which would generally last from about
1:00 P.M. to 3:00 P.M., as the Italians have lunch not so much to eat
as to get together with other people, socialize, and discuss a variety
of things. Then, drowsy from the wine that would inevitably be
served with the meal, I would take a siesta until about 4:00–4:30 P.M.
when I would again get up, go for a walk and make a renewed
attempt at my selected work. But, alas, in vain, as again the telephone would ring or people drop by to chat and make plans for
supper and for the rest of the evening. At about 8:30–9:00 P.M. we
would have dinner, which would last a good hour and a half or two,
and then we would go dancing or improvise a party at someone's
house which would last well into the night, at times even until 2:00

or even 2:30 A.M. This was the renowned Italian "Dolce Vita" or "Dolce far niente" ("sweet doing nothing") which was very enjoyable but equally unproductive. With this lifestyle, which I enjoyed, I clearly got nowhere with my chapter and could not be creative no matter how much I wanted to. Thus, I decided to take drastic measures.

I had a friend, a beautiful and rich but eccentric girl, who had inherited a lot of money on her 21st birthday and who had built her dream "refuge," a true "eagle's nest" in the Swiss Alps above St. Moritz where I usually went skiing in the winter. The house was carved in the rock of one of the peaks and had huge panel glass windows with a panoramic view of the Alps and of the town of St. Moritz that was absolutely "out of this world." The house, however, had no telephone, radio, or television and had no access road. It was located about half a mile from the terminal point of the highest telepheric and could only be gotten to by foot, following a little path that led to it, or by helicopter, having a little landing pad in the back. I asked if I could spend a week or two there to do my writing and was given the keys to the house. The next day I left by bus and got to the house with my books, papers, and typewriter, as well as with some food provisions, and settled in. The next day, I got up early, went for a walk, and settled to work, which went very well. The following day, I followed the same procedure and did my best and most creative work. The third day, however, I noticed that something was wrong. My concentration was wavering and I seemed to have exhausted by "creative vein" of the previous two days. I felt restless, tense, and depressed. Thus, I did little creative work and went, instead, for a long walk and did a lot of physical exercises, retiring early to bed with a good novel to read. The fourth day I was in very bad shape and had no idea what might have happened to me, except that I might have caught a "bug" from some of the mountain goats that were freely roaming about. I was very tired and listless. I could not bring myself to do any quality work at all, and was very depressed and "drained out." It was difficult for me even to fall asleep, and I distinctly remember having nightmares. When I woke up the fifth day, I felt no better, even worse in fact, and so I decided that I must be sick and should go to town to consult the local doctor who had office hours from 8:00 A.M. to 12:00 P.M. I took the telepheric down and, on my way to the doctor, I "bumped into" one of my old friends who did not even know I was in St. Moritz. I told him that I was quite ill and was on my way to see the doctor, but he succeeded in convincing me to have some "Apflesaft and Kuchen" with him at a local tearoom before I went to see the doctor so that we could chat a little and "catch up" with each other before I went off to bed to recuperate from my strange illness.

The next thing I knew was that my friend was looking at me in a very strange way and that the Swiss Cuckoo clock in the background indicated that almost two hours had gone by. Then I realized that I had been speaking in a monologue with very high psychic pressure for more than an hour and a half. But, the most astonishing thing I discovered was that *all my symptoms had left,* that I had found my "old self" again and was, in fact, feeling quite good. I discussed my sudden transformation and "healing" with my friend and, of course, did not go to the doctor as I had intended. What had happened was that I had just learned, through the famous "verstehen approach," or experientially in my own being and consciousness, a most important sociological principle: the vital function of human interaction for the proper functioning of my human consciousness. At that point, everything became clear to me. I had just come from Milan where I had had, if anything, *too much human interaction* by constantly seeing and talking to many people to the situation in St. Moritz where I was quite alone, without as much as a human voice, and thus completely cut off from all human interaction. Moreover, I had been practicing meditation and other spiritual exercises to get the necessary insights and the creative urge which had made me far more sensitive to what was happening within myself thus intensifying the normal psychological functioning of my psyche. The final result was that I learned a great lesson which I had never forgotten. Just as food is indispensable for the proper functioning of our physical body and our physical well-being, so is human interaction indispensable for the proper functioning of our psyche and our psychological well-being.

As a result of this experience and other similar experiences, I have become existentially aware of the true meaning of one of the deepest and oldest teachings of the spiritual tradition. Namely, that to become a full and "holy person," an awakened and actualized human being, *one needs to be able to interact meaningfully with the whole of humanity;* that to truly know and understand all of the parts and psyche, one has to know and to understand all of the different types of persons that together constitute humanity. This great and ancient insight is now fully substantiated by the modern social sciences when they claim that anthropology, sociology, and history hold up a great mirror to Man wherein he can see actualized and expressed the extraordinary richness and complexity of his own human nature; that in Man is contained the essence of humanity. To understand the former, consider now the following:

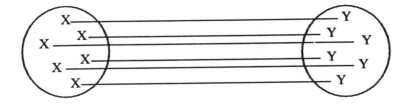

In the human psyche and in the personality of every human being there are many facets, aspects, and latent potentials which are denoted by the symbol "X." In human societies there are many different types of person who are denoted by the symbol "Y." In order for a person to actualize his or her human faculties and potentials it is necessary that that person interacts with another person who then brings out certain aspects, facets, and potentials of that person. For example, if we take love or hatred, we find that every person has a certain potential and ability to experience love or hatred but it takes a certain kind of person in a certain kind of role relationship to bring it out, to actualize it and experience it. We always have the potential and carry it with us, but to "draw it out," "incarnate it," and "live it" human relationships are indispensable.

Moreover, at the psychosocial or human level, as at the physical level, in Man's soul or human consciousness, as in Man's body, there are two basic processes of interaction: the visible and the invisible, the gross and the subtle, the conscious and the unconscious. Physically, a human being interacts with nature by eating and drinking its raw materials, but he also interacts with nature by breathing her invisible atmosphere, a process which is even more important for his survival than the former as shown by the respective lengths of time he can remain alive without eating, drinking, and without breathing. Psychosocially, Man interacts with humanity with his various interpersonal relationships, but he also "breaths" and "responds to" the *human or psychic atmosphere* generated by the various members of his community. And this "psychic atmosphere" is just as vital for his well-being and growth as breathing is for the well-being and growth of his physical body. This is something which is often overlooked or neglected by lay persons and social scientists alike.

In the sixties, seventies, and eighties we have become alarmingly aware of the profound and devastating effect that the pollution of our earth, water, and air has upon the health, well-being, and growth of Man. But we have not yet become aware, at least collectively, of the equally important and devastating effect that our psychic atmosphere has upon the psychic health, well-being, and growth of Man. This remains the task of future and psychically more mature generations. Man is responsible for and affected by not only what he eats, drinks, breathes, and says and does, but also by what he thinks, feels, desires, and wills.

The spiritual traditions have taught from time immemorial and sensitives, mystics, and seers have long known experientially that a human being's aspirations, thoughts, feelings, and desires emanate radiant and creative energies which have vibrations, a life, and even a color of their own which can be directly and experientially perceived by those who are sensitive to them; that they create atmospheres, which can be felt by many, seen by some, and which have an impact and psychosocial consequences on all living beings long after those who have generated them have left or died. As a matter of fact, every *living being,* whether plant, animal, or human, has an "aura" or radiating fields of interacting forces which can be perceived by those who are "sensitive" and "seen" by those who are clairvoyant. Plants have one such "aura" or energy field which is called the "life," "vital," or "etheric" field; animals have two, the "etheric" and the "astral," or "emotional" field; human beings have three, the "etheric," the "astral," and the "mental" fields; and spiritually awakened humans develop even a fourth one, the "spiritual" field. Thus, every object which comes into contact with a living being, every room, house, community, city, and nation, and even the whole world have "auras" or distinctive "psychic atmospheres." This means that every object or place that a human being comes into contact with, touches, or lives in, acquires an energy and vibratory field, which is quite complex and subtle in its nature and dynamics, and which interacts with, being affected by and affecting, all other such fields. In the recent past, this fact has now become scientifically recognized even by people who are not "sensitive" or "clairvoyant" as "screens," "cameras," and sophisticated electronic devices have been developed which can reveal objectively the existence, strengths, and impacts of these "energy fields." Hence, the time has now come for social scientists to become aware of such "energy fields" and to investigate scientifically their nature, dynamics, and functions, which is what some pioneers in this field are already doing.

As I have mentioned time and again in various lectures and writings, Man is literally a walking and living radio and television receiving and transmitting station. He continually radiates and absorbs psychic energies of various types and thus "bathes in" and feeds the psychic atmosphere of the room, house, and community he lives in. Today, we talk a great deal about the pollution of our earth, water, and air, and the impact this has upon our ecosystems, our societies, and even our personalities. This is nothing compared to the pollution of the psychic atmosphere in which we live which has a devastating effect especially upon the more sensitive and psychospiritually developed person. All the fears, anxieties, greeds, lusts, frustrations, and anger of so many people, dealing with their economic, emotional, professional, political, and personal lives engender a variety of problems: confusion, sickness, and suffering. Thus the time has come to become aware of these subtle energies and influences, to bring them into our field of consciousness, and to find antidotes for them, to neutralize them, and transform them into positive energies and influences.

The central point here is that Man constantly interacts, though usually subconsciously, or without being aware of this, with the psychic atmosphere of the room, house, and community in which he lives, giving and taking from it and thus being deeply, though subconsciously, affected by it at the psychological, social, and cultural levels. This affects his holistic health, state of being, and performance in various areas, and it explains why, all over the world and in every culture, there are beliefs and claims that certain places and certain people have "good" or "bad" atmospheres and influences. Thus every community and society have their share of "sanctuaries," "healing or inspiring places," and "haunted houses" as well as their share of Saints, Sages, Heroes, Healers, and "psychic vampires," negative or destructive persons.

Human Interaction: Its Technical, Comprehensive, and Sociological Analysis

The time has come for us to put *human interaction*, the specific domain of sociological analysis, under our "magnifying glass" or "microscope." There are 7 basic points to be noted when dealing sociologically with the concept of human interaction. These are:

1. Human interaction is the *analytical unit of sociology* or the specific domain that sociology studies.
2. It implies two or more people doing something with each other.
3. Human interaction is not the interaction between physical bodies, rather it is the interaction between human consciousnesses.

4. When two or more human consciousness interact with each other, specifically, we have the meeting of *mind with mind, heart with heart,* and *will confronting will. As* human interaction brings about a *creative psychic synthesis,* the above three-fold exchanges bring about *new ideas, new feelings* or emotions, and releases *new creative energies.*

5. Even though human interaction has been studied in a systematic fashion for almost two centuries, it is still, to a large extent, a process that is not fully understood and harnessed in terms of the energies and potential it can liberate.

6. This is because it is a process that is far more complex and intricate than most people, including social scientists, realize for it occurs not on one but on three distinct levels:

   a. at the *conscious* level where images, words, and deeds are transacted;

   b. below the threshold of the conscious level, at the *subconscious* level where various impulses and materials are transacted; and

   c. above the conscious level, at the *superconscious level* where other, qualitatively different, impulses and materials are transacted.

7. Finally, while there are many possible applications of the cumulative knowledge of the process of human interaction that has been gathered over the last two centuries, two specific applications stand out. These are:

   a. the *therapeutic function* of human interaction that has been explored and used by psychosomatic medicine and psychiatry in seeking to heal those who are not well; and

   b. the *self-actualization* of human interaction that has been explored and utilized by religion, the spiritual traditions, and now humanistic and transpersonal psychology in seeking to expand the human consciousness of the participants and to actualize human potentials and faculties.

Thus, at the *psychosocial level* as well as the *biopsychic level,* Man is in a state of constant and subtle interaction with his sociocultural environment and the psychic atmosphere of the place in which he finds himself. Moreover, without this process of constant interaction with his sociocultural environment and its psychic atmosphere, Man's human nature, his human consciousness, could neither be born, maintained nor be further expanded and developed.

Finally, at the spiritual level, the same basic principles and laws are at work: Man is constantly interacting, receiving and giving, with the invisible ocean of spiritual Life and Energies which surround him at all times, but of which most people are still unaware. For a human being lives and moves, and has his being not only in a physical, sociocultural, and psychic environment, but also in a *spiritual environment* whence matter and Life, and the very Source and Essence of his human consciousness (knowledge, love, and creative energy) originate and draw their being and essential substance.

The fundamental implication of this is that the same basic principles and laws that apply to the *biopsychic,* or physical dimension, and to the *psychosocial,* or human dimension, also apply to the *spiritual* dimension: *spiritual consciousness* is born, nourished, and further expanded through *spiritual interaction.* Spiritual consciousness is a fourth and qualitatively higher and different level of consciousness than the three levels most human beings are born with: the sensory, the emotional and the mental ones. It involves becoming aware of and bringing into consciousness our superconscious and our essential Self with their potentialities and faculties. When activated, they enable a human being to realize experientially that he or she is a spiritual, immortal being with a great reservoir of as yet untapped energies, potentials, and faculties. This greatly diminishes personal and existential fears and anxieties while increasing one's energies and creative expression. They also give one a direct personal experience of God, the ultimate reality, and his Wisdom, Love, and Designs for humanity and for oneself, thus literally transforming one's perceptions, definitions, and responses to daily experiences and life on earth. Spiritual interaction is, basically, what is generally called *Prayer* which is a profound but little understood science and art, the science and art of becoming consciously connected with God and the Self, with essential reality and which implies an energy, Light, and consciousness exchange, expansion, and transfusion.

Thus, in conclusion, we can say that: as Man's physical body is made up of and constantly sustained by the raw materials of nature; as Man's consciousness is made up of and constantly nourished by human interaction: the vital, emotional, and mental exchanges between two or more embodied consciousnesses; so Man's spiritual nature is made up of and unfolded by spiritual Energy, the Divine Light, and the very Life of God. The Biblical passage; "in Him we live, and move, and have our being" is thus literally and scientifically true on all three great levels of man's being, at the physical and human as well as the spiritual, and at the structural as well as the functional levels of being. Without this constant interaction, exchange, or give and take between Man and the Cosmos, Man could neither have been born, continue to exist and live, nor further develop himself and achieve his perfection. This is why the great spiritual traditions rightly claim that there are three great Sources of life, love, and inspiration for Man—Nature, Humanity, and the Spirit. And this is why, historically and experientially, three basic forms of mysticism or communion have manifested *natural mysticism,* or the love of and communion with nature; *social mysticism,* or the love of and communion with human beings; and *spiritual or transcendental mysticism,* or the love of and communion with God.

Man began his long ascent and earthly evolution by being more aware of and sensitive to nature and by drawing the greatest part of his life forces and inspiration from nature. In the last few millenia of human evolution, he has progressively abandoned nature and lost most of his natural "contacts" becoming more aware of and sensitive to his fellow humans, from whom he now derives the greatest part of his conscious stimulation, inspiration, energies, and satisfaction (what I call "Love Vitamins"). In the future which is now "at hand," however, Man will turn back to God, to the ultimate reality within and without himself and to the Self, and draw from the Spirit his ultimate source of life, love, consciousness, and joy. And, in the light of his awakened and growing spiritual consciousness, he will rediscover, but this time at a higher level and through a different perspective, both Man and Nature, the whole of Reality reconciled and properly harmonized in full self-consciousness and cosmic consciousness.

A last important point to be mentioned and analyzed in this chapter is the nature and dynamics of "egoism" and "altruism." Egoism or selfishness was always seen by traditional morality, philosophy, and religion as constituting the essence of "evil" and "sin" whose ultimate consequence was death: unconsciousness, slavery, and decay. Modern social science and the experimental method can now explain why in a rational and demonstrable way—simply because egoism actually implies "turning upon oneself" and closing the gates of the Soul or of human consciousness to the great process of interaction with Nature, with Man, and with God! Because it implies refusing to give and, therefore, to receive in a living exchange or circuit, at all levels or, rather, preventing the nourishing currents and tides of life from flowing through and nourishing and expanding his being. Altruism and selflessness on the other hand, were seen as constituting the essence of "good" and "virtue" whose ultimate consequence was a life more abundant: a fuller consciousness, freedom, and self-expression. Modern social science and the experimental method can also now explain why in a rational and demonstrable way. Altruism actually implies "turning toward the Cosmos" and opening wide open the gates of the Soul or human consciousness to the great process of interaction with Nature, with Man, and with God. It implies letting life, with its many energies, materials, and experiences, flow freely through our being both nourishing and perfecting it. This is one of the reasons why it has been stated. "If you want to receive, give!," "if you want to be loved, learn to love first," and "if you want knowledge and understanding, seek and ask." This is also why the Scripture say, "Those who seek life for themselves (who are selfish and egotistical) shall lose it while those who willingly give their lives for My sake (who are selfless and altruistic) shall find it more abundant!".

Chapter 5

An Integral Theory of Human Consciousness: The Nature, Structure, And Functions Of The Psyche

In the previous chapters, we have seen how Sociology studies *human interaction* which engenders, through a *creative psychic synthesis, both human consciousness,* in the microcosm, and *human culture,* in the macrocosm. Human consciousness and human culture are, therefore, both the product of the human spirit and genius and the result of human interaction within a stable and enduring network of human relationships which is called "society." In this chapter, we shall turn and focus our magnifying glass or microscope upon *human consciousness,* the distinctive feature of human nature, in order to analyze it objectively, systematically, and experientially. To do so in a truly scientific fashion we must begin by embodying our integral theory of human consciousness in the larger perspective of a general theory of human nature, or basic set of assumptions as to what Man is as a whole.

A General Theory of Human Nature or Basic Sets of Assumptions Concerning What Man Is Both Structurally and Functionally

After many years of systematic studies, analyses, and experiential observations concerning what Man, the Wonder and Synthesis of Creation, is, drawn from many perspectives and traditions which include the philosophical, sociological, psychological, anthropological, and spiritual traditions of East and West, tested in my own personal experiences and those of my students, I have concluded that:

1. Man is, himself, the greatest, the first and the ultimate *instrument* for gaining objective and subjective systematic knowledge and understanding of any kind, be it of the physical dimension of Nature, of the psychosocial dimension of Man, or of the spiritual dimension of God. This is the modern and scientific equivalent of the great and timeless Greek Injunction "O Man, Know Thyself . . . and thou shalt know the Universe." For we are the ultimate prism through which all awareness,

knowledge, and understanding must necessarily flow. It is our consciousness and its senses and faculties which filter and construct all perceptions of reality generating what is called our "cognitive universe." And our consciousness, with its related senses and faculties, is a dynamic, changing, and evolving system. It can move up or down the vertical qualitative axis of our being, expanding or contracting, moving towards the superconscious or the unconscious, coloring and fashioning our total perception, definition, and responses to what we call "reality."

2. At this point in history and evolution, Man is not yet a finished product but, rather, *an incomplete being undergoing an evolution,* a self-actualization and Self-realization process.

3. Today, this human evolution, self-actualization and Self-realization process must become, evermore, a conscious and willed process in which we are the *co-creators* of our being and becoming, or destiny, with Nature and God as our Fields and Partners.

4. Man, therefore, is not yet a unified, multidimensional, and integrated being; he is a very complex and still largely unknown non-integrated being-in-the-making who is composed of at least three basic dimensions or natures:

    a. *the physical body:* his animal or biopsychic nature;
    b. *the psyche:* his human or psychosocial nature; and
    c. *the Spirit or Divine Spark:* his true but as yet unknown Self.

5. Interestingly enough, our knowledge of man decreases and our understanding of ourselves diminishes as we move from the *physical* to the *spiritual* dimension.

6. For the social sciences as a whole, Man is neither what he looks like nor what he owns but, after, the *life that flows through him* whose flower is *human consciousness* ever growing and expanding to new quantitative and qualitative levels.

7. Thus, the social sciences do not focus upon and study directly either Man's animal nature or his spiritual nature, that is man's biopsychic or spiritual dimensions. That is the task of biology, on the one hand, and of theology or of the emerging spiritual sciences, on the other. What they do focus upon and investigate systematically is *Man's human or psychosocial nature:* the nature, genesis, dynamics, and expressions of human consciousness.

8. Man did not make his body or generate his Spirit. The first he received from Nature, which is the "mother of his body," while the second he received from God Who "buried a part of Himself in human nature" and Who is the "Father of his Spirit."

But his human or psychosocial nature, his *human consciousness* (which the Ancients called the "Soul"), he *must forge and fashion by himself* as the Son of Nature and of the Spirit. In other words, he must become the Mother and Father, the Creator, of his own "Soul" for which bears ultimate responsibility.

For a very long time in human evolution (which involves tens if not hundreds of thousands of years) Man's character, his personality, the growth and unfoldment of his consciousness, was left up to external agents and to "tradition" backed by "Custom"—to external physical and sociocultural forces working upon him *ab extra*. Thus it was the climate and the geography of his nation working through his physical body, and the culture of his nation or tribe working through his primary groups that forged and fashioned, *ab extra,* his personality and human consciousness. To a large extent, it was the *biopsychic unconscious* and the *sociocultural subconscious* that structured and directed his life and being, his behavior and inner states of awareness, and that determined his destiny (the classical Greek view of human evolution was that Man evolves from *Physis* (where he is ruled by his instincts) to *ethos* (where he is ruled by reason and the culture of his group), to finally unfold *Logos* (when he will acquire genuine integrity and autonomy and be ruled, *ab intra*, by his intuition).

The great challenge of our present times is for Man to learn how to progressively emancipate himself from his bondage to the "elements" and to traditions and sociocultural customs, from the slavery to his biopsychic unconscious and sociocultural subconscious in order to assume the consciousness and responsibility of forging and fashioning his being and becoming, *ab intra*, from within. In the present age, Man is called to *become himself* (see APOCALYPSE NOW, Llewellyn Publications, 1988), to realize his true Self and its powers. And this can only be achieved through the action of the human self operating at the conscious level and, increasingly, through the action of the spiritual Self operating at the superconscious level which must break through into man's field of consciousness. The key elements and driving energies of the unconscious and of the subconscious, in other words, must be *raised to the level of his consciousness and human self,* while the key elements and the vitalizing and life-giving energies of his superconscious must be *brought down to the level of his consciousness and human self.* This is the true and ultimate aim and purpose of Man and of his life on earth: *to know himself so as to complete himself,* TO CONSCIOUSLY UNITE WITH HIS TRUE SELF TO ALLOW HIM TO EXPRESS HIS ATTRIBUTES IN CREATION.

The Concept of the Psyche: Its Nature, Structure, and Functions

The social sciences focus upon, study, and work mainly with Man's human nature, with his *human consciousness* in its multidimensional aspects and expressions. Hence, it is very important that we define specifically and technically what we mean by the concepts of *human consciousness*, its nature, structure, and functions. To do so, we shall turn to *Psychosynthesis*, developed in the last half a century by Roberto Assagioli, M.D. and his associates, which offers us a recent sophisticated and integral *Model of the Psyche*.

The Nature of the Psyche

The "Psyche" is the modern term used to denote the "Soul" or Man's human nature—his *consciousness*. It is the "bodies," the instruments or vehicles through which human consciousness flows and manifests itself. The Psyche is thus the matrix, the "house" or "temple" of human consciousness. Practically speaking, it can be subdivided into three basic categories: the animal, human, and spiritual "Soul" which are better known today as the *unconscious*, the *conscious*, and the *superconscious*. It is composed of what the Ancients called the "Four Elements" and what modern mystics and spiritual scientists call the "energy and consciousness bodies," namely, the *etheric, astral, mental,* and *spiritual "bodies"* or "vehicles" of expression. While these cannot be seen by the naked human eye or even detected by microscopes, which only operate upon the physical or horizontal dimension, they can be seen by clairvoyant sight, felt by sensitive people, and detected by Kirlian photography and other such procedures of the emerging field of parapsychology. Modern social sciences have, by and large, not studied them and have even denied their existence, choosing instead to focus on what they have called the *structure*, or component parts, and the *functions*, or expressions, of the Psyche.

The Structure of the Psyche

According to the psychosynthetic Model of the Psyche, the structure of human consciousness can be diagrammatically represented by the "Egg of Psychosynthesis" which looks as follows:

The Egg of Psychosynthesis Representing Its Structure

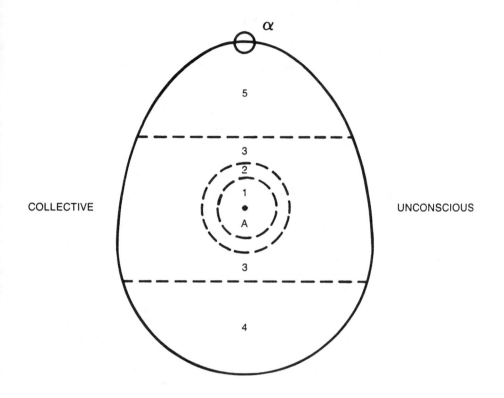

A. *The Human Self:* The center of pure consciousness and will located at the center of the field of consciousness.

B. *The Spiritual Self:* The "true" but as yet unknown essential or spiritual Self. That part of God or the ultimate reality that is embedded in the superconscious of all human beings and which has been known by various names in different religious and spiritual traditions; e.g., The Christ-within, the Atman, the Divine Spark.

    1. *The Field of Consciousness:* The stream of awareness or all of the materials a person is aware of at a given point in time; the seven Functions of the Psyche: willing, thinking, feeling, intuition, imagination, biopsychic drives, and sensations which manifest through speaking and acting and which derive their energies from the human self and the personality.

2. *The Preconscious:* Those levels of human consciousness and materials which stand on the very threshold of consciousness and which can be brought into the field of consciousness by an act of the will.

3. *The Subconscious:* This area of human consciousness can be subdivided into the higher and lower subconscious involving those levels of consciousness and materials which have been "forgotten" and pushed into this area for permanent storage by the *amnesia mechanism.* It is here that all the things that a human being has ever seen, said, felt, done, or experienced since birth or even conception are permanently stored away. It is the great "archives" or memory bank of the personality, which cannot be brought into the field of consciousness by a simple "act of will."

4. *The Unconscious:* Those levels of consciousness and materials lying below the threshold of consciousness and deriving their energy from the biopsychic organism. It contains both the energy of "life" behind the biopsychic drives, impulses, or what used to be called "instincts," and the highly emotionally charged materials which have been repressed there by the amnesia mechanism because they are too painful, threatening, or anxiety-arousing to the ego. This is the area where the essence of *psychopathology* can be found, for these emotionally charged materials gather energy or "libido" in the unconscious, build up their "pressure" and then reappear in the field of consciousness by *somatizing* (affecting the biological organism) or *psychologizing* (manifesting as compulsive behavior).

5. *The* Superconscious: Those levels of human consciousness and materials lying above the threshold of consciousness and deriving their energies from the spiritual Self or the Divine Spark. It is thence that come the basic energies and drives manifesting as inspiration, intuition, creativity, and altruism. It is the fountain-head or "home" of wisdom, saintliness, heroism, and of all the higher impulses that can be found in human nature.

The Star or Flower of Psychosynthesis
Representing Its Functions

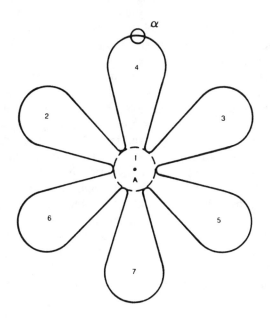

1. *Willing:* The focused energies of the self. The ability of a person to say "yes" and to say "no" to himself and to others. This is the central function of the psyche as it connects the energies of the human self to all the other functions. Like a battery it can be "charged" or strengthened and "discharged" or weakened according to whether we *use it* or not.

2. *Thinking:* The ability to develop thoughts and ideas, to gain a cognitive grasp of outer and inner reality, and to communicate these thoughts and ideas through a verbal or written medium.

3. *Feeling:* The ability to experience emotions: powerful energies welling up from the unconscious, the subconscious, and the superconscious impinging upon the field of consciousness and eliciting a response such as love, fear, anger, awe, wonder, gratitude, etc.

4. *Intuition:* Its etymological meaning is to "see from within" or the "teachings from within." It implies the ability to go from a question or problem to the answer to that question or problem without going through the in-between logical or empirical analysis. This is the function that links up the psychological with the spiritual part of our being, which connects the field of

consciousness with the superconsciousness, and which makes available to the ego the higher energies and impulses.

5. *The Imagination:* The image-making function which has a *reproductive* and a *creative* function as well as an *objective* and a *subjective* side. The imagination, through the process of visualization, can reproduce anything we have ever seen, done, or experienced as well as create new patterns and possibilities. Together with the emotions, it is the great energizer of the personality.

6. *Biopsychic drives:* These are the impulses which used to be called "instincts" such as hunger, thirst, fatigue, the sexual drive, and anger. They are, specifically, the energies behind such drives which originate in the unconscious to impinge upon the field of consciousness and elicit there an adaptive response the pressure of which increases with time. Their basic task is to function as an "alarm" mechanism designed to make sure that the basic needs of the biological organism are brought into consciousness and attended to, to ensure the survival and proper functioning of the physical body.

7. *Sensations:* These comprise the five basic senses: seeing, hearing, smelling, touching, and tasting plus the newly discovered ESP such as telepathy and, eventually, also clairvoyance, clairaudience, Out-of-the-Body Experiences and others. They are powerful external physical stimuli impinging upon the field of consciousness and eliciting a sensory response.

According to the model proposed by Psychosynthesis, the personal journey of self-discovery, self-mastery, and self-integration involves progressively and systematically expanding the field of consciousness to the point where, eventually, the entire "Egg" or higher and lower unconscious will be made conscious. This journey begins with an exploration of the field of consciousness, with a cognitive and experiential knowledge and understanding of the seven Functions of the Psyche and of their related psychological processes; namely, Willing and Concentration, Thinking and Meditation, Feeling and Devotion, Intuition and Invocation-Evocation, Imagination and Visualization, Biopsychic Drives and Energy Transformation and Direction, Sensations and Outer and Inner Observation.

From there, it continues through the use of guided imagery and the "guided daydream" to a systematic exploration and harnessing of the energies and materials of the Preconscious, Subconscious, the Unconscious, and the Superconscious. It is through such work and the training of many professional and lay persons along these lines that a true modern science of consciousness will emerge paralleling the Ancient Hindu science of consciousness called the "Antakharana."

Chapter 6

Sociology, an Overview: The Nature, Functions, Purpose, Methodology and Status of Sociology

As one scans the files of sociology and reads sociology books, one will find to one's amazement perhaps, that there are almost as many definitions of what sociology is and does as there are sociologists. This reminds one of the Eastern Saying that there are "as many doctrines of spiritual enlightenment as there are Gurus!" This can be explained by the fact that sociology is a discipline that is relatively young, covering a very larger territory where one can have many different perspectives and personal interests; that the social sciences are, qualitatively, quite different from the natural sciences in that, here, there is not one right or wrong answer, but many different answers that come from looking at social reality from different perspectives that are more or less comprehensive; and that sociologists have something of the "artist" in them which makes them creative and prolific at the cost of "concept diffusion."

The first basic question one might ask at this point is, "Where does the word "Sociology" come from, who coined it, when, and for what reasons?" It was first coined by the French Father of Sociology, Auguste Comte, who in 1829, in his major work, *A Course of Positive Philosophy,* changed the name of the emerging science of man and society from "Social Physics" to "Sociologie." The word "Sociology" comes, etymologically, from the Latin word "socio" or "societas," meaning "society," and from the Greek word "logy" or "logia," meaning "the study of." Thus, "Sociology" literally means "the study of society." But Comte had other reasons for coining this new concept to designate the science of Man and Society. On the one hand, he wanted to clearly emphasize that sociology is not a *natural* but a *social* or *human science,* and "Social Physics" was too clearly and closely linked with Physics which is a natural science. Human beings, Comte argued, cannot be studied in the same way inanimate objects are studied. A great gulf separates them and that is *human consciousness* which, when actualized and developed, can become a causal and creative agent, filtering, defining, and acting upon external incoming stimuli and one's perception of reality, and leading towards "free will" and voluntarism thus away from *determinism* which is the "iron law?" of the natural sciences. On the other hand, Comte also had a "passion for excellence" and wanted to instill that "passion for excellence" in his students. Now, the word "Sociology" is a composite word composed of a Latin prefix and a Greek suffix, thus it should remind its students of the Romans and of the Greeks. The Greeks had a distinctive genius for philosophy which, during the Renaissance, led to the development of science and the experimental method. The Romans, on the other hand, had a genius for creating laws and a great society which culminated in the Roman Empire. Comte hoped that the students of sociology would combine the Greek genius for Science with the Roman genius for creating a great society, thus bringing about the Good Man, living the Good Life, in the Good Society!

Auguste Comte defined sociology as the "abstract theoretical science of social phenomena" which, today does not mean much to us. Herbert Spencer defined sociology as a kind of super-science which does not make any observations on social phenomena, but which unifies and integrates the observations and generalizations made by the other social sciences at a lower level of abstraction— which also does not mean too much for us today. Georg Simmel conceived of sociology as the "study of the forms of human actions in society," while Emile Durkheim named sociology the "scientific study of social facts." James Vander Zanden in his text, *Sociology: A Systematic Approach,* thought of sociology as the 'scientific study of human interaction," where human interaction is viewed as the "mutual and reciprocal influencing by two or more people of each others feelings, attitudes, and actions." Finally, my own informal definition of sociology is "the disciplined study of human interaction: its nature, causes and consequences" where the greatest products of the creative psychic synthesis occur when two or more consciousnesses interact together are the actualization of *human consciousnsss,* in the individual, and the creation of *culture,* in society.

At this point, I would like to amplify and specify this informal definition by giving you my formal definition of sociology:

> *Sociology is the scientific observation, description, and analysis of human interaction, as influenced by and influencing social institutions and social groups, and the understanding of the causes and consequences of social action within society.*

In this definition, each concept that is used has a specific and precise meaning which is technically defined and which can tell us, using as few concepts as possible, what sociology is and does. Thus, in analyzing this definition, we see the following points:

1. This definition tells us something about the nature of sociology; namely, that it is both *scientific* and *humanistic,* and, specifically, at what levels it is and should be scientific and at what levels it is and should be humanistic. Thus, at the *observational, descriptive,* and *analytical* levels, it is and should be scientific, while at the *explanatory* and the *interpretative* levels it is and should be humanistic. The scientific school obviously focused upon and emphasizes the observational, descriptive, and analytical levels and identifies explanation with analysis in causal terms. The humanistic school, on the other hand, focuses upon and emphasizes explanation and interpretation, linking explanation with interpretation.

2. The concept "human interaction" should bring to the student's mind all that he or she has learned about it; namely, the seven basic points we discussed in our lecture on human interaction.

3. The words "influenced by and influencing" should remind the student of the "concomitant variation" type of causal relationships that operate in the world of human affairs; specifically, that while human interaction influences social groups and social institutions, it is also influenced by them (think of the relationship between Man and Society where Society molds and fashions most persons but is also molded and fashioned by some people).

4. The concepts "social institutions and social groups" should bring the structural-functional approach to the student's mind as "social institutions" is a structural word while "social groups" is a functional word. The structural-functional approach is the mainstream of contemporary sociology, which is based on the Shakespearean analogy of "society being like a theater play" where the two major component parts are the actors, the *persons* involved, and the *script,* their ideas which tell them who they are and how they are to act. Thus, the structural-functional approach analyzes society in terms of *people* and their *ideas.*

5. The concept "understanding" should remind the student of the two basic forms of knowledge that are used in sociology: *scientific knowledge,* or knowledge *ab extra,* obtained through observation, readings, and lectures, and *understanding,* or knowledge *ab intra,* from Max Weber's *Verstehen approach,* obtained through direct personal experience of a given social situation as a thinking, feeling, willing, speaking and acting person. It should also remind the student of the scientific school which aims at gathering *knowledge* and the humanistic school which aims at unfolding *understanding.*

6. The concepts "causes and consequences" should bring to the student's mind the basic way in which sociology proceeds, namely to focus upon the nature and characteristics of a given social phenomenon, to then *look into* the past to find the *causes* that made it what it is or that causes it to function the way it does, and then to *look into the future* to attempt predicting its possible *consequences* for the actors and the social system as a whole.

7. The concept "social action" should remind the student of the great objective of modern sociology, finally realized by Talcott Parsons in the 50's, to develop a *theory of social action,* to explain in a systematic and objective sociological fashion why people behave the way they do.

8. Finally, the concept "within society" is included, even though implied and tautological, to emphasize society's greatest teaching, namely that human beings are *social beings* and not *isolated beings,* that they live and develop their human consciousness and identity in stable and enduring groups called "societies."

By going over this formal definition of sociology which I am proposing to you, you can see that it meets all the modern criteria for a good social science definition. It tells us, by using as few words as possible, via concepts that are precisely and technically defined, exactly what sociology is and does.

The House of Science

The best image I can find to describe *modern science* and its composition is that of a house . . . which has a foundation, a first and second floor, and which is now in the process of developing a roof.

20th & 21st Centuries **Spiritual Sciences:** focus on the *Spiritual* dimension

18th & 19th Centuries **Social Sciences:** focus on the *human* dimension

16th & 17th Centuries **Natural Sciences:** focus on the *physical* dimension

15th & 16th Centuries **Scientific Method:** focus on *Methodology*

During the Renaissance, in the 15th and 16th centuries, the *scientific method,* also called the *Baconian* or *experimental method,* was conceived and developed as the most systematic and objective way of acquiring knowledge. In essence, the Scientific method substituted for *authority* and *tradition, direct observation* and *personal experience* letting the *facts* be the foundation for theory and explanation rather than seeking to fit facts into pre-existing theories and basic assumptions. This new method was then first applied to the study of *Nature,* of the physical dimension of Reality, of the biological organism of man and of the world in the cosmos. This was done by turning our *physical senses,* basically *seeing* and *hearing,* and *using* our *reason,* basically *analysis* and *synthesis,* to study nature and harness its materials and energies to control the physical world and raise our standards of living. Thus, in the 16th and 17th centuries the *natural sciences,* astronomy, physics, chemistry, biology, and geology were developed engendering technology and industrialization. Then, this new method was applied to the study of *Man* and of his relationships with other human beings by adding *direct personal experience* as thinking, feeling, willing, speaking, and acting beings to the senses and reason. Thus, towards the end of the 18th and 19th centuries the *social sciences,* psychology, sociology, anthropology, economics, and political science were developed in the hope of bringing about a conscious, free, responsible, and actualized Person to live the Good Life in the Good Society where freedom, equality, justice, and human brotherhood would reign. But this has not happened yet; in fact many perceptive modern thinkers and writers are now questioning the whole concept of "progress" and the possibility of "establishing the Kingdom of Heaven on earth," or of creating utopias through the use of reason, education, and science. Some are even arguing now that things are getting "worse" and not "better" and that science, which yields knowledge and power might be the enemy rather than the friend of human beings! This indicates to me that something *vital* was missing in that whole equation, that in order to truly develop the *whole of our being* and *function in the whole of creation* in a harmonious way, so as to perfect our being, fulfill our destiny, and achieve true happiness, something essential is still lacking.

That vital and essential "something," which I now see as emerging in the focus of our consciousness and priorities is the SPIRITUAL AND MORAL ELEMENT which alone will enable us to establish RIGHT RELATIONSHIPS; first *within ourselves,* between the different and conflicting parts of our intricate being; then with *other human beings,* and finally *with God,* the ultimate Source and Essence of all there is, including Man and the Universe; and *with Nature* which is truly our "matrix" or "Mother" and which we are presently raping and polluting with disastrous consequences for ourselves and the world in which we live. Thus, I postulate that, at the end of the 20th century, or in our time, and at the beginning of the 21st century, a new group of "sciences" will be developed which I call the "Spiritual Sciences" that will focus upon and study the *Spirit* in Man and in the Universe. This is what I call the "roof of the House of Science" and, obviously, a house that has no roof is an unfinished and vulnerable house! I see plenty of "empirical evidence" for the emergence and development of this new set of sciences and am personally actively involved in bringing this about.

What these sciences will finally be called, I do not know. Several names come to mind—"parapsychology," "paraphysics," "bionics," "psychotronics," "Spiritual Science" but it is still too soon to say. The sociocultural conditions to make this happen are, essentially, very simple: enough men and women, possibly with academic or scientific credentials, will have to develop their higher levels of consciousness and faculties, have new and genuine personal experiences dealing with this dimension, and be motivated and willing to explore, charter, and harness it with the same method that yielded such abundant fruits on the physical and human levels. Tapping into this dimension and reaching higher levels of self-actualization and Self-realization would also, necessarily, imply developing Wisdom and Love which is what the modern world lacks most!

The Four Central Postulates of Modern Sciences

Modern science rests upon four basic assumptions, or self-evident truths. If one accepts all four such assumptions, then science does make rigorous, logical sense, but if one does not accept one or more of these assumptions, which cannot be proven one way or the other in a rigorous philosophical or empirical manner, then science does not make sense and could be seen as an "organized fantasy" or a "self-contained logical system." These assumptions are:

1. that the world exists;
2. that we can know the world through our senses;
3. that empirical phenomena are causally connected; and
4. that men can communicate and accumulate knowledge through symbols.

Let us begin by looking at the first assumption in a systematic manner. Does "the world" or an external, objective reality, independent of our consciousness really exist? There is really no rigorously satisfying way of proving or disproving this as one could always accept the solipsistic position that only the self exists and that everything else is but a projection and creation of the self. Rene Descartes, who coined the famous dictum "cogito, ergo sum," states that while he was working on writing one of his books, the disturbing thought came to him: "Am I truly awake and thinking and writing this or am I dreaming?" And, "is human life really more than a dream, or a dream within a dream?" This came to be known as "Descartes' demon" for, indeed, there is no way of proving in a rigorous and scientific manner that "life is not a long dream" and thus that the external world and waking consciousness do, indeed, exist. For there is no human experience that we cannot dream about, while there are things we can dream about but not experience in external reality such as flying or going through a door or a wall.

As for the second assumption, the same situation applies. Can we know the world through our senses? Do our senses truly reveal "reality" to us, or only a "part of reality." Do they fashion and construct their own subjective "reality?" Philosophers such as Plato came to the conclusion that sensory knowledge is the least certain of all the kinds of knowledge we can acquire. For example, if you consider the floor on which we are now all standing: your eyes tell you that it is made of matter which is at rest and which appears as one solid entity of a greyish color. But if we take a powerful microscope and look at the same floor with increasing powers of magnification, we shall see this very floor completely transform its substance and appearance. It will end up by being composed essentially of space rather than matter, to be made up of billions of particles which are in a state of motion, and its very color will transform itself to appear black with bright streaks through it. And so, you could raise the question, "What is really this floor? The way it appears to our naked eyes? Or the way it appears at 100 or 1,000 or 100,000 powers of magnification?" Or is it yet something quite different? Our senses give us *phenomena* but, as they are presently functioning, they can never reveal the *noumena*, or things as they really are. For my part, I have no problem in accepting that our senses reveal *some aspect* of reality but never the *whole of reality*. Those aspects of reality which our senses reveal to us, however, are enough to enable us to function in the world in an organized and meaningful fashion.

When it comes to the third assumption, again we encounter the same situation. In the present and in the past, empirical phenomena do appear to be causally connected; i.e., the same cause always yielding the same effects. But, will they continue doing so in the future? This is a question which we cannot answer in the present, even though we make the assumption that this will be so. Take for example the sun. The sun rises in the morning and sets in the evening and has been doing so for many years. We can assume that the sun will rise and set tomorrow and in the near future, but what about the distant future when science itself tells us that the sun will either turn into a nova and burn us or that it will exhaust its fission fuel, hydrogen. For practical purposes we can assume that empirical phenomena are causally connected but we cannot prove this in a philosophically rigorous fashion.

Finally, when it comes to the fourth assumption, the same conditions still apply. We assume that we can encode and decode valid knowledge in our numbers and concepts which can be interpreted in the same fashion by other, properly trained, human beings. But what about poets, lovers, and mystics who tell us that their deepest and most important experiences and realizations cannot be translated into word or number which greatly distort and limit them? Again, my position would be that we can encode or decode *some knowledge* but not *all knowledge,* and that this "some knowledge" is sufficient to build a cumulative and valid scientific system.

Concerning the nature and functions of science, Vander Zanden (SOCIOLOGY: A SYSTEMATIC APPROACH, Ronald Press, 1965) gives us a few valid insights:

1. Science can be viewed as implying two things: a way of organizing and transmitting knowledge, and a series of well-defined rules whereby scientific knowledge is acquired—the criteria of scientific *validity* and *reliability.*
2. Science also orders knowledge into a system of interrelated propositions which have the form: If . . . Then . . . And these propositions must be:
   a. empirically verifiable;
   b. of repetitive nature or *nomothetic;* and
   c. significant in terms of some theory or explanatory scheme.
3. Sociology, as a science, is concerned with developing a set of valid propositions to describe and explain the observable uniformities in man's behavior as a member of society.
4. Science, as a method, provides us with an approach to the entire empirical world, the world that is susceptible to man's experience. It is characterized by objectivity in observation and analysis, and by precision, cumulative development, and systematic analysis such that its conclusions are independent of the values, beliefs, and biases of the scientist.
5. Science deals with what is, with the empirical world of what exists rather than with what ought to be, the world of values and ideals. Its purpose is not persuasion or conversion but demonstration. Science can never tell us what to desire or to want, what values or ideals to adopt and pursue, only how to achieve what we want and desire in the most economical and efficient way. It does not offer us *ends* but shows us the best *means* we can use te achieve our ends. As such, science is *ethically neutral* and *value free.*

6. Finally, Vander Zanden concludes that science can do three things for human beings:
   a. it can offer *means* for realizing certain values and goals;
   b. it can offer *alternative means* for realizing certain values and goals, calculating the relative costs and implications for each alternative we choose; and
   c. it can provide means for *predicting* the consequences of choosing a given course of action or adopting certain values and beliefs.

7. In conclusion, during the Renaissance some of the most perceptive and creative minds developed the *scientific method* which was, subsequently applied systematically to the study of Nature and of Man and Society, unfolding the natural sciences and the social sciences which replaced the Cosmology and Anthropology of the Ancients. Such as it was conceived, science gives us *knowledge* and *power,* but not *Wisdom* or *Love,* and it narrowed its domain of investigation to include only the physical and rational worlds but excluding the spiritual and moral worlds, thus dismembering both reality and human nature that is a synthesis of reality. Collectively, we embarked on the path that would give us objective knowledge of and control over the natural world . . . which then spilled over into the human world. Science can thus be compared to a *big computer* or a *powerful machine* which can give our ego the power to obtain what it wants, but not the wisdom and the love to use that power harmoniously and to ESTABLISH RIGHT RELATIONS with ourselves, with other human beings, with Nature and with God. It privileged the masculine polarity of developing the physical and rational aspects of our being but at the neglect of the feminine polarity of emotion and intuition. It made us powerful and selfish and, in the process, drained all true meaning, purpose, awe, wonder, and "joie de vivre." As Max Weber aptly put it, it gave us the world but led to "disenchantment" with the very world we gained power over.

Now the point is not to "turn back the clock," to "go back to an agrarian and rural form of pre-scientific and pre-industrial life," or to disavow science, technology, and industrialization which have given us, in the West, our higher standards of material life and more free, discretionary time. Rather, it is to learn how to use *wisely* and *lovingly* that knowledge and power that we have painstakingly acquired over the last five centuries. And to do so, we must now expand our consciousness into the higher realms and potentials of our nature and of reality, develop our spiritual consciousness wherein the true heart of genuine Morality lies so as to re-establish our lost harmony with Reality.

Science utilizes the scientific method to gather its data and reach its conclusions. Let us now turn to the scientific method to analyze it in its nature and how it operates. It consists of five basic concepts which define it and describe its operations. These are:

1. *Theory:* A group of interrelated propositions, linking central concepts gathered from general observations which explains a certain set of phenomena and allows for prediction. It is the theoretical framework which links many observations and includes several hypotheses to explain the nature and behavior of a certain set of phenomena.

2. *Hypothesis:* An "educated guess" as to why something is the way it is or behaves the way it does. To be "scientific" hypotheses must be tested by observation and integrated within a theory.

3. *Observation (personal experience):* This is where the scientist begins the scientific process: either by making observations in the external world or by analyzing personal experiences he has lived and the understanding he derived from these, in the case of the social sciences. Observations and personal experiences should both test existing hypotheses and generate new hypotheses and theories. There is a continuous flow, or feedback, between theory and observation, using *induction* to arrive at natural laws and then *deduction* to predict future behavior.

4. *Experiments:* Both the natural sciences and the social sciences use laboratory experiments to test some of their hypotheses and corroborate their theories. But the social sciences use laboratory experiments much less than the natural sciences, and this for three reasons:

    a. the greater complexity of human nature and human behavior resulting from the unfoldment of human consciousness and "free will;"

    b. the moral question as to whether it is ethical or not to experiment with human beings. The consensus of opinion and the professional ethic of the social sciences today is that it is ethical to use human beings as subjects for social science experiments provided that two conditions are met:

        1) that the subjects be willing to participate in these experiments; and

        2) that they be given a reasonable knowledge of the nature and purpose of the experiment.

c. *The Hawthorne Effect: The* fact that the experimental situation becomes itself an intervening variable in the process one is observing. In other words, when human beings know that they are being observed and analyzed, they don't behave the way they would normally behave.

What social scientists normally do, especially those who belong to the "humanistic camp," is to look for *natural experiments* in the annals of anthropology, sociological or psychological abstracts, or in historical records of ancient or modern societies, to find situations that approximate what they are trying to investigate.

When they do carry out experiments, social scientists proceed in the following manner:

1. They must identify a question or problem to research.
2. Then they select a *target population* for the study of this question or problem.
3. As the target population is, generally, much larger than what they can possibly test and analyze, they draw a *sample* from that population which can range from a *random sample* to a *representative and typical sample.*
4. The sample is then subdivided into two or more *homogeneous groups* called respectively the *experimental* and the *control group(s).*
5. The members of both *control* and **experimental** groups are then tested with a *questionnaire* or an *interview* for their attitudes and/or behaviors pertaining to the question that is being researched before the experiment has actually been carried out and their responses are assumed to be fairly similar.
6. The members of the experimental group(s) are then subjected to the experiment or exposed to certain situations, or stimuli, while the members of the control group(s) continue with their normal activities.
7. At the end of the experiment, both the members of the experimental and control groups are tested once again respective to their attitudes and behaviors pertaining to the question that is being researched. Now the attitudes and behaviors of the members of the experimental group(s) are expected to have changed while those of the control group(s) should not have changed. The differences in the members of the experimental group, before and after the experiment, and the differences between the members of the experimental group(s) and those of the control group(s) after the experiment has been carried out are *assumed to represent the impact of the experiment.*
8. *Checks for validity and reliability:* These are, respectively, *qualitative* and *quantitative* checks. Validity checks that it is,

indeed, the factor or cause that is assumed to have caused the change which has indeed done so and not other factors or causes, thus avoiding *spurious correlations*. Reliability, on the other hand, checks that, should the same experiment be carried out under the same conditions, the results would be the same. The more alike the results are the greater is the reliability and the more they are spread apart the lower is the reliability.

Scientific Language

It is very important to draw a distinction and not to confuse the three basic sublanguages that exist in every language and which are:

a. The *language of everyday speech* whose units are *words*. Words are media or instruments to convey and elicit thoughts and *feelings* which, in semantics, are called *denotation* and *connotations*.

b. The *language of science* whose units are *concepts*. Concepts are media or instruments to convey and elicit only *thoughts*. Here a rigorous empiricist would insist that each concept have only *one denotation* with an *empirical referens*.

c. The *language of religion and poetry* whose units are *symbols*. Symbols are media, or instruments, to convey and elicit thoughts, feelings, and *intuitions*. The essence of a symbol and its major function is to activate the *intuition*, or the inspirational flow, which means that the same symbol can be used many times, each time bringing through a new and different set of meanings and correspondences which grow and transform themselves with the expansion of human consciousness and new human experiences.

Now, to my mind, the basic conflicts and divergences between science and religion (e.g., evolution vs. creation and the span of time involved in the Seven Days of Creation) are due not so much to the "truth" or "error" of one approach as to *semantical confusion* to interpret *symbols* as *concepts*. For, in fact, religion, philosophy, and science are three equally valid and complementary approaches to the same reality.

Dealing with scientific language, Robert Merton wrote, "It is time to distinguish between jargon and that essential of all disciplined thought: technical language. Technical language is a more precise and condensed form of thought and communication than colloquial language. It is designed to fix definite meanings in which each word has, ideally, only one denotation and is deliberately deprived of connotations. Jargon, in contrast, is a wordy imitation of the former."

James Vander Zanden makes five basic points regarding scientific concepts.

1. The first step in the mastery of formal sociology, as of that of any discipline, is the *mastery of its basic concepts*. For these are the very tools with which the sociologist works and they serve both to define the relevant phenomena he will study and to differentiate his discipline from others.
2. Concepts provide the terms in which problems are posed and solved. Obviously, our concept-bank and the quality of the concepts we use are all-important to raise the questions that interest us as well as to find answers to these questions.
3. What then are concepts exactly and how do they differ from the words of ordinary speech? Concepts are *intellectual constructs* devised by the human mind to describe and render reality and human experience meaningful. Though they may refer to purely hypothetical entities or processes which cannot be directly observed, concepts do ultimately emerge from some kind of observation or experience which they represent. Furthermore, concepts are not, like facts or propositions, true or false; they are more or less useful *heuristic devices* which help us to get at the problems and questions that interest us.
4. Thus, in defining and utilizing basic sociological concepts, we are *defining the nature and limits of the sociological perspective* and we render explicit those particular aspects of social reality with which we are concerned. By focusing our attention upon selected aspects of reality, concepts in effect tell us *what to look for*.

The Status or Relationship of Sociology to Other Academic Fields

Sociology has a particular and intimate relationship with two of the other social sciences, psychology and anthropology, and with three of the humanities, philosophy, history, and literature. To develop a systematic and objective "theory of society" we need to have a theory of personality, which sociology borrows from psychology, and a theory of culture, which sociology borrows from cultural anthropology.

Like the other social sciences, sociology studies certain aspects and facets of human nature and human behavior through the use of the scientific method. Specifically, it studies the "inter-organismic psychic processes" or human consciousness as it arises out of human interaction and manifests in human interaction. Psychology, on the other hand, studies the "intra-organismic psychic processes" or human consciousness as it unfolds and expresses itself in the human organism. Finally, anthropology studies the biological organism in its various stages of growth and development, and the growth and articulation of human consciousness, social organization, and human culture; in other words, the whole broad range of human nature, human behavior, and human culture but without, as yet, including the spiritual dimension!

The humanities also study certain aspects and facets of human nature and human behavior, and human culture, but without the use of the scientific method. Sociology is also connected with and has an intimate relationship with Philosophy, from which it borrows its conceptual apparatus and its theoretical frameworks. It is from the philosophy of science and from empiricism that sociology has learned how to develop technical and precise concepts and how to create scientific theories.

Philosophy is primarily concerned with rationally understanding reality in its totality, giving it an order, meaning, and purpose as it is apprehended by human experience and reflection. The philosopher begins with ultimate principles or assumptions which may or may not have an empirical foundation and then attempts to explain and give a meaning to reality as a whole in terms of these principles. From history and literature, sociology gets a great deal of data and information which it then processes, analyzes, and interprets in terms of its own theoretical framework. History also seeks to understand and describe interacting human beings, but it studies them as a sequence of concrete and unique events, situations, and processes (it focuses on the ideographic aspects) while sociology studies them as patterns of recurrent variables (that is, it focuses on the nomotheric aspects). Literature studies the real or fictionalized and dramatized human vicissitudes, passions, aspirations, and dramas of concrete groups and individuals in concrete sociocultural settings. Sociology can utilize this information, which it analyzes with its own theories, to gain further knowledge about certain kinds of people and their sociocultural environment.

In conclusion, recapitulating and telescoping the central points of this chapter, we can say that:

1. The nature of sociology is first and essentially scientific in its observations, descriptions, and analyses, but it can also be humanistic in its explanations and interpretations.
2. Sociology functions or operates through the use of the scientific method and by developing its own concepts and models.

3. The purpose of sociology is, basically, to describe, analyze, and explain the interaction of Man within a social structure and to bring systematic insights and understanding of the laws and processes which are at work in man's social nature and life.
4. The methodology of sociology is heavily borrowed from that of the natural sciences but is also developing along its own distinctive lines (the Verstehen approach and participant observation).

Finally, though a discipline in its own right, sociology is intimately interconnected with the other social sciences, borrowing a theory of personality from psychology and a theory of culture from cultural anthropology. Sociology also has a close connection with the humanities, deriving its conceptual apparatus and its theoretical frameworks from philosophy and much of its data from history and literature.

Chapter 7

A Conceptual Analysis of Sociology

In this chapter, we shall provide a detailed analysis of the conceptual backbone of modern sociology in its structural-functional approach, which constitutes the mainstream of contemporary sociology. We shall look at the interrelationships that exist between the master concepts of *Society, Personality, and Culture* and how these concepts are organized in three distinct systems each of which is described by four basic concepts.

Scientific sociology is based upon two central assumptions derived from general observations; namely:

  a that human beings are "social beings" and not isolated creatures; and

  b. that the behavior of human beings shows regular and recurrent patterns.

To my mind, the first is self-evident and constitutes the central teaching of sociology; that all human beings are, by nature and necessity, *social* or *interacting* beings who live in society and not as isolated beings in nature. Sociology does not believe in the existence of true hermits or persons who live without any form of human interaction as this would imply the slow starvation of their human consciousness and their return to an "animal state." In my various travels, I have come in contact with a few "hermits" or "anchorites," particularly on Mount Athos in Greece, but these are very rare exceptions as well as exceptional persons who have opened up their spiritual consciousness and are thus able to live in another dimension and to interact with spiritual beings. Should a human being decide to become a true hermit, he has two basic options: to become "mad" and return to the animal level or to unfold his spiritual consciousness and "break through" into another dimension of being which is not accessible or real to most people.

The second assumption implies that human behavior can be subdivided into two basic categories: those behavior patterns that are *ideographic,* that happen only once and that are studied by history, and those behavior patterns that are *nomothetic,* that occur more than once and that are thus repetitive. These are the patterns that are focused upon and studied by sociology for, should a social phenomenon occur only once, how could one abstract a "law," a cause and effect relationship from it from which to predict future behavior?

In a previous chapter, we stated that modern sociology is closely linked with two other social sciences: *psychology,* from which sociology borrows a theory *of personality,* and *cultural anthropology,* from which sociology borrows a theory of *culture.* This is because sociology really studies the *interrelationships between society, personality, and culture,* or *human interaction,* which generate *human consciousness* in the individual and *human culture* in society. Let us begin by defining in a very simple but technical fashion the three master concepts of *society, personality,* and *culture* and then analyze their interrelationships:

> *Society* is a set of interacting *human beings.*
> *Personality* is the set of the *structure* and *functions of the psyche.*
> *Culture* is a set of interrelated *ideas.*

In studying the interrelationships between society, personality, and culture, what sociology really studies is people, their consciousness, and their ideas.

There are three basic axioms which describe these interrelationships.

a. Culture is internalized, partially and differentially, by the personality system acting through the social system. This means, basically, that the ideas of culture are transmitted into individual personalities through their interactions with other human beings. The words "partially" and "differentially" imply that no one human being can transmit a whole culture to another human being, only a group of persons can do that; and that even those aspects or items of culture which are transmitted by one person to another are "filtered" and "interpreted" through the specific values, personal experiences, and theoretical framework of that person.

b. Culture is a projection and externalization of the personality system acting through the social system. This means that the great ideas which are institutionalized by society into its "culture" come, ultimately, from a personality system or human consciousness. But, that unless their creator interacts with other people who understand, accept, and, in turn, transmit these ideas to others, they will never become "institutionalized" or part of that society's culture.

c. Society is a projection and objectification of both the personality system and the cultural system. This means that people interact in specific ways with each other in a given social system because of the way their human nature and personality are constituted and because of the particular norms, beliefs, and values they have internalized from a particular cultural system.

The three systems formed by society, personality, and culture are the following:

Social Science:	Psychology	Sociology	Anthropology
Approach:	Analytical	Functional	Structural
Essence:	Human Consciousness	People	Ideas
Master Concepts:	Personality (Personality system)	Society (Social system)	Culture (Cultural system)
Conceptual	Subpersonalities	Social Groups	Social Institutions
Breakdown	Needs and Ideals	Roles	Social Positions (Statuses)
	Structure and Functions of the Psyche	Individuals	Behavior Patterns: Norms, Values, Beliefs, and Symbols

The Structural-Functional approach of modern sociology is thus the study of *people* and their *ideas* with an implicit theory of personality.

The Structural-Functional Definition of Society or the Sociocultural System

Unfortunately, there is some conceptual confusion and diffusion in modern sociology concerning the concept of "Society." Three different terms have been and are used almost synonymously, these are: "Society," "the Social System," and "the Sociocultural System." "Society" can be used to mean only *people* or also *people and their ideas* and is generally used with the latter meaning. "The Social System" is generally used to mean only *people* but also has been used to mean *people and their ideas*. But the term "Sociocultural

System" is used meaning only and clearly *people and their ideas*. I would suggest making the term "Society" to be synonymous with the term "Sociocultural System" and to use both to imply *people and their ideas*, and the term "Social System" to mean only *people*.

The Structural-Functional definition of "Society" or the "Sociocultural System" is that SOCIETY IS A DYNAMIC SYSTEM IN EQUILIBRIUM. This means that the Sociocultural system is a set of functionally interrelated parts and subsystems working as a whole where one set of forces tends to maintain it at rest, or in equilibrium, while another set of forces tends to set it in motion and change it. Here, Society can be seen as the resultant of two great and oppressed forces:

a. the forces that make for social integration, that tend to preserve the status quo, and to maintain the existing equilibrium; and

b. the forces that make for social change, that tend to transform the system through social, political and economic reforms.

The central sociological insight here is that too much social integration, or preservation of the status quo, and too much social change, or transformation, are equally unhealthy for its members and for society as a whole, leading to different forms of social pathology.

If we look at the political dimension of Society we could say that, in the United States, the Republican Party or, more specifically, the *conservatives*, are behind the forces that make for social integration, and that the Democratic Party or, more specifically, the *liberals*, are behind the forces that make for social change. Moreover, the American Constitution implicitly recognized this great insight of modern sociology in producing a Two-Party System.

The social pathology that would ensue from anyone of these two great and opposed forces gaining too much power and thus destroying the dynamic balance that should always exist between integration and conservation and change and transformation is the following:

a. Should the conservatives truly take over the system and freeze change, what would happen is that the unfoldment of human consciousness and the creative self-expression of individuals would become blocked and build up pressures and tensions that would result in either a *sociopolitical revolution* (if these forces were expressed in an *extraverted* fashion) or in escapes into the worlds of fantasy or "madness" (if these forces were expressed in an *introverted* fashion).

b. Should the liberals truly take over the system and introduce changes and transformations that are too rapid what would happen is that anomie, anarchy, social conflict and a breakdown in communication between the generations would inevitably ensue, leading to a state of moral decay, unbridled individualism, and hedonism.

If we look at the United States over the 20th century, I would come to the conclusion that we went through three great phases: from 1900 to the end of the 1930's, the conservative forces prevailed and blocked the system, leading to the New Deal which, from the 1940's to 1980, witnessed the opposite extreme where the liberal forces prevailed, generating the present economic and intellectual climate that changed again in 1980 with Ronald Reagan's election. Will we now finally achieve a healthy balance and equilibrium between these two great and opposed forces or will the conservatives also go to an extreme and bring in their wake, sooner or later, the other extreme? This is something which is yet undetermined.

The optimum point of balance between these two great and opposed forces is not something static but dynamic which changes with different systems and conditions and which must always be sought by persons of vision and true statesmanship.

The next question we can now ask is, "If the sociocultural system is a dynamic system in equilibrium, what about the personality system? Can it also be conceived and analyzed as such?" The answer is also clearly "yes." The personality system is a dynamic system in equilibrium, being the resultant of two great and opposed forces. These, however, can be conceptualized differently. Erich Fromm in *The Art of Loving* provides one very interesting answer. He argues that these two great and opposed forces essential for the proper growth and functioning of the personality system are "conditional love", provided by the father, and "unconditional love", provided by the mother.

"Conditional love" says I love you because of what you do, therefore, what you do is very important. If you obey me, live up to my expectations and, basically, do what I want you to do, I will love you a lot. But, if you do not obey me, live up to my expectations, and are not successful, I will not love you. Conditional love thus provides the essential *motivation* for working hard, making sacrifices, and actualizing one's potential. As such, it is the most potent "fuel" for achieving success but it has a price and this is *emotional insecurity and instability*. It drives one to great achievements and a high standard of living, such as the one we have in the United States, but it leaves one very insecure, unfulfilled, vulnerable to stress, over-achievement, and psychopathology.

"Unconditional love," on the other hand, says I love you because of what *you are,* therefore, what you do is unimportant. I will love you regardless of whether you obey me, live up to my expectations, and do what I want you to do or not, and whether you are successful in the world or not. Unconditional love thus provides the essential *emotional security to* be oneself and love oneself, and to allow the process of self-actualization to unfold spontaneously and organically in the psyche and life of a person. As such, it is the most potent "integrator of the psyche" and healing force there is, as it provides *relaxation* and *stimulation,* peace and life, but it also has a price and that is to make it very easy for a person to live below his potential and capacities, and to settle for a lower standard of living such as the one we have, for example, in Mexico.

It is because of this basic conception of the healthy growth and functioning of the personality system as the resultant of conditional and unconditional love that Fromm takes a negative view towards one-parent families: one parent cannot provide, at the same time, conditional and unconditional love, motivation and emotional security. My personal position on this issue, however, is that it is not the father that is the "channel" for conditional love and the mother the channel for unconditional love but, rather, the *male* and the *female* principles which can be found, developed, and integrated within the *same person* but on the condition that that person has reached, or is in the process of pursuing, *self-actualization.* For it is the male principle that embodies and expresses activity, life, aggression, dynamism, severity, and accountability while the female principle embodies and expresses nurturance, receptivity, peace, mercy, and forgiveness, that focuses on *being* rather than on *doing.* Thus, for most people who are still living unconscious lives and who are not yet self-actualized, Fromm is right that the one-parent family is not healthy for the child; but for the few persons who are living conscious lives and who are actively pursuing the process of self-actualization and Self-realization, this is not true, as the male aspect could channel and express conditional love while the female unconditional love! And, obviously, the "mix" between these two great and opposed forces is a *dynamic process,* varying from person to person and at different points in one's life cycle.

One could also view the two great and opposed forces that fashion and structure the personality system as being other than conditional and unconditional love, as being, for example, "freedom" and "discipline," "introversion" and "extraversion," "supraversion" and "infraversion." If a child is more mature, responsible, and evolved and that child does not have the "psychosocial soil" to express himself/herself, to experiment, and to be creative, his/her life forces, creativity, and self-expression will be thwarted and damned up with dire psychosocial consequences for his/her growth, well-being, and becoming. On the other hand, if a child is not mature, responsible, or evolved and does not get more freedom, that freedom will be abused so that the child will abuse himself and others and then hate his parents for not having "loved him" enough to provide the right guidance and discipline with equally disastrous psychosocial consequences. In a democratic and egalitarian society such as ours this could raise a very thorny problem; that of treating differently children who are, in fact, *different* in terms of their *level of being* and *consciousness.* And this is where the activation of the intuition and the recognition of the spiritual dimension on the part of the parents, and of the society at large, could play a vital role; namely, to recognize and take into account the fact that human beings have four and not three ages: the *biological, emotional, mental,* and *spiritual.*

As we have seen previously, the structural-functional approach is grounded in the Shakespearean analogy that society is like a theater play with is two fundamental component parts of the *actors,* or the people involved, and the *script,* or their ideas. Moreover, it has its origins and roots in the very beginning of sociology when this modern discipline was born at the end of the 18th and the beginning of the 19th century. When Auguste Comte layed the foundations for this new "science of man and society," he patterned it around the then flourishing science of *biology* from which he drew much of his inspirations and his conceptual model. As biology has two great branches, *Anatomy* and *Physiology,* Comte subdivided sociology into its fundamental branches of *social statics* and *social dynamics.*

Social Statics, paralleling Anatomy, studies those aspects and conditions that allow for the existence of society and for the harmony in Man's relationships that make right human relations possible. For Comte, the basic focus of Social Statics is the *theory of order* which, today, is called a *theory of social integration* that provides the foundation for *social cohesion* and for the *division of labor.* Comte's rough theory of Social Statics has slowly evolved and articulated itself into the contemporary theory of structural analysis that focuses on social integration.

Social Dynamics, paralleling Physiology, studies the forces and processes that make for social change, which he called a *theory of Social Progress* and which we call today *Functional analysis* that provides the foundation for social and cultural transformation.

In Comte's subdivision of sociology into Social Statics and Social Dynamics, we also find his answer to the great Hobbsian question that stands at the very core of sociology; namely, *How can Society exist and why does it change? The* modern answer to this fundamental question is the Structural-Functional approach. Moreover, Biology, in its two great branches of Anatomy and Physiology, also raised two fundamental questions that were picked up and incorporated by the Structural-Functional approach; firstly, "What is the nature of a given Phenomenon?", "What are the component parts that make it up?" and, secondly, "What is its *structure?*" And, what are the functions of these parts, what do these parts do, and how do they contribute to the proper functioning of the whole? This is exactly what we find in the Structural-Functional approach under the headings of *structure* and *functions*, or raising the questions, "What is this phenomenon and what does it do? The Comtean answer to the basic questions of Social Statics and Social Dynamics, or how can society exist and why does it change?, can be found in his concepts of *Consensus Universalis* and the *Law of the Three Stages.*

Consensus Universalis basically means to achieve universal consensus or agreement by making everyone think in the same way; namely, in a positive or scientific fashion which is what sociology will teach people. Specifically, to achieve Consensus Universalis according to Comte one must teach people to:

a. *Order their thinking* which will
b. *Order their feelings* which will
c. *Order their willing,* or decisions, which will
d. *Order their behavior,* which will bring about
e. Social integration.

Psychological Dimension: The Spiritual Regeneration of Man. Social Dimension: The Reconstruction of European Society

And, for Comte, it is sociology which will teach people to think in a positive, or scientific, fashion which will enable them to order their thinking which will realize his twin grand aims for sociology: the spiritual regeneration of Man and the social reconstruction of European Society.

The Law of the Three Stages is the progressive passage of both the individual and of society through the three great stages of thinking and conceptions of the world; namely,

a. *Theological,* which pertains to the child and to primitive societies which see the causes of all events, natural and social, to issue from Spiritual Beings or Gods.

90

b. *Metaphysical* which pertains to the adolescent and to traditional societies which see the causes of all events, natural and social, to issue from Metaphysical Principles.

c. *Positive or Scientific* which should characterize the adult and modern industrial societies which finally give up the search for the ultimate ground of being, for *noumena,* and which are content with *phenomena,* and which impute the causes of all events, natural and social, to Nature and natural laws derived from disciplined observations and the generalizations obtained from watching the cause and effect sequence. These empirical, natural laws, moreover, while greatly limiting and restricting our search for truth and reality to their positive or empirical elements will also give us the *power of prediction* that characterizes true science and that will enable us to achieve mastery over nature and over our standards of living and destiny.

Thus, schematically put, we have:

	Social Statics:	theory of social integration: Consensus Universalis.
SOCIOLOGY		
	Social Dynamics:	theory of social change: Law of Three Stages.

Finally, as Vander Zanden puts it simply, "Culture refers to the customs of a people while Society refers to the people who are practicing the customs. Culture represents the fabric that enables human beings to interpret their experiences and to guide their actions while Society represents the actually exiting network of social relations among people."

Chapter 8

Patterns of Culture (1) Norms

The cultural system is grounded upon and made of four fundamental kinds of ideas which are its "building blocks" or "units." These are, as we have already seen, *norms, values, beliefs,* and *symbols.* Of these, *norms* are the most important ones for they are the "cultural units" that *make viable and meaningful human interactions possible.* It is viable and meaningful human interactions that make society possible which, in turn, makes sociology possible. So let us now put norms under our "magnifying glass" and analyze them in a comprehensive, objective, and sociological fashion.

Sociologically speaking, norms are the rules that tell us what is appropriate and inappropriate behavior; norms also tell us who we are and who other people are, and what we can mutually expect from one another in given social situations. They are the prescriptions and proscriptions that tell us what we should, ought, or must do, or not do. They are the *social expectations* internalized by the members of a society and institutionalized by their sociocultural system. There are two basic kinds of norms:

a. *Formal norms* which come from the value-system of a social system and which are imposed upon its members and which they must obey if the system is to be viable and function properly.

b. *Informal norms* which come from the actors themselves, from their on-going interaction, and which many times, can clash with the formal norms and replace them at a later date.

Seen in this light, the central social institutions of a society: the Family, Religion, Polity, Economy, and Education are *sets of basic norms* which have crystallized over time and articulated themselves through certain social agencies. Ely Shinoy, for example, states, "Social institutions are normative patterns which define what are felt to be proper, legitimate, or expected modes of action or social relationships" and "Social institutions are a set of interrelated norms which are centered around some type of human activity or major problem such as providing subsistence, shelter, caring for children, or maintaining order and harmony in the group."

Norms have also been subdivided into two basic categories: *Folkways* and *Mores*. Folkways are conventional practices, accepted as appropriate but not strongly sanctioned by a given society. Mores, on the other hand, are those norms which, being seen as essential for the survival and proper functioning of the society, are strongly sanctioned and conformity to which is expected and formally enforced. These two really form a *continuum* with each being at the opposite pole of the other. Two basic criteria can be operationalized and used to distinguish them.

a. *The degree of importance* attached to certain norms by society such that mores are very important and folkways less important.

b. The *severity of the sanctions* attached to certain norms and the means by which these are enforced. Mores being strongly sanctioned through *formal means* and folkways being less strongly sanctioned through *informal means*.

Examples of folkways are such things as shaking hands when meeting people, brushing one's teeth after eating or washing one's hands before eating. While examples of mores are injunctions such as not killing, stealing, or betraying one's country to a potential enemy.

Amongst folkways, we also have *Fads* and *Fashions*. Fads are basically folkways that last a short time with a limited acceptance from a certain group of the society. Examples would be songs, dances, clothes, etc. Fashions, on the other hand, are folkways that also last a short time but which enjoy a widespread acceptance within society (examples are car designs, architectural styles, and clothing). Finally, we also have *laws* which are a special body of norms. Mores and folkways are spontaneously and collectively enforced by the members of a society, while Laws are enforced by a special and legitimate agency (the police and the court system). Thus, the differences between them lies with *who applies the sanctions*. Primitive societies have mores that, in Traditional and Modern societies, are, little by little, transformed into laws. Laws can also be subdivided into *Customary* and *Enacted Laws* which differ primarily in the origin of the norms. Customary Laws arise in a more or less gradual and unplanned fashion while Enacted Laws arise in a deliberate and planned way, by fiat from the Legislature. When societies become larger, more heterogeneous, and are faced with major social change Enacted Laws become a necessity and are part of the modernization, bureaucratization, and specialization tendencies.

For Society and Culture to survive, and thus for Personality to survive and to actualize itself, basic human needs, both primary and secondary, must be fulfilled (Adaptation), mutual expectations must be validated (Integration), and a basic harmony of social interests must exist (Goal Achievement). And this is what shared and institutionalized norms make possible.

Social Change: Although Mores and Folkways tend to change relatively slowly, they do and must change. In the last 80 years morals and manners have undergone significant changes and may yet undergo even more drastic ones in the immediate future as we pass from the Piscean to the Aquarian Age. Change is a general phenomenon of social life which involves all areas and aspects of society including norms, values, beliefs, and symbols; i.e., culture. The question is what happens to people when "Foul becomes Fair and Fair becomes Foul" or when "yesterday's vices becomes today's virtues?"

Social Conformity is *obedience to socially accepted norms.* Society has three basic mechanisms to bring about such obedience; i.e., conformity to the customs and the rules of a group:

a. *Socialization:* Through education and social interaction, we internalize the norms and values of the social group and society in which we live.

b. *Social controls:* Our conformity to existing norms is constantly *reinforced, positively* for abiding by them (gaining money, acceptance, prestige, and power) and *negatively* by sanctions which are applied, formally or informally, for their violation (being deprived of acceptance, money, prestige, and power).

c. *Ignorance and unconsciousness:* Most of the time, people are unaware of possible alternative modes of behavior and other options.

As a member of a society and of different social groups, we continually interact with others. It is through this social interaction that norms are transmitted. Many of these norms we *internalize,* that is, we incorporate into our personality so that they become second nature to us. As members of a society and of social groups, we acquire a self-identity, recognition, security, and affection—we develop a feeling of *belongingness* and thus regard that society and those groups as *our* society and groups. Thus we look upon *their* norms as *our* norms. This is the core dynamic of *socialization* which brings us to conform willingly, without special rewards or punishments—*to make us want to do what society requires of us.* Quoting C. W. Mills discussing Parsons' Social System (*The Sociological Imagination,* New York: Grove Press, 1959):

"How is the social order possible? Because of commonly accepted values (and norms). When people share the same values (and norms) they tend to behave in accordance with the way they expect one another to behave. Moreover, they often treat such conformity as a very good thing—even when it seems to go against their immediate interest (this is the essence of the social contract!). That these shared values (and norms) are learned rather than inherited does not make them the less important in human motivation. On the contrary, they become part of the personality itself. As such they bind society together for what is *socially expected becomes individually needed.* . . . Let us imagine something we may call the "social system," in which individuals act with reference to one another. These actions are often rather orderly, for the individuals in the system share standards of value and of appropriate, and practical ways to behave. Some of these standards we may call "norms;" those who act in accordance with them tend to act similarly on similar occasions. Insofar as this is so, there are "social regularities," which we may observe and which are often quite durable. Such enduring and stable regularities, I shall call "structural." It is possible to think of all these regularities within the social system as a great and intricate balance. That this is a metaphor I am now going to forget, because I want you to take as very real my concept of "social equilibrium." There are two major ways by which the social equilibrium is maintained; and by which—should either or both fail—disequilibrium results. The first is *socialization,* all the ways by which the newly born individual is made into a social person. Part of this social making of persons consists in their acquiring motives for taking the social actions required or expected by others. The second is *social control,* by which I mean all the ways of keeping people in line and by which they keep themselves in line. By "line," of course, I refer to whatever action is typically expected and approved in the social system. The first problem of maintaining social equilibrium is to *make people want to do* what is required and expected of them. That failing, the second problem is to adopt other means to keep them in line."

In addition to *socialization* and *social controls* it usually does not occur to most people, who are still unself-actualized, that alternative standards of behavior do exist. The norms of our society and social groups constitute the guideposts, the social tools that enable us to relate to others in a meaningful fashion and to carry out our daily functions. We may also realize that it "pays" to conform to the expectations of others in terms of acceptance, praise, and affection and that it is "expensive" not to conform in terms of ostracism, dislike, fines, and being put in jail.

Non-conformity or Deviance

Every norm, even the most strongly sanctioned one, usually has a "zone of flexibility," variability, or tolerance. Thus, we may expect certain kinds and degrees of *over* and *under-conformity* which constitutes *deviance.* At times, the behavior of people exceeds the tolerated margin and they become *deviants.* This is because norms are criteria which tell us what people *should* and *must do* but not what people *actually* do and because people do have free will and never internalize all the norms of their society completely. Thus, the discrepancy between the ideal normative prescription and the actual behavior of individuals which falls *beyond the range of the tolerated margin of flexibility* constitutes nonconformity or deviance.

In all human societies not only do we find the coexistence of a real and ideal normative system but we also find a patterned evasion of norms such that a norm is overtly accepted but covertly violated on a large scale with the tacit acceptance, or even approval, of the social group, provided the violation is kept concealed—for, should it become public, it would be punished. Here, two contradictory norms apply to a given situation; the first, the overt and sanctioned norm; the second, the covert and tacitly approved norm (examples: prohibition and bootlegging, sexual chastity vs. clandestine affairs and prostitution, and honest government vs. graft and corruption). Strong pressures may be brought to bear by different groups in order to ensure both systems of norms. And this would lead to norms becoming vague, ambiguous, or contradictory which, in turn, would lead people to become confused, feel guilty, "have a bad conscience," and become depressed. This is the state of things that Durkheim called "Anomie" and which can have 3 basic meanings.

Anomie at the *sociological level* means a state of *normlessness* where there are no norms at work that are clearly defined or where the norms are contradictory or ambiguous.

Anomie at the *psychological level* means a state of *rootlessness,* of not belonging to any group, of not having any solid reference points, and of being cast adrift on the ocean of life. As James Vander Zanden puts it:

"It is the state of mind of one who has been pulled up by his moral roots, who has no longer any standards but only disconnected urges, who has no longer any sense of continuity, of folk, of obligation. The anomic man has become sterile, responsive only to himself, responsible to no one. He derides the values of other men. His only faith is the philosophy of denial. He lives on the thin line of sensation between no future and no past."

Anomie at the *cultural level* means the *discrepancy between the cultural goals given by society to its members and the socially approved means by which different groups can achieve them.* Robert Merton, who identified this third type of anomie (*Social Theory and Social Structure,* New York: Free Press, 1957), defined it as, "the disparity between the goals held out to members of a society and the institutional means by which these goals may be achieved." If human beings cannot achieve the goals which society has presented to them, and which they have internalized, by legitimate means, they may resort to illegitimate means or to other ways of reacting.

For example, in the United States most people have internalized the value of *success* and of a *middle class way of life,* but not all of them enjoy the same access to legitimate means for realizing them. Lower class and minorities find themselves handicapped by little formal education, few social contacts, and scarce economic resources. These people have internalized the same goals (that is, success and a middle class way of life) as more privileged groups in society but do not have the same opportunity to use legitimate means to achieve them. Thus, they will become angry, frustrated, and may become non-conformists or deviants to achieve them.

Richard Cloward ("Illegitimate Means, Anomie, and Deviant Behavior," ASR, April 1959) extends this hypothesis to say that not only the gap between the American Dream and the legitimate means to achieve it may lead people to use illegitimate means, but also that, for some people, even illegitimate means are unavailable (for example, access to criminal means may require social connections with other criminals, technical skills, and certain personality characteristics which some people lack). What happens then? Cloward, drawing upon Merton's basic insight, develops a 6-fold paradigm:

> *Normal Person:* Buys the goals and has the legitimate means to achieve them.
>
> *Criminal:* Buys the goals but uses illegitimate means to achieve them.
>
> *Innovator:* Uses legitimate means but changes the goals.
>
> *Retreatist:* Does not buy either the goals or the means but "retreats" into his own private world of fantasy, alcohol, drugs, sex, or poverty.
>
> *Ritualist:* Gives up the goals but preserves the legitimate means and lives an empty ritualistic life where he goes through "all the motions" but has no real rewards.
>
> *Rebel:* Rejects both the goals and the means but develops new ones.

Sociologists have noted that not only *under-conformity* but also *over-conformity* constitutes *deviance* and is punished. This is because both of them interfere and threaten the smooth operations and predictability of society. For example, people who commit themselves excessively to the prescriptions of the moral or religious code, even when such code may enjoy the highest prestige, may be regarded at times as "Saints" and "Heroes" but at other times as "fanatics," "heretics," and "troublemakers." The person who over-produces in a factory or is never ill may be reprimanded by his union for threatening his fellow workers. Finally, the person who takes literally the injunction not to kill may be put in jail for draft dodging.

People who find themselves caught in frustrating and conflict laden situations may form groups whose norms dictate patterns of behavior that are seen as deviant by the culture at large, and deviant norms may be transmitted to new members thus forming *deviant contra-cultures.*

For example, take the *professional thief.* He must possess specialized "skills," be smart, and have the appropriate "social contacts." He lives in the underworld where he, too, must conform to special norms that are often brutally enforced.

Chapter 9

Patterns of Culture (2)
Values, Beliefs and Symbols

In our daily life we continuously evaluate objects, acts, ideas, feelings, and events in terms of their desirability, value, and merit. Our entire selection of activities, friends, recreation, study, employment, and all our judgments are permeated with values.

Definition: Values are criteria or conceptions used in defining what is real, what is important, and what is desirable. They define what is real, good, beautiful, desirable, moral, and worthwhile for us, as well as their opposites. In short, they are criteria for what we love.

Basic Differences Between Values and Norms

A. Norms are rules for behavior while value are criteria for evaluating the desirability of things.
B. Values can be held by a single individual but norms cannot.
C. Norms always contain some types of *sanctions* but values do not always.
D. Norms come from the value system of the social system, that is, norms are derived from values.

Values represent the individually held or commonly shared conceptions of what is desirable—what we or others feel and think is good and worthwhile. Norms define the rules by which we have to abide in social action or be subject to sanctions for their violation. Both are subject to social change.

Functions of Values

Values commonly shared by people have a *cohesive* and *integrative* function for society. They constitute a "social glue" knitting people together and enabling them to understand each other and communicate with each other. When people share a common view of what is right and wrong, good or bad, beautiful and ugly, desirable and undesirable, they tend to experience a sense of social solidarity, of sympathy, and of communion. Primitive and Traditional Societies were highly integrated by commonly shared values while Modern Industrial Societies have become pluralistic and poorly integrated.

Basic American Values

1. *Individualism:* the belief in the infinite value and worth of Man as an individual which is derived from the belief in the immortality of the Soul of Man.
2. *Success and Achievement:* the stress is put upon personal achievement, proving one's worth by what one does and what one can achieve—improve one's being and standard of living.
3. *Materialism:* tendency to evaluate things in concrete, material, and monetary terms—quantitative emphasis: the biggest, largest, best.
4. *Progress:* belief in the perfectability of Man and Society. This can be seen as the driving force in American history.
5. *Work and Activity:* belief in the work ethic, the ennobling power of work. Through Reason and Work, Man can achieve what he wants.
6. *Rationality:* great emphasis on the rational approach. Reason and Science are the new God leading to time-saving, effort-saving, and efficiency.
7. *Democracy and Humanitarianism:* emphasis on egalitarianism and helping those who are underprivileged or disfavored.

Actually, Individualism and Success sharply clash with Democracy and Humanitarianism which could explain the periodic changes between the political left (Democracy) and the political right (Individualism).

Beliefs are ideas concerning inner or outer reality and any of its component parts which may be true or false, empirical or non-empirical.

Beliefs are really ideas concerning facts and, as such, they are distinguished from values by the possibility of testing them. Beliefs may be true or false but, more often, it is a question of their *degree* of truth or falsity. While not all beliefs are amenable to scientific verification, many are. Finally, beliefs, like norms and values, are not static but dynamic—they alter and are subject to social change.

Functions of beliefs: Beliefs make life, human experiences, and the world understandable to those who hold them. They tell people about the nature of their being, of society, of the world, and of their place therein. They provide a meaningful framework for people to relate to and understand others and life in general.

The beliefs of a society tell its members about their history: their friends and enemies, their Gods and Devils, their heroes and villains. They tell people about the processes and structure of their society, about internal differentiation, how they came into being and why they differ from other societies. They tell people how to get ahead in life or fall behind, about disaster, illness, birth, marriage, and death. They also fulfill the function of tension management for a society and its members. They provide a rational framework for appraising, understanding, and dealing with occurrences that might, otherwise, pose a severe threat and constitute a source of great anxiety. Most people need beliefs and "illusions;" to strip them of all their "false beliefs," or "illusions," might have a devastating psychological effect upon them . . . as I personally found out at one point in my life! Like norms and values, beliefs bring about social cohesion and social integration and fulfill the function of integration.

The Self-fulfilling Prophecy: strongly held beliefs that are acted upon tend to bring about what they postulate. W. I. Thomas once stated that, "If men define . . . a situation as real, it is real in its *consequence.*" Human beings do not only respond to the objective features of a situation but also, and *especially,* to the *meaning* that situation has for them. Thus, the act of *defining* something is also the *formulation of a prophecy:* the definition is a self-fulfilling anticipation which will bring about the conditions whereby the definition (prophecy) will be realized. For example, lack of faith to pass an examination will lead to anxiety which will jeopardize its outcome and block effective studying, or defining a group or being inferior will lead to cut expenses to educate this group and thus lead its members to become *de facto* less competent. What a self-fulfilling prophecy really is . . . is a false definition of a situation which leads to its creation and concretization.

Symbols: Practically all forms of human interaction depend on symbols. Symbols are the very vehicles and tools that make human interaction possible: through them we influence and are influenced by other people, we accumulate and communicate knowledge. Thus, it is symbols that make it possible for us *to become* and *to maintain ourselves as human beings,* as well as to actualize our various potentialities and faculties. Our very human existence depends upon communication which is rooted in symbols. Our whole knowledge and education depend essentially upon an accumulation and transmission of information which is based on symbols.

Definition: Symbols are any sign, act, object, or sound which has come to stand for something else and the meaning of which is socially standardized.

Symbols are also the bridge between the known and the unknown, the profane and the sacred, the Conscious and the Super-conscious.

The functions of symbols: Symbols make communication possible through language and technical signs (in the life of Helen Keller, the introduction of language brought about an intellectual and emotional "revolution!") The acquisition of language (which is an integrated set of meaningful symbols) is very closely related to the process of *socialization*—of the acquisition and internalization of the patterns of one's culture. Words are tools that serve as categories, "handles" by which to view the world, describe what goes on in our consciousness and experiences, and communicate with other people. They enable us to conceive of the world as orderly and predictable.

Language stands for things that human beings experience, but it also determines *what* they will experience. Different cultures will emphasize different areas of human experience.

From the spiritual viewpoint, the nature and functions of symbols can be amplified to cover the following aspects:

1. Symbols, which include images and archetypes, are the "Forgotten Language of the Unconscious, both Lower and Higher" which are used by the Scriptures and the Rituals of all Sacred Traditions.

2. They are *multi-dimensional;* that is, they do not have one set of meanings that is pre-established and socially standardized like the language of everyday speech and the language of science. Being a *function of human consciousness,* they have many sets of meanings, correspondences, and practical applications which are "open to infinity," unfolding with the expansion of human consciousness, and bursting forth with new emergent levels that can be linked, analogically and homologically, with Man, with the World, and with the manifold expressions of human experience.

3. They function as a bridge or link between the known and the unknown, the knowable and the unknowable, the conscious and the unconscious.

4. They can both *reveal* and *unveil,* or *cover* and *veil,* the truth or process which they represent and act as media to convey to others.

5. Each symbol has to be "worked upon" and "made to come alive" in the consciousness of the person using it. Hence, each symbol could be seen as a "mine" which has to be individually "mined" to yield its treasures, or as a "tree" which has to be "fed," "nurtured," and "grown" to give its fruits. Therefore, no one can hand a symbol "already worked out" to another person for then it would be a concept, or a word, but not a true symbol. The implications of this are that each person has to become actively involved with a symbol and use all the functions of his Psyche to "make it come alive" and to get it to "yield its treasures" which vary and grow with the level of consciousness, human experience, and degree of maturity of the person using it.

6. Each symbol, moreover, has a threefold nature: it has a *body*, the image or glyph, a *soul*, its growing, unfolding, and emergent interpretations and applications, and, finally, a *Spirit*, the Life or Energies it is connected with. What can and is transmitted from one generation to another, from one person to another, is its *body*. Its soul has to be nurtured and organically grown by the person who receives it and lives with it. Finally, its Spirit is the ultimate treasure, or gift, it will bestow upon those who have worked diligently with it and who are ready to receive it.

7. To pierce through the many veils of symbols and archetypes, on the different planes of being and levels of consciousness, we need to involve our whole being, give it our entire attention, and utilize effectively the major functions of our Psyche: *willing, thinking, feeling,* and *imagination*. Thus, we should learn to concentrate and direct our entire attention to the chosen symbol (willing), meditate on its various meanings, correspondences, and practical applications (thinking), visualize it (imagination) and to pour all our emotions into it eliciting new feelings from it (feeling).

Concentration can be practiced and further amplified through the proper use of symbols. Visualization can train as well as open up our creative imagination. Meditation can be practiced and developed through the use of symbols as well as it can reveal, by degrees and in various steps, the inner meanings and correspondences of the symbol. Love and devotion can be directed to the symbol and elicited from the symbol in higher octaves when Prayer is applied to it and when the symbol is used in Prayer. Finally, the intuition and the breakthrough of the higher energies and levels of consciousness can be channeled and modulated through the proper use of symbols and archetypes. A symbol or archetype can also be used *theurgically* to create, or bring about, a new state of consciousness, a new state of being, and a new reality: *the incarnation of the spiritual power,* in Man and in the World, to which it corresponds. And here it is the twin processes of *invocation* and *evocation* that are used. Thus, a whole curriculum of psychospiritual development, leading to spiritual awakening and realization, can be drawn from their proper use.

Chapter 10

Social Positions and Social Roles

Social Positions and Social Rules:
General Observations

Thus far, we have examined four basic kinds of ideas—norms, values, beliefs, and symbols—that are very important to sociology, noting that they constitute the *smallest units,* or the "building blocks" making up the abstract and all inclusive concept of *Culture.* Yet, as atoms combine and organize into larger units molecules so do these cultural units tend to link up with each other to form larger structured units. These cultural units are not usually found at random within a society but coalesce together to form a *social position* (or place) within a given culture as individuals learn to play key *roles* in that society.

The concepts of social position (or status) and social role derive from certain basic observations about the nature of social institutions and social groups. *Human beings fill or occupy positions and play or perform roles.* A social position (or status) is thus a kind of "identification tag" which places people in relation to each other and which implies some kind of role (two sides of the same reality). Thus, each person occupies many positions and plays many roles.

As one considers the variety of social norms, or standards of human behavior, it becomes apparent that relatively few of them apply universally to all people. This point can be illustrated by one of the most basic and universal norms: "thou shalt not kill." The person who kills is guilty of one of the most serious crimes and, if caught, subject to the most severe penalty. Yet this rule does not apply to certain persons occupying certain positions and performing certain roles. The policeman in execution of his duty, the soldier in battle, the public executioner carrying out the legal edict, and at times and in certain places even the betrayed husband—all these may kill without fear of being subject to criticism and sanction; indeed, we do not even define their acts as "murder."The central fact of this illustration is that the social institution, that is, the norms, do not apply to people occupying certain positions and performing certain roles. The terms used in our illustration, policemen, soldier, and public executioner, refer to social positions and social roles. Each social position carries with it a set of rules and norms which prescribe how the person who occupies it and plays that role should and should not behave. Thus, social position and social role are really two sides of the same reality. A *social position* is the place an individual occupies in the social system relative to other positions and which describes what a person is in that capacity. *Social role* is the pattern of behavior expected from the holder of that position which describes what a person does.

The Nature of Social Positions

A social position is the location or place within culture that is made up of a set of norms, values, beliefs, and symbols and which have as their purpose the regulation of the behavior of its occupant. As James Vander Zanden puts it, "It is the socially identified position one occupies in the social structure which entails expectations of behavior which are institutionalized." Let us take, for example, the social position of the *nurse*. What are the distinctive norms, values, beliefs, and symbols that make up her social status in American society?

a. *Basic Norms*
   1. Must be permissive and understanding (female qualities) yet emotionally uninvolved and strict about rules.
   2. Must adhere to the professional ethics.
   3. Must respect and hold in confidence all information given as such.
   4. Must advertise health products in accordance with allowed norms.
   5. Must not use professional knowledge for ends that are detrimental to the public good.
b. *Basic Values*
   1. Life is the ultimate value and must always be preserved.
   2. Suffering is undesirable and evil, and must thus be minimized.
   3. All human beings, regardless of color, race, religion, and class are equally sacred and valuable.
   4. Scientific knowledge and formal education are the best tools for being effective at alleviating human suffering and must be cultivated.
c. *Basic Beliefs*
   1. Nursing is a feminine profession where one must be able to display kindness, gentleness, sympathy, and patience.
   2. Must hold basic conceptions of how to deal with and treat sickness.

3. Must hold basic notions of psychodynamics and of patient-nurse relations.
   d. *Basic Symbols*
      1. The white uniform, hat, and shoes, and perhaps, a Red Cross embroidered on the uniform or on a pin.

The Status-Set

Every social position has its complementary position or positions. The position of a father has no meaning except in relation to his children and that of a professor apart from his students. Thus, every social position usually has more than one position associated with it and these, collectively, are called the *status-set*. Its sociological definition is: "An array of interdependent, complementary social positions associated with a given social status."

As an example, the social position of a medical student is tied to an array of other social positions which make up his *status-set*. These are professors, physicians, nurses, psychotherapists, social workers, etc. The norms of his social position prescribe that he should relate in a different way to the occupants of these complementary positions. Thus, social positions form an interlocking system in which each unit molds and influences the other units of the system with a reciprocal effect. The norms associated with a given social position define the rights and duties, the privileges and responsibilities of that position.

Another example is the American wife who is expected to do certain things for her husband, home, and country (even though these expectations have lately been debated and contested)! She is expected to cook, clean, decorate and take care of the home, provide companionship, be sexually available and interested, serve as a hostess, and bear children. The duties of the social position of "wife" are reciprocally also the *rights* of the status of "husband," and conversely, the *rights* of the wife are the *duties* of the husband (e.g., economic support, emotional security, attention and affection, company, sexual access and fidelity, and help in supporting and raising the children).

Ascribed and Achieved Position

A central feature of a social position is the rank in society which it confers upon its holder. Both the social position and the rank it confers upon its holder can be obtained through two basic mechanisms: **ascription** and **achievement**. In ascription, it is society that places an individual in a certain position with a certain rank; in achievement it is the individual himself who achieves that position and its attached rank.

All human societies are confronted with a constant "stream" of new babies who need to be placed in social positions. These new babies cannot be ignored or left to their own devices and society, too, needs new members to fill social positions that open up or that are vacated by death or other reasons. And here society is caught on the horns of a dilemma. On the one hand, the formation of a person's habits and attitudes begins at birth. Thus, the earlier the training begins, the better, for the more complete will his eventual social adjustment be. On the other hand, however, individuals differ greatly in their capacities and abilities, and there is no way of telling who the truly gifted will be. Thus, the longer the allocation of social positions is postponed, the better society can place the individual in the position for which he/she is best suited. Every society is, therefore, confronted with making a choice between these two options. The way out of this dilemma is to assign some positions to an individual independently of his/her unique capacities and abilities-these are the **ascribed positions**. While allocating other positions to an individual on the basis of his/her unique qualities and abilities, social statuses that will be secured through individual choice, competition and performance-these are the **achieved positions**.

As Kingsley Davis notes, "The fabrication of an infant for future positions must begin as soon as possible for preparing a child for his membership within society. It is a long and tedious process, and it pays to start the training as soon as possible, while the child is still in his most plastic phase. Nor can the child be left culturally vacant for any extended period of time. Paradoxically, the fabrication of a child for many future positions cannot start until he already has a position."

The basic conceptions concerning the norms, values, beliefs, and symbols of a social position are already standardized and formalized by society before the birth of the child. Thus, they exist apart from the child until, by virtue of the socialization and social control processes, they become internalized and incorporated in his personality.

Ascribed Positions

These are not controlled by or voluntary on the part of the individual but thrust upon him at birth, independently of his/her capacities and abilities. There are four major reference points that are used by human societies for ascribing social positions. These are:

1. *Sex—the* biological reality of the individual;
2. Age—infancy, childhood, adulthood, and old age carry different norms;

3. *Family Relationships*—father-child, mother-child, brother-sister, etc.; and,
4. *Birth into various socially established groups*—class, caste, religion, race, political groups.

Achieved Positions

These are not thrust upon the individual but voluntarily pursued and achieved; e.g., that of doctor, professor, engineer, dentist, etc. All human societies do recognize individual accomplishments and grant achieved positions . . . but some more than others!

Trade Off Between Ascribed and Achieved Positions

Ascribed Positions provide security, stability, predictability and stagnancy, while Achieved Positions provide challenge, mobility, and motivation but at the cost of anxiety, guilt, demoralization, and social alienation. As one sociologist put it, "The achieved status probably represents both the most efficient use of human potential and the greatest threat to the individual's security." Thus, a good balance between the two is necessary, changing with time and condition.

The Nature of Social Roles

While the emphasis of social position falls upon what *people should ideally do,* that of social roles falls upon *what they actually do.* As we defined social positions to designate the positions an individual occupies in the social system, so we can now define a social role as *the behavior expected from the holder of a certain position.* The concept of a social role is by no means a recent one. We already find it in Shakespeare's notion that "All the World is a stage . . . and all men and women merely players, with their exits and their entrances. And one man in his time plays many parts." The long ancestry of the idea of "social role" does not mean that this concept has been used in a systematic way in the past. What is new in this concept, as with all other scientific concepts, is the attempt to *systematically organize our knowledge,* to test our insights with empirical evidence, and to further our knowledge by pushing beyond these insights. Thus science consists not merely of perceptive and penetrating insights but of orderly and cumulative developments of knowledge.

The theatrical role suggested by the words "All the world is a stage" exists independently of individuals who must learn their lines and acquire the appropriate gestures and manners. Social roles are learned as individuals acquire the culture of their group even though social roles may become so much a part of their personality that they are played without awareness of their social characteristics. Most social positions and roles emerge from the process of *collective living,* of social stratification, and of the division of labor which entail a differentiation of positions and roles, of duties and privileges. As there is a *Status-set* so there is also a corresponding *Role-set.* Social positions exist apart from individuals but social roles do not because they are the actual performance of the individual.

Role-Conflict

In playing their roles, individuals may become exposed to incompatible behavior expectations—they may experience *role conflict* or role strain. There are five basic types and sources of role-conflict or role-strain. These are:

1. An individual maybe confronted with the obligations of a social status that he finds incompatible or uncongenial with some of his personality traits; as an example, the male nurse who has been socialized to be independent, aggressive, and impatient and who finds that this social role calls for being patient, tolerant, and gentle.

2. An individual may be confronted with conflicting obligations stemming from his simultaneously occupying two social positions; as an example, being a teacher and a friend to the same person. As a teacher, one is expected to be fair, impartial, and not emotionally involved, but as a friend, the opposite is true as one is expected to be partial, emotionally involved, and to help one's friends.

3. A social position may have a number of complementary positions associated with it—a Status-set—so that the occupant of one position may find himself in several role-relationships with different individuals which are mutually exclusive and contradictory; as an example, the Italian physician ("Medico della Mutua") who is under pressure from his clients to grant them medical dispensations but is employed by the State to insure an adequate level of health and prevent abuses of the system by workers.

4. A social position may demand several responses in relation to another position, responses that may be mutually contradictory; as an example, a nurse who is expected to be a surrogate mother and an effective leader; i.e., affectionate and permissive but also efficacious and strict.

5. Status ambiguity. Here the role strains result from the fact that the position an individual occupies lacks clarity and precision of definition, that is, the norms are vague and ambiguous; as an example, the American adolescent. The transition from

childhood to adulthood is vague. In other societies this transition might be made easier by puberty rites or *rites de passage.* The American adolescent does not really know what society expects of him/her. Thus, he falls prey to anxiety and searches for guide-posts, social anchorages, and standards that will bring a minimum of order and security in his/her life.

Roles and Personality

The position we occupy, and hence the roles we play, have a major impact and consequences for the development and proper functioning of our personality. They confront us with many demands and elicit from us a variety of attitudes, emotions, and overt actions—thus impacting our personality and the formation of our self-image and Weltanschauung. As an example, a person who has a very sedentary life, doing bureaucratic paper work, unless that person compensates in other ways, will tend to be in poor physical shape and to have difficulty in relating to people . . . rather than paper.

Conclusion

We have seen how norms, values, beliefs, and symbols agglutinate to form distinct, socially recognizable and structured, *social positions.* These social positions (or statuses) constitute a social location within a culture while *social roles* represent the actions of individuals. Whereas social positions define what people *should do,* social roles indicate what they *actually do.* Every social position has its complementary positions—*the Status-set*—just as every social role has its complementary roles—*the Role-set.* All human societies must place their members within their distinctive network of social positions, and such placement is done either through *ascribed* or *achieved* positions.

Individuals usually play their role within the limits of the tolerated range of variations prescribed by a society. Role-strain, however, may occur, stemming from five basic sources: the social position being incompatible with the individual's personality, the person occupying two conflicting positions, conflicting role-relationships with a status-set, conflicting demands within one role-relationship, and positional ambiguity.

Chapter 11

Social Institutions

The Nature of Social Institutions

Institutions are strategic channels through which human life is patterned, stabilized, and made predictable. They constitute an indispensable element of human life for, should they be destroyed, society itself would die.

While norms, values, beliefs, and symbols represent the smallest units, or construction blocks, social institutions make up the largest. Just as "behavior patterns coalesce to form a social position, so social positions agglutinate to form social institutions. As an example, the position of mother, father, husband, wife, child, son, daughter, grandfather, aunt, nephew, etc., fuse within a much larger structural whole making up the social institution of the *family*.

The Organic Analogy

The field of biology was very important for early sociology which took it as a major frame of reference. Thus, beginning with the smallest units—norms, values, beliefs, and symbols—we can see that culture is made up of progressively larger units—social positions and institutions. Turning to the biological analogy, we can see that living organisms begin with the cell, cytoplasm, nucleus, and cell-membrane—that could be compared to norms, values, beliefs, and symbols at the cultural level. We would then note that cells bind themselves together in such a way as to form various kinds of "tissues"—social positions—and that social positions interconnect to form organs—social institutions. Social institutions are, therefore, *the major instruments of social life*. They provide us with an appreciable degree of regularity, efficiency, and predictability in ordering our daily activities. They are the means by which the essential tasks of social life are organized, directed, and executed. Thus they can be defined as "a set of norms, values, beliefs, and symbols defining and organizing a large part of human behavior."

Structure and Function: System Analysis

In order to properly understand the nature of social institutions and their place and role in social life, it could be useful to introduce the concept of *system* which now plays a key role in many sciences. A "system" is a structured arrangement made up of interdependent and semi-autonomous parts all working as a functional whole (e.g., a solar system, an atomic system, or a system of ideas). Following this line of thinking, we can conceive of culture as making up an ideational system the central parts of which are institutions.

Basic Features of a System

1. It is composed of heterogeneous and semi-autonomous parts.
2. It is structured by functionally interrelated parts constituting an integrated whole.
3. It contains a variety of forces, or processes, operating within itself.
4. Though in a state of constant change, or flux, a system is a relatively lasting entity as its parts, or subsystems, are in a state of "dynamic equilibrium."
5. It is delineated by boundary lines, within which it retains its structural-functional entity.

Within system analysis, considerable attention is paid to the various *functions* which are performed by the system's parts.

The sociological definition of "function" is, "those observed consequences that make for the adaptation or adjustment of a given system." And the basic tasks of system analysis are:

1. to ascertain the functions required by the system if it is to survive and operate efficiently;
2. an evaluation of the structure through which these requirements are met; and
3. an examination of the compensating, or alternative, mechanisms that operate to meet the necessary functions should the normal mechanisms fail.

Within the context of this approach, sociocultural phenomena are viewed as related to one another so as to constitute a whole and as performing a function for the whole or some of its parts.

If a sociocultural system is to persist through time, it is essential that certain functions be performed (these are called the "functional prerequisites"). For example, goods and services must be produced and distributed; social control, basic goals, and protection must be ensured; children must be reproduced, socialized, and cared for; and social consensus and solidarity, health, and welfare must be preserved. To carry out these functions, certain structures—

116

social institutions—are essential as they constitute the principal cultural instrument through which functions are performed. Thus:

a. the economic institution produces and distributes goods and services;
b. the political institution protects citizens from one another, from enemies, and defines national goals;
c. the religious institution helps to provide social cohesion and social solidarity; and
d. the family institution reproduces, socializes, maintains, and socially places children.

As we saw in the "organic analogy," social institutions can be compared to the *organs* of the biological organism. They meet the vital requirements necessary for the survival of the system (biological, psychosocial, sociocultural, and spiritual).

These are called the "functional prerequisites" of which T. Parsons gave a very good definition and analysis in his "AGIL system" and which have been conceptualized by Bennett and Tumin as:

1. the maintenance of biological adequacy (Adaptation—the economy);
2. the reproduction of new members (Pattern Maintenance—the family);
3. the socialization of new members (Tension Management—the family);
4. the production and distribution of goods and services (Adaptation—the economy);
5. the maintenance of internal and external order (Goal Achievement—the polity); and,
6. the maintenance of meaning and motivation (Integration—the polity).

Alternating and Compensating Mechanisms

The functional requirements of sociocultural systems can be met in different ways as illustrated by *cultural variability*. Society "selects," as it were, its particular solutions from a wide range of cultural possibilities. But, however wide this range is, it is always limited—by man's biopsychic nature and by the nature of the physical and sociocultural environment. Also, should one institution fail to meet the functional requirements of the system another institution may assume this function much in the same way as when one organ in our body fails, another takes over that function or part of it. For example, the American family, undermined by social and geographical mobility, has failed in its traditional function of caring for the aged so that government and religious institutions have

117

stepped in, assuming that function through social security, retirement programs, and nursing homes.

Functions and Dysfunctions

While *functions* are those observed consequences that make for the adaptation or adjustment of a given system, *dysfunctions* are their counterpart which lessen the adaptation or adjustment to the system. But, a unit of a system—a norm, belief, position or institution—may be functional as well as dysfunctional and, at times, play both functional and dysfunctional tasks.

Take the institution of religion. Religion is functional to the extent that it promotes social cohesion and solidarity, encourages elements of a society to adopt common ends and values, providing, so to speak, an ideological and emotional *glue,* and fosters self-actualization and Self-realization in its members. It may also, on the psychological level, make human suffering more bearable and aid in the emotional adjustment to disappointment, death, and disaster. Yet religion may also be dysfunctional. Where different religions coexist in the same society, there often develops conflict between them that may impair social integration (that is to say, just as religion can *unite* people it can also *separate* them)! And religious doctrines may be at odds with secular values (e.g., birth control).

From a sociological viewpoint, neither functions nor dysfunctions have any ethical or moral connotations. Sociologists do not evaluate what is "good" and "bad" for a particular person or for society, rather they analyze the consequences and implications of certain actions, beliefs, and social structures—which they call *functions* or *dysfunctions*. What procedures do sociologists use to obtain knowledge about functions and dysfunction? One possibility is to set up a *mental experiment*—to assess within broad limits, what would happen if a position or an institution were eliminated, interrupted, or substituted. Here we can "think away" the part and calculate the consequences. Another possibility is to use the *comparative approach,* that is, to compare two situations that are alike, except for the part in question. Finally, we can observe the consequences when *a part of the system breaks down*—when the behavior associated with it is not adhered to (wars, revolutions, and crises often unveil profound insights as to the nature and consequences of functions and dysfunctions).

Manifest and Latent Functions and Dysfunctions

Manifest functions are those consequences which are deliberately intended and recognized by the participants in a system; *latent functions* are those functions which are neither intended nor recognized. This distinction shows that the conscious motivations for social behavior are not identical with the behavior's objective consequences and that both must be accounted for. As an example, take the ceremonials amongst the Hopi Indians to produce rain. These do not, in fact, produce rain (manifest function) but they do fulfill a number of latent functions at the psychological level. They provide an occasion for the tribe to get together and engage in common activities which promote social cohesion and social controls; they provide for Tension Management, the release and channeled expression of emotional tension and stress; and they provide an escape from reality and the reassurance that the Hopi can understand and control the forces of nature.

Latent Functions and Value Judgments

As moral evaluations tend to focus on the manifest functions of a structure or process, we should expect that an analysis of latent functions would often run against moral judgments. As an example, political machines are generally viewed as being "bad" and "immoral" as they violate a number of moral codes. If so, why do the political machines continue to exist? Because they perform positive functions which are not adequately covered by other existing structures (the American government has decentralized power by a system of "checks and balances" thus making it difficult to achieve rapid decisions and effective action. The political machine counterbalances this by "streamlined" decisions and actions). The political machine also transforms the impersonal and distant politics into more personalized government. Finally, the political machine provides services for "illegitimate" businesses that *do create jobs*.

Robert Merton, for example, writes, "Any attempt to eliminate an existing social structure without providing adequate alternative structures for fulfilling the functions previously fulfilled by the abolished organization is doomed to failure. To seek social change, without due recognition of the manifest and latent functions performed by the social organization undergoing change, is to indulge in social ritual rather than social engineering."

The Concept of Equilibrium

Any system is assumed to have a tendency to achieve a balance among its various parts and the forces that are operating within and upon it. The notion of equilibrium implies that, in spite of internal changes and external forces impinging upon the system, the latter remains in balance. We can also find three basic types of equilibria:

a. *Neutral* equilibrium—a ball on a flat plane;

b. *Stable* equilibrium—a ball fitting at the bottom of a cup; and,

c. *Unstable* equilibrium—a ball on the rim of two cups; a small disturbance here can produce considerable and rapid change.

Interrelationship Between Institutions

All cultural phenomena are, in fact, interconnected. Thus change in one of the parts has consequences for all the other parts and for the whole. Each of the social institutions directly influence and are influenced by all the others.

Chapter 12

Human Culture: An Overview

In a world in which a great many human beings of very different ways of thinking, feeling, willing, speaking, and acting with very different belief systems and life styles are brought into ever-closer contact with one another; and in a world where another World War would probably extinguish life on this planet and where human beings are facing ever-more complex problems and rising psychosocial stress, it is becoming increasingly more important to be able to answer the following fundamental questions:

a. What common grounds exist between human beings at different nations and cultures?
b. What differences exist between such human beings?
c. What are the sources of these differences?
d. How deep and how irreconcilable or reconcilable are these differences?
e. What are the means by which human beings of one nation and culture may come to understand those of another and may be able to establish right human relations with them?

The answer to such questions rest largely with understanding the nature and dynamics of *human culture.* To put it briefly, *culture* can be seen as the *total way of life,* the "designs for living," the ways of thinking, feeling, willing, speaking, and acting that a human being acquires as a member and "product" of one concrete society—of the creative psychic synthesis brought about by their interactions with each other. Culture consists in the idea systems (religious, philosophical, and scientific), the beliefs, customs, self-image, and Weltanchauung which makes a person an American rather than an Italian, a member of the upper class rather than the lower class, and a Christian rather than a Buddhist. Culture, therefore, is a systematic and objective study of the ways in which human beings differ in their sociocultural lives and creations, of the reasons why they differ, and of the possible ways in which they may understand other people with other cultures and levels of consciousness. The concept of culture is one of the most illuminating and practical contributions of anthropology, like the concept of *evolution* was for biology, the concept of *gravitation* was for physics, and the concept of *libido* was for psychology. This concept can greatly enhance our understanding of Man, his consciousness, his motivation, and his life-style. It dates back to the end of the 19th century and to the early 20th century. This basic concept has now been incorporated by sociology which has reconceptualized it by focusing upon appropriate aspects to suit its particular analytical and explanatory purposes.

Like the concept of sociology and other basic concepts in the social sciences, it has not one but many different and complementary definitions suggested by different thinkers and writers. For example, Clyde Kluckhorn in *Mirror for Man* looks at human culture as:

"The total way of life and human expression of a people: the social legacy the individual acquires from the group. . . . That part of the environment which is the creation of man and that makes man human: a blueprint for all of life's activities. . . . Culture arises out of human nature and its forms are restricted by man's biological nature and by the environment (the climate and geography) in which he lives, but it also channels, develops, and concretizes (stimulates or inhibits) man's biological processes and nature. All men undergo the same fundamental existential experiences—birth, helplessness, loneliness, illness, and death—but *how they do it* (and *view it*) is a cultural question. . . . The essence of the cultural process is *selectivity* (the focusing of one's attention and priorities), both conscious and unconscious."

Ruth Benedict in *Patterns of Culture* sees human culture as:

"What binds men together; it is a set of techniques for adjusting both to the external environment and to men. . . . It produces as well as fulfills needs."

James Vander Zanden in his *Sociology: A Systematic Approach* defines culture as:

"The socially standardized ways of thinking, feeling, speaking, and acting that man acquires as a member of society."

For our purposes, I would like to amplify our formal definition of culture to include both a structural and a functional aspect, that is:

Culture is the socially standardized way of thinking, feeling, willing, speaking, and acting that man acquires as a member of society, and the artifacts and social structures he produces.

Culture functions as a blueprint for survival—physical, psychological, social and spiritual—which enables man to meet social expectations, to solve his basic existential problems (needs and ideals), and to develop and actualize many of his faculties and potentialities.

If we put these definitions under our magnifying glass and analyze them in detail, here is what we have. Culture is the product of the creative psychic synthesis brought about by human interaction which is the meaningful articulation and externalization of human consciousness which becomes institutionalized by society. As such, it involves three basic dimensions:

a. *The ideational dimension* involving the creation of thoughts and *idea systems* such as our religious, philosophical, scientific, political, and economic systems. This dimension really constitutes the essence of culture which is an objectification of human consciousness.

b. *The interactional dimension:* various forms of *social organizations* based on values and norms that regulate the specific forms of human interaction in a given society.

c. *The material dimension: artifacts* or man-made implements and objects, tools, machines, houses, clothes, weapons which can be produced directly by human beings or indirectly by machine.

Culture, moreover provides human beings and human societies with:

a. order and organization;
b. motivation and incentive; and,
c. meaning and purpose.

These, in turn, enable human beings in various physical and social environments to create A PSYCHOSOCIAL COSMOS OUT OF CHAOS: to unfold a social and personal identity (to know who they are and who other people are), to find different meanings and purposes for their lives, and to organize their mutual lifestyles.

Culture also functions as a total blueprint for his personal and collective survival and for realizing personal and collective ideals at the physical, psychological, social, and spiritual levels. At the *physical level,* survival implies being able to meet one's basic, or primary, needs, and aspirations such as obtaining food, shelter, and protection from the elements and other living beings. At the *psychological level,* survival means essentially to experience one's self as a being endowed with value, dignity, and autonomy; i.e., *to love oneself.* At the *social level,* survival implies being perceived and treated by others as a being endowed with value, dignity, and integrity; i.e., to be loved by others. And at the *spiritual level,* survival entails finding meaning and purpose which enable one to find a right relationship to oneself, to others, to God and to Nature. Finally, while most anthropologists and social scientists define the functions of culture as being essentially those of ensuring biopsychic and sociocultural survival; i.e., adapting to the physical environment and adjusting to the sociocultural environment, I would add to this the realization of ideals and aspirations and the actualization of one's human potentials and faculties. For the true purpose of life on earth is not only for Man to survive but also to become more than what he is, to grow, unfold, and actualize his potential, and to realize the designs of the Spirit in Creation. Survival, important as it is, is a *means* to a *greater* end which is *self-actualization* and *Self-realization*. This can be demonstrated empirically where we find human beings who have everything to "survive" and to have a comfortable material and psychosocial life and yet who are far from being happy or fulfilled, becoming bored, jaded, and even sick whereas other human beings who have a "hard physical or psychosocial life" can find meaning, fulfillment, and joy in their precarious existence.

The Nature of Culture

The concept of "culture" designates an abstraction, an ideal type, of a high degree of generalization. Like "evolution" or "gravitation," culture is an intellectual construct of the human mind which serves to look at, analyze, and explain sociocultural phenomena. What the social sciences study are the manifestations of human consciousness and behavior which the concept of culture unifies, analyzes, and explains such as Man's words, attitudes, actions, and artifacts. Culture also refers to, unifies, and explains patterns of human behavior which are essentially psychic, or super-organic, even though they manifest themselves in words, actions, and objects. Culture is thus an all-embracing phenomenon which permeates and structures all human activities. Culture exerts an influence in society through the various social institutions it shapes and crystallizes and is *internalized* by individuals who, in turn, educate and socialize new members of society.

The Characteristics of Culture

Culture has six distinctive features:

1. *Culture is learned* and is not instinctive or innate; it is acquired by Man from the group into which he is born and in which he is raised and springs forth from his psyche rather than from his biological organism or instincts.

2. *Culture is transmitted from generation to generation.* It represents in Man and serves many of the functions that instincts fulfill for animals. It helps him to adapt to his physical environment and to adjust to his sociocultural environment as well as to develop and actualize his faculties and potentialities, to find meaning and purpose in life, and to realize his Self. Man is born into a social tradition and culture represents his social legacy that will help him to develop and channel his biological heredity.

3. *Culture is socially shared.* Cultural patterns are learned and shared by human beings living in organized groups and "standardized" by social pressures. Cultural patterns can be seen as group norms and habits.

4. *Culture is gratifying.* It helps both to generate and to satisfy human needs, be they biological, psychological, social, or spiritual. Every human group has culturally defined and acquired drives which can be even more powerful than those rooted in the biopsychic drives (e.g., to be successful, to obtain honor or status).

5. *Culture is adaptive.* Culture is, necessarily, structured and regulated by forces that originate outside of itself (e.g., geography, climate, and social conditions) and to which it helps Man to adapt and adjust. People have to adapt to their physical and sociocultural environment if they are to survive and to realize their ideals.

6. *Culture is integrative.* All the manifold parts and subsystems of a culture tend to form a consistent, coordinated, and interrelated whole. Moreover, cultural patterns shared in common by human beings tend to integrate and synthesize their norms, values, beliefs, symbols, expectations, and action.

The Observed Dimensions of Culture

Culture has three basic sets of what social scientists call its "observed dimensions or structures:" the *Ideal* and *Manifest,* the *Overt* and *Covert,* and the *Explicit* and *Implicit.*

a. The *Ideal* and *Manifest* dimensions: Cultural patterns can be observed two different levels: the Ideal level expressing how people say they behave or should behave and the Manifest level expressing how they do, in fact, behave. And it is a well-known fact that there is always a discrepancy between these two levels. Both must be taken into account and properly evaluated by social scientists.

b. The *Overt* and *Covert* dimensions: The Overt aspects of culture refer to those elements of culture which can be *empirically perceived*—words, actions, and artifacts. The Covert dimensions, on the other hand, refer to those aspects of culture which cannot be empirically perceived, to the internal activities of human beings which cannot be directly observed or discovered (e.g., values, sentiments, fears).

c. The *Explicit* and *Implicit* dimensions: The Explicit aspects of culture refer to those elements of culture which can be easily verbalized, described, and discussed. The *Implicit* aspects of culture, on the other hand, refer to those components of culture which cannot be verbalized and conceptualized, but which are lived (e.g., rules of grammar, performing a certain sport, or attitudes which have become like a "second nature").

The Implications of Culture

1. *Do animals possess a culture?* No, only human beings have cultures which are a distinctly human phenomenon. Animals have "societies" but no truly *human culture*. At best they have a "proto-culture." They do live in organized societies such as anthills or bee-hives and they can learn certain patterns, but they neither have a language nor a history. Animal societies go on repeating the same patterns generation after generation as these patterns are instinctually controlled and not culturally regulated.

2. *Culture and biological processes:* Culture channels, molds, and modifies a large area of biological functioning. On a very general and abstract level, culture is influenced by biology, climate, and geography but never in concrete and specific ways. If Man is to survive he must, necessarily provide for his basic biological needs of hunger, thirst, fatigue, sex, elimination, and temperature control, but there are almost infinite specific ways of doing so. Human beings must eat, for example, but what the eat, how they prepare what they eat, how they get their food, and whom they eat it with is a cultural question. Culture can both inhibit and stimulate primary needs and even create new secondary needs; the cultural beliefs can lead a person to explore and develop new aspects of the universe and of his self. Strong beliefs backed by powerful emotions can even kill a person!

Ely Chinoy, in *Sociological Perspective*, writes:

"Both the universality of generalized cultural patterns and the diversity of more specific patterns call for explanation. We pointed out earlier that most human behavior is learned rather than inherited, and that culture determines what people learn. The invariable recurrence of certain cultural patterns suggests the likelihood of a close relationship between culture and the biological nature of man. To what extent or in what way, we may ask, is the nature of culture determined, shaped, or influenced by man's organic characteristics? The structure and functioning of man as a biological organism provides (to use Parson's terminology) "points of reference" or "foci" around which universally found cultural patterns inevitably develop. These foci consist of such things as the structural and functional differences between the sexes, and the fact that human infants are for a comparatively long time dependent upon others for survival, the organic drives generated by hunger, thirst, and sex, and the processes of maturation and aging, and the fact of death. These biological facts form the basis upon which many universal elements of culture are built—for example, child care and child rearing, or the techniques of securing food and drink. But again it should be noted that there is no uniformity in *how* men deal with these facts. Human biology, as Kluckhorn has put it, "sets limits, supplies potentialities and drives, provides clues which culture neglects or elaborates." Biological universals, however, do not provide all the points of reference around which men develop their culture. An examination of even the partial list quoted above of patterns found in all groups will indicate many that one cannot easily relegate to biological factors. Such things as bodily adornments, cosmology, courtship, folklore, decorative arts, and dancing appear far removed from innate drives or basic needs. Instead, we must search for an explanation in the fact of *collective living,* a fact which we have already emphasized as basic to our analysis. The discovery of the social foci for cultural patterns constitutes one of the major theoretical problems of sociology."

3. *Culture and perception:* We never really "see" the physical universe about us as it really is. Rather, our picture of the world and of material objects therein is the result of the creative interaction between the physical universe (external, physical stimuli), our nervous system and sense organs, our level and quality of human consciousness, and what we have learned in our past experiences— all of which are structured by culture both in its foci and in its interpretations.

Sociocultural influences affect perception in a very decisive way. Perception is highly selective and involves a good deal of focusing, adding and omitting. A well-known social science experiment demonstrated how if one projects a luminous line on a black surface and then asks participants how long the line is most of them will give a length that is closely related to the first answers that were given. Large distortions can be obtained if a number of people are asked to deliberately exaggerate the length of the line but without telling the members of the experimental group about this.

4. *Culture and emotions:* Culture has a very profound impact upon what triggers off emotions within us and how we express our emotions. Some cultures like the Dionysian cultures of the South and of the romantic movements strongly privilege and emphasize

our emotional life. Here, it is very desirable to be a "passionate" and an "emotional person" and to fully acknowledge and express our wide range of emotions such as love, anger, fear, awe, sympathy, etc. For life, here, is apprehended in an essentially emotional way. Other cultures such as the Apollonion cultures of the North and of the Classical and Rational movements strongly privilege and emphasize reason and self-control, fearing and denying strong emotions which are seen as "barbarian" and threatening to the psychological organization of the psyche and to the integration to the psychological organization of the psyche and to the integration of the social order. A new and more holistic culture is emerging in the Aquarian Age, in the Human Potential Movement, and in holistic and preventive medicine which emphasizes owning our entire nature and finding a *harmonious expression* of all functions of the psyche and of all our energies and drives.

5. *Cultural universals:* While most cultural items, ideas, and beliefs are perceived as being relative and culture bound, there are certain cultural universals but at a very high and general level of abstraction and expressed in a *symbolic* and *analogical* fashion and not in a descriptive and analytic fashion. For example, the family, religion, eating, sleeping, dancing, and various archetypes could be considered cultural universals.

Take, for example, one of the Ten Commandments: "Thou shalt honor thy Mother and thy Father." In its concrete and specific interpretation of respecting and obeying one's biological mother and father, this Commandment is certainly not a cultural universal as it is relative to certain cultures, historical periods, social classes, values, and norms. But, taken in its symbolic and archetypal sense of becoming aware of, and entering into a proper relationship with the physical part of one's being, or the biological organism (the "mother") and with the spiritual part of one's being, or the Divine Spark (the "father"), and with the female (the "mother") and the male (the "father") principles of one's nature, they are, indeed, cultural universals. Cultural universals always refer to the broad, overall, and symbolic categories and never to the specific, analytical contents of culture.

6. *Subculture and Contraculture:* By studying many different cultures and different subsystems of these cultures, social scientists have discovered that there exists not only a great deal of *inter-cultural variability* but also a great deal of *intra-cultural variability*. Thus, sociologists have developed two basic concepts, or ideal types, to describe and analyze the intra-cultural differences; *subculture* and *contraculture*.

A *subculture* refers to the variations in culture which differ from the major culture by stressing some aspects more than others, and which thus separates a group of persons in their ways of thinking, feeling, willing, speaking, and acting from the society at large without bringing that group to reject the larger culture. As examples of subcultures, we could cite the artistic or scientific communities or the YUPPIES.

A *contraculture,* on the other hand, refers to those variations in cultural patterns which set a group of persons against the larger society in its basic ways of thinking, feeling, willing, speaking or acting. Rather than being a "variation on a theme" as the former, the contraculture involves a rejection and denial of the basic traits and themes of the larger culture.

As examples of contracultures we have extremist political groups, certain religious sects, and delinquent gangs. The members of a contraculture, who are often caught in frustrating and conflict-laden situations, react by creating ways and values which are the *opposite* of those of the society at large.

To conclude our theoretical discussion of human culture, let us again quote Ely Chinoy:

"Man is not the only "animal" who learns to act instead of knowing more or less automatically what to do. Dogs can be taught a good deal and can learn from experience, as can horses, cats, monkeys, and apes. But, by virtue of his greater brain power and his capacity for language, man possesses greater flexibility of action than other animals; he can do more to control the world about him, acquire a greater variety of knowledge, and transmit what he learns more effectively. Man is the only "animal" who possesses culture proper."

From my viewpoint, the basic difference between a human being and an animal is that animals adjust *autoplastically* to their environment (i.e., they change themselves to adapt to their environment) whereas Man adjusts *alloplastically* to his environment (i.e., he changes his environment to suit his nature, needs, and aspirations). Animal societies are instinct-bound, repeating the same basic patterns over and over and thus lacking a true "history," whereas human societies are regulated by their culture and do have such a true "history." Finally, Man, through the expansion of his consciousness and the transformations of his culture can *transcend himself* and reach higher levels of being and functioning for which he is responsible. He has the freedom that requires responsibility and integrity to create countless human and social experiments on his path to self-actualization and Self-realization. Finally, while, at best, some animals can become "domesticated" and imitate their human companions, human beings can break through into qualitatively different and higher levels of consciousness and being which will eventually bring about the "Spiritual Man of tomorrow," the fully actualized and realized Being he was intended to be by the supreme Force and Intelligence that created him.

Having analyzed briefly but systematically the nature, dynamics, and functions of human culture, let us now turn our attention to some concrete and practical examples of how culture works and of the differences it brings about in human life.

1. The anthropologist Clyde Kluckhorn reported that he once met in New York City a young American who was born and raised in China and who thus had internalized a Chinese culture. While he was a white caucasian like most New Yorkers, he was quite lost there and was unable to become acculturated in his new sociocultural environment and thus eventually returned to China!

2. Japanese soldiers were excellent and dedicated soldiers who were, for the most part, willing to die for their country. Yet, once they became prisoners of war and interacted with Americans they suddenly changed their alliance and became quite willing to help the American war effort: lacking the proverbial "individualism" of Americans, they felt as though they had "died" and had been socioculturally "reborn," and thus were now an organic part of American society.

3. While visiting the countryside of Iran, I decided one day to interview some Iranian women and ask them about how they felt sharing their husband with up to three other wives. The first genetic response I got through the interpreter was; "why do you ask such a silly question?" It is quite obvious why a God-fearing and good man who truly cares for his wife would acquire other wives! "Only a selfish man who did not care for his wife has only one wife . . . out of avarice and lack of consideration!"

One woman argued that it was a universal trait of human nature to want to do less work rather than more work. If a man has but one wife, she ends up doing all the work at home and with the children whereas if he has more than one wife, they will share the work.

Another woman asked whether all human beings would not prefer to have another person, of roughly their own age, to keep them company and have fellowship with rather than being along with children while her husband works in the fields.

Yet another woman, who appeared as a budding political scientist, stated that while a man was physically stronger and would dominate her if pitted alone against her, he would be much more reasonable if he had to deal with more than one woman. This would reestablish a healthy "balance of power" which would ensure a more satisfying and lasting relationship.

Finally, the last woman claimed that only another woman could really understand a woman and that everyone really needs a "confidant" or someone who really understands and to whom one can open up without fear of misunderstanding. The typical jealousy and possessiveness of Western persons seemed to be completely absent here. Since then, I have discovered that there are other human societies (e.g., the Alor, Chuchee, and Muria) where women actually urge their husbands to take other wives.

4. I once had an American friend who went to visit mutual friends in Spain. While in their house he expressed great interest in a painting and was told that it was his and that he could take it (on the principle that "my house is your house." He took this statement literally, and took the painting with him when he left, and was "quite surprised that he never heard from them again!"

5. But the best illustrative story of the influences and differences of culture is one that happened to me in Italy many years ago, and which could have only happened in Italy! At the time, I was studying at the University of Denver and had invited a friend of mine to spend the summer at my parents' villa in St. Margherita, on the Italian Riviera. To get to Italy, we took a boat in New York and on that boat we each met a girl we really liked so we made plans to see each other in Italy; and, as the girls were on a tour that would spend three days in Florence, we decided that that would be the place we would meet. I knew Florence well as I had been a student there for one and a half years and thought that this would be the ideal place to meet. So a month after arriving in St. Margherita, we took the "vespas" we had bought to drive around the Riviera and headed for Florence. We went to the same hotel where the girls were staying and had a happy reunion with them. The first day we were in Florence we went to visit many of the high spots of the City such as the Ponte Vecchio and the Palazzo della Signoria, then went to a Tratoria for lunch and to a good restaurant for dinner. The following day we did much of the same, but ended up at a nightclub overlooking the City near Piazzale Michelangelo. While dancing and guzzling good sparkling Italian wine we decided to have an "unforgettable adventure," to do something we had never done before and would be able to tell people about for a long time, and little did we know that Destiny had already prepared something much better than we could have ever imagined or planned. At that point there were six of us for we had met another American, the day before, who decided to date a girl who was on the same tour, and to come with us. In between dances, we decided to play a game and see how each of us could propose something unusual for that "unforgettable adventure."

Many plans were thrown on the table, but, as I knew the city and its possibilities well, mine was finally adopted.

What I proposed was the following. We would go down by the Arno River and take some canoes that were always by the waterfront and that belonged to a man who lived in a cabin nearby. Then, we would go down the river to the small waterfall and up the river to where a nightclub played music all night and thus have an almost complete panoramic view of the city from the river. Everyone was quite enthusiastic about our agreed upon adventure and so we set off. The canoes were exactly where I had expected them to be, with their oars in; the cabin of the owner was dark; and it was about 11:30 P.M. Each couple took one canoe which was gently pushed into the water, and we set off on our journey, but not without the girls giggling a great deal, a trivial fact which, however, turned this little escapade into a truly "unforgettable adventure." Slowly and carried by the current, we paddled down the river taking in the moonlit and brilliantly illuminated sky-view of the city. About an hour later, we reached the first waterfall which made us turn around and leisurely we rowed up the river, this time up to the point where the other nightclub was located. On the way, however, we lost my friend from Colorado and his date. As we reached the area near the nightclub, we threw overboard the little anchor every canoe had in its bottom and relaxed, drinking another bottle of good tuscan wine, and settling comfortably to listen to the good music that was reaching us from the shore and to watch the moon and the slumbering shape of the city in the distance.

How much time elapsed, I do not know and did not care, but, at a certain point, I saw the canoe of my friend from Denver coming up the river with two other boats filled with people. He was calling my name and was gesticulating, but I kept looking at the people who filled the other two boats and who soon appeared to me to be distinctly Italian Carabinieri, the elite Italian police. As the three boats finally came up abreast with ours, I realized what had happened. The girls' giggles had woken up the owner of the canoes who had then called the police to report that three of his boats had been "stolen" by strange people. I pretended not to speak Italian and to be an American like all the rest, even though I spoke better Italian, at that time, than English for I had decided that, under the circumstances, that might be the best course of action. We were then taken back to the point where we had taken the canoes, and an English-speaking Carabiniere asked us why we had "stolen" the boats to placate the irate and sleepy owner who was looking at us shaking his hand. I told them that we had not "stolen" the boats but "rented them" and asked what the fee was for that. When we paid the fee, which had doubled for the night use of the boats and

given the owner a nice tip, the whole matter might have been resolved then and there, robbing us of the best part of the adventure.
But it was not, as one of the Carabinieri asked us for identification
and pointed out that, as the three girls were 20 years old, they had
broken the city-imposed curfew of 1:00 A.M. for foreign girls who
were not accompanied by adults. The three of us obviously did not
qualify as "adults" in that situation. Consequently, we were all
taken in a police paddy-wagon to the hotel to get the girls' passports. The streets of Florence sure looked different at 4:30 A.M. seen
from the perspective of a racing police paddy wagon with its sirens
blasting!

When we arrived at the hotel, the girls' French tour leader was
woken up by a dutiful concierge who felt he had to report this matter. As she came to meet us at the reception desk, she looked very
sleepy and even more angry and her anger seemed to have been
especially directed at me! Fortunately, there were the peerless
Carabinieri to restrain her or I don't know what would have become of me! The girls got their passports and we were all taken to
the police station with the tour leader who insisted on not leaving
the girls out of her eyes and who, naturally, had misunderstood the
whole situation. At the police station, we told our story to an
amused police sergeant who told us that we three men and the tour
leader could go back to the hotel (but in different taxis!) while they
would keep the girls until they could report the incident to the
American Consulate.

A few hours later, after some deep sleep, I was awakened by
my date who told me a most incredible story of what happened to
them. Apparently, at around 6:00 A.M., many of the police reported
for duty and started making all kinds of comments and whistling
when they saw three lovely American girls sitting in the main hall.
This disrupted the normal routine of the police station and the sergeant then, apparently, sent the three girls to a large cell to restore
order. A police lieutenant happened to be passing by when he noticed the girls in the cell. He began speaking to them in English,
which he knew fairly well, then left and came back with other
Carabinieri who brought some wine, a mandolino and other musical
instruments, and they all sang and danced for a couple of hours.
The girls were then taken back to their hotel in a squad car as a
petition had obviously been made for the case to be dropped as they
were, quite clearly, "very nice persons!" And this story, a most unforgettable adventure which probably got told many times to many
people back home. I contend could only have happened in Italy
which has very different customs than other countries and the
United States in particular!

Chapter 13

Parsons Theory of Social Action

Ever since its birth in the late 18th century, sociology has attempted to explain in an objective, systematic, and sociological fashion why people behave the way they do. Talcott Parsons was the first sociologist to offer a coherent, integrated, and sociological theory to explain human behavior. Thus, his theory of social action is his greatest contribution to modern sociology and modern sociology's greatest addition to our cognitive universe. This theory was articulated and published in the mid 50's in two main works: *Toward A General Theory of Social Action* and *Selected Papers On A Theory of Social Action*. It is this theory that I will analyze and summarize in the following pages. As it is quite complex and written in heavy sociological jargon or "parsonese," I will begin by presenting the practical implications of his theory contained in the "Practical Paradigm for the study and analysis of social action" and then will move on to discuss his "Theoretical Conceptual Framework for the study and analysis of social action."

The Practical Paradigm for the Study and Analysis of Social Action

According to Parsons, any social situation involving conscious, meaningful, and goal oriented behavior, defined as "social action" can be observed, described, analyzed, and explained by the following paradigm:

1. *Actors:* These are the people who are involved and who should be observed and described in terms of standard sociological variables such as number, age, sex, education, occupation, socioeconomic status, religion, ethnicity, etc.
2. *Setting:* This is the place where the action occurs and which should be accurately described as it is assumed to have an impact upon human consciousness which has an impact upon human behavior.

The first two variables, Actors and the Setting, are the objective variables which can be found in the world and observed empirically. While the following three variables—Goals, Means, and Norms—are the subjective variables which can be found only in the consciousness of the actors.

3. *Goals: Instrumental or Expressive:* These are what the actors want, their ends or objectives. The basic assumption here being that if people do something and act, it is because they want to get something.

   Instrumental goals are the things we do to get something else; for example, working in a factory to get the money to pay for rent, food, and leisure. Here, the rewards are extrinsic, lying not in what we do for its own sake but in order to get what we really want.

   Expressive goals are the things we do for their own sake; for example, going out for dinner and then dancing with someone. The assumption here is that we enjoy that person's company and dancing. Thus the rewards are intrinsic; the satisfaction or "pay-off" being in what we actually do.

Sociologists should find out what are the actors' goals, both instrumental and expressive, and describe them accurately.

4. *Means: Rational and Irrational:* These imply the ways in which the actors go about getting what they want.

   Rational means are simply those ways of getting what we want effectively and economically.

   Irrational means are ways of getting what we want which either do not get us what we want or which do but in a much more expensive, time-consuming, or energy-expending way than was necessary.

Sociologists should find out what are the means, both rational and irrational, which are used by the actors to get what they want and describe these accurately.

5. *Norms: Formal and Informal:* These are the rules that regulate the interactions between the actors as they pursue their goals through various means.

   Formal norms are the rules that are imposed upon the actors by the situation in which they find themselves and which come from the value system of the social system. For example, they would be the "house rules" that students would get when signing up to live a school dormitory.

Informal norms are the rules that emerge from the interaction itself and which are created by the actors. Many times, informal rules can mitigate or change the formal rules as, for example, during prohibition when it was lawfully forbidden to drink but people did it any way, at all levels of society, making a point to "keep this to themselves."

Sociologists should find out what the rules are, formal and informal, that regulate the interactions of the actors they are studying and describe them accurately.

Thus, a sociologist studying the social action involved in a classroom would take a notebook and on the first page enter the rubric "actors" and then proceed to list all the information he can get by direct observation and by asking questions. This would include how many actors there are, their sex and age, their educational level and occupations, their ethnic affiliation and religious affiliation, their socioeconomic status and, perhaps, also their residence. On the second page, he would enter the rubric "setting" and then proceed to describe the room itself and its location in the school. On the third page, he would enter the rubric "goals" and proceed to list the instrumental and expressive goals of the actors by observing them and asking them questions and then, perhaps, cross-checking these. On the fourth page, he would enter the rubric "means" and proceed to list and describe the means, rational and irrational that the actors use to achieve their goals. Finally, on the fifth page, he would enter the rubric "norms" and then proceed to conceptualize and list the formal and informal norms that regulate and structure the actors' interaction. On the basis of this accumulated data, he would then describe, analyze, and explain the instance of social action he is studying.

The Theoretical Conceptual Framework for the Study and Analysis of Social Action

This is the "philosophy" or "rationale" behind the practical paradigm. It involves basic insights which are:

1. *The central axiom of social action theory:* this states that THE FRAME OF REFERENCE OF ACTION INVOLVES *ACTORS,* A *SITUATION OF ACTION,* AND THE *ORIENTATION* OF THE ACTORS TO THAT SITUATION.

The *actors* are, of course, the people involved, and the situation is the *setting* or the place where the action occurs. Sometimes, Parsons also includes *norms* under the situation viewing them as the objective constraints imposed by the social system upon the interacting actors. The actors and the situation constitute the objective variables that can be observed empirically by the sociologist.

The *orientation* of the actors to their situation includes the goals, means, and norms of the actors. Here norms are viewed as the *subjective* elements operating in the consciousness of the actors as these depend, ultimately, upon the consciousness and will of the actors to be implemented and enacted. This is the subjective component of social action as it takes place in the *consciousness of the actors* where it must be ferreted out and conceptualized.

2. *The basic postulate of social action theory is that* SOCIAL ACTION IS DEFINED AS BEHAVIOR ORIENTED TO THE ATTAINMENT OF GOALS OR ENDS IN SITUATIONS BY MEANS OF THE NORMATIVELY REGULATED EXPENDITURE OF ENERGY OR MOTIVATION; AND THAT ANY BEHAVIOR THAT INVOLVES SOME AWARENESS OF A GOAL IS SO ORGANIZED AS TO CHOOSE THE MOST ECONOMICAL AND EFFICIENT MEANS TO REACH THIS GOAL.

3. *There are four basic points that characterize the concept of social action.*

    a. In social action, behavior is oriented to the attainment of goals or ends; that is, that behavior is conscious, meaningful, and purposeful involving, directly or indirectly, human interaction,

    b. It takes place in situations,

    c. It is normatively regulated,

    d. It involves the expenditure of energy or effort.

4. *There are two basic sets of forces that blend in the consciousness of the actors to determine and regulate their behavior.* Parsons calls these the *motivational orientation* and the *value orientation.* The motivational orientation represents those forces that come from the personality of the actors and which are, therefore, *psychodynamic* in nature. These are *energy, drive,* and *needs.*

The motivational orientation is defined by Parsons as "the actor's evaluation of a situation which can or cannot satisfy his need-dispositions. It is those aspects of the actor's orientation to his situation which are related to actual or potential gratification or deprivation of his need dispositions." And it includes three basic modes or conscious ways of reacting to them.

    a. *The cognitive mode:* the process by which an actor perceives an object. It is the actor's definition of an object and placing it in the whole scheme of his knowledge.

    b. *The affective* (cathectic) *mode:* the process by which an actor attributes emotional meaning and significance to an object.

c. *The conative* (evaluative) *mode:* the process through which an actor chooses one object instead of others to satisfy his needs to the maximum.

The value orientation represents those forces that come from society and which are, therefore, sociocultural in nature. These are *goals, means,* and *norms.*

The value orientation is defined by Parsons as "that part of the actor's situation which compels him to choose between several accepted ways of behavior. It is the actor's commitment to certain cultural standards or criteria of selection." It also includes three modes or conscious ways of reacting to them:

a. *the cognitive mode:* knowing the cultural standards related to the situation at hand;
b. *The affective* (appreciative) *mode:* the process by which an actor emotionally assesses a situation as one which can or cannot gratify his needs; and
c. *the conative* (moral) *mode:* the evaluation of the effects and consequences which the choice of some types of action will have on the actors and on the system as a whole.

What Parsons means by the foregoing is essentially the following: One can picture human nature, the body and the psyche, as an energy generating and transforming system. It is as if there were a fountain-spring in our bodies and psyches which pours forth energy on a continuing basis. This energy generates drives or pressures which are experienced as basic needs which must be satisfied if we are to continue functioning properly. These needs are physical, such as hunger, or psychosocial, such as affection, and they drive us to do something about satisfying them. Moreover, one can *think* (the cognitive model), *feel* (the affective mode), and *make decisions* (the conative mode) about them. Society or the sociocultural system in which we live then brings a set of sociocultural forces which enable us to define what these drives or needs are, in terms of concrete and specific goals to be pursued to satisfy them, the legitimate means we can use to satisfy them, and the norms or rules we must abide by in satisfying them. And one can also *think* (the cognitive mode), *feel* (the affective mode), and *make decisions* (the conative mode) about them.

A concrete and specific example at the level of biopsychic needs is *hunger.* As time goes by our body generates energy that we experience as a drive. Society then comes in and tells us that this is "hunger" and that we can relieve this hunger by eating. It tells us what kinds of foods are available for us, how we can cook them and eat them, how we can work to earn the money to buy this food or grow it, and what norms or rules we should live by in our interactions with other human beings in order to achieve the foregoing.

A concrete and specific example at the level of psychosocial needs is *affection*. As time goes by, our psyche feels loneliness that we experience as a drive. Society then comes in and tells us that this is a need for affection and that we can get affection by entering into intimate relations with one or more human beings, what are the legitimate ways in which to give and receive affection, and what norms or rules we should live by in our interactions with other human beings in order to achieve the above.

All of the foregoing can be schematically represented by the following formula:

Cognitive: thinking

SOCIAL ACTION—Human Consciousness   Affective: feeling
(human behavior)

Conative: willing

Personality: Energy, drives, needs.

Society: Goals, means, norms.

Chapter 14

The Four Functional Prerequisites: Parsons AGIL System

As we saw in a previous chapter, the Structural-Functional Approach goes all the way back to the origins of sociology and has its roots first in biology and later in psychology. The central postulate of this approach is that THERE IS AN ANALOGY OR CORRESPONDENCE BETWEEN THE BIOLOGICAL ORGANISM OF MAN AND THE SOCIAL ORGANISM, OR SOCIAL SYSTEM, SO THAT, ROUGHLY SPEAKING, THE BASIC LAWS AND CENTRAL CONCEPTS DESCRIBING THE FORMER ALSO APPLY TO THE LATTER. A derivative assumption of this postulate is that HUMAN AND SOCIAL EVOLUTION CAN BE REGARDED AS THE "ADAPTATION OF AN ORGANISM TO ITS ENVIRONMENT, PHYSICAL, SOCIAL, AND CULTURAL" which comes from biological evolutionary theory and which can then also be applied to spiritual evolution. Here, functional theory asks, "how can the biological and social system adapt to its environment, how does it operate, what functions does it fulfill and, in particular, *what mechanisms and processes ensure its adaptation, adjustment, and proper functioning?*

Thus, one of the great questions and contributions of the Structural-Functional Approach is to ask, "HOW DOES THE BODY, PHYSICAL OR SOCIAL, ADAPT TO ITS ENVIRONMENT? WHAT ARE THE BASIC PROCESSES WHICH ENABLE IT TO SURVIVE? This great question finally articulated itself in the theorem of the *functional prerequisites.* According to Parsons, there are four basic functions that all sociocultural systems must perform in order to be viable, function properly, and to survive. These have become known as the AGIL system and are the following.

1. *Adaptation:* Human beings who are the "units" of the sociocultural system, must adapt to their physical environment by meeting basic physical needs which are the needs for food and shelter, clothing and protection. And, it is through the division of labor and the *economy* that these needs can be met. The sociologist must, therefore, study the particular and concrete

articulation of the economy of any social system to see how this works and succeeds in meeting these basic needs.

2. *Goal Achievement:* To live together, survive, and achieve their highest ideals, human beings pursue certain goals, instrumental and expressive, which are provided by political and economic systems. Here, the sociologist must, therefore, study and conceptualize the basic goals provided by either the political system, in a secular society, or the religious system in a sacred society, or a combination thereof.

3. *Integration:* The various actors and cultural items of the sociocultural system must be integrated through a common normative, value, belief, and symbol system in order to function properly and for meaningful human interaction to occur. The members of a sociocultural system must create a meaningful psychosocial cosmos out of chaos. This is done by internalizing and acting out a common culture and *education,* controlled by the political or religious system, which is the social institution that provides for integration.

4. *Latency: Pattern Maintenance and Tension Management:* An ongoing social system is composed of human beings who die, become sick, or withdraw, therefore, new members must be inducted and socialized into the system if it is to survive and continue to be viable. This is done through *reproduction* and *immigration.* New babies and human beings of other social systems must be acculturated and socialized into the new system. And it is the *family* which does this for newborn babies while it is the school and the marketplace which does this for members of other social systems. The family is the social institution which allows for the reproduction, early socialization, and emotional nourishment of new members.

Here, the sociologist must analyze the concrete and specific economic, political, religious, educational and family system of a given social system to see how these vital functions are taken care of, for should even one of them break down, the whole system would slowly fall apart and disintegrate.

Chapter 15

Durkheim's Theory of Suicide

Emile Durkheim towards the end of the 19th century asked himself a very simple, basic, yet tragic question: *Why do people commit suicide?* Who are the people and what are the basic factors that lead them to take their own lives? This question was all the more significant for Durkheim as, being an offspring of the Enlightenment, he was a rationalist and a positivist who did not believe in a life after death and thus who saw suicide as being total and final: the end of the life, consciousness, and identity of the person who committed it.

To answer this very fundamental question and get his research underway, Durkheim went to the library to do preliminary research. This led him to three basic observations and conclusions, namely:

a. that suicide is a universal phenomenon which occurs in all societies at all times;

b. that the rates of suicide remain pretty much the same year after year with but a slight change; and

c. that this slight change, in fact, is a progressive increase in the rates of suicide per hundred thousand of population.

The last observation and conclusion led him to become pessimistic about Western civilization and to really question the 18th and 19th century notion of "social progress" which assumed that reason and the light of science would dispel the last remaining "superstitions," "inequalities," and "ignorance" and that things would get better and better. This assumption, in fact, had been one of the main premises and sources of motivation for the establishment of a science of Man and Society that Auguste Comte called "Sociologie" and which would eventually bring about the Good Society in which the Good Man could lead the Good Life. But Man is not essentially a rational being as the "Philosophes" of the Enlightenment had assumed and thus reason, science, technology, industrialization, urbanization, universal education, higher education, and more research do not necessarily lead to higher qualitative standards of human living! Man is also an instinctual, emotional, and spiritual being with the forces of Good and Evil, of Life and Death, ever-struggling and contending with each other in his being. More knowledge and power, obtained to the detriment of Wisdom and Love could well lead in the opposite direction as we painfully realized in the 20th century with two World Wars, industrial pollution, and the arms race. Were Durkheim to have lived another 60 years, he would have seen his worst fears confirmed as the rates of suicide, amongst many other negative trends, have greatly increased and are still rising, especially amongst teenagers in the USA. The great dream and vision of the future of the rationalists, positivists, socialists, and materialists have been shattered by the dramatic events of the 20th century as they were essentially based upon a partial and incomplete understanding of human nature and human behavior.

Durkheim's next step was to go back to the library and to do extensive research on existing studies and explanations of suicide. His conclusions were that, in his time, there existed three basic theories or explanations of suicide, namely:

a. *The biogenic theories* which saw the cause of suicide lying in a malfunctioning of the biological organism. Here, it is something that goes wrong with the body (e.g., a tumor in the brain, an endocrine imbalance, or a dysfunction of the central nervous system) which causes a person to take his life.

b. *The psychogenic theories* which imputed the cause of suicide to a malfunctioning of the psyche. Here it is temporary insanity, compulsive behavior, massive depression or introflected aggression that leads a person to take his life.

c. *The ethico-religious theories* which imputed the cause of suicide to the Devil. The reasoning here is that a person commits certain "sins" which cut him off from God's grace and protection so that in comes the Devil, leading that person further and further into "sin" until such time as the Devil can come and claim that person's "soul" through suicide.

Reflecting upon these different explanations and theories of suicide, Durkheim came to reject all of them and to propose, instead, his own theory or explanation which is:

d. *The sociogenic theory of suicide* which assumes that the true cause of suicide is *society* or the quantity and quality of a person's human relationships.

The reasons why Durkheim rejected the existing theories of suicide and felt compelled to formulate a sociogenic explanation are manifold, but two basic reasons stand out. First, he had a strong vested interest in helping sociology become a valid and recognized academic field. Thus, he felt that, if he could prove that suicide was *a social* rather than a physiological, psychological, or cultural phenomenon, that it was a collective rather than a personal and individualistic fact, he would go a long way towards establishing sociology as a *bona fide* academic discipline. Second, and most important, his sociogenic explanation of suicide was a direct and logical outgrowth of his theory of human nature. Durkheim saw Man, essentially, as a Homo Duplex, as a being with two basic natures: the body or *biopsychic nature* which is the product of nature and biological evolution and the mind or *psychosocial nature* which is the product of society and sociocultural evolution. Durkheim argued that if we want to understand the human nature, the human consciousness of a person: the ways in which that person thinks, feels, and wills which determines his behavior, one *must understand* his network of *human relationships* which give birth and nurture his human consciousness. Now, clearly, to take one's own life one must *think about it,* have *strong feelings and emotions about it,* and make the *decision to end his life.* And *to obtain* the key to unravel the interrelated psychological processes one *must understand and analyze* the social life, the quantity and quality of human relationships, which determine it. This is perfectly logical if one accepts Durkheim's theory of human nature.

Durkheim sent teams of researchers to collect data about suicide from the *official records* of hospitals and police stations first in Paris, then in other French cities and provinces, and finally abroad. And he set himself to analyze and interpret the data that was collected for him. In so doing, he asked himself another fundamental question; namely, are all suicides the same or are there different types of suicide generated by different types of human motivation? The answer to this question can be found in Durkheim's typology of suicide which distinguishes between three primary types, the *egoistical,* the *altruistic,* and the *anomic,* and one secondary type, the *composite. The* fundamental difference between the primary types of suicide lies in the *motivation* that leads a person to take his own life.

Durkheim's Typology of Suicide

A. Egoistical: Here a person takes his own life for himself because life has become too hard to bear or because the person refuses to go on living with a certain situation or without something which he defines as being vital. The cause of this type of suicide is *undersocialization,* not having people to interact with who really love and care about the person and whom the person really loves and cares about. Examples would be a person taking his life because he has an incurable cancer, because he lost his money, or because his mate has left him.

B. *Altruistic:* Here a person takes his own life in the *alleged belief* that one or more persons will benefit, either materially or psychologically, from one's death, and because he interacts so much with them and *loves them* so much, that when the right circumstances present themselves, he is willing to offer his life. For Durkheim, the cause of this type of suicide is *oversocialization,* interacting so much with people and loving them so much that one is willing to give one's life for them. Needless to say, I do not, personally, regard this type of suicide as a true form of *suicide* but rather as a form of personal sacrifice, whether justified or not, and whether effective or not, for the well-being of others. Examples would be Kamikaze pilots, taking one's life when captured by the enemy and holding sensitive and important information that could be revealed under drugs or torture which would damage one's nation or army, and a woman who would throw herself under a car to save a child at the cost of her own life.

C. *Anomic:* Here a person takes his own life not because life is too hard to bear or because other people might benefit from this, but because *life has lost its meaning and purpose.* The cause of this type of suicide is *poor socialization.* Here, Durkheim focuses not upon the *quantity* but rather the *quality* of human interaction. One can have relationships with others, and even many of them, but if their quality is poor, if they are shallow, superficial, and exploitative, then the "nourishing currents of society" can no longer feed and actualize one's consciousness, and thus one would be unable to find true meaning and purpose in his life and decide that life is not worth living. A person who has most of what the material and social side of life has to offer but who has lost his sense of meaning and purpose and his "joie de vivre" would fall into this category.

D. *Composite:* Any kind of suicide which is not clearly egoistic, altruistic or anomic falls into this "catch-all" category. Examples here would be a Buddhist Monk who sprays himself with gasoline which he sets on fire or a person who kills himself to "punish" his loved ones who have not given him the love or attention he sought.

Durkheim's Basic Rationale Behind His Typology of Suicide

In articulating his theory of sociogenic suicide and developing his typology of suicide, Durkheim made the following basic assumptions; namely that:

1. *Love is the life-giving force par excellence.* That is, it is love, the ability to love and being loved that will give one the desire and strength to want to go on living in spite of life's hardships and injustices.
2. *No one can live in this world without suffering.* Given the nature of Man and of the world, all human beings at some time or other and to a greater or lesser extent will suffer and undergo hardships, problems and difficulties. Thus, when these sufferings and hardships occur, it is crucial for one to have someone to love and be loved by . . . if one is to want to go on living.
3. *Love can only be generated and circulated through human interaction.* In other words, love is a distinctively human energy that can only be given and received from human beings.

    Here, I feel that Durkheim is too narrow in his approach in confining love to human interaction. While this is certainly true for most human beings at this point in time and the "line of least resistance" to love and to be loved, one can also give and receive love from God and nature through spiritual and physical interaction.

Having set up his typology of suicide, Durkheim proceeded to test the most common category of suicide which is egoistic suicide by formulating subhypotheses which he tested with the data that he had available. His core hypothesis was that *there is an inverse correlation between the degree of social cohesion and social solidarity that a person has with one or more persons and the likelihood that this person will commit an egoistic form of suicide.* In other words, when sufferings, injustices, and hardships arrive if one is loved by other persons and can love other persons the likelihood of committing suicide, on a statistical basis, will go down. But if one finds oneself alone, the likelihood will go up. The specific and concrete hypotheses that Durkheim formulated to test this main hypothesis with his data were that:

1. a person who is single, divorced, or widowed is more likely to commit suicide than a person who is married; and his data corroborates this;
2. a person who is married with children is likely to commit suicide than a person who is married without children; this, too, is corroborated by the available data;
3. a person who belongs to a religion will be less likely to commit suicide than a person who does not belong to a religion; this also checks out;
4. a person who belongs to a socially oriented religion such as Catholicism or Judaism will be less likely to commit suicide

than a person who belongs to a more individualistic type of religion, such as Protestantism; and this checks out; and

5. finally, a person who belongs to a club, an organization, or a professional association will be less likely to commit suicide than a person who does not. This, too, checks out.

Thus, Durkheim's main hypothesis on Egoistic suicide was substantiated by the data that he had collected as he found evidence to back up each of his subhypotheses.

By looking at his data, Durkheim found some seemingly "strange facts" concerning suicide patterns. The more important ones are that:

a. suicide rates go down in the winter and up in the summer; and

b. the three days during which there is the greatest likelihood that a Christian will commit suicide is Christmas, Easter, and his birthday.

In both instances, Durkheim explained these patterns by invoking the visibility of one's *aloneness* or *togetherness*. In the winter everybody stays indoors as it is cold and dark, thus the visibility of one's aloneness or togetherness goes down. But in the summer, when it is warm and the daylight is long everyone goes outdoors where the visibility of one's aloneness or togetherness goes way up. The same is true for the three crucial days of the year: Christmas, Easter, and one's birthday. During those days, society expects and thus one expects to be *together with loved ones,* but if one does not have any loved ones, then this becomes much more visible and painful. And statistics also showed Durkheim that the poor are *less likely to* commit suicide than the rich because they generally have a richer network of human relationships.

The Core Weaknesses and Strengths of Durkheim's Study of Suicide

Durkheim's study of suicide, from our perspective, has two basic weaknesses and two basic strengths.

Weaknesses:

a. *Methodologically,* Durkheim used *official statistics* of suicide which were gotten from hospitals and police stations. These grossly *underrepresent* the total number of suicides as relatives and friends of suicide cases have always tried to disguise a suicide as a natural cause or an accident for moral or practical reasons: morally because a suicide created a moral failure for the family, and practically because insurance policies are not paid in the case of a death that is self-inflicted.

b. *Theoretically*, Durkheim used a *monocausal explanation* of suicide by imputing a sociogenic cause for it: it is *society* or, rather, the quantity and quality of one's human relationships that are the best explanatory factor for suicide.

Today, after the work of Max Weber, we no longer use monocausal explanations of social phenomena but, rather, we use a *multicausal* explanation such that there is not one but many factors, all interlinked, that cause social phenomena.

For example, should I set up a theory of suicide I would postulate that there are at least five basic factors that are involved in causing suicide, each of which might be the determining one under different circumstances. These are:

1. *A biogenic element:* something going wrong with the body or body physiology.
2. *A psychogenic element:* something going wrong with the mind or the psyche—temporary insanity or overwhelming self-destructive emotions.
3. *A cultural conflict element* (which is the present day explanation for the old ethico-religious theories): powerful conflict between two value systems which create unbearable guilt, fear, and despair.
4. *A sociogenic element:* lack of love generated by loneliness and a lack of deep and meaningful relationships.
5. *The age of the Soul, the spiritual element* (Peter Roche de Coppens' factor): a "young soul" who has not had many earth-life incarnations is much more likely to resort to suicide when things "get tough" than an "old Soul" with many such incarnations with possible previous suicides for which one has paid a heavy price.

Strengths:

a. *Methodologically,* Durkheim has given us a classical *research design model* which we are still using today. That is, Durkheim has taught us and shown us the way to do sociological research.
b. *Theoretically* or substantially, Durkheim has pointed out for us the importance of the social element in suicide, that is the importance of understanding the quantity and quality of one's human relationships. From this, we have learned that a pre-suicidal person, or a person who is inclined to resort to committing suicide should never be *left alone*.

While most elements of the social phenomenon of suicide can easily be comprehended by us today, the ethico-religious theory or explanation, which we would reconceptualize today under the heading of "cultural conflict," is the least understandable. To throw light on this explanation, let me tell the following true but sad story.

Several years ago, I was told by some Amish friends the following story. A bright and beautiful Amish girl was sent by her family to Franklin and Marshall College in Lancastor, Pennsylvania. There, she met a young man who was not Amish but with whom she became friends and with whom she started to go out. Now the Amish are a strictly *endogamous* group and so her family began to warn the girl to "be very careful" of what might develop with her non-Amish friend as their relationship could have no "happy final ending." But she, having a mind of her own and really liking this young man, continued to see him. Little by little more and more social pressure was put upon her to make her "understand" what she was doing and desist from her "deviant ways." The "cold shoulder" of her parents and relatives, however, drove her further away from them, and brought her closer to her boyfriend. They were never invited together to any family or religious functions and she found herself ostracized to a large extent from many social events.

A few months before he was to graduate from Franklin and Marshall, her boyfriend told her that he was "fed-up" with this situation, that he really loved her and wanted to marry her, and that he was moving to Philadelphia. He invited her to come with him. He told her that he did not think that they were being treated fairly and that, as they loved each other they should be free to marry. When she announced this marriage proposal to her family she was told that she knew very well that this could not be, that it was against their beliefs and norms and that, should she go ahead with this, she would be "shunned" by her family and community. Torn between her family and her love, her need to affirm herself and the traditions by which she was raised, she chose to move to Philadelphia with her boyfriend but not to marry him as that would have been the last rejection of her childhood values and upbringing. They settled there and he went to work but she became more and more moody and depressed, being torn by her inner conflict and guilt. Finally, one day, her common-law husband had a frank talk with her and told her that he could not "go on like this," that something was wrong as she was always unhappy, indrawn, and moody. Love, he said, should bring happiness and life and not the opposite. Thus, she had a choice: either to pull herself together or to go their separate ways. Naturally, this kind of "ultimatum" achieved the opposite effect and merely intensified her inner conflict and guilt. One day, he could stand it no longer and, unable to understand what was truly going on within her, he left telling he that her parents were right and that they should not be together. A few days later she turned on the gas stove and committed suicide. When told by the police of the death of their daughter, her parents were very sad but stated emphatically that they had predicted what would happen all along. The Devil had gotten into her because she had sinned against God Who had then withdrawn His grace and protection from her, and had finally claimed her soul. This is a sad and tragic but typical example of the ethico-religious explanation of suicide where the putative cause is seen to be the Devil. We, of course, would interpret this as the result of *cultural conflict* which finally destroyed her personality and her physical life.

To conclude this analysis of suicide, I would like to tell you, but from the standpoint of the Spiritual Tradition and not from a sociological perspective, what happens to a person who commits suicide. You can take this story as a "fairy tale," as a working hypothesis, or as a possibility to be further explored through your own research and personal experiences. The "data" for this explanation comes from three basic sources:

a. a growing literature in the field of thanatology, parapsychology, and the New Age Consciousness;
b. from people I personally know who have the higher faculties necessary to explore this from the standpoint of personal experience; and
c. finally, from my own personal experiences.

The first thing that happens to a person that commits suicide is to be in for quite a "shock." For the person does not "die" completely but "wakes up" on another state of consciousness to realize that life, awareness, and sensitivity do go on after "death." Most people who commit suicide actually either consciously or unconsciously expect this to be "the end" of their problems and sufferings, but it is not. For those who still, implicitly or explicitly, believe in the traditional "heaven" and "hell" of organized religion, there is another shock. Neither devils come to carry them off to hell nor angels to take them to heaven. Instead, the person finds himself in a "no man's land," "limbo," or "prison" for a *certain period of time,* which could be hours, days, months, or even years in "earth time," but which is certainly not eternal and which does not come to an end where the normal "process" will then begin.

During that period of time and for as long as that person remains in this "no man's land," he will be going through a very hard time . . . of his own making and not inflicted upon him by an "avenging Deity." This for three reasons:

a. Because of the emerging realization that he has thrown away a priceless opportunity to grow and learn valuable lessons. At this point, the person who finds himself in that state realizes that Life is much larger and greater than he had realized hitherto and which goes way beyond incarnate life. Thus, that *all human experiences,* even the most painful and horrifying in human terms such as a painful and terminal disease, political injustice and persecution, torture, helplessness, aloneness, etc., all have a *deeper meaning and purpose* the ultimate end of which is personal growth, transformation, and the freeing up of new energies, faculties, and possibilities. This realization could be compared to having thrown away a lottery ticket that had just won a million dollars!

b. Because of the impossibility, while in that state, to express oneself constructively and creatively which is one of the deepest human drives, the frustration of which can cause very deep anguish, pain, and unhappiness.

c. Because of the impossibility, while in this state *to give and receive love* which is absolutely essential for one's well being and sense of personal fulfillment. Not being on earth anymore, since the person has destroyed the physical expression of his being on that dimension, and not being able to rise to the spiritual worlds on account of the life force that still keeps pouring into his psyche, that person is temporarily cut off from loving . . . which is very painful, especially in that discarnate state of being.

After a certain point of time has elapsed, which is very difficult to evaluate in earth terms, since *time is a function of human consciousness* and can flow much more slowly when one is unhappy and depressed or much faster when one is happy and creative, the person who has committed suicide will then go through the "normal process" occurring after physical death. According to the teachings of the Spiritual Tradition and my own personal experiences of them, this process unfolds in three distinct phases which I have termed:

a. going to school;
b. having a vacation; and
c. going back to school.

The first phase, or school, involves first beholding and then feeling and experiencing one's entire life unfolding *backwards* from the time one died to the time one was born. This time, however, one's perceptions and feelings are heavily colored by two factors which were not present when one was living one's life on earth. The first is that now, for the first rime, a person can understand and locate in a larger perspective some of the most inexplicable and puzzling "facts" about one's life which can only be so grasped from the perspective of spiritual consciousness (which, however, can be achieved by an incarnate person who has realized spiritual consciousness). This would include why one was born into a certain family, race, religion, country, socioeconomic status, a man or a woman, and with a certain genetic baggage and educational opportunities; why one has certain "puzzling" effects occur to one in one's life: great success or failure, fame and fortune or anonymity and poverty, love or loneliness, betrayal or help on the part of certain "trusted persons," etc. The second is that now the person can *see* and *feel* the *impact and consequences* of his words, feelings, and deeds towards others. So that should one have done "good," he will see and feel that good in others and their lives, or should one have done "evil" he can also see and feel that "evil" in others and their lives. Should one have exploited others, used them, or caused suffering and sorrow to them, he will now develop a very strong urge and desire to come back and rectify the wrongs he has consciously or unconsciously set in motion—which is a powerful force to bring one back into incarnation or earth life! At this point, the first phase would end and the second begin.

Following the "judgment day," the "hall of judgment," or the "Scales of Tahuti" as the first phase is called by various traditions, comes what is known as "going to heaven." There are as many different types of "heaven" as there are different religions and even branches of the same religion. To cite just a few examples amongst the best known or most striking ones we have:

a. The American Indians believed that when one died after having led a good life, one would end up in the "Great Hunting Fields" where one would enjoy hunting bisons in beautiful fields.

b. The classical orthodox Christian view is that one would find oneself in the presence of God with Angels and other beings singing His praise.

c. Some Arabian tribes believe that heaven consists in finding oneself in a beautiful oasis in the desert with a cool breeze blowing through, plenty of cool water to drink, and where women would remain virgins no matter how many times they were made love to!

d. My personal conception of heaven and what I feel will befall me after I pass on is that I will be on a very large and high mountain, reminiscent of the Swiss Alps, with many ski trails I could ski on all day long to find myself in the evening at the bottom where a large pot of Swiss cheese fondue will be brewing around which there would be many good wines and all my dear ones gathered.

The most astonishing thing about all these different conceptions of heaven is that *they are all true*. This because in this state of being one's mind and imagination are, indeed, *creative powers* with the ability to manifest and objectify one's being, environment, and events. Whatever we believe in, think about, imagine, and want weaves the reality into which we live! There is one special point to be mentioned about human beings, however, and this is that one will have the people and the kinds of relationships one wants, but that they will be figments of one's imagination and not real human beings unless there is *true love* between them and they find themselves on the same level of consciousness and being! And when this is the case, then one *accepts people exactly as they are expecting nothing other than that they be themselves!* Any kind of expectation or demand we put upon human beings will be gratified . . . but by creations of our own minds and imagination and not by real "live" beings. Herein also lies a very important point or lesson for those who want to achieve *true love* while incarnate on earth: one must be able to accept the person in his totality without any demands or expectations, and leave that person his full freedom to truly be himself. After a certain period of time has gone by, which can again range from days to many years, the second phase will come to an end and the third begin. More advanced and evolved Souls do not tarry long in these "heavens" for they are eager to continue their work and service to God and human kind. Hence, it is mainly unevolved Souls or Souls who have suffered a great deal on earth and experienced many deprivations and frustrations who tarry there for a long time.

The third phase or "going back to school" as I have called it, involves *preparing the lessons and experiences for the next incarnation on earth* with the help of Spiritual Powers and within the parameters established by one's level of evolution and one's most important objectives, as defined from the standpoint of spiritual consciousness. This implies selecting and identifying one's future parents, sex, events, and challenges which one will then have to experience while again incarnate on the physical plane. Not all of one's life experiences are thus "prepared" and "selected," but the most important certainly are . . . which is why Sages and Saints never complain about what they have to face on earth and can truly thank God for all that happens to them . . . because they realize that they have, themselves, chosen these experiences for their own growth and development! An important point to be made

here is that our perspective and choice are very different, sometimes even opposed, when seen from the spiritual viewpoint and
when seen from the human viewpoint. While incarnate on earth,
most human beings are, indeed, governed by what Freud called the
"pleasure-pain principle," seeking pleasure and avoiding pain. But
from the spiritual viewpoint, the basic standard is not security,
love, health, happiness, wealth, or all the things that the human
ego wants and craves but, rather, personal growth, transformation,
and genuine service to God and Man. Thus, an evolved Soul may be
quite ambitious when on the spiritual planes and choose a very difficult life with a great deal of insecurity, frustration, and pain in
order to evolve and grow faster. But, once incarnate, he may find
this to be a little bit too much to bear!

This third phase, too, then comes to an end and the Soul then
waits for the appropriate time and circumstances when it will be
able to come back to earth in the right family to live and incarnate
what it has selected for itself.

Chapter 16

Max Weber's Protestant Ethic and the Spirit of Capitalism

The life and work of Max Weber, the greatest and most influential German sociologist centered around 3 major themes:

1. the study and analysis of the origins and distinctive features of Western civilization;
2. the study and analysis of the relationship between religion and economic activities, or the impact of ideas and ideals upon social and material conditions; and
3. the study and analysis of the interrelationships between religion and social stratification.

The Protestant Ethic (1903–06)

The Protestant Ethic focuses on the impact of ideas and ideals upon human behavior and of religious ideals upon economic activities. This was his first major work after his recovery from a devastating nervous breakdown and is, perhaps, his most famous and controversial book. It is his classical contribution to modern sociology that every student of sociology must be well-acquainted with. Here, Weber proceeded upon 4 basic lines of investigation.

a. He explored in depth the psychosocial orientations of human beings and their religious basis which he had uncovered in previous historical and economic studies.
b. He sought to relate the connection between ideas, ideals, and human behavior and their impact upon social and material conditions, thus challenging the *monocausal* approach by substituting a *multicausal* explanation which is the current one.
c. He began a long series of studies in the sociology of religion by determining the impact of religious values and beliefs upon social structures, human conduct, and economic pursuits.
d. He began to articulate his theory of historical development, his vision of the progressive rationalization of human thought and human relationships, and the ensuing "disenchantment with the world," loss of meaning, purpose, and joy.

The first core question that Weber asked is, "Can ideas and ideals have an impact upon social, material, and economic conditions?" And his answer was, yes, but not directly, rather indirectly. Ideas and ideals do have an impact upon our human consciousness, the essential functions of which are *thinking, feeling,* and *willing.* Thus, ideas and ideals can change and transform our consciousness, our ways of thinking, then feeling, and finally willing. And these, in turn, will transform our behavior which will transform the world or social, material, and economic conditions. Thus, if enough people buy certain ideas and ideals, share them with others, and live in accordance with them, their collective behavior will transform the world.

Weber applied this basic line of thinking to the "Protestant Ethic" and the "Spirit of Capitalism." His basic thesis is that *the central ideas and ideals of the Protestant Reformation were one of the major contributory factors to bring about the modern capitalistic system.*

This does not mean that the core ideas and ideals of the Protestant Reformation created Capitalism rather than incarnating God's Kingdom on Earth, which was their manifest intent. Rather it means that, because enough people bought these new ideas and ideals and because they lived by them, they made possible the conditions which resulted in the modern capitalistic system. These core ideas and ideals of the Protestant Reformation, according to Weber's interpretation of them, were the following:

1. Martin Luther brought a *new conception of Work* as *"Beruf"* or *calling.* That is, instead of viewing work on earth as a result of the Fall of Man and as a *means to material survival* in this world, it should now be seen as a way to worship the Creator which is just as desirable and effective as prayer and contemplation. The net impact of this new conception of work is to revaluate and greatly increase the importance of work for one's being and life. Should one accept this view, then once would logically work better and more thus *earning more money.*

2. *The Reformation brought in a new emphasis on Puritanism.* Criticizing the Catholic Church for its worldly emphasis and corruption, the Reformation put a great emphasis on puritanism and asceticism to distinguish itself from the established Church and show concrete parameters to establish its superiority to Catholicism. To live a simple and austere life was the model given by Jesus and His Apostles and should thus be emulated by all practical Christians. If one buys this view, then one will live a more simple, austere, and ascetical life

giving up luxuries and the "pleasures of the world" and, thereby, *save more money by spending less*. If one earns more and spends less, then one ends up with an economic surplus which is called *"capital"* and capital is the essence of capitalism!

3. *The Reformation repealed the then existing usury laws which forbade* Christians to lend money to other Christians and charging an interest for it. During the Middle Ages the usury laws did exist and were enforced so that only Jews and Muslims could be money lenders, which considerably hampered commercial activities and commerce. With the coming of the industrial and commercial age tremendous pressures were generated to free up capital investments which was made possible by the Reformation's repeal of the usury laws. This meant, practically, that now one *could invest one's capital and get a decent rate of return for it*.

4. *John Calvin put forth his theory of Predestination* whereby it was God alone Who decided who would and who would not be saved and not human effort. This meant that human beings could do nothing to *earn Salvation* through their own efforts as it was purely the work of Grace. What they could do, however, was to find some criteria by which to evaluate whether they were amongst God's Elect or not. If one bought this conception, one would have a great psychological pressure to know where one "stood with God." Calvin felt that success on earth was such a criterion for, should God have predestined one to go to Heaven, His Guidance and Blessings would be upon one also in this world, and this would result in *being successful*. The question then becomes, how does one measure success? Money is a very likely answer to this question, for money is one way of quantifying worldly success. Thus, it became very important for those who bought this conception of Predestination to be wealthy, not because *money would buy their way into Heaven* but because it would be an indication that one had been blessed by God.

In conclusion, the core ideas and ideals of the "Protestant Ethic" meant, practically, that one would work harder and better, thus earn more money; but spend less as one would lead a simple, austere, ascetical life, thus save more money which would lead to an economic surplus known as "capital;" now this capital could be invested to earn more money as the usury laws were repealed; and, finally, one would have a great psychological pay-off to be wealthy as this would be an indication, according to Calvin's theory of Predestination, that one was one of God's Elect. Such is Max Weber's core thesis when he claimed that the Protestant Ethic was *one of the main contributory factors* to bring about the modern capitalistic system.

Chapter 17

Socialization: Becoming a Member of Society and Becoming Human

Man becomes human, that is, a mature, rational, social, and productive member of society, through the process of socialization.

Socialization is simply the network of social interaction through which a human being acquires the ways of thinking, feeling, willing, speaking, and acting, as well as the basic skills, that are essential for effective participation in a given society.

Man is not born human: he becomes human through his meaningful human relationships. As Robert Park put it, "It is only slowly and laboriously, in fruitful contact, cooperation, and conflict with his fellows that he attains the distinctive qualities of human nature." Both society and the individual are mutually dependent on this unique "process of psychosocial amalgamation" whereby the sentiments and ideas of a culture are joined to the capacities and needs of the human organism.

The process of socialization is not yet fully understood at this time, but provides a common meeting ground for all the sciences dealing with man—biology, psychology, sociology, and anthropology. All of them have a common interest in the subtle alchemy through which a human biological organism is transformed into a social being.

Not all learning, however, is socialization, for some learning is irrelevant to the motivation and skills necessary for participating in society. Sociology focuses upon social interaction and is primarily interested in *how* an individual becomes a functioning member of society. Socialization is the process which enables the individual to acquire the culture of his group, that is, the norms, values, beliefs, and symbols of his group by occupying certain statuses and playing certain roles.

At the very heart of the socialization process we find the emergence and development of the human *self,* of our personality and being, as both *object* and *subject*. The human self is a *psychological* (psychic) and not a physical or spiritual entity. It is not something which exists prior to or apart from a *sociocultural environment*—it is a social product which can exist only in a social matrix. Beginning with an "oceanic, undifferentiated stream of consciousness," the child slowly acquires self-consciousness by learning how to distinguish between the *self* and the *world,* animate and inanimate nature, and finally the "I" and Others in different human relationships. At first, "all is one" for the child who then individuates and slowly develops a sense of "I" by differentiating between "thinking, feeling, and willing" and possessions, between the animate and inanimate environments, and by "locating himself" in different social relations.

How can we effectively get "outside of ourselves" in such a way as to become a reflecting object to ourselves? Charles Cooley gave a classical answer to this question with his concept of the "looking glass self." How do we develop and crystallize a human self? By our human relationships with others in which we *look at ourselves through their eyes* and internalize their perceptions, conceptions, and, especially, treatment of ourselves. Here, he says, there are three basic steps.

a. An act of imagination and visualization: how do I look in the eyes of others?
b. Imagining how others perceive me and judge me, my human self.
c. The emergence of self-feelings experienced through the judgment and relationships with others. Our self-appraisal and liking or disliking tends to mirror that of others . . . if I am accepted, liked, and approved of by others, I will develop a feeling and attitude of self-acceptance, self-liking, and self-respect. Otherwise, not. In other words, I will judge myself as others judge me!

According to George Mead, the key to the development of self is to be found in *language.* Through the use of language, which conveys and elicits thoughts, feelings, energies, and intuitions, a person arouses the same tendencies in himself that he does in others and, in this fashion, puts himself in the place of others, of the "Significant Other" in particular. Socially standardized symbols enable the individual to carry on an internal dialogue; he hears himself, he talks to himself, he responds to himself. Thus can an individual judge how a person will respond to him by how he himself responds to the words he utters.

As *language* is the first vital element for effective socialization, *acting out* the behavior and attitudes of others through playing games is the second. Through acting, the child adopts the attitudes, responses, and behaviors of the persons whose behavior he is enacting. A game constitutes a social situation that requires all the participants to know what the others expect. Here, the response of every player to every other player is organized in terms of definite rules. By grasping the rules of the game, the child acquires within himself an organized system of positions; and can participate in the mutual responses that constitute the actual game. According to George Mead, the persons, or social group, that gives the individual his sense of self, or identity, is called the *Generalized Other*. The attitude of the Generalized Other is the attitude of the entire group. It involves the individual's organized conceptions of the expectations of those who interact with him within a given sociocultural context. Although we acquire our concepts of these expectations from particular people, *Significant Others* (Mother, Father, Teacher), these expectations are generalized to embrace all people within similar contexts.

Man is not born actually human, he is born potentially human and will translate that potentiality into actuality through his network of social interactions. Born a social blank, at the personality level, a human being can acquire those ways of thinking, feeling, willing, speaking, and acting essential for social living only from others who already are the bearers of that culture. This is why childhood experiences have the greatest importance in shaping the human personality. The first and most important socializing agency in the child's life is the *Family*, which provides him with his most durable and intensive social relationships and even more—with the very model for all future human relationships.

The methods and mechanisms through which parents transmit the cultural patterns of their culture to their children are:

a. *Imitation:* the child models his behavior on that of his parents.
b. *Reward and Punishment:* positive and negative reinforcement for appropriate and inappropriate behavior.
c. *Didactic teaching:* telling and showing the child what and how he is to do things that are required of him.

Then comes the *Peer Group* as the second socializing agency which is made up of people who are roughly the same age and equal to the individual. The Peer Group serves two basic functions:

a. to give the child experience with egalitarian relationships; and
b. as a vehicle for the transmission of cultural patterns that cannot be acquired from those in authority positions—folkways, fads, secret knowledge and ways of achieving personal gratification.

Finally, we have *Adult Socialization*. Socialization is really a never-ending process that continues throughout the life cycle of an individual, through his friends, superiors, colleagues, etc. Here both normal and deviant behavior are acquired in the same way: through socialization and social controls.

Chapter 18

Social Stratification

All known human societies rank people in a vertical hierarchy that differentiates them as being "superior" or "inferior," "top dogs" or "underdogs," and "higher" or "lower" than someone else.

Social "stratification" is a term borrowed from the science of geology which differentiates between different "strata" or "layers" in its sedimentation and rock formation. Social stratification, or differentiation, is generally carried out on the basis of 10 classical variables which are: sex, age, race, religion, health, marital status, family membership, conformity to norms, physical characteristics, occupation, and education. In different societies, at different times, different criteria among this basic list have been emphasized as being the most important.

From a "spiritual perspective" and assuming that the core functions and dimensions of a human being are his/her capacity to *know and understand,* to *feel and to love,* and to *will, to create, and to do,* one could set up a threefold stratification system where people would be classified and differentiated in terms of these capacities. Here, Geniuses would be at the top of the *knowledge* pyramid, Saints at the top of the *love* pyramid, and Creators of various types at the top of the *will/creation* hierarchy. The great problem with "elites" and hierarchies is that they normally end up by being "selfish" and pursuing their own personal and self interests (including those of their families) rather than the interests of the nation and of the whole!

Kingsley Davis and Wilbert Moore have proposed a "classical" theory of social stratification based on the traditional economic theory of the market mechanisms of Supply and Demand. The essence of this theory runs as follows:

1. All human societies have unequal rewards attached to different social positions, thus all societies *are* **stratified.**
2. Human societies must concern themselves with providing organization and motivation in their members. And they must do this on two basic levels:

a. Instill in suitable individuals the desire to fulfill certain positions.

b. Once they are in these positions, they must make sure that their occupants will want to act out the associated roles; i.e., *conform.*

3. Thus, human societies must have a *reward system* they can use as a motivating factor. And, they must have a way of distributing these rewards differentially according to positions. "Power, in the broader sense of the term, is generally the motive . . . which leads to basic inequality."

The most universal and basic types of *rewards* used are:

a. *Wealth*—the amount of money or income a person gets.

b. *Power*—the ability to realize one's will against the resistance of others (which includes political, military, economic, social, religious, or intellectual power).

c. *Status*—the ability to command prestige, esteem, or admiration from others.

It is interesting to note how one type of reward can, generally, lead to the others or be "exchanged" for the others. Thus if one has wealth one can generally get power and prestige, or if one has power one can use it to get wealth and status, as status can be used to get wealth and power.

From the standpoint of conflict theory, Tumin noted that social stratification involves certain "dysfunctions" the most important of which are:

1. When social stratification is based on *inherited positions,* it serves to limit the possibility of discovering and utilizing the full range of talent and creativity available in a given society.

2. Social stratification distributes favorable and unfavorable self-images unequally and thus promotes inequality and injustice.

3. This inequality and injustice generates hostility, frustrations, and demoralization in the lower classes.

Basic Types of Social Stratification Systems

Basic types of social stratification systems: the Class-Caste continuum. Social stratification and social positions can be allocated either on the basis of birth (ascription) or of capacity (achievement). Classical India had a Caste system that was based fully on ascription while the USA has a Class system based primarily (but not solely) upon achievement. In theory, what we have in the USA is *equality of opportunity.* Karl Marx and the communists, on the other hand, wanted a classless society (at least in theory) that was based upon the famous saying, "From each according to his abilities, and to each according to his needs." The Israeli Kibbutz system may have come closest to achieving material equality but not psychosocial equality which is even harder to achieve.

Empirical approaches to the study of social stratification are based upon 3 primary methods.

a. *The objective approach* (Lloyd-Warner): Here, the focus is upon 3 core variables, *occupation, education, and income* which are used to define 6 categories—upper Upper, upper Middle, lower Middle, upper Lower, and lower Lower class.
b. *The subjective approach* (Richard Centers): Here, classes are psychosocial groupings, essentially subjective in character and subdivided into 4 classes: Upper Class, Middle Class, Working Class, and Lower Class. A person's class is part of a feeling on his part of belonging or identifying with something larger than himself. Here, a person basically ranks himself and tells us where he thinks he belongs.

Social mobility is defined as the "movement of individuals or groups from one stratum of society to another." There are 4 basic factors that affect mobility rates:

a. different fertility rates—population trends;
b. changes in the ranking of positions (social change);
c. the opening up of new positions; and
d. change in values, norms, and legal restrictions.

For social mobility to occur, individuals must aspire to getting into better positions and be willing to pay the price to achieve them. Ethnic groups vary in their rates of upward mobility. These differences can be explained in terms of the individuals':

a. *Motivation*—this instills the desire in the individual to achieve and to reach higher levels of being and of living. It springs from the individual's education, character, and Soul.
b. *Values*—these can both stimulate or inhibit social mobility.
c. *Aspirations*—these spring from the individual's education, character, or Soul.

Finally, let us quickly look at and define some of the major social processes next to that of *socialization* and *social stratification;* namely, those of *conflict, competition, cooperation, accommodation,* and *assimilation.*

Conflict is defined as "a social process in which individuals or groups seek to realize their goals by neutralizing, injuring, or eliminating their rivals." Conflict involves both *functions* (setting group-boundaries, enhancing group solidarity, and acting as a "safety valve" for society as a whole) and *dysfunctions* (weakening or destroying the social fabric of a society by breeding hostility, tension, and insecurity).

Competition is a social process in which individuals or groups seek to realize their goals through established norms and roles that define what is fair and legitimate.

Cooperation is a social process in which individuals or groups seek to realize their goals through mutual aid. In the USA, we have the polar tendencies of strong competitive and individualistic strivings with cooperation and mutual help.

Accommodation is a social process in which individuals or groups seek to reach an adjustment whereby conflict may be temporarily or permanently avoided. It is a cohesive force acting between individuals or groups, involving "antagonistic cooperation," compromise, arbitration, mediation, and toleration.

Assimilation is a social process in which groups with diverse cultural and behavioral patterns become fused together in a social unity and common culture. Two basic possibilities exist here; either one group may completely absorb and integrate the other or both may contribute to forming a new culture; for example, "America seen as God's Crucible, or the great *melting pot,* where all the races and cultures of Europe are melted and reformed."

Chapter 19

The Future of Modern Sociology and Its Role as a "Foundation" for the Development of a Comprehensive "Philosophy of Life" and Art of Living

As it stands today, in its various branches and theoretical frameworks, Sociology is the *disciplined study of human interaction* and of its major fruits, *human consciousness* in the *microcosm* and *human culture* in the *macrocosm*. In order to gain systematic knowledge and understanding of human interaction, whose creative psychic synthesis brings about the unfoldment of human consciousness, Sociology must, necessarily, study a central dimension of *Man* and of the *World* in which Man lives.

As we saw earlier, Sociology does not focus upon the biological organism, or "animal nature," which is the domain of biology, nor does it focus its attention upon the Divine Spark, or "spiritual nature," which is not even recognized by all sociologists and which, in any case, would be the domain of the theologian or of the spiritual scientist. What Sociology studies and focuses upon is the *psychosocial nature,* or human consciousness, as it arises from human interaction and manifests in human interaction. Likewise, Sociology does not study the *physical environment* in which we live, which is the province of the physicist or of the geologist, nor does it study the *spiritual environment* in which we "live, and move, and have our being," which is not even recognized by materialistic scientists. What it does investigate is the *sociocultural environment,* or *people* and their *ideas.*

Seen in this light and through this perspective, Sociology has many major *theoretical* and *practical* contributions to make to the emerging synthesis of human knowledge, manifesting through a comprehensive philosophy of life, and to self-actualization and sociocultural improvement, manifesting through an integral art of living. Specifically, Sociology can make distinctive theoretical and practical contributions by the systematic development of:

In the Microcosm, or Man:	*In the Macrocosm, or World:*
a. Self-knowledge.	a. Knowledge of our sociocultural environment.
b. Self-mastery.	b. Development of sociocultural skills.
c. Self-integration.	c. Sociocultural integration.

Moreover, Sociology can also make distinctive contributions for learning to discern, conceptually and existentially, the aspects, forces, and agents that are **psychosocial** and **sociocultural** in nature from those that are **physical** or **spiritual in nature.** And, it has many vital and unique contributions to make for realizing our personal and collective growth and self-actualization, for achieving true healing, harmony, and enlightenment at the **human** level.

The really **essential** sociological insight is that a **human being** is a **social being** which means three basic things:

a. that without human interaction, a human being could neither be born, survive, nor achieve his self-actualization on the physical, human, and spiritual levels;
b. that human interaction brings about a creative psychic synthesis unfolding a **new reality** with new elements that can only be realized through human interaction; and
c. that the psyche is an organ of interaction, meaning that human potentialities and faculties are elicited, brought out, and translated from potentiality into actuality through **human interaction.**

Since the three major foci of modern Sociology, seen through this perspective, are *human interaction, human consciousness,* and *human culture,* let us now put each of these concepts under our magnifying glass to summarize, in technical and specific terms, what they are and what they do. As we have seen in previous chapters, each can, interestingly enough, be described in terms of 7 basic concepts.

Human Interaction

1. Is the analytical unit of sociology, or what sociology focuses upon and studies.
2. Means two or more people doing something with each other.
3. Is not the interaction between two or more **bodies** but, rather, the interaction between two or more **human consciousnesses.**

4. Here we have, specifically, the interaction or exchanges between:
   a. *Mind and mind,* which creates new *ideas;*
   b. *Heart and heart,* which creates new *emotions;* and,
   c. *Will and will,* which releases new *energies.*
5. Though it has been studied and investigated by social scientists for about two centuries, human interaction still remains a *largely unknown process* which is far more complex than it was earlier thought to be.
6. This is because human interaction involves transactions, or exchanges, on three levels.
   a. *On the conscious* level, it involves the exchange of *images, words,* and *deeds.*
   b. On the *subconscious level,* or below the threshold of awareness, it involves the exchange of energies, impulses, and biopsychic materials.
   c. On the *superconscious level,* or above the threshold of awareness, it involves the exchange of energies, impulses, and psychospiritual materials.
7. While there are many basic functions and practical applications for our present day knowledge and understanding of human interaction, from my viewpoint, two are really crucial. These are:
   a. The *therapeutic function,* or healing the sick, harnessed and focused upon by psychiatry and psychotherapy.
   b. The *self-actualization function,* or expanding, deepening, and heightening human consciousness, harnessed and focused upon by religion and the spiritual disciplines.

Human Consciousness

In **structural** terms, it is composed of:

1. The human self
2. The spiritual Self
3. The field of consciousness
4. The preconscious
5. The subconscious
6. The unconscious
7. The superconscious

While in **functional** terms it entails:

1. Willing
2. Thinking
3. Feeling
4. Intuition
5. Imagination
6. Biopsychic drives
7. Sensations

Human Culture

1. Is the greatest objective creation of human interaction.
2. Is all the things a human being can do that a monkey cannot do.

3. Is the distinctively "human" way of adapting to one's physical environment and of adjusting to one's sociocultural environment.
4. Structurally, it entails three basic dimensions:
   a. the *ideational:* human ideas and idea-systems (religion, science, and philosophy)
   b. the *interactional:* various forms of social organization (how people relate to each other).
   c. the *material:* the various artifacts or man-made implements and tools.
5. Functionally, it provides a *blueprint for survival:*
   a. physical: enable your biological organism to continue living.
   b. psychological: love yourself.
   c. social: love others.
   d. spiritual: love Life and perceive meaning in all that happens.

   This enables human beings to solve their basic human problems; to meet social expectations, and to survive in a multidimensional, holistic fashion.
6. Provides models, tools, and "road-maps" by which human beings can develop and actualize many of their faculties and potentialities.
7. Is the essential medium, or "process", through which human beings can complete their evolution and destiny, becoming **co - creators** of the world and of their Selves with God and Nature.

Finally, Sociology also seeks to describe, analyze, and explain human behavior, **social action,** in terms to two basic streams of forces that meet and blend in the consciousness of the actors. These are the *psychodynamic* processes, originating in man's own personality and providing energy, drive, and needs, and the *sociocultural* processes, originating in society and providing goals, needs, and norms. This theory of social action, however, is based on a **homo duplex** conception of human nature which does not include and account for the **spiritual** dimension. As human consciousness expands and unfolds, there will be not only a "voice of the body" versus a "voice of society" within the individual, but also the "voice of the Self" that he will have to learn to recognize, integrate, and account for. Thus, at higher levels of consciousness, *psychospiritual* processes will emerge and thus have to be accounted for and integrated in this perspective.

Now Sociology is called to broaden, deepen, and heighten, its own outlook by looking both into the microcosm and into the macrocosm, and, especially, at **qualitatively different** ("higher" and "lower") **levels of consciousness and of being.** The very "right relationships" it sought to study and promote for human beings in society, it must now apply to its own **cognitive growth and development.** Thus, it must take into account, assimilate, and integrate both the latest developments of the New Physics and those of Parapsychology, with particular attention being paid to the consciousness of human beings who are unfolding **spiritual consciousness** and reaching higher **levels of being** with *emergent faculties, energies, and capacities.* While continuing to privilege and emphasize **human relationships,** it must also connect these human relationships with **physical** and **spiritual** ones, with the lower and pathological end of the spectrum of human behavior as well as with the higher "supernormal" end. This is what will, eventually, enable us to put together, through an **interdisciplinary** and **multidimensional** approach, the much needed comprehensive **philosophy of life** and **art of living** which will find their roots in a true and living **Science of Man,** with its twin practical applications of an *Art of Prayer* (the Love of God, or Worship) and of an *Art of Service* (the Love of one's fellow human beings, or Social Action).

To this end, I have included, at the end of this work, in appropriate appendices, as "stepping stones" and "practical models" of what can be done, basic materials I have used in lectures and workshops which constitute "fragments" and "stepping stones" towards articulating this Philosophy and Art of Living. For, as Lester Ward aptly put it for true students of all times: "Science must benefit Man, enrich his Life, and ennoble his Character."

Chapter 20

Conclusion

In this work, I have put together over 20 years of materials that I have used teaching one of my very favorite courses, Introduction to Sociology, as well as a few other courses and various lectures and workshops I have given dealing with human nature, human behavior, and human destiny—and how we can consciously cooperate with our own evolution and becoming. I have been faced with difficult choices in that I had to reconcile many opposites, contradictions, and **paradoxes.** I have consciously chosen to use a **synthetic approach** based on linking together and relating to each other very disparate bodies of knowledge and objectives. Specifically, I wanted to blend the very best of classical sociology, with contemporary sociology, and where I see sociology moving in the future; I wanted to relate in a unified and coherent framework the major conclusions, principles, and teachings of sociology with those of other social sciences, and of the emerging **spiritual** sciences, or transpersonal perspective. I have sought to relate what one might call the "exoteric" and the "esoteric" approach, very simple findings with highly sophisticated conclusions, and the truly essential and most thought-provoking aspects of the discipline with a comprehensive and wide-angle view that would satisfy the requirements of a healthy, balanced, traditional and New Age Introduction to Sociology course. I have also sought to link together theory and practice, principles and live stories and illustrations, and finally the academic intellectual requirements with more existential, practical aspects. In most of the exams that I give, and I only give essay-question exams in the social sciences because of the nature and the complexity of the subject matter as well as the basic situations and demands that my students will be faced with in their lives, I ask three basic things:

a. That students provide a definition of something, or that they can demonstrate that they know it and can discuss it.
b. That they apply it to a concrete specific aspect of sociocultural reality—that they can work with it.

c. Finally, that they relate it to themselves and to their daily lives being able to relate theory to life in terms of their selves and biographies.

And it is these criteria that I have kept in mind in writing the present work.

Thus, in a nutshell, this work is meant to be a clear and simple synthesis and elucidation of basic traditional, contemporary, and future sociology, seen both as a science and as an art. To do this I have used a "holistic" or "integral" approach based on general systems' theory and synthesis with the addition of the spiritual dimension of both human nature and Life. Needless to say, this work is a "point of departure," a "first attempt," and a very tentative approach that seeks to be cumulative and systematic, and not the mature synthesis—which is yet to come. Its merit is that it integrates a large body of very disparate facts, information, and discoveries that are now being made in many fields, in many places, by many people that suggests a growing quantitative and qualitative expansion of human consciousness and a major paradigm shift that could radically transform and alter our conception of ourselves, of the universe, of Life, and of knowledge itself—that could result in a veritable cognitive revolution or transformation! There are, however, well authenticated roots and traditions in sociology that indicate that the very founding fathers of the discipline were, in fact, attempting the very thing that I have proposed and carried out in this work—from Auguste Comte, Spencer, and Ward to Emile Durkheim, Max Weber, and Pitirim Sorokin—all of whom, in one way or another, looked upon themselves as "Men of Destiny," as "prophets" in the modern world, and as philosophers and synthesizers of human knowledge as well as healers and doctors of society and of human relations.

This work thus began with a brief consideration of what sociology is, what it does, and why it does what it does—of what might be its specific domain and concrete contributions. It then continued with an analysis of the concept of sociological perspective, of its current application to, and articulation in, the field of sociology—of the macroperspective focusing on society and the microperspective focusing on small group interaction; of the structural-functional, conflict, and interactionist perspective which I embedded and integrated into what I termed a "holistic perspective with a spiritual thrust." We then went on to examine the "World of Sociology" in terms of the discipline, the people who are drawn to it and practice it, and the basic impact of practicing and living sociology upon one's consciousness, attitudes, and behavior. We continued by dedicating 3 very important chapters to interaction, which I termed the "Law of Life, Love, and Growth," seeing it in its physical, human, and spiritual aspects. The major consequence of human interaction and its "creative psychic synthesis" for the individual, is the unfoldment of human consciousness while their major consequence for society is the development of culture. We then tried to define and analyze, specifically and concretely, what sociology is (its nature), what it does (its functions), why it does what it does (its purpose), how it does what it does (its methodology), and its relationship to other academic fields and places in our cognitive universe—with its future and promise examined in subsequent chapters.

We have continued our systematic analysis and investigation of human interaction of man's psychosocial nature, and of the sociocultural environment in which we live, through a conceptual analysis of sociology, and of the structural-functional approach in particular, in terms of both its conceptual break down and of the interrelationships that exist between the social system, the personality system, and the cultural system—between people; their consciousness, their ideas, and their relationships. Then, we went on to an examination of some of the major theories and contributions of the greatest classical and contemporary sociologists, including Emile Durkheim's *Suicide,* Max Weber's *Protestant Ethic and the Spirit of Capitalism,* and Talcott Parsons' *Theory of Social Action.*

Finally, we looked at two major social processes, *socialization,* or "becoming a member of society and becoming human" and *social stratification,* how people perceive and relate to each other in terms of money, power, and prestige. We focused briefly on the very "quintessence" of sociology and at some of its possible future developments and unfoldments. Finally, in the appendix, I have included a basic theoretical framework for the "Study, Analysis, and Interpretation of Social Theory," as well as some of the most important lectures and workshops I have given on psychosocial and biopsychospiritual processes, and the creation of a "Comprehensive Philosophy of Living" and of an "Integral Art of Life" which should be the finest fruits of all academic and intellectual endeavors of the end of the 20th century.

Today, wherever we happen to be in this troubled but beautiful planet of ours, we are living in a most extraordinary period of transition, crisis, and renewal. The century that follows WWII, roughly from the 1950's to the 2050's, will witness some of the most massive quantitative and qualitative changes in the entire history of the human species. In the cultural and cognitive realms, in education, research, and the sciences, more literature will be produced and greater changes will take place than ever before.

One of the major changes is that our cognitive universe will look very different say 50 years from now than it does today: from analysis we will move to synthesis, from the ever-proliferating and fragmenting fields and subfields with their various specialties, we will move towards an *organized synthesis* of all of human knowledge—at least insofar as the methodology to learn and gain knowledge, and the basic principles and insights of various disciplines are concerned! And from a materialistic, positivistic, and rationalistic standpoint we will move towards a spiritual, integral, and intuitive stance.

This "organized synthesis" will reconnect specialists and generalists, and will culminate in a comprehensive philosophy of life and an integral art of living as its finest outgrowth. This philosophy and art of living will be grounded in a general theory of human nature, a specific model of the psyche, and a structural and functional theoretical framework to organize and integrate our knowledge and understanding of ourselves, of the universe, of Life, and of our purpose and destiny in this world.

Before the Renaissance there was such an organized synthesis of human knowledge (albeit a partial one!) that found its culmination in philosophy (in its etymological meaning of the "Love of Wisdom"). Here, philosophy related and interpreted the specialized knowledge of the three great fields of human endeavor: **Theology,** dealing with God in the Universe and the Spirit in human nature; and focusing on the spiritual dimension of reality; **Anthropology,** dealing with human beings in the world and human consciousness in human nature, and focusing on the human dimension of reality; and, finally, **Cosmology,** dealing with Nature in the world and with the biological organism in human nature, and focusing on the physical dimension of reality.

At this point in time, I see again efforts being made, in many fields and by very different people, to arrive at such a synthesis—in a larger and more comprehensive scale than ever before. This, of course, was the dream of the Encyclopedists such as Bayle, D' Alembert, and Diderot and of the founding fathers of sociology such as St. Simon, Comte, and Spencer. But the spirit of the times, the positivistic, empirical materialism and rationalistic emphasis on Reason and Analysis made this impossible and led to ever greater fragmentation and specialization. Today, however, with the rediscovery of the spiritual dimension and a paradigm shift towards synthesis and establishing *right relationships* between various parts and ever greater wholes, both in the macrocosm and in the microcosm, this profound and perennial aspiration of human beings might well finally realize itself.

In this new United Nations of academic disciplines, encompassing both the sciences and the humanities, sociology, after nearly two centuries of struggling and growing, is finally finding its "rightful

178

place under the sun" and its specific "niche" and role in the family of the social sciences. In this work, I have sought to bring out and analyze the essential nature and the most important functions of sociology, in this emerging "holistic perspective with a spiritual thrust," for human beings who are striving to live in a conscious, productive, and responsible way, both as professionals and as lay persons. By way of conclusion, and in summary, sociology is and does the following:

1. Sociology is the "disciplined study of human interaction, its nature, causes, and consequences."
2. It studies a specific dimension of human nature, called the human or psychosocial nature of human beings, that is human consciousness as it arises out of human consciousness and manifests in human consciousness. And it studies a specific dimension of the world in which we lived, called the sociocultural environment or "people and their ideas."
3. It examines systematically the interrelationships between Society (people), Personality (consciousness), and Culture (ideas) so as to be able to describe, analyze, and explain social action, why people behave the way they do.
4. It investigates major social structures and social processes such as social institutions and socialization, social stratification, conflict and cooperation, conformity and deviance.
5. Finally, sociology presents us with a basic theoretical perspective—the Sociological Imagination—and various "tools" or "instruments"—concepts, hypotheses, and theories, as well as research guidelines and criteria of verification—with which to study, in an objective and objective way, any social phenomenon.

The main goal of sociology, in doing the aforementioned things, is to make available for us greater self-knowledge and understanding as well as knowledge and understanding of the world in which we live, so that we may use this knowledge and understanding to gain greater self-mastery and control over our destiny. This, in turn, should lead to self-integration and self-actualization and, eventually, to Self-realization.

The early and first main objective of the "Science of Man and Society," or sociology, was to bring about the Good Society in which the Good Man could live the Good Life. This was generally assumed to mean the unfoldment of a Utopia, in which all people would be free from external oppression and internal wants, secure, able to actualize their potentials and to express themselves to the fullest possible extent, and to be essentially, happy. Today, in the light of an expanding human consciousness and of an emerging spiritual science, we may redefine these very human but *childish* dreams and wishes in a new fashion, reframing them, as it were, to mean:

"Develop ourselves, individually and collectively, by actualizing our faculties and potentialities, and by unfolding higher, spiritual, states of consciousness, wherein we will finally be able to answer the "Riddle of the Sphinx," the "Enigma of the Universe," and the "Puzzle of Life"—Who am I? Where do I come from? Where am I going? What is the meaning and purpose of my daily experiences? What am I to achieve in this life?

This new mindset, perspective, or conception of the world, called the "New Age" or the "Aquarian Age" by some people, is geared not so much to give people what their human egos want—money, health, power, love, leisure, etc., as it will be to lead a person to understand and accept all the parts and aspects of his/her being and all the facets and experiences of Life as being meaningful and purposeful—as having some "Good" to be learned and assimilated. Here, the basic dichotomies of Day and Night, Winter and Summer, Joy and Suffering, Life and Death, Poverty and Affluence, Sickness and Health will be reconciled and integrated at a higher level. Fear, frustration, anger, injustice, violence, envy, jealousy, and greed will slowly diminish and change as acceptance, gratitude, appreciation, patience, contentment, and joy will increase."

Here, sociology has a major role to play in the "Family of Academic Disciplines" that will work together to bring this about. Perhaps the best single specific description of the distinctive contributions that sociology can make to this growing and maturing "family of the social sciences" and to concerned human beings living in the present era, is that given by C. W. Mills in the first chapter of his *Sociological Imagination* (Grove Press, New York, 1959):

"Nowadays men often feel that their private lives are a series of traps. They sense that within their everyday worlds, they cannot overcome their troubles, and in this feeling they are often quite correct: what ordinary men are directly aware of and what they try to do are bounded by the private orbits in which they live; their visions and their powers are limited by close-up scenes of job, family, neighborhood; in other milieux, they move vicariously and remain spectators. And the more aware they become, however vaguely, of ambitions and of threats which transcend their immediate locales, the more trapped they seem to feel.

Underlying this sense of being trapped are seemingly impersonal changes in the very structure of continent-wide societies. The facts of contemporary history are also the facts about the success and the failure of individual men and women. When a society is industrialized, a peasant becomes a worker; a feudal Lord is liquidated or becomes a businessman. When classes rise or fall, a man is employed or unemployed; when the rate of investment goes up or down, a man takes a new heart or goes broke. When wars happen, an insurance salesman becomes a rocket launcher; a store clerk, a radar man; a wife lives alone; a child grows up without a father. Neither the life of an individual nor the history of a society can be understood without understanding both.

Yet men don't usually define the troubles they endure in terms of historical change and institutional contradictions. The well-being they enjoy, they don't usually impute to the big ups and downs of the societies in which they live. Seldom aware of the intricate connection between the patterns of their own lives and the course of world history, ordinary men do not usually know what this connection means for the kinds of men they are becoming and for the kinds of history-making in which they might take part. They do not posses the quality of mind essential to grasp the interplay of *man* and *society*, of *biography* and *history*, *of self* and the *world.* They cannot cope with their personal troubles in such ways as to control the structural transformations that usually lie behind them.

The very shaping of history now outpaces the ability of men to orient themselves in accordance with cherished values. And which values? Even when they do not panic, men often sense that older ways of feeling and thinking have collapsed and that newer beginnings are ambiguous to the point of moral status. It is any wonder that ordinary men feel they cannot cope with the larger worlds with which they are suddenly confronted? That they cannot understand the meaning of their epoch for their own lives? That—in defense of selfhood—they become morally insensible, trying to remain altogether private men? Is it any wonder that they come to be possessed by a sense of the trap?

What they need, and what they feel they need, is a quality of mind that will help them use information and to develop reason in order to achieve lucid summations of what is going on in the world and what may be happening within themselves. It is this quality, I am going to contend, that journalists and scholars, artists and publics, scientists and editors are coming to expect of what may be called the *Sociological Imagination.*

The sociological imagination enables its possessor to understand the larger historical scene in terms of its meaning for the inner life and the external career of a variety of individuals. It enables him to take into account how individuals, in the welter of their daily experiences, often become falsely conscious of their social positions.

Within that welter, the framework of modern society is ought, and within that framework the psychologies of a variety of men and women are formulated. By such means the personal uneasiness of individuals is focused upon explicit troubles and the indifference of publics is transformed into involvement with public issues.

The first fruit of this imagination—and the first lesson of the social science that embodies it—is the idea that the *individual can understand* his own experience and gage his own fate only by *locating himself within his period,* that he can *know his own chances in life* only by becoming aware of those of all individuals in his circumstances. In many ways it is a terrible lesson; in many ways a magnificent one. We do not know the limits of man's capacities for supreme effort or willing degradation, for agony or ecstacy, for pleasurable brutality or the sweetness of reason. But in our time we have come to know that the limits of human nature are frighteningly broad. We have come to know that every individual lives, from one generation to the next, in some society; that he lives out a biography, and that he lives it out within some historical sequence. By the fact of his living, he contributes, however minutely, to the shaping of his society and to the course of its history, even as he is made by society and by its historical push and shove. The sociological imagination enables us to grasp history and biography, and the *relation between the two within society*. That is its task and its promise. To recognize this task and this promise is the mark of the classical analyst.

No sociological study that does not come back to the problems of biography, of history and of their intersections within a society has completed its intellectual journey. Whatever the specific problems of the classical social analysts, however limited or however broad the features of social reality they have examined, those who have been imaginatively aware of the promise of their work have consistently asked three sorts of questions:

1. What is the essential structure of this particular society as a whole? What are its essential components, and how are they related to one another? How does it differ from other varieties of social order? Within it, what is the meaning of any particular feature for its continuance and for its change?

2. Where does this society stand in human history? What are the mechanisms by which it is changing? What is its place within and its meaning for the development of humanity as a whole? How does any particular feature we are examining affect, and how is it affected by, the historical period in which it moves? And this period—what are its essential features? How does it differ from other periods? What are its characteristic ways of history making?

3. What varieties of men and women now prevail in this society and period? And what varieties are coming to prevail? In what ways are they selected and formed, liberated and repressed, made sensitive and blunted? What kinds of human nature are revealed in the conduct and character we observe in this historical period? And what is the meaning of human nature in each and every feature of the society we are examining?

Whether the point of interest is a great power state or a minor literary mood, a family, a prison, a creed—these are the kinds of questions the best social analysts have asked. They are the *intellectual pivots of classic studies of man in society*—and they are the questions inevitably raised by any mind possessing the sociological imagination. For that imagination is the *capacity to shift from one perspective to another*—from the political to the psychological; from the examination of a single family to the comparative assessment of the national budgets of the world; from the theological school to the military establishment; from considerations of an oil industry to studies of contemporary poetry. It is the capacity to range from the most impersonal and remote transformations to the most intimate features of the human self—and to see the relations between the two. Back of its use, there is always the urge to know the sociological and historical meaning of the individual in the society and period in which he has his quality and his being.

That, in brief, is why it is by means of the sociological imagination that men now hope to grasp what is going on in the world, and to understand what is happening in themselves as *minute points of the intersections of biography and history within society.* In large part, contemporary man's self-conscious view of himself as at least an outsider, if not a permanent stranger, rests upon an absorbed realization of the social relativity and of the transformative power of history. The sociological imagination is the most fruitful form of this self-consciousness. By its use men whose mentalities have swept only a series of limited orbits often come to feel as if suddenly awakened in a house with which they had only supposed themselves to be familiar. Correctly or incorrectly, they often come to feel that they can now provide themselves with adequate summations, cohesive assessments, comprehensive orientations. Older decisions that once appeared sound now seem to them products of a mind unaccountably dense. Their capacity for astonishment is made alive again. They acquire a *new way of thinking,* they experience a transformation of values: in a word, by their reflection and by their sensibility, they realize the cultural meaning of the social forces.

It is true, as psychoanalysts continually point out, that people do often have "the increasing sense of being moved by obscure forces within themselves which they are unable to define." But it is not true, as Ernest Jones asserted, that "man's chief enemy and danger is his own unruly nature and the dark forces pent up within him."

On the contrary: "Man's chief danger today lies in the unruly forces of contemporary society itself, with its alienating methods of production, its enveloping techniques of political domination, its international anarchy—in a word, its pervasive transformations of the very nature of man, and the conditions and aims of his life . . . I believe that the social sciences are becoming the *common denominator of our cultural period,* and the *sociological imagination our most needed quality of mind.*"

To the Sociological Imagination of C.W. Mills I would like to add the following beautiful quote from Annie Besant that adds the "holistic perspective with a spiritual thrust" with a vertical emphasis to balance the horizontal emphasis of the former:

"If we were in the habit of identifying ourselves in thought, not with the habitation we live in but with the Human Self that dwells therein, life would become a greater and serener thing. We should brush off troubles as we brush the dust from our garments, and we should realize that the measure of all things happening to us is not the pain or pleasure they bring to our bodies, but *the progress or retardation they bring to the Man within us;* and since all things are matters of experience and lessons may be learned from each, we should take the sting out of our griefs by searching in each for the wisdom enwrapped in it as the petals are folded within the bud."

Basic Theoretical Framework for The Study, Analysis, and Interpretation of Social Theory

In this appendix, we shall articulate and analyze our major instrument for the analysis and development of social theory, namely *a theoretical framework* encompassing the fundamental assumptions upon which social theory is grounded and showing explicitly the central questions, dimensions, and variables that make up its structure as well as the major schools of social theory that developed over time. This is the core instrument that should enable you to analyze social theory in its various formulations and expressions as well as to formulate your own social theory.

The Three Great Objects of Man's Thought and Knowledge

Traditionally, for primitive and traditional societies, there were three great objects for Man's thought and knowledge. These are:

	Macrocosm	*Microcosm*	*Discipline*
Cognitive	God	Spirit	Theology
Universe	Man	Psyche	Anthropology
	Nature	Body	Cosmology
			Philosophia

This resulted from the fact that human consciousness, or Man's attention, can turn three ways:

	Object	*Philosophy*	*Culture*
Mind:	Spirit (God)	Idealism	Ideational
	Itself (Man)	Rationalism	Idealistic
	World (Nature)	Empiricism	Sensate

In modern industrial societies true and substantial philosophy that related and integrated Man's entire cognitive universe was lost as was an experiential and "living understanding" of the first great object: God, or the Spirit. From a Trinity, Man became a *Homo*

Duplex composed of a body (biopsychic nature) and a mind (psycho-social nature) relegating God and the spiritual dimension of his own nature to fantasy and wishful thinking because social scientists were, at that point, unable to empirically experience these. Cosmology then became the natural sciences that studied various domains and areas of nature through the scientific method; Anthropology became the social sciences which studied Man (human nature, human behavior, and human consciousness) through the use of the scientific method and by developing their own distinctive methods and procedures such as the *Verstehen* approach and participant observation; finally, Theology became quite "anemic," lost its former status and predominance, was relegated to the "humanities" and culminated in the "Death of God theology," that is, in the disappearance of God and the spiritual dimension from human consciousness and preoccupation. In the post-industrial or information society, which we are now entering, and in the emerging Aquarian Age, God and the spiritual dimension will manifest themselves again and now become "empirical," that is, amenable to direct personal observation and experience but in varying and unfolding degrees. This will lead to the creation of the *spiritual sciences* which will complete the "broken trinity" and make possible a new Philosophia, or cognitive synthesis of human knowledge, integrating all dimensions of human nature and reality, physical, psychosocial, and spiritual.

The Three Great Orientations of Man's Thought and Attention

Analytically and topologically speaking, there are three great orientations that human thought and attention have taken culturally and historically and which were embodied in their most succinct fashion in the three great Greek Ideals and Injunctions. These correspond to the focusing upon and articulation of the "three royal functions of the Psyche," thinking, feeling, and willing or seeking *Knowledge, Love,* and *Creative Power* and are:

a. *Man, Know Thyself* (and thou shalt know the Universe) or *seek to become aware of, know, and understand the various aspects and dimensions of Reality,* of the World, in terms of its physical, sociocultural, and spiritual environment, and of Human Nature in terms of its biopsychic, psychosocial, and spiritual natures.

b. *Man, seek Harmony with Thyself* (and Thou shalt find harmony with the Universe) or *seek to unite with, to find the right relationships or harmony with the various aspects and dimensions of Reality;* of the World in terms of its three great Objects: God, Man, and Nature, and of Human Nature in terms of the Body, the Psyche, and the Spirit.

c. *Man, be the Master of Thyself* (and thou shalt be the master of the Universe) or *seek to control, master, or dominate* the various aspects and *dimensions of Reality* in terms of its physical, sociocultural, and spiritual environment, and of Human Nature in terms of its biopsychic, psychosocial, and spiritual natures. Here, however, we find a great paradox. While Man must seek to develop and actualize his will to the fullest possible extent to achieve self-actualization, when he will finally have done so, he will have to offer his will to God's Will or attune the human with the Divine Will! For while Man must be "male" in regards to his lower self, he can only be "female" in regards to the Higher Self, and must find Harmony, or Love, God, Man, and Nature, and not control or exploit them for the selfish ends of his ego or lower self!

When we turn our attention to and study the historical articulation of these three great orientations, we find that Man has always been concerned with his relationship with God, the Spirit, Man, the Psyche, and Nature, the Physical Universe, in terms of knowing or understanding them, loving them and finding harmony with them, and mastering or controlling them. These relationships, however, with their focus and quality, have varied and changed with changing times: value-systems, existential experiences, transformations of human consciousness, population increases, and technological, economic, and sociopolitical developments in various societies. On the whole, however, we find the following topology:

a. *In primitive societies* the focus was upon seeking harmony, a right relationship or union with God, Man, and Nature.
b. *In traditional societies* the focus or emphasis shifted to seeking to know and understand God, Man, and Nature.
c. *In modern industrial societies* the focus shifted again to seeking *prediction* (scientific knowledge) and *mastery* or control of Nature and its physical energies and materials and, later, of other human beings (politics, socialization, psychotherapy, and management techniques).
d. Now, *in the emerging post-industrial or information societies,* the focus or emphasis is again changing to one of understanding and seeking harmony with one's complex human nature and human relationships, and to seeking understanding of and harmony with God, the spiritual Self, and the spiritual dimension. Thus, after five centuries of seeking knowledge to gain power and mastery over Nature and Man which began

with the Renaissance, reached its apogee during the Age of Enlightenment, and finally declined at the end of WWII, we are finally to realize again and want *Wisdom* and *Love* at the onset of the Aquarian Age.

As Emory Bogardus put it (*The Development of Social Thought,* David McKay, 1966):

"Today man faces a world in which his social problems are becoming increasingly more complex and intricate. As a result, he is perplexed beyond description and his thinking often ends in confusion. Upon the success of the social scientist, as well as of the layman, in mastering the intricacies of social thinking and the fundamental issues of collective living depends the further development of humanity, if not the very life of civilization. The most fundamental issues here lie, on the one hand, in understanding the genesis and development of social theory in its historical unfoldment and, on the other, in establishing a bridge or feed-back process of communication between social theorists and those who apply and practice social thinking."

To this, the great British historian, Arnold Toynbee adds (*An Historian's Approach to Religion,* Oxford University Press, 1956, p. 186):

"No human soul can pass through this life without being challenged to grapple with the mystery of the universe. If the distinctively human impulse of curiosity does not bring us to the point, experience will drive us to it—above all, the experience of suffering. In casting about for an approach to the mystery in a westernizing world midway through the 20th Century, we might well take a clue from our 17th Century western predecessors, who opened up for us a view that still holds us under its spell today. So far, mankind has never succeeded in unifying the whole of its experience of the universe in which he finds himself. We can see the universe from different angles and from each of these it wears a different aspect. From one angle we see it as a spiritual universe; from another as a physical universe; and from either of these two we can drive a tunnel into one flank of the great pyramid. But our tunnels driven through these from these two directions have never met yet, and neither of these two approaches by itself, has enabled man to explore the mystery more than partially; neither of them has revealed its heart. Midway through the 20th Century, we Westerners are still exploring the universe from the mathematico-physical angle that our 17th Century predecessors chose for us. In order to choose it, they had to wrench themselves away from the spiritual approach which Christianity had followed since Socrates and the prophets of Israel. This radical change of orientation required of the 17th Century Western mental pioneers who made it, a great effort of thought, and the spectacle of their prowess should inspire us to follow their example now, at their expense. The time has come for us, in our turn, to wrench ourselves from the 17th Century mathematico-physical line of approach, which we are still following, and to make a fresh start from the *spiritual side.* This is now once again the most promising line of approach of the two if we are right in expecting that, in the atomic age which opened A.D. 1945, the *spiritual field of activity,* and not the *physical one,* is going to be the domain of freedom."

And Pitirim Sorokin concludes (*Basic Trends of Our Times,* College and University Press, 1964, p. 196):

"The mysterious forces of history seem to have given man an ultimatum: perish by your own hands or rise to a higher moral level through the grace of creative love. . . . Since the real curative agent in mental disease is love in its various forms, many eminent apostles of love have been able to cure the mental disorders of legions of persons, although these altruists did not have any special psychiatric training. Their sublime love and supraconscious wisdom have been an excellent substitute for "little or no love" and for the professional training of ordinary psychiatrists. . . . Love not only cures and revitalizes the individual's mind and organism but also proves itself to be the decisive factor of the vital, mental, moral, and social well-being and growth of an individual."

To these, I would add the very gist, or quintessence, of the greatest minds of our century such as Teilhard de Chardin, Bergson, Aurobindo, Eliade, Campbell, Jung, and Assagioli which can be summarized by saying succinctly that *human beings and human cultures will either rediscover the spiritual dimension and the power of love and make these the unifying and integrating principles of their psyche and lives or degenerate to the level of a barbaric age and die out.*

Bogardus saw five great lines or avenues of investigation for human thought which he conceptualized as follows:

a. First we have the *spiritual orientation* towards the invisible, supersensory spiritual world which characterized primitive societies:

"Primitive man conceived of a personal universe peopled with spirits. Throughout history, man has been a religious being, trying to solve the problems of a universe peopled by Spirits or Gods, or by One supreme God. This type of thinking has produced polytheisms, monotheisms, and theocracies. It has formulated theological creeds and resulted in bitter ecclesiastical controversies."

b. Then came the *philosophical orientation* towards life: interpreting all human experience by reason and the senses which characterized traditional societies.

"Irrespective of religious needs, man has endeavored to think out his relations to the whole universe, animate and inanimate. He has philosophized. He has tried to reduce to a few far-reaching concepts this baffling, intangible as well as tangible, universal environment. He has searched for reliable grounds for explaining his relationships to the universe. He has sought unity in change and monism in multiplicity. He has proclaimed that blind change itself is Lord of all, or he has found solace in creative evolution. He has put Man at the apex of all creation or he has asserted that all is vanity. At any rate, he has sought ultimate meanings in as unbiased an interpretation of which he is capable."

    c. This led to the *humanistic orientation* where the focus of man's thought and investigation became Man himself and the structure and dynamics of his consciousness.

"From the far-flung horizons of religious and philosophical systems of thought, Man has directed his concentrated and prolonged attention in an opposite direction. He has turned this thought upon itself. He has maneuvered his thought processes introspectively. He has puzzled long and diligently upon the structure and functions of thinking and behaving."

    d. This, in turn, brought about the *scientific orientation* which aimed at the *prediction* of empirical phenomena and the harnessing and control of the physical resources and energies of Nature.

"Man has sought to fathom the material secrets of the earth. Since the Industrial Revolution in England, inquiring minds have focused tremendous energies upon attempts to understand and harness the physical elements. Rocks and strata of rocks have been caused to yield a wealth of ores, and subterranean caverns have been made to pour forth reservoirs of oil and gas. Modern transportation has been made possible by man's knowledge about steam, gasoline, and electricity. Mechanical inventions have followed one another in unanticipated fashion, paying awe-inspiring tribute to the thought-power of man. Abstract thinking has given man a marvelous degree of control over the material side of life. In other words, science has become the God of mankind in many fields. Scientific thought has added immeasurably to the conveniences and comforts of life."

    e. Finally, came the *social orientation* which redirected Man's thinking and concern towards understanding and being able to predict human relationships which degenerated into the attempt on the parts of some to control them.

"Recently, the problems of man's adjustment to his fellow men has received worthy attention at the bar of scientific thought. Social scientific thinking has acquired increasing accuracy during the present century. For millennia man has pondered hard over his relation and obligation to God, as well as to His universe, over the nature of his thought processes and of his mind, over ways and means of acquiring individual success through a manipulation of the material resources of the earth. Incomprehensible as it may seem, it is true, however, that man has neglected almost wholly until recent decades, the very heart of all truly successful living, namely *his relation and obligation to his fellow men and to society.* Social thinking, or the analytical thinking about the nature of social life, its trends and its problems, has been so ignored. Social thinking, the *center of all complete thinking,* has been so little perfected that the world today is suffering beneath a staggering load of ills that few seem able to diagnose accurately. In the present age, however, the need is great for scientific social thinking about the whole gamut of social ills."

What Bogardus has delineated for us is really the progressive transformations and narrowing of human consciousness in its involutionary arc which has now shifted to the evolutionary arc. Man's level of being, level of consciousness, and the focus of his thinking is now going full circle; beginning with a dim and oceanic awareness of the whole of external and internal reality in its threefold expression of spiritual, human, and physical; it has led through analytical thinking to a narrowing of attention focusing more and more upon the physical dimension. Now through synthetic thinking the attention is, once again, expanding from the physical to the human, to culminate in the rediscovery of the spiritual dimension. Primitive Man was not, as many thinkers of the last 3 centuries thought, an immature child who was reacting more emotionally, imaginatively, and intuitively to reality, projecting and objectifying his own fears and aspirations onto the screen of the cosmos. He was progressively losing his perceptions and experiences of the whole of reality to focus upon an ever narrowing band of it; only to discover that the true secret of life and meaning could not be found in the physical dimension but in the life and consciousness that ensoul and permeate the physical dimension and which nature and origins lie in higher and more interior levels which are generically called the "spiritual dimension." Thus, from a preoccupation with his relation to God and the universe, with the nature of human consciousness, and with the exploitation of the natural resources of the earth, Man is turning, once more, to study and examine his relation to his fellow human beings. Today, growing and unfolding human consciousness is seeking a new definition and synthesis of reality in terms of its social and spiritual dimensions. And this leads us to our first and most fundamental definition of social theory as *the understanding of Man's relation to man, and to man-made social structures and artifacts, their nature, genesis, dynamics, key dimensions, and agents, and their psychosocial consequences for man and society.* And it can either focus upon seeking to *understand,* find *harmony,* or *control* these. Auguste Comte developed a motto which goes to the very heart of this enterprise: "Voir pour Savoir, Savoir pour Prévoir, Prévoir pour Pouvoir" or "to See (and Experience) in order to Know, to Know in order to Predict, and to Predict in order to Control."

The Two Basic Kinds of Knowledge
in the Social Sciences

These stand at the very root of the distinction between the scientific and the humanistic schools in modern sociology and are:

a. *Knowledge ab extra or extroverted knowledge* which is gained through observation, measurement, and experimentation. It is a descriptive and analytical knowledge that is based upon statistics and probabilities. It is the *Esprit de Geometrie* of Pascal which yields prediction and power that are at the heart of *scientific knowledge.*

b. *Knowledge ab intra or introverted knowledge* which is gained through introspection and participant observation. It is an analogical and symbolic knowledge that is based upon sympathy and personal experience. It is the *Esprit de Finesse* of Pascal which yields phenomenological *understanding* or *Verstehen.*

Social Thought and Modern Sociological Theory

Social thought has existed and been formulated so long as human beings have been capable of thinking, asking questions, and wondering about Reality, themselves, and the nature and origins of the World, Man, and God. But, before the birth of modern sociology at the end of the 18th century and the beginning of the 19th century, social thought was inextricably intertwined with other humanistic disciplines such as religion, philosophy, literature, and political science and lacked a well defined methodology and field of investigation. When modern sociology was born, social thought became conscious of itself, organized itself around one central discipline, sociology, and acquired a well-defined and specific methodology.

The Fundamental Problems and Key Issues of Social Thought

Margaret Vine wrote:

"Social theorists, regardless of the times in which they lived, raised, and pondered upon, the answer to *similar basic problems.* The conceptualization of the central issues and the classification of the basic answers to them (the fundamental problems and key issues of social thought) has made an organic continuity and unity in social theory possible."

From the humanistic viewpoint, for Margaret Vine, these fundamental problems and key issues of social thought are:

1. *The person as a social unit.* What is Man's social nature and his relationship to society? (Theory of human nature and human consciousness.)

2. *Social forces and processes.* What is the nature and origin of human society? How can society exist? What is the genesis, unfoldment, and articulation of the social bond? (Theory of social integration.)
3. *Social structures.* What is the structural organization of society? What are the basic "units" that make up society? (Structural analysis.)
4. *Persistence of social structures.* How is a human being transformed into a social and rational being able to function within a given social system? What are the basic mechanisms that ensure the existence of society and by which society can insure the conformity of its members? (Theory of socialization and social controls.)
5. *Social change.* What is the nature and the causes of social change? What factors determine social change and constitute the "motor of history?" (Theory of social change.)
6. *Sociology and Methodology.* What is the discipline that can unify the basic answers to the above questions and provide an adequate and integrated methodology to do this? What is the nature and function of sociology? What is the analytical unit of sociology and the methods it can utilize to gain valid knowledge? (To understand the fundamental forms of social thought.)

Fundamental Problems and Key Issues of Sociological Theory

Nicholas Timasheff wrote:

"The foundation of every empirical science is *observation* (and *experience* in the social sciences). Its result is a proposition stating that, at a given time and place, a particular phenomenon or occurrence has taken place. Individual observations are then compared and give rise to a classification showing similarities and differences from which generalizations, statements of invariance, or "laws" are abstracted."

Looking at sociology from the viewpoint of the scientific school, Timasheff asserts that the foundation of any science, whether natural or social, and, therefore, of sociology, must be the *scientific method* which substituted authority and tradition with observation and personal experience that can be duplicated and verified under laboratory conditions. As we saw in a former chapter, the scientific method is anchored upon 5 basic concepts which describe its nature and operations. These are:

1. observation and personal experience;
2. the formulation of hypothesis;
3. the construction of theory;
4. experimentation; and,
5. checks for validity and reliability.

Timasheff is careful to point out, however, that theory cannot be derived from observations, generalizations, and personal experiences merely through rigorous induction. That the construction of a theory is, in fact, a *creative achievement* as there is always a qualitative "jump" beyond the strict evidence of the senses, a *hunch* or *intuition* corresponding to the creative effort. But he is also careful to point out that this creative intuition which stands behind all theory must, according to the scientific method, be subjected to empirical verification and corroboration, which will either prove, disprove, or modify the theory.

In a "mature science" like physics or biology, there is one highly abstract theory or set of theories which are organically interrelated and mutually complementary to explain a very wide array of known observational facts. This state of maturity, reached after long and tedious efforts over centuries has not yet been reached by sociology, or any of the social sciences, which deal with a far more complex set of phenomena underpinned by human consciousness which can become a causal and creative agent when actualized. Thus, sociology and the other social sciences are still characterized by an unusually large number of conflicting and paradoxical theories and propositions of a lesser degree of abstraction.

Careful inspection of social theory of the past and present show that it is grounded upon certain fundamental problems and key issues which, from the scientific viewpoint, can be formulated as follows:

1. What is Man and how has he become what he is?
2. What are Society and Culture?
3. What are the basic units into which Society and Culture can be analyzed?
4. What is the relationship between Society, Culture, and Personality?
5. What are the key factors determining the state or change of a Society, Culture, and Personality?
6. What is Sociology and its basic theories and methodology?

A careful analysis of the fundamental problems and key issues of both social thought and modern sociological theories, seen from the viewpoint of the humanistic and scientific schools, show that their substance is really the same though it has been conceptualized in different ways. From these, we can therefore abstract and formulate what I call a *Practical Paradigm for the study, analysis, and evaluation of social theory*. This practical paradigm can be used both to evaluate existing social theory or to formulate one's own in a mature and rigorous fashion.

194

The Practical Paradigm for the Study, Analysis, and Evaluation of Social Theory

This practical paradigm rests upon a set of 5 basic assumptions, or subtheories, which are:

1. *A theory of human nature* which, in turn, rests upon 3 subtheories:
   a. A theory of human cognition . . . what constitute valid scientific knowledge? Epistemology.
   b. A structural theory of Man's being . . . what is Man, how did he become what he is, and what can he become in the future? Anthropology.
   c. A theory of Eudaemonia or self-actualization . . . how can Man develop himself to the fullest possible extent so that he can make his highest contributions to others and, thereby, live the most conscious, creative, and productive life?

2. *A theory of the nature of Society* which, in turn, rests upon a set of two basic assumptions:
   a. How can society exist? What are the mechanisms and forces making for social integration?
   b. What are the basic structures and key functions of society and social institutions? What is the common value system and its externalization and objectification?

3. *A theory of the nature of History* which, in turn, rests upon a set of two basic assumptions:
   a. How does Society change? What are the mechanisms and forces making for social change?
   b. Why does Society change? Psychosocial versus sociocultural mechanisms and forces involved.

4. *A theory of the Socialization of Man* which, in turn, rests upon a set of two basic assumptions:
   a. How is the biological organism of Man transformed into a social, rational being?
   b. What are the mechanisms responsible for the genesis and unfoldment of Man's psychosocial nature and self?

5. *A theory of the nature, scope, and function of Sociology:* its theories, and methodologies which, in turn, rest upon a set of two basic assumptions:
   a. Key assumptions and conceptions of the nature, function, and purpose of Sociology.
   b. What are and should be its major contributions to Man's cognitive universe.

Thus, to critically evaluate any existing social theory or to creatively construct one, one can use the above-described practical paradigm and ask the questions: What are the author(s) basic assumptions and conceptions, which should be made explicit and clearly conceptualized, concerning:

1. a theory of human nature;
2. a theory of the nature of society;
3. a theory of the nature of history;
4. a theory of the socialization of Man; and,
5. a theory of the nature, scope, and function of sociology.

Are these adequate, comprehensive, properly integrated, and compatible with the ever-advancing frontiers of human knowledge? Are they able to satisfactorily explain and interpret contemporary events and developments? Can they adequately relate and explain all available facts of both observation and human experience? Or are they still anchored upon obsolete, incomplete, and *a priori* 19th century assumptions? Are they so structured as to be closed or open-ended to incorporate new and emerging facts and developments?

A careful review of the fundamental types of social theory that have emerged in the 20th century reveals that there are 3 basic approaches or schools of thought. These are:

a. *The materialistic school* which views Man as being essentially a unidimensional, biopsychic being struggling to survive and express himself in this world.
b. *The psychosocial main stream-school* which views Man as being essentially a Homo Duplex with a biopsychic nature, arising from Nature, which must be organized and directed by the psychosocial nature which arises from Society.
c. *The spiritual school* which views Man as being essentially a Homo Triplex, or a trinity, with a biopsychic, a psychosocial, and a spiritual nature.

The materialistic school, represented by such well-known social thinkers as Karl Marx, Herbert Spencer, Vilfredo Pareto, and B.F. Skinner is definitely obsolete and declining with the growth of humanistic psychology and sociology which have uncovered a great wealth of facts and evidence showing that Man is more than an "animal" or a purely biopsychic being. The psychosocial school, represented by most of the rounding fathers and classical as well as contemporary figures in sociology, is still the mainstream approach that has the widest consensus and body of research. The spiritual school, represented by some of the greatest minds of our century such as Henri Bergson, Max Weber, Mircea Eliade, Pitirim Sorokin, and Roberto Assagioli, is still small but definitely a growing and emerging school that promises spectacular growth and development in the future. It is supported by a growing body of evidence and facts coming out of such widely different fields as nuclear physics, humanistic and transpersonal psychology, and the rediscovery of the ancient spiritual traditions.

Werner Starks' Fundamental Forms of Social Thought

In the early sixties, Werner Stark published an important work in social theory entitled *The Fundamental Forms of Social Thought*. In this work, he argues, after having made a careful study and analysis of social thought throughout the ages, that there are three fundamental sets of assumptions and basic conceptions of social thought. Drawing from Wilhelm Dilthey and Pitirim Sorokin, he calls these:

a. *The Mechanistic School* which draws its fundamental truth and reality-giving experience from *inanimate life*. This approach draws its model, inspirations, and basic concepts from physics and mechanics. The focus is on homeostasis or equilibrium and on classical cause and effect relationships. Thinking in this view is nominalistic, atomistic, individualistic, and contractual. Society is seen as a multiplicity of individuals who alone are real and appears like a great big *machine* composed of pieces put together by Man's mind.

b. *The Organismic School* which draws its fundamental truth and reality-giving experience from *animate life*. This approach draws its model, inspirations, and basic concepts from biology and physiology. The focus is on process and stimulus-response. Thinking in this view is holistic and organismic. Society is seen as *an organism* the whole of which is greater than the sum of its parts. Here, there is a common life and a "great chain of beings" permeating the whole of society which is seen as an *entity sui generis*.

c. *The Cultural School* which draws its fundamental truth and realty-giving experience from *Man, from human consciousness*. This approach draws its model, inspirations, and basic concepts from psychology, history, and philosophy. The focus is on dualism and moral conflict between body and mind. Thinking in this view is holistic and integral. Society is seen both as a psychic unity and as a psychic multiplicity, as a *psychic process*. Society is the product of human interaction, human consciousness, and human will. It is both objective, or outside the individual, and subjective, or inside the individual. Society here is viewed as an *exteriorization of human* consciousness, the core of which are common values and norms, habits and customs.

Stark links the Mechanistic and the Organismic Schools with the Scientific School of Sociology and the Cultural School with the Humanistic School and does not further differentiate the emergent spiritual approach in the Cultural School. Finally, he argues that there can be no convergence, at a higher level of abstraction, between the Scientific and the Humanistic Schools and thus that one must make a value-choice and take a position in either one or the other of these camps. This because he sees an unbridgeable chasm in the following assumptions these two camps make concerning:

a. *A theory of human nature:* seeing Man essentially as an animal and being totally bound by the deterministic model of nature (the Scientific School) versus seeing Man as a human being as a being of will and reason and endowed with a human consciousness which, when actualized, can become a causal and creative agent, who can then rise above or transcend nature (the Humanistic School).

b. *A theory of the nature of society:* seeing society and culture as being purely a natural product, the latest creation of nature (the Scientific School) versus seeing them as a human phenomenon, the product of human interaction, human consciousness, and human will (the Humanistic School).

c. *A theory of the nature of history:* seeing the "motor" of social change as being controlled and determined by extra-human forces (the Scientific School) versus seeing them as being controlled and determined by Man's will and ideas or human forces (the Humanistic School).

d. *A theory of the nature and purpose of sociology:* focusing essentially upon scientific knowledge or knowledge *ab extra* and obtaining the knowledge and expertise to "know what is the common good and the best for society" (the Scientific School) versus focusing upon understanding or knowledge *ab intra* and helping each individual develop himself to the fullest extent possible and realize his highest ideals (the Humanistic School).

I do not accept this viewpoint and feel that there can, indeed, be a valid convergence and synthesis, at a higher level of abstraction, between the Scientific, the Humanistic, and the Spiritually oriented Schools which depends on the level of being and consciousness of the actors who are involved. So long as we are dealing with unself-actualized persons and persons who are living at an unconscious level, the approach of the Scientific School might be the most pertinent and efficacious to describe existing conditions but, as people grow and become more and more conscious and in control of their being and their lives activating their human consciousness, then the Humanistic becomes more appropriate to end with the Spiritually-oriented School in the case of persons who have undergone or are undergoing a valid form of spiritual awakening. Every School and legitimate approach is valid and useful but limited to a certain type of person and circumstances that gave rise to it. And, as we move up and down the vertical scale of consciousness and shift our field of consciousness, different theories and approaches are needed and become more or less useful.

Fundamental Assumptions for a Practical and Dynamic Course In Social Theory

A practical paradigm for the "Creative Process" applied to social theory. Why should one study, evaluate and create social theory? Only to gain a greater knowledge and understanding of sociocultural processes, to better know and understand oneself and the sociocultural milieu in which one lives? No, I feel that we are not only *spectators* but also *actors* in the joint creation of a psychosocial cosmos, in the development of our personality and character as well as our society and culture. If we consider the following assumptions about human nature and the creative process, we can better understand the nature and purpose of social theory. These assumptions are the following:

1. *That Man comes unfinished and incomplete from the hands of Nature*:
    a. What begins as *natural evolution* must lead through personal growth and transformation to *rational and social evolution* (the point at which we now are and which is "underpinned by human will and ideas") to culminate in *spiritual evolution,* the challenge of our times.
    b. That is to say, Man is at first guided by nature and his instincts, but then he must emancipate himself from nature and make himself and fashion his own being and destiny through his own human powers, eventually to reach his perfection and the fulfillment of his destiny through the guidance and inspiration from the Spiritual Powers both within himself and in the Cosmos.
2. *Genesis leads to Telesis:* that is, unconscious evolution gives birth to conscious evolution wherein Man must take charge of himself and of his becoming, and forge the core of his being, life, and destiny.

3. *The creative process* by which Man can make and transform himself and his environment is the following. Three basic elements are used in 3 sequential steps.

    a. *The development of vision,* ideas and ideals of what he wants and wishes to become.

    b. Then, *the activation of love, desire and feeling* for this vision.

    c. Finally, *the application of will-power and action* to incarnate these in his life, being, and world so that: MAN'S VISION OR IDEAS AND IDEALS, VITALIZED BY HIS LOVE AND FEELINGS, AND REALIZED BY HIS WILL AND ACTIONS CAN AFFECT, CHANGE AND TRANSFORM HIS BEING, HIS CONSCIOUSNESS, AND HIS ENVIRONMENT, PHYSICAL, SOCIAL, AND CULTURAL.

The Genetic Paradigm for Studying Objectively and Systematically Social Theory

If we wish to truly understand a given social theory and evaluate it in a larger context, we must take the following steps and make the following investigations:

1. the theorist's life and personality;
2. the major influences on his life and works;
3. his major works;
4. his sociological system: theory and methodology;
5. his major contributions to social theory and sociology and our current criticism of them; and,
6. application of the Practical or Analytical Paradigm to his social theory.

Final Note

A few years ago, the Sociology Department of Duke University did a study on "Peace of Mind" which revealed several factors as being crucial for achieving emotional and mental stability. These are:

1. The absence of suspicion and resentment. Nursing a grudge was a major factor in unhappiness.
2. Not living in the past. An unwholesome preoccupation with old mistakes and failures leads to depression.
3. Not wasting time and energy fighting conditions you cannot change. Cooperate with life, instead of trying to run away from it.

4. Force yourself to stay involved with the living world. Resist the temptation to withdraw and become reclusive during periods of emotional crisis.
5. Refuse to indulge in self-pity when life hands you a raw deal. Accept the fact that nobody gets through life without some sorrow and misfortune.
6. Cultivate the old-fashioned virtues—love, honor, compassion, and loyalty.
7. Don't expect too much of yourself. When there is too wide a gap between self-expectation and your ability to meet the goals you have set, feelings of inadequacy are inevitable.
8. Find something bigger than yourself to believe in. Self-centered, egotistical people score lowest in any test for measuring happiness.

The Fundamental Questions of Life: How to Answer Them

Everywhere, today, life is becoming more and more complex and difficult! The solution of one problem gives birth to further problems and, as soon as a crisis is resolved more appear on the horizon. In the USA, as well as in Europe, we are afflicted by what Alvin Toffler has appropriately called "overchoice". In the family, at work, in education as well as in one's leisure, in religion, medicine, politics, and in psychotherapy, there is a tremendous confusion and many conflicts due, precisely, to this "overchoice" to this great "personal freedom" where *all is possible but hardly anything can be realized!* This is the result of many factors and, particularly of the tremendous accelerating transformations of society since the second half of the 20th century, the radical change in basic values and moral principles, and the decline of the "controlling power" of the great social institutions such as the family, the state, religion, and education. No wonder, therefore, if the individual, abandoned to himself and "adrift on the ocean of life", is not happier and more actualized by this new "freedom" and "power of self-expression" but, rather, in prey to a great psychosocial "stress", to a permanent existential anxiety, and to an ever-growing insecurity.

In this state of confusion, anguish, and generalized disarray, many people turn toward all kinds of modern "authorities" and "experts"; educators, psychiatrists, psychotherapists, or Gurus of new cults. . . but without better or more effective results. Others throw themselves into new studies or personal growth workshops but with no better end results. Others yet, launch themselves into a new "love quest", in intimate relationships that are just as "disposable" and "ephemeral" as everything else in our post industrial society. Thus, religion, psychotherapy, counselling, and, above all, education are in a state of "generalized crisis". . . as we are! This is, perhaps, why, in the USA, education is coming back to "basics" and why we *now we see* appearing in intimate and affective relationships, the phenomenon of "tough love" replacing "soft love" . . . which emerged towards the end of the first half of the 20th century as a result of the "progressive and democratic" movement in education and philosophy. This is also why, today, I would like to discuss with you what I call the "Fundamental Questions of Life" which have, unfortunately, been *drowned* in the extraordinary intellectual, but *anarchic*, development of our times. These questions are the following:

1. *The Enigma of the Sphinx* (the question of identity): Who am I? Where do I come to do on earth and what is the meaning of my life?
2. *How can I discover and create a system of values and of moral principles* which correspond to my level of consciousness and being? So as to live a conscious and responsible life and "become what I am"?
3. *How to identify and choose my "work" or profession?*
4. *How to find and choose a life mate,* the person with whom I will live?
5. *How to develop and live a "philosophy of life" and an "art of living"* which truly correspond to my being and our age?

These questions are truly fundamental for two reasons: First, because they constitute the true "foundation" for living a conscious, responsible, and autonomous life; and second, because they are truly "universal" and valid for societies and cultures of all times and places. It is at the very "heart" of religion and education of all people that we find these "questions", presented in a more symbolic or allegorical fashion. It is when the "wisdom" of the ancients became the "knowledge" and then the "technical expertise" of modern people (that is, since the Renaissance and, especially, since the "Age of Reason") that the analysis and the direct development of the "great questions" became, more and more a "personal question" . . . a "personal question" submerged by many other preoccupations.

I would like at this point to state, in a clear and explicit fashion, my central thesis concerning these "fundamental questions":

To answer these "questions" in a serious, comprehensive, and satisfactory way, it is imperative to develop *another state of consciousness* than the one we are normally functioning in—to develop *spiritual consciousness!* This because "below", in the lower state of consciousness, there are no truly valid solutions and answers. To find these we must, necessarily, "move up", reach higher states of consciousness.

Let me develop and analyze this thesis a little further. A normal human being "functions with" and "integrates" three qualitatively different levels of consciousness: *Sensory consciousness* which brings us in contact with the physical world, *Emotional consciousness* which brings us in contact with the emotional/astral world, *Mental consciousness* which brings us in contact with the mental world. But, human beings, as well as the universe, also have the potentiality to unfold higher levels of consciousness, in particular, *spiritual consciousness* which can get to the very "heart" of our Self and of Reality. Hence, it is, paradoxically, only when we become aware and activate our *spiritual* dimension, and the *spiritual* dimension of the universe, that we will finally be able to answer in a mature and holistic way all the basic questions that our mind can raise. And, specifically, who we are, what is the universe, life and death, good and evil, etc. Nature, however, has endowed us only with the first three dimensions of consciousness which manifest spontaneously in normal and healthy human beings. The other one, the most important one, involves a *transformation of our state of consciousness and being, a conscious growth, and a psychospiritual transformation of our psyche.* It is probably because of this that religion has always affirmed: "Seek ye first the "kingdom of heaven" (spiritual consciousness) and all "these things" (the answer to the fundamental questions of life) will be given to you".

Until now, science has searched for the key to the mystery of life and of the universe in matter with the use of *observation* and of *reason;* medicine seeks the etiology of diseases and the key to health in the human body through *scientific experimentation;* philosophy and education seek for the meaning of life and the actualization of human potentials through a *rationalistic* and *positivistic* approach; and, finally, economics, political science, and psychology seek personal and social integration using the same approach and methods . . . and with the same results! The universe, human behavior, and the basic existential problems are expanding and complexifying while the answer given to certain questions and problems merely *raise new questions and problems*. There is one essential thing which is missing and which is, at least for me, the *true key and answer to* this baffling situation and that is SPIRITUAL CONSCIOUSNESS . . . which *alone* can truly get to the "heart of reality," both internal and external. For, without spiritual consciousness, there would always be an "essential dimension" missing and we would apprehend but the "shadows" of reality!

The fundamental question is thus: How to awaken and unfold the spiritual consciousness of human beings—how to understand and "put into action" the great process of PSYCHOSPIRITUAL TRANSFORMATION? This will be the specific subject of another lecture/workshop. In this lecture/workshop, I am merely stating my essential thesis which lies at the core of the perspective I am suggesting.

Once a person has developed this spiritual consciousness, at least up to a certain point, or adopted the perspective that a person who has unfolded spiritual consciousness, how would one look at and answer these "fundamental questions"? What is the holistic conception that can help us give truly satisfying and meaningful answers to these questions? Drawing from my own personal experience and the conclusions of my own studies, I would say propose the following:

1. *The Enigma of the Sphinx:* the question of human identity. The Sphinx, a mythical animal, was a symbolic fashion to represent human nature. It was made up of three essential parts: the body of a lion, representing the *animal nature* of man; the human torso and head, representing the *human nature* of man; and the wings of an eagle, representing the *spiritual nature* of man. The Sphinx thus represents the *synthesis* of both human nature and of human consciousness and of their progressive unfoldment: the development, coordination, and perfecting of the physical body and of the instincts/impulses, then of the astral and mental bodies (emotions and thoughts) and, finally, of the spiritual body or body of Light (intuitions and inspirations)—the birth of the inner Christ and the awakening of spiritual consciousness.

One of the major problems of our times is, indeed, that of the *crisis of identity* which we can find everywhere: in the clergy, in social workers, in educators, in medical doctors, in women . . . in men—in short, in the *modern person.* This person, left to himself, cut adrift from the great social institutions, and "emancipated" from traditional values, at times even from the family, asks himself where he comes from, where he is going and what he has come in this world to do. A progressive expansion of human consciousness, an intensification of sensibility, and an explosion of inner energies, together with a geometric growth in leisure time, a freedom and an overchoice always growing . . . have brought this identity crisis to its paroxysm. To be able to fully *live,* and even to survive psychologically, one must be able to answer the universal and perennial "enigma of the Sphinx" (Who are you? Know yourself. . . and you will know the universe!). Without this, it is literally impossible to create a psychosocial cosmos (a psychological and social organization and order) that is truly valid and effective.

The first answer to this "fundamental question" is that *no one else,* except the *individual himself,* can possibly answer this question because the true "answer" can only emerge from a *personal, interior and organic work.* Moreover, if the individual does not do this "work' and does not answer to HIS INTERNAL SPHINX, he will be "devoured" by the powers which flow through his being seeking to answer the great Life-call of everyday living. That is, his personality will become "disorganized" and "overwhelmed" by his *personal unconscious* and by the *sociocultural subconscious* just as the mythical Sphinx devoured those who could not answer its "enigma" or great question ("who is the being who walks on four feet in the morning, on two feet at noon, and on three feet in the evening?").

Finally, to truly answer in an effective and satisfying way to this great question, one must undergo a *psychospiritual transformation*—one must expand one's consciousness to reach the "Sacred Mountain" of the Superconscious and the awakening of spiritual consciousness. To attempt to answer this great question in a "sensory", "emotional", or "mental" way simply does not work. At best, it will only *temporarily* quench the metaphysical thirst of man for Being and for the Sacred Fire of Soul . . . which is awakening and which is propelling him forward with its own language of "stress, anxiety, and inner distress".

2. *How to discover and create a system of values and of moral principles* which correspond to my level of consciousness and being? So as to live a conscious and responsible life, and "become what I am"?

After the question of one's own identity comes that of creating a psychosocial "spine" the substance of which is a *value system* and an *ethical system*. This is truly a "fundamental step" to live a conscious and autonomous life, and to develop one's character and to build personal integrity. For a human being can live in three essential ways, following the three "integrating and unifying principles" that the Greeks called *Physis, Ethos,* and *Logos.* That is, following one's *instincts and impulses,* one's *reason and culture,* or one's *intuition.* At this point in our evolution, we have gone beyond the "stage" or the instincts and impulses, which correspond to nature and to the animal stage, but we have not yet reached the spiritual stage where *love* and *intuition* will be our unfailing guides, making us conscious of the Will of God or of the Self.

Until World War II, it was basically society, the state, and the church which imposed a system of values and of moral principles, transmitted by the family and the school, which the individual accepted and followed, more or less, unconsciously. After World War II and 1968 in particular, traditional values and moral principles have all been "questioned" and, largely, rejected by many people, the young in particular. This has created a situation where the individual, today, finds himself in a state of "axiological anomie", that is, without a system of values, of moral principles, and of norms enjoying a large social consensus. He lacks, therefore, a psychosocial "spine" to organize his life and his being, to create a psychosocial cosmos. Hence, he falls back unto actions that are far more *impulsive reactions, emotional or imaginative reactions* than *rational and coherent actions.* Without this central value system and moral system, the individual is like a little boat lost in the ocean of life . . . and without a compass!

This situation thus demands *personal work,* work to sift out, select, and recreate a new value system and system of moral principles which are coherent with the level of consciousness and the type of personality of the individual. And for this kind of work, the activation of the intuition, spiritual awakening, and the ability to contact one's own superconscious are essential . . . as they are essential to answer the "enigma" of one's own Sphinx! To merely draw from the cultural, social, philosophical, and religious traditions of the past is no longer enough. These can provide valuable "elements" and "options"; but to unite and integrate these in an organic and coherent system, adapted to one's own being and life in the modern world, can only be the result of *personal work*—of personal work that leads to *spiritual consciousness* wherein each person must become his or her own *artist* and practice "Soul-Sculpture".

3. *How to identify and choose my "work" or profession?* This is another "fundamental question" to which one must provide one's own answer. For one's occupation is not only a means to ensure economic and social survival; it is also, and more and more so, a *way to express oneself in a creative and constructive way, to make a valuable contribution to society, and to mold and unfold one's own personality.* Prostitution exists just as well at the level of one's occupation as it does at the level of sexual and affective exchanges. To enter into an intimate relationship with a person who is not "on our wave-length" and who does not "correspond to the deepest part of our being" can be very detrimental for our health, creativity, and happiness. I would argue that the same holds true for our occupation. Prostitution can exist on many levels and in many domains of human expression—love, work, and knowledge in particular!

To seek to earn as much money "as possible", to have the greatest amount of "professional power", or to get into a particular sector of the economy simply because it is the up and coming sector, these are all forms of "prostitution" which one pays dearly for in the long run . . . in terms of one's holistic health, growth, creativity, and happiness.

How then, can one identify and find one's occupation or "work"? This implies a certain amount of *self-knowledge* as well as knowledge of the society in which one lives—of its basic mechanisms and opportunity structures. It also requires a certain amount of *self-mastery,* a great deal of patience and perseverance, and certain personal and economic sacrifices. Finally, it also requires a specific *goal* or objective, towards which one can move slowly, to achieve it one day when one has acquired the necessary skills and when the moment is "appropriate". To discover and identify this occupation or "work" one must also know one's *Dharma,* what one has come to do in this world, one's strengths and weaknesses, and the be able to progressively develop the aptitudes that are required for this occupation. This requires, in other words, to have *activated one's intuition,* to be able to contact the superconscious, and to have awakened, at least in part, one's spiritual consciousness. In short, it requires the same "essentials" as do the other questions!

4. *How to find and choose a life-mate,* the person with whom I will live? The true "core" of mental health and happiness consists in three great principles: To have *someone to love . . . truly!* To have *a job to do . . .* the right one! And to have *hope in a better future!* The choice of the "right partner", of a person with whom we are truly compatible, is one of the most important questions of our life . . . with extremely important consequences for our health, creative self-expression, happiness, and for all that we will do or not do in this world! Undergirding this choice, we also find an economic, social, and personal growth aspect which will define our "life's project", what we will do and what we will become.

To give in to sexual, emotional, social, or other pressures (to loneliness and the "availability" of another person) is very dangerous and can be paid for dearly later on. A conscious and harmonious choice is absolutely imperative. For the entire "morality" and "future" of a marriage can be summarized in one essential point: *right initial choice!* Hence, how can we make this "basic choice" in a conscious and satisfactory way? In the past, it was the *objective* dimension that was most important (as it still is in certain oriental and third-world societies)—a religious, ethnic, or social compatibility where the family of the two people played an essential role. But, beginning with the 20th century, it is the *subjective* dimension which is now privileged: the personal choice of a person one "falls in love with", or whom we really "like"! This can bring "happiness" and function over the short run, but rarely for the long run! Thus, new criteria and social mechanisms are now becoming imperative which could bring about a *synthesis* between the *objective* and the *subjective* dimension. For example, one could use astrological, clairvoyant, and psychological counselling; one could make an analysis of the basic values, predispositions, and personality type of the two prospective "partners" and of the "elective affinities" they have with each other. Amongst these new criteria and social mechanisms, I would privilege a deep *self-knowledge* and *knowledge of the different types of persons,* the activation of the intuition, the experiential contact with the superconscious, and the awakening of spiritual consciousness.

5. *How to develop and live a "philosophy of life" and an "art of living"* which truly correspond to my being and our age? All of what we have been discussing and arguing for can be found in a

"philosophy of life" and an "art of living": that the individual must forge and fashion *for himself* as the true *synthesis of his knowledge.* A "philosophy of life" and an "art of living" which are suited and in "lock-step" with his own level of consciousness and being, with his sociocultural milieu, and with our own times-where *spiritual awakening* plays a primordial role. At the "heart" of this effort and synthesis, we find a personal *Philosopher's Stone* which will enable the individual to *accept all the various parts and aspects of his being* as well as *all the parts and aspects of the world in which he lives.* So that he may be able to face, in a positive and constructive way, all the trials, adventures, and situations that he may encounter in his daily life. This also means to be able to find and understand the meaning and purpose of all the great "lessons" and "situations" one will be facing in one's life. Particularly, it means the ability to transform *destructive suffering* (destructive because perceived as *"un-just"* or "without meaning and purpose") into *creative suffering* (perceived as being meaningful and as enabling one to become more than what he was before going through this suffering).

The foundation of the "philosophy of life" and of this "art of living" rests upon *self-actualization* and *Self-realization,* that is, upon:

a. *A systematic self-knowledge,* or knowledge of human nature and human consciousness, that is, upon the
   - Systematic exploration of one's own field of consciousness with its 7 functions;
   - Systematic exploration of the preconscious (of the materials which one can bring into one's field of consciousness through an act of the will);
   - Systematic exploration of the subconscious (of our entire lived experience since our conception);
   - Systematic exploration of the unconscious (the great reservoir of biopsychic energies and of repressed traumas);
   - Systematic exploration of the superconscious (of the psychospiritual energies and materials such as intuitions, inspirations, creative breakthroughs, and heroic deeds).
b. *A systematic self-mastery,* of one's human energies and faculties, or the progressive unfoldment of the power of:
   - *Concentration,* the use of the will;
   - *Meditation,* the use of thinking;
   - *Devotion,* the use of feeling;
   - *Visualization,* the use of the imagination;
   - *Invocation-Evocation,* the use of the intuition;
   - The direction and transmutation of biopsychic and then psychospiritual energies and materials;
   - *Observation,* exterior and interior, the use of sensations.

c. *Systematic self-integration,* "personal psychosynthesis" and the creation of a new, conscious and mature, personality: become the "artist of one's self" and to practice "Personality Sculpture" and "Soul Sculpture".

As you can see, there are no easy, "ready-made" solutions to answer the "fundamental questions of life", but a great and long personal work of the transformation of one's level of consciousness and level of being—of *bio-psycho-spiritual transformation* of what one *is* and of what one *knows.* For me, this is truly the greatest challenge of our times and the most important and exciting adventure to which we are all invited . . . and to which I would like to invite each one of YOU TODAY! Here is a great goal and objective to which we can consecrate ourselves, our lives, our energies, our time, and the very best of our personal faculties and potentialities . . .

Appendix C

Consciousness Checklist

The Consciousness Checklist described below is a practical instrument we have derived from Roberto Assagioli's *Egg of Psychosynthesis* which represents, diagrammatically, and describes the *structure* of the human Psyche. Its seven basic categories or questions are drawn directly from the Field of Consciousness and its seven functions: Willing, Thinking, Feeling, Intuition, Imagination, Biopsychic Drives, and Sensations. It is a most important psychological tool designed to enable the Candidate to develop his/her capacity for inner observation and to monitor what is really happening in his/her Consciousness, to note and evaluate the qualitative and quantitative changes and psychospiritual transformations that might occur as the result of particular work being done, using Ritual or practicing other psychospiritual exercises.

It is the primary tool, operationalized from Psychosynthesis theory, for self-observation and consciousness-examination we are offering the reader and Candidate. As such, it should be properly memorized and understood in sequential order, and then used before, during and at the end of doing the entire range of individual exercises. Its proper use will enable the Candidate to systematically become aware of his/her inner state, of the processes and materials at work in his/her Field of Consciousness, and of possible transformations that will occur therein. These should then be noted mentally and/or in his/her workbook.

This is a tool that I have used not only for esoteric/spiritual work but also for psychological, human growth, and psychotherapeutic purposes, and which has yielded excellent results. Its merit is to be, at the same time, simple and practical as well as systematic and exhaustive, tapping not only quantitative but also qualitative possible changes.

Consciousness Checklist

1. What *sensations* are you presently aware of in your field of Consciousness?

   a. Seeing
   b. Hearing
   c. Tasting
   d. Smelling
   e. Touching

   What sensations are particularly strong, and which are weak?

   Where do these sensations come from?

   Realize that you are *not* these sensations, but that they are tools for you to contact the Physical World.

2. What *biopsychic drives* or *impulses* are you presently aware of in your Field of Consciousness?

   a. Hunger
   b. Thirst
   c. Fatigue
   d. Sexual Arousal
   e. Anger or Aggressiveness

3. What *emotions* and *feelings* are you presently aware of in your Field of Consciousness?

   a. Joy
   b. Sorrow
   c. Love
   d. Fear
   e. Excitement
   f. Depression
   g. Other

   What emotions and feelings are particularly strong, and which are weak? Where do these come from?

   Realize that you are *not* these emotions and feelings, but that they are tools for you to use and that *you* control them, that they are not really a part of your true being, but act as a source of great energy and drive, joy or sorrow.

4. What *images* or *symbols* are presently activated in your imagination?

    a. Natural
    b. Human
    c. Spiritual

What images are particularly strong, and which are weak?

Where do these images and symbols come from?

Realize that you are *not* these images and symbols, but that they are tools for you to reproduce the other functions of the Psyche and experiences you have or could live.

Presently, is your image-making function strong or weak?

5. What *thoughts* or *ideas* are presently going through your mind?

    a. Of the Past
    b. Of the Present
    c. Of the Future

What thoughts and ideas are particularly strong, and which are weak?

Where do these thoughts and ideas originate?

Realize that you are *not* these thoughts and ideas, but that they are tools for you to use to express yourself on the Mental level, and that *you* can control them.

6. Is your *intuition* presently active in your Field of Consciousness?

    a. Spiritually
    b. Mentally
    c. Emotionally
    d. Physically

If it is active, what is it telling you?

Does any part of your being oppose or thwart your intuition?

Can you distinguish between your intuition, emotions, imagination, and biopsychic drives?

Realize that you are *not* your intuitions but that these are tools for you to contact the deeper and higher parts of your being and of life.

7. What are you presently *willing?*

   a. Physical objects
   b. Emotional objects
   c. Mental objects
   d. Spiritual objects

How well can you presently use your will and ability to concentrate upon the above objects? In your outer work and inner work, are you able to do what *you* want and not to do what *you* do not want?

What is preventing you, if anything, from presently using your will efficiently?

How can you develop your will further?

The Love Vitamin Theory

Official modern medicine, which is technically called *allopathy,* is now undergoing a very basic, qualitative, transformation; it is moving from a "medical model" that focused on psychopathology to a "growth and wellness model" that focuses on holistic and preventive hygiene. In other words, instead of waiting until a person falls sick to then intervene to remove the illness, we are now going, more and more, in the direction of seeking to understand and apply the basic laws of health and well being that focus on the whole person, physical, psychosocial, and spiritual, that will prevent a person from falling sick in the first place. These laws are fundamentally few and simple, and can be summarized as follows:

a. *Nutrition:* eating the right quantity and quality of food for one's age, personality, type, and life style.
b. *Sleep:* getting the right amount of sleep, which means not *too much* or *too little* sleep every day, and good quality sleep.
c. *Physical exercise:* making sure that one exercises one's body enough through exercises, sports, or other physical activities.
d. *Sexual and love life:* getting not too much or too little sex and, especially, good quality sex. This is a dimension which is still very much misunderstood and greatly abused at the present time, sexual education not withstanding.
e. *Emotional and mental life:* getting in touch with one's emotions and thoughts, through self-observation and introspection, and learning how to deal with negative emotions and thoughts to transform them into positive emotions and thoughts, and making a conscious effort to cultivate positive emotions and thoughts.

To these five well-recognized and analyzed dimensions, I would personally add *two additional ones* which, though intimately interconnected with the five aforementioned ones, are also distinct from them, namely:

f. *Social life:* the quantity and quality of one's relationships with significant others, the basic composition of one's *psychosocial network,* and the energies and cultural materials which are exchanged in one's human relationships.

g. *Spiritual life:* getting in touch with one's Higher Self and with ultimate reality to balance, harmonize, and vivify one's entire being and life. Paradoxically, this dimension, which is the kingpin of the whole structure, is often either neglected, identified with emotional and mental life and with the psychosocial and sociocultural dimensions, or the last one to be recognized and properly developed.

The Ancient Sages fully recognized that a human being is a very complex microcosm composed of four basic dimensions which they termed: Earth, Water, Air, and Fire, or the physical, emotional, mental, and spiritual dimensions which are all interconnected and interacting with each other in a feedback loop. At the forefront of the modern holistic and preventive medicine movement, or wellness movement, stands the basic conception of human nature as, indeed, involving four basic quadrants, all of which have to be recognized and taken care of if health, well-being, growth, and self-expression are to be achieved. Our civilization, however, still has a very large bias toward the *physical* and *mental* dimensions, which are overemphasized, to the neglect of the *emotional* and *spiritual ones.* Thus, for example, in education our fundamental thrust and concern deals with *physical* and *intellectual* training and development neglecting, if not starving and poisoning, our *emotional* and *spiritual* aspects, for which we pay an exceedingly high price in anti-social, destructive, irrational, and pathological behavior on the part of an ever-increasing number of people. Medicine also focuses upon the physical body and bio-chemistry and only recently with the psychological and social aspects.

Evolution, however, is not standing still but moving forward. Our human consciousness is developing and expanding; our needs, concerns, and aspirations are changing with new and emergent ones appearing all the time. Slowly, but surely, we are moving from a medicine of the physical body to a *medicine of the energy bodies* (see Dr. Janine Fontaine, *Le Medecin des trois Corps,* and *La Medecine du corps Energetique*). As the education, hygiene, and medicine of the *physical body* is improving, we are slowly shifting our "center of gravity," the focus of our problems, needs, and concerns, to that of the *emotional body,* or energy body, with an entirely new host of problems, diseases, and challenges.

It is within this general sociocultural and evolutionary framework that I would place my "Love Vitamin Theory," one of the latest, most exciting, and challenging areas of research and personal experimentation that I have undertaken in the last few years. In a nutshell, the central postulate of this theory is:

What physical vitamins are to our physical organism, "Love Vitamins," or energy exchanges, are to our human consciousness: they are absolutely vital and indispensable components for our well-being, continued growth, and self-expression.

If our physical body lacks what we call today "vitamins" (A, B, C, E, etc.) it will not be able to function properly and will cause many problems (vulnerability to various diseases, increased fatigue, diminished capacity to activate the immunological systems, and lower performance, not to mention faster "aging"). If our "emotional body" or, more specifically, our four "energy bodies" lack what I call "love vitamins" they, too, will be unable to perform their various functions and enable our consciousness to function at its best, and will lead to dysfunctional syndromes and behavior patterns which can be changed and alleviated as soon as those energy exchanges are reintroduced—something which can be demonstrated empirically or scientifically. Thus:

Do you ever feel *depressed* (that great enigma of modern medicine)?

Do you ever feel down, tired, chronically exhausted with no "sparkle," vitality, and sense of exhilaration or "joie de vivre?"

Do you ever feel exasperated, "on edge," irritable, beside yourself (désaxé), with a very low threshold of frustration so that the least thing that goes wrong makes you over-react, feeling angry, frustrated and blue?

Do you ever feel very shy, unable to express yourself, affirm yourself, or overwhelmed by circumstances or the wishes and expectations of others?

Do you ever feel *bored* and drained of all your creativity and ability to be yourself and express yourself, to create, bring beauty, meaning, purpose, and goodness in your being and life, and in this world?

Do you ever feel alienated from yourself and from reality, fragmented in many pieces that you cannot synthesize and control, thus saying and doing things that are not really "you" and which you will regret later?

I could go on and add a lot to this list, but the above should suffice to indicate situations and states of being that we all have experienced and which I directly impute to a *lack of "love vitamins"*—as they can easily and rapidly be corrected when these "love vitamins" are introduced. Why do you feel that way? My theory would say because you are lacking or are deprived of your essential "love vitamins!"

Have you ever felt one of the above described states and conditions; i.e., depressed, washed up, unbalanced, drained out, irritable, bored, uncreative, and really "not yourself," or simply, "in pieces?" And then something happens! You meet someone, someone comes that you really get along with or greatly admire, or you fall in love and, bingo, something "magical" occurs. Your consciousness is transformed, your feelings change and come alive again, your energies return, you rediscover your "self" and reacquire your "joie de vivre;" the demons that oppressed you are exorcised and you become a new person—what you *really* are. Unconsciously, perhaps, you have received a good dose of "love vitamins" and they have immediately gone to work in *your consciousness, transforming it,* and you become a "new person" or, rather, what you *really are* but were unable to remember and express. When you "fall in love" or when you meet a spiritually awakened person, you then receive a "megadose" of "love vitamins" and the effects are dramatic and powerful, as well as immediate, something which can also lead to a disorganization of your personality or your life when you let yourself be emotionally driven!

Ancient or traditional medicine, which always viewed a human being as a biopsycho-spiritual being, has long recognized this and modern psychotherapy and psychosomatic medicine is now beginning to rediscover and reaffirm this more and more explicitly. The central causal agent is always the same: AN EXCHANGE OF LOVE VITAMINS CHANNELED BY A VERY POSITIVE FORM OF HUMAN INTERACTION. This is why it is now said that it is the *relationship between the therapist and the client* that is the true *curative agent* and not the expertise of the doctor or the various techniques which are being used. Religion and the sacred traditions have always recognized this explicitly, though they may have expressed it through a different vocabulary and set of practices. This is why God is said to be Love and why Saints, the heroes of love, have been such great and effective healers even though they may have been very simple and uneducated persons. Even one of our popular songs affirms this when it states that "All we need is love!"

Practically and experientially speaking, what are these "love vitamins?" Where do they come from? What do they affect in our being? And, how are they transmitted? This is what constitutes the structural and functional, or scientific part, of my "love vitamin theory."

The sacred traditions of East and West have long taught, spiritually awakened persons know and have been working with, and the latest schools of psychotherapy and human growth are now rediscovering and slowly demonstrating that a human being has not only a biological organism but also four basic energy bodies: the vital or "etheric body," the emotional or "astral body," the intellectual or "mental body," and the "causal" or "spiritual body," which NEED TO BE FED, TO BE EXERCISED, TO BE EXPRESSED, AND TO BE CARED FOR JUST AS THEIR PHYSICAL BODY DOES. And, that if this is not done, a heavy price is paid in terms of personal malfunctioning or functioning below one's capacity, of illness, and self-alienation and fragmentation. Homeopathy, acupuncture and acupressure, therapeutic touch and massage, the laying on of hands and spiritual healing together with many of the "parallel" or traditional forms of healing have long recognized this, being essentially ENERGY MEDICINES rather than physical medicines . . . and the medicine of the future will unquestionably be a medicine of the energy bodies (including chromotherapy, music therapy, art therapy, and psychotherapy).

In each case, an *interaction,* an energy exchange, bringing about a creative psychic synthesis is necessary. For life always manifests and flows in the creative tension generated by the interaction of a "male" and "female" polarity. In each case, there is a *transmitter,* a *receiver,* and an *energy exchange.* At the vital or "etheric level," the essential agent is touch, physical touch, which is why touch is so important. At the emotional or "astral level," the crucial agent is the generation, reception, and exchange of emotional energies which involve all the functions of the psyche. At the intellectual or "mental level," the causal agent is the generation, reception, and exchange of ideas, mental energies and materials which also involve all the functions of the psyche. Finally, at the "causal" or "spiritual level," the active agent is *contact,* the transmission of spiritual energies and materials. In terms of my "love vitamin theory," I would say that there are 28 different kinds of "love vitamins" or L1 to L28 (there are 4 different kinds of energy bodies each of which have been subdivided into 7 different octaves or levels of functioning). The sacred traditions have long taught and now modern parapsychology and transpersonal psychology are rediscovering these energy bodies stating that a plant, a tree, or an herb has one energy body, the "etheric one" and thus can transmit L1 to L7s; an animal has two energy bodies, the "etheric" and the "astral ones" and thus can transmit L1 to L14s; a normal human being has three energy bodies, the "etheric, astral, and mental ones" and thus can transmit L1 to L21s; and, finally, a spiritually awakened human being has four energy bodies, the "etheric, astral, mental, and spiritual bodies," and thus can transmit L1 to L28s.

These fundamental truths were known by the sacred and the religious traditions of various peoples who have sought to teach and to operationalize them in various ways. Thus, for example:

It is known that eating certain kinds of foods or herbs, walking barefoot in the grass, and putting one's back against a pine or oak tree can transmit certain healing energies that will calm, balance, and re-energize a person better than a tranquilizer or a tonic and without the side effects of the latter! Pet therapy has now emerged whereby pet animals will be taken to sick people, prisoners, or old people, who will greatly benefit from this by becoming more balanced, less aggressive, and better able to express themselves. Psychotherapy and positive human relations are well-known for their equilibrating, relaxing, stimulating, and overall positive effects in changing in a person's consciousness and state of being. Finally, it is also well-known that contact and interaction with a spiritually developed person can have very powerful healing, consciousness transforming, and lifegiving consequences for persons who can find these persons.

In each of these cases, I would argue that a basic exchange and transmission of "love vitamins" has occurred (L1 to L7s in the first case; L1 to L14s in the second case; L1 to L21s in the third case; and L1 to L28s in the fourth case) which can explain many things which, otherwise, would not be properly or rationally understood and ascribed to "magic," "chemistry," or particular affinities or sympathies.

When these "Love Vitamins" do flow and manifest themselves between two living beings, they always have *three basic experiential features;* they bring *"Peace"* or RELAXATION, the "female pole" (and who, today in our superstressed civilization does not need deep, genuine, holistic relaxation, not only of the body, but of the emotions and mind as well?"); "Life" or STIMULATION, the "male" pole (and, again, who today could not use a little more energy and life?); and finally, *SELF-EXPRESSION,* the ability to get in touch with and manifest one's Self, which is the essence of true CREATIVITY (who could not be a little more himself or herself and genuinely creative?). This is something which every person and, therefore, every one of YOU, can and should experience for themselves under the proper conditions and which will be the ultimate "proof" or "corroboration" of the validity of my "love vitamin theory." Sociology, which is one of my professional disciplines, clearly teaches in one of its major axioms that HUMAN INTERACTION BRINGS ABOUT A CREATIVE PSYCHIC SYNTHESIS; i.e., that when two or more people come together, there is a creative exchange between mind and mind, which gives birth to new ideas, between heart and heart, which gives birth to new emotions, between will and will, which liberates new creative energies. This, in a nutshell, is a simple and beautiful manifestation of my "love vitamin theory" in action between normal nonspiritually awakened persons!

The final, and perhaps, the most important point is: should this "love vitamin theory" of mine appeal to you intellectually and should you want to test it out and experience it personally to benefit from its various implications, how can you go about it? Or, more simply put, if you want to get your daily dose of "love vitamins" how and where can you get them? There is a very simple, practical, and integrated way of doing this which I call the "Love Vitamin Generator" and which is the practical side of this theory. All that is required is a small group of men and women of good will and the knowledge of the basic techniques designed to generate and circulate "love vitamins" on at least three levels—the etheric, the astral, and the mental.

These people should form a circle and, preferably sit down. Find a comfortable, relaxed position, close their eyes and make an effort of introversion; i.e., deliberately withdraw their attention and energies from the outside physical world to refocus them on the inner, psychological world—the field of consciousness. Then, deliberately let go of the past, and the future, of their fears and anxieties as well as their desires and aspirations and become fully present in the here and now. At this point, they should focus their attention upon their hands, the left hand and the right hand, and experience an exchange of human warmth, of light, life, and love which I call "warm milk" and which will automatically and naturally flow, balancing their energies by giving of those energies they have in excess and receiving of those energies they lack. Nothing more than *physical touch* and *receptivity* and *sensitivity* to etheric energies is required. To pass on to the next level, the emotional or "astral level," the participants should then focus their attention on their *head area* and visualize there a pulsating, radiating sphere of dazzling white light. Then let a ray of that light descend into their *heart area* and awaken, activate the heart to then extend a ray of the same light and energies to their *left shoulder,* then left arms and left hands and circulate that light and those energies *three times* from *left to right.* Then, they should focus again on their heart area and extend a ray of the same light and energies to the *right shoulder,* then to their right arms and hands and circulate that light and those energies three times from *right to left.* During this phase, *all of the functions of the psyche* should be used as much as possible—concentration, meditation, devotion, visualization, and invocation and evocation in particular for, here, one will get out of this exercise in direct proportion to what he puts into it. Finally, for the mental phase, they should bow, mentally to the person on their left saying "Namaskara," the Divine in me greets and recognizes the Divine in you." As they are vibrating the word "Namaskara" they should visualize the flame of a candle slowly formulating and enveloping that person and experience Light, Love and Light flowing to that person and then returning to them. This should be done for all the persons making up the circle or, at least seven times, if there are more than seven persons. Again, all the functions of the psyche, or psychospiritual muscles should be used as much as possible at this level. If there are spiritually awakened persons, the next level, the *spiritual level,* will automatically be triggered on and activated by "spiritual Contact."

The basic process at work here is the same for all levels; first, the "etheric level," then the "astral level," followed by the "mental level," and finally the "spiritual level" are affected so that energies on these levels are *balanced,* properly *aligned, and recharged* or energized. As the three or four basic levels are touched and their corresponding "love vitamins," the LI to LTs, then the L7 to L14s, the L14 to L21s, and, perhaps, even the L21 to L28s are awakened, circulated and exchanged each person should personally feel and experience a physical, emotional and mental relaxation followed by a physical, emotional, and mental stimulation, culminating in genuine self-expression or creativity on all levels that are affected.

There really is no way to adequately describe this process and what happens. It must be personally undergone and experienced to be truly understood and integrated in one's being. But, this is a very simple and practical way to get one's basic love vitamins which will make one come alive, become aligned to his whole being and his higher Self, as well as those of others. For it is a well-known truth that Love and Life are identical and that it is LOVE which is the greatest integrating, healing, and Life-giving force both within one self and in the universe.

To conclude, let me say a few basic things about the nature and dynamics of love. All the great Mystics, Sages, Seers, and Saints, as well as the true Philosophers, have unanimously stated that *love is the single most important thing there is in oneself, in the world, or anywhere else because love is the very essence of God, Man, and Nature, of Reality and, therefore, of Life, Health, Happiness, and Self-Expression.* It is LOVE that is the ultimate life-giving and healing force. As Love is the ultimate reality, both in the microcosm and in the macrocosm, EVERY HUMAN BEING IS THUS CAPABLE OF LOVING AND OF BEING LOVED.

Love is an energy, vibration, and essence that can be consciously experienced in countless degrees of quantity and quality, that can be generated, circulated, given and received. It is a multidimensional food or nourishment for all the parts and levels of our being. Like God, Man, and Nature, Love is a TRINITY which can best be represented like a sun having *light, warmth,* and *life.* When the Heart-Center is activated, it does, indeed, look like a true, pulsating, vibrating, shining INNER SUN, to clairvoyant sight. When experienced at the conscious level, Love always manifests three distinctive characteristics which are PEACE, LIFE, and CREATIVITY i.e., it will *relax us, stimulate us, and facilitate true Self-expression.*

To learn the theory of Love, to acquire the skills of loving, and to master the art of loving, there are three vital prerequisites one must develop and possess which are self-knowledge, self-mastery, and self-integration. For our perception and conception of Love, as well as our ability to Love and be Loved, are a direct function of our level of consciousness and of our place on the scale of being. Thus, it is only by changing and expanding our consciousness that we can change and expand our conception and experience of love. Our bodies, Psychospiritual Centers, limbs, and words, are ultimately but conductors, channels, "hoses" and "wires" through which the light, energy, fire, vibration, and essence of love can flow to others and be expressed by oneself. Love and Life are ONE and, therefore, as the ultimate yearning of the human soul is to BECOME MORE ALIVE, the fulfillment of this yearning can only come from loving more consciously, fully, and audaciously!

The same message has been conveyed to us by countless thinkers, in their own distinctive words and ways, from St. Paul to Sorokin, Fromm, Buscaglia, and many others. And, this is why Sorokin stated many times:

Without a minimum of living unselfish love, all the fashionable prescriptions for the elimination of the ills of humanity cannot achieve their task. . . . Since the real curative agent in mental disease is love in its various forms, many eminent apostles of love have been able to cure the mental disorders of legions of persons, although these altruists did not have any special psychiatric training. Their sublime love and supraconscious wisdom have been an excellent substitute for "little or no love" and for the professional training of ordinary psychiatrists. . . . Love not only cures and revitalizes the individual's mind and organism but also proves itself to be the decisive factor of the vital, mental, moral, and social well-being and growth of an individual. . . .

If love can be viewed as one of the highest energies known, then, theoretically, at least, we can talk about the *production or generation, the accumulation (or loss), the channeling, and distribution of this particular energy* . . . . The mysterious forces of history seem to have given man an ultimatum: perish by your own hands or rise to a higher moral level through the grace of love.

And, St. Paul could state in his famous Epistle to the Corinthians:

Though I speak with the tongues of men and angels, and have not love in my heart, I am become as sounding brass or a tinkling cymbal. And though I have the gift of prophecy, and understand all mysteries and all knowledge; and though I have all faith, so I could remove mountains and have not love in my heart, I am nothing.

Appendix E
The Muscles of Human Consciousness

It has now been over 30 years that I have been active in the Human Potential Movement, the Consciousness Circuit, and Various Esoteric Groups both as a leader and as a participant. I have attended and been a lecturer at a great number of symposia and lectures, and have joined many psychological and spiritual groups dedicated to human growth and spiritual development as the *Leitmotiv* of my personal and professional life has always been "the study of human nature for its conscious development" or "the expansion of human consciousness and the achievement of spiritual consciousness." I used to have a great deal of enthusiasm and very high hopes and expectations for this kind of endeavor and for the people I would meet at these gatherings and who joined these groups. While my enthusiasm for and dedication to human development and spiritual awakening have remained and, in fact, grown and intensified over the years, my hopes and expectations for what people could actually achieve by attending these groups, symposia, and lectures have considerably diminished. For, I noticed that, just as in the world where most people seek financial wealth and social status but few actually achieve it (about 5% according to the latest statistics) so in the Consciousness Circuit great are the hopes and promises but few are the results! Most people attend symposia after symposia, lecture after lecture, taking various "courses" and applying different techniques, or they join one or more "esoteric" or "spiritual organization" or yet they find and follow one or more "guru" but soon settle down in a new routine with VERY LITTLE CHANGES IN THEIR LIVES AND BEINGS. Many lectures and several years later, they are still basically WHERE THEY WERE BEFORE IN TERMS OF THEIR EVERYDAY LIVES, STATE OF CONSCIOUSNESS, AND LEVEL OF BEING! The only thing that really "happened" is that they found and accepted a few new "ideas" and "beliefs" to meditate upon and to discuss with their friends; ideas and beliefs such as reincarnation, the subtle bodies, the psychospiritual centers, the various auras, more evolved human beings, meditation, prayer, and ritual. As these have, basically, remained in their "head" and have not "descended into their hearts" and been "enfleshed in their lives" or, in other words, as they have basically heard, read, or discussed these ideas and beliefs but not *felt them or incarnated them,* little has actually happened in their lives and beings and not much basic change really occurred. Many of these people will later either fall into a given routine of mechanically reaffirming certain ideas and principles, with no actual connection with their real lives or they will become disenchanted and drop out altogether from the Consciousness Circuit and become disillusioned and disappointed in the "spiritual quest" as many other people have become disillusioned or burned out in the quest for "money and status." A most interesting book to read along these lines is Robert de Ropp's *Warrior's Way,* which is his own personal "spiritual biography" and odyssey through many New Age Groups and Spiritual Organizations. The basic question one can ask at this point is WHAT HAS GONE WRONG? WHY HAVE 80 MANY HIGH IDEALS AND LOFTY OBJECTIVES FAILED TO DELIVER WHAT THEY PROMISED?

The answer to this fundamental question came to me, by analogy, when one day I was reflecting upon my diary and meditating on what happened to a dear friend of mine and myself in the Summer of 1958, and it came in a genuine flash of intuition which illuminated a most important principle for me and which provided the foundation for this lecture. At that time, my friend and I were students at the University of Denver and we had been invited by my parents to spend the summer in Europe. During that academic year, we had worked very hard on our course work and, being quite ambitious, in our quest to make the Dean's List and to achieve academic distinction, we had completely neglected our physical bodies, doing no exercise or sport, eating and drinking too much, and leading a very sedentary and intellectual life—but a very unbalanced life. My parents who knew what was going on, at least in my case, were very eager that we use the summer to get back in "good physical shape" and get involved with different sports to achieve this. To this end, they provided us with the best available instructors for snow-skiing in Switzerland, water-skiing on the Italian Riviera, and for playing tennis. Our instructors were, indeed, excellent and very dedicated persons but all their efforts availed naught! We could see what they were doing; we understood what they were telling us; and, we could have written superb papers on the principles and techniques involved in all three sports, but *our bodies were absolutely not capable of following through and of doing what our minds and wills were telling them to do!* It was at this point that the Swiss ski instructor really got at the **heart** of this question when he told us in a flash of intuition and recognition, "Boys, you are in bad physical shape! Before you do anything else and waste your time and mine, GO AND BUILD AND COORDINATE YOUR PHYSICAL MUSCLES."

This, of course, was the answer! For over a month we did just that. We went to a gymnasium and learned and practiced all kinds of physical exercises designed to build and coordinate our physical muscles until they got back in good shape. Then, we went back to our old instructors and were able to carry out their instructions and to have our bodies DO what they were told to do, and thus we learned a much better technical snow-skiing, water-skiing, and tennis. A breakthrough had occurred which broke the deadlock into which we had fallen and which opened the key to the door we wanted to get into. The same breakthrough happened to me later as I was considering the PSYCHOLOGICAL AND SPIRITUAL BLOCKS OR DEAD-ENDS INTO WHICH SO MANY PEOPLE HAVE FALLEN, and provided me with the answer to the basic question I raised before, "What went wrong with all these spiritual idealists and enthusiasts?"

The answer is, of course, DO WE NOT ALSO HAVE CONSCIOUSNESS OR PSYCHOSPIRITUAL MUSCLES? AND, SHOULD NOT THESE MUSCLES ALSO BE TRAINED AND COORDINATED BEFORE WE CAN EXPECT ANY KIND OF GENUINE CHANGE AND GROWTH TO OCCUR IN OUR CONSCIOUSNESS AND BEING? Naturally, we do have such muscles so that the basic question now becomes, "What are these muscles and how can they be properly developed and coordinated so that they can be applied in human growth and spiritual awakening?" To answer these questions, in a disciplined and systematic way, we must first ask ourselves, "What is *human consciousness* and what is *its structure and functions?* Just as if we wanted to develop and coordinate *physical muscles* we should first ask ourselves the question, "What is our *physical body* and its *anatomy and physiology?* The latest model of the human psyche is, as far as I am concerned, that proposed by Psychosynthesis developed by Roberto Assagioli. In formulating and then articulating the now famous "Egg of Psychosynthesis," describing the structure of the psyche, and the "Star or Flower of Psychosynthesis," describing the functions of the psyche, Assagioli has put together the most comprehensive, up-to-date, and sophisticated model of the human psyche. In a nutshell, *the structure of the psyche* is composed of 7 basic elements which are The Human Self, the Spiritual Self, the Field of Consciousness, the Preconscious, the Subconscious, the Unconscious, and the Superconscious—while the *functions of the psyche* are also seven; namely, Willing, Thinking, Feeling, Intuition, Imagination, Biopsychic Drives or Impulses, and Sensations.

The central thesis and basic postulate of this lecture is that the most important muscles of our consciousness are those associated with willing, thinking, feeling, imagination, and intuition. And that these muscles are just as important for mundane or physical endeavors as they are for psychological or cultural endeavors and for spiritual endeavors. These, in other words, are the *core psychospiritual tools for successful living and for the expansion of human consciousness and spiritual awakening.* Without a minimum amount of training and coordination of these muscles NO EXERCISE, technique, or consciousness raising and spiritual development program can truly get underway, let alone succeed! For as the Spiritual Tradition has rightly put it in a nutshell, "First, we must *know* something, then we must *feel* it, and only at that point can we *live* it in order to *become* it." These muscles of our consciousness or, as I have called them "the core psychospiritual tools for successful living" are truly the ABC, the foundation for all conscious change and personal growth on *any* level. These are:

1. *Concentration* associated with *willing* or the "focused energies of the self," the "ability to say 'yes' and to say 'no' to ourselves and to others" or, in other words, to *know what we want and to know what we don't want.* The Will can be compared to a battery that can be charged as well as discharged and Concentration is, in itself, a science and an art.

2. *Meditation* associated with *thinking* or "thinking in a focused and disciplined way about any subject, mundane, human, or spiritual." And Meditation can also be considered a science and an art that has to be properly understood and mastered.

3. *Devotion* associated with *feeling* or "directing one's emotions and opening one's heart and energizing whatever subject one is concerned with." The ability to express devotion or to put one's heart into a subject of one's choice is a science and an art that has to be cultivated and developed.

4. *Visualization* associated with *imagination* or "the ability to create images or symbols to represent what one is concerned with" and allow these images and symbols to "come alive" and to unfold in one's consciousness. To visualize properly is, likewise, a science and an art which are now being rediscovered with the study and application of "mental imagery."

5. *Invocation-Evocation* associated with *intuition* or "the ability to focus all of one's attention or *concentration,* one's thinking or *meditation,* one's feeling or *devotion,* and one's imagination or *visualization* upon a given topic or subject and then empty one's consciousness to receive the energies and impressions that might then flow into it at that point. The proper training

of the intuition and the mastery of invocation-evocation is not only a science and an art but, perhaps, the most important psychospiritual work one can do to contact one's Higher Self and obtain guidance and conscience from *within* in these turbulent times when all external authorities and experts are slowly crumbling!

Concentration, Meditation, Devotion, Visualization, and Invocation-Evocation must be cultivated and developed first *individually* and then *concomitantly* when one reaches the stage of training of the Intuition which requires the previous mastery and coordination of the first four to enable one to work with Invocation-Evocation. What Religion and the Spiritual Traditions call FAITH and to which they give so much importance is really a Triangle of the focused and coordinated use of Concentration-will, Meditation-thinking, and Devotion-feeling ("Thou shalt love the Lord Thy God with all thy *heart,* all thy *mind,* and all thy *soul*") with the *visualization of the proper images and symbols at its base.* The image of the *Pyramid* can also be used wherein the *four corners and angles* of the Pyramid represent, respectively, Concentration-Willing, Meditation-Thinking, Devotion-Feeling, and Visualization-Imagination, which thrust upward toward the top and point of the Pyramid, forming a grand Invocation, to be answered by Evocation— then descend in the center of the Pyramid as true Inspiration or Intuitive Insight and Energy.

The final question I will address myself to in this lecture is *how* can we concretely and practically develop and train in ourselves and apply in our daily lives these "muscles of our consciousness" or "core psychospiritual tools," first *individually* and then *collectively and simultaneously* in the opening of the Intuition? Obviously, each one could be the object of an entire lecture and even a book, so I shall try to be brief and focus upon only a few of the most important guidelines and exercises that will enable each of you to use your own personal experience of the reality and development of each of these "muscles" and "tools."

1. *Training of the Will and Concentration:* The Will is the key function of the psyche as it relates the energies of the self to all the other functions. It is neither a great deal of raw energy nor a blind determination to do what one wants to do at any cost. Rather, like the director of a play, the Will focuses, directs, and utilizes all the energies and resources of one's consciousness and of one's human environment to achieve the goals and objectives that are wanted and focused upon. More than a physical or biopsychic energy, the Will is a *psychospiritual energy,* the energy of life of the self, working through the psyche and the biological organism to accomplish

and realize one's objectives. As such, it is the key to one's *freedom* and *integrity* as a human being.

a. Learn to focus upon, or concentrate upon, a physical object, then a feeling, a thought, an image, and finally a symbol or a basic theme.

b. Learn how to say "no" to others, to desires and longings in yourself, and to various inducements of circumstances, no matter what the attraction or the temptations offered—for, whenever we resist ourselves or others, or deny ourselves, we *charge our will* and, conversely, whenever we "give in" to temptations and desires, and seek "instant gratification," we weaken our will.

c. Learn to reflect upon and determine what you really *want* and *don't want* and then make sure that you *pursue what you want* and *avoid what you don't want*. Never abandon a plan, project, or undertaking you have carefully selected and in which you believe because of the difficulties or the time involved. If something is worth starting, it is worth completing.

2. *Training of Thinking and Meditation:* Thinking is getting a *cognitive grasp of the outer and inner universe.* It implies developing thoughts and ideas about what exists and what is happening both outside and inside of our being so that we can become *more conscious* of outer and inner reality and make sense out of them. Here, it is vital to remember a most important psychological law: *the psychospiritual energies of the psyche will follow and energize whatever we are thinking about or directing our thoughts toward.* Indeed, we become what we think or contemplate! *Meditation* is the process by which we think in a systematic and disciplined way and it involves 3 basic inner aspects: *reflective, receptive,* and *contemplative* meditation.

Reflective meditation involves organizing all our thoughts, ideas, and experiences—all that we know, have learned and experienced—about a given subject in a clear, coherent, and integrated way. It means bringing all the materials that pertain to our chosen subject from the subconscious and the preconscious into the field of consciousness so that we can "behold them" and become aware of them.

Receptive meditation involves clearing and emptying our minds of all our acquired knowledge and experience about our chosen subject so that new insights, associations, and information may be received. Here, the main process is to "let go," to relax and become fully receptive, once our attention has been fixed upon a given subject.

Contemplative meditation is the *spiritual* dimension of meditation. It follows the first two steps and involves *expanding our state of consciousness,* through a chosen spiritual exercise, so that we can now "behold" our chosen subject in an altered state of consciousness, "become at-one with it," and let the materials pertaining to it now flow from the superconscious into the field of consciousness. It is "inspired and intuitive thinking" about our given subject so that new aspects and insights may be gathered from the superconscious and the Divine Spark.

The topics one can choose for meditation are as many and as wide as life itself; they can be *qualities* such as joy, courage, peace, love, wisdom; *the symbols of basic prayers* such as Heaven, Father, Kingdom, or a whole prayer; *life goals and plans* or the *ideal model* of a personality one would like to develop.

3. *Training of Feeling and Devotion:* While *willing* produces energy and life, *thinking* yields knowledge and understanding, *feeling* awakens *love* and the ability to have and to express *deep emotions,* or to "feel deeply" about whatever we focus our attention upon. *Life, knowledge,* and *love* are truly the "food of our inner being" and indispensable components for any person to be properly equilibrated, psychologically integrated and humanly fulfilled—to be able to live as a full human being.

Feeling is the ability to evoke emotions, to feel deeply and passionately about something, to be truly moved from the heart by whatever we focus our attention upon.

Devotion is the process of expressing and focusing emotions and feelings about a given subject of our choice. To feel deeply and passionately about something we must involve our will, images, thoughts, and symbols that stir up something in our make-up and that will open the doors of the Deep Mind.

What we need is a good meditation on our own emotions; what does and does not "move us." Then, we must discover and utilize the images, thoughts, symbols, and the particular situations and relationships that evoke profound and genuine feelings from us. Through *prayer* and *beauty* we can also energize and amplify the quality and intensity of our emotional responses. The name of a person, the image of someone we love or really admire, the recall of a particularly emotionally charged event—all of these can be powerful helps to cultivate devotion.

4. *Training of Imagination and Visualization:* Just as the power of *observation* is crucial to gather knowledge about the physical world and to orient ourselves in that world, so the power of inner observation, or *visualization* is crucial to gather knowledge of the inner worlds.

The imagination is the *image-making faculty* and *visualization* is the power to see things with the "eye of the mind." Imagination has both a "female," or reproductive nature, and a "male," or creative nature (the ability to reproduce on the "screen of the mind" anything one has seen or experienced and the ability to create new things, events, or stories). The imagination and the power of visualization have an immense *evocative and awakening power* for our emotions, thoughts, and even our intuition, by reasoning with and opening up the various regions of the psyche (the subconscious, unconscious, and superconscious) with their related energies, vibrations, and states of consciousness. The essence of visualization is *full concentration and absorption in the fantasy one is living* which acts as the key to unlock the doors of the unconscious and of the superconscious.

The basic exercise to develop the imagination and the power of visualization is "guided imagery" or the "inward journey;" for, just as we can take journeys in the outer, physical world, so we can also take inward journeys in the psychological and spiritual worlds of the psyche. The most important "inward journeys" involve:

a. Taking a trip to the sea and exploring its depths; taking a trip to a mountain to find the Temple of Silence or the Temple of the Sun, or a Guardian of the Mysteries; and taking a trip under the earth to explore its caverns and depths.

b. Encounters with other beings during the trip—human, animal, or angelic, and dialoguing with them, giving them something and receiving a present from them.

c. One can take these beings with oneself in moving through the psychological space going up or down, and watching the transformation that are likely to occur in them or in oneself.

While one is taking an "inward journey," it is very important to study oneself and to observe any changes that may occur in one's state of consciousness, and to be able to describe them. One should also bear in mind that every being and event encountered represents, analogically, a part of one's being and life.

5. *Training of Intuition and Invocation-Evocation:* Concentration, Meditation, Devotion, and Visualization are the central psychological "muscles" or "tools" which form the base from which the 5th, *Intuition,* with its twin processes of *Invocation-Evocation,* is to emerge to crown the whole edifice.

Intuition means "seeing from within" of the "teachings from within." It is the bridge or channel that links up the field of consciousness with the superconscious, and the human self with the spiritual Self. This is why it is the only faculty that is half psychological and half spiritual in nature and that links up the psychological with the spiritual dimension of our being like a true "ladder of Jacob." Genuine spiritual Illumination, true spiritual Initiation, or Divine Revelation, must ALL come through the channel of the intuition which must be open for such purpose. For once the channel of the intuition is open and the spiritual Energies (the Light, Fire, and Life of the spiritual Self) can flow through it, they will enliven, quicken, and *bring to life* all the other functions and literally transform man's consciousness, translating him from the realm of nature to the Kingdom of God. Then, and only then, will a person be guided from *within* and receive all the answers to the most basic questions and problems of life from his own Higher Self rather than from various external experts and authorities!

To activate and open up the *Intuition* a sequential process known as *Invocation-Evocation* is used. In Invocation, the first 4 functions of the psyche—willing, thinking, feeling, and imagination—are used in a *synchronous fashion* so as to concentrate all our attention upon the Spiritual Self residing in our "Head-Center," direct all our thoughts and meditations to Him, send Him all our love and feelings, and visualize Him in our favorite image or symbol. This creates an upward-thrusting triangle with *Concentration* and *Meditation* at the outer two angles, *Devotion* at the center, and *Visualization* at the base. Another basic image or model that can be used is that of the Pyramid where Concentration, Meditation, Devotion, and Visualization form the 4 angles meeting at the top from which evocation or the Intuitive Energies flow down the center of the Pyramid. When this is done to the best of our present abilities, *Invocation* will be answered by *Evocation* which is the down-pouring of spiritual Energies into our field of consciousness wherein spiritual Life energizes our human will and concentration, spiritual Light, illuminates our meditation and thinking, spiritual Fire warms and expands our feelings and devotion, and spiritual Vision opens up and crowns over visualization. Ultimately, however, it is important to remember that Intuition with its accompanying *Inspiration and Revelation are spiritual gifts* and not human or psychological achievements. As such, a life of devoted prayer, selfless service to others, and proper perspective and balance in all the things one does, is, perhaps, the best way to obtain the gift of true Intuition which only the spiritual Self can bestow.

The core exercises to develop and train the Intuition are:

1. *Guided Imagery, the Inward Journey:* ascent in psychological space and meeting/dialogue with a Sage, an Angel, the Light, or the Sun.
2. *Inner Dialogue:* conversation with a symbol of the Superconscious and/or the spiritual Self.

3. *Letter to the Higher Self:* expressing aspirations, fears, and needs.
4. *Prayer:* practice of *Silence* and *Ritual* to maximize *sensitivity* and *receptivity* and the down-pouring of *Light* and the *spiritual Energies.*

Crucial here is also to learn how to listen to and recognize the "voice of Intuition" when it does manifest itself and to cultivate Peace, or systematic relaxation, and Life, or systematic stimulation, in our whole personality.

The Two Faces of Human Suffering: Creative or Destructive?

Human suffering is unavoidable and universal. It is an integral part of the "human condition" and, therefore, no human being can escape it while alive in this world. Sooner or later, and in one way or another, each person will encounter and experience suffering in its thousand aspects and faces. But, we have a choice, an **essential choice:** to live and experience suffering and pain, on various levels of our being and in different ways in a **creative** or **destructive** fashion, as a **friend** or as an **enemy**, as a benevolent or as a malevolent trial. This choice is truly *fundamental* in terms of its implications and consequences on the biological organism and on the psyche. And it depends, largely, on our *level of consciousness and being*, being a direct **function** of them.

If we accept suffering, whatever its nature and manifestations, and if we invoke the *help of Heaven,* Grace, the spiritual Energies which can expand our consciousness and raise our vibrations, then suffering is **creative** and **benevolent**; if, with their help, we succeed in "understanding the incomprehensible", in "accepting the inacceptable", and to face the test of the unknown, of "death", and of pain . . . then suffering can become a friend and positive. But, if we refuse suffering or if we attempt to confront it **unaided**, with our own will, reason, and resources, then suffering can be very destructive and malevolent; if we get "up tight", **revolt**, or let ourselves fall prey to anxiety, fear, or frustration, then suffering can become our enemy and be very negative, and it can do us a great deal of harm physically, psychologically, and spiritually.

The essential objective of the lecture/workshop will be to explore and analyze the nature, psychodynamics, and the consequences of suffering in its multiple "faces" and manifestations. It will be, also, and especially, to explore the "alchemy", the work, and the internal transformations which can transform suffering from being destructive to being constructive—from being lived without "justice" or "meaning" or with a "meaning" that enables us to accept it. And it is precisely this "change of paradigm", the result of a qualitative expansion of our consciousness, which can radically transform our perception and conception of suffering—from being destructive and deleterious to being creative and helpful. Then, suffering and pains caused by illnesses, accidents, "radical transformations", and "deaths" will be lived at the **sacred** level in an **initiatory** way which will transform them into "friends".

Lived at the creative and positive level, suffering is truly the "motor of evolution", of the "expansion of human consciousness", for it will "sensitize" us, revealing our own being with its various reactions, limitations, and capacities. Lived at the level of the instincts, of the impulses and emotions—of the "human self"—suffering is a "psychic poison" and a source of toxins which can poison our psyche and our body. Here, suffering can harden us, "close" us up, and make us sick, bitter, aggressive, and evil.

What is suffering and what are its manifestations in a human being? Suffering is a "state of being", a "state of consciousness" which can affect all the functions of our psyche (one or two more than others) and which can manifest on the *4 fundamental levels of our consciousness and being*—on the physical, emotional, mental, and spiritual levels. Suffering is, likewise, a power that can make "conscious" the unconscious, which forces us, by its **intensity** and **acuity,** to become aware of certain things which would, otherwise, have remained buried in the unconscious. Thus, suffering implies a very strong *intensification* of our consciousness and focalization of our attention.

Suffering can also work as an "alarm system" to indicate to us, through its own "language", that there is "some work to be done"— that one must "change certain things" and pay attention. It also helps us to discover our limits and capacities . . . and to focus upon our higher faculties and energies . . . when there are no "solutions" "below" and that we are "stuck", apparently without "hope". It also helps us to better understand the Laws of Life, and of our own being, and to develop empathy and sympathy towards others.

At the physical, sensorial level, suffering is characterized by a tension, a pressure, and a disharmony which engender physical pain. This physical pain is thus an "alarm system" which demands that our attention be directed towards the "painful part" of our body and that "something" be done or changed. Emotional suffering is characterized by strong, "cutting" emotions which, again, create a disharmony and a tension in our consciousness. This disharmony and tension also act as an "alarm system", telling us that something must be done at the *emotional* level.

Mental suffering is characterized by mental confusion and disharmony—being pulled in different directions by several contradictory choices. This is another "alarm signal" that something is not functioning "right" at the mental level . . . which requires our attention and a *transformation*. Finally, spiritual suffering, "existential anguish", is characterized by a sense of "malaise", "anxiety", by a sense of "isolation", "abandonment", and "loss". Loss of what? Of *Divine Light* and of the conscious contact with our spiritual Source and Essence—with our Self! This, too, is an "alarm signal" that tells us through the "malaise" and the "pain" it is creating, that we must change or do "something" . . . in our **being** and in our **lives.**

According to the above definitions, we can conclude that human suffering is a *disharmony*, a *tension*, and a *malaise* which, acting on the physical, emotional, mental, and spiritual levels, acts as a sort of "alarm signal" to bring us out of our normal "routine" and to tell us that *something must be done and "changed"*. What must be done or changed? Learn a lesson, the causes of which may go back to the distant past, or have the opportunity to take the "next step" in our evolution by facing more difficult circumstances and, thereby, developing and actualizing new *faculties* and *potentialities* of our being and consciousness. Or yet, end dysfunctional behaviors or attitudes we may have which are harming us as they no longer correspond to our present nature, level of consciousness, or "vibratory level".

Where does suffering come from and what are its causes? Human suffering has two major causes or "agents": first, human beings themselves and then God. For most people, most of the time, suffering has one basic cause and origin: **one self!** It comes, or manifests itself in its "own time"—which we call an "accident", a "coincidence", or, simply "bad luck". Its origin and cause, here, can only be found in the *person himself,* in what he did, or failed to do, in the past.

All religions and sacred traditions have always affirmed that, "As man sows, so shall he reap"! The law of justice, of Cause and Effect, or of "Karma" as it is called in the Orient, proclaims the same basic truth, but in different words. Modern science, today, states the very same truth, but using different words: Cause and Effect follow each other as a reaction follows action . . . in an absolute and unfailing way. And yet, human beings, in the domain of suffering and of trial, continue to claim that these are but an "accident" or "bad luck"! Even this has a cause and an origin—the very low level of consciousness of such people and the fact that their psyche, their human consciousness, is still half "asleep". What we must always remember, especially when we are *personally involved,* is that **all human consciousness always has a *cause and a reason*** and that this cause and reason can, generally be found in *man himself!*

Just as there are different kinds of human suffering (physical, emotional, mental, and spiritual), so there are different "direct causes" of suffering. Suffering can come through the "instrumentality" of accidents, illnesses, other people; through the family into which we are born; the society and the age in which we live; as well as from frustrated desires and expectations. In all these cases, we should always ask ourselves the following fundamental questions: "Why was I there, at that time and in that place? Why was I attracted by that person? Why was I born into that family, at that place in that time? If we take some time to reflect and meditate about what is happening to us and why, we shall soon discover that the causes go very deep into our being . . . and very far into the past. Should we be able to retrace these and to become conscious of them, we would eventually discover that it is we who have created these causes and "set them into motion"!

The suffering that comes from a human being, comes as a result of what he has *done* or of what he has *not done*. A human being can abuse himself or other persons . . . and must reap its consequences. He may have abused his body, his emotions, his mind, or have misused his spiritual energies and faculties . . . which brings unavoidable consequences to be reckoned with. He may have abused other persons, consciously or unconsciously; he may have harmed others, generated animosities, or exploited others who now "settle their accounts" . . . most of the time without even being aware of this!

In other instances, he may have misused the opportunities that presented themselves. He may also not have developed certain faculties and capacities (e.g. intelligence, prudence, discernment, strength, or intuition) and may now find himself "cut adrift" in a world which requires these capacities from him. This problem is even more complicated at the mental level by the fact that memory is still an "embryonic faculty", little developed . . . and which covers only "this life" which is but "one day in the great School of Life"!

If, on the other hand, suffering comes through other persons— through their ignorance, egoism, immaturity, or even meanness— the following question could then be asked: "Why did I meet that person"? "Why was I attracted by that person"? "Why did I get involved with this person and did not recognize the "dangers" and "implications" of this involvement"? Here, too, the answers are many. It could be Karma, Destiny, that we had an "account" to settle with that person that comes from the distant past; or it could come from our own immaturity or our own desires and values. One could have "lessons" to learn, through this relationship, which will bring much to us and enable us to make great progress, even if it is painful and difficult. It could also be that this person attracts a certain part of our own being . . . and that, in order to satisfy this part, one forgets all the other parts, as well as all the "warnings" that are given. Or there may yet be other factors at work.

While most of human suffering is self-created, there are also sufferings which are not . . . which are sent by the Higher Power! These cases are still quite rare and touch, generally, only people who are quite "evolved" at the human and spiritual level . . . yet they also exist. In such cases, Divine Providence, through its multiple "agents" and "human laboratories", sends many "problems", "difficulties", and "obstacles" to an individual . . . so that he may learn how to face them and to overcome them! At times, Divine Providence sends also persecutions, betrayals, slanders which a person must "accept" and "bear" to "discover certain things" in himself, to develop certain faculties or actualize a certain potential. Far from being the sign of "divine wrath" (which exists only in the mind and in the imagination of human beings), these situations and difficulties are, in fact, the sign of a "divine blessing"; they constitute a *benediction and a special "privilege"* which God sends to those who are near to Him, who are His "friends" . . . for their own good . . . and to "accelerate their progress".

As witness of this truth, we have the unanimous declaration of all the great Saints and Sages, of all times, and of Christian Martyrs in particular . . . who offer a striking example of this truth. These have, without exceptions, considered hardships and very difficult situations (thus, **suffering**) as particular "gifts" from Heaven (because, having developed their spiritual consciousness, they could perceive and comprehend their experiences in a totally different way than persons who had not). Even the Sacred Scriptures tell us, in a very clear and explicit way: "Those that God loves a lot, He chastises a lot". This is also why the authentic Orders of Chivalry, of all times, recognized this truth, which they enshrined in their famous motto, "let us be worthy of great adventures, let us be worthy of great battles, let us be worthy of great **sufferings**"! (Actually, these Orders of Chivalry constituted a genuine spiritual and initiatory school in the deepest meaning of these words).

Why are sufferings and difficulties a "Gift from Heaven"? Because they demand the maximum of our capacities and resources . . . and, therefore, awaken, activate, and bring out many aspects and potentialities of our personality which would, otherwise, remain latent or unknown! Because they are the true "school" of character, nobility, and of spiritual chivalry! Because they lead us, little by little, to realize the spiritual sense of the famous Roman motto "Nihil Humanum Alienum a me puto", that is, nothing that is human will be foreign or alien to me—from now on. I will not feel threatened by or fear **any human experience** so that no human experience will be able to make me fall into a state of deep anxiety, despair, or **self-alienation!** But, to achieve this we are forced to keep a conscious contact with the spiritual Energies and the Light which, **alone,** can help us to realize this. It is at this point and only at this point, that a human being becomes truly *free,* truly **universal,** truly a **MAN** with the whole of Life and the entire earth opening up to him.

What are the "functions" and the meaning of human suffering? Suffering has multiple meanings and functions, the most important of which are the following:

1. It helps us to distinguish between "Good" and "Evil"; that is between what brings Life and what brings Death.
2. It brings to us and unfolds **conscience** and **responsibility;** that is, that every *action* brings *consequences* which we have to undergo, and that that which we do unto others, we do unto **ourselves** because, on the higher levels, we are all ONE.
3. It helps us to develop **sensibility** and **sympathy** (which is its social equivalent).
4. It functions as an "alarm signal", at the essential levels of our being and consciousness, to "force" us to pay attention to certain things and to change certain dysfunctional behaviors and attitudes.
5. It "awakens us from our state of lethargy and torpor" and "forces" us to find answers . . . to our pains and problems; to understand why we are confronted with a certain situation, and to find solutions. It acts, therefore, as a strong "motivating and propelling force" to make us mature and grow; and it "forces" us to use all of our resources, to develop our faculties, or to ask the help of the Higher Powers—and thus to alternate between the "male" and the "female" polarity of our being.
6. It demands "all we have got", the best of ourselves . . . and, when our human resources are exhausted, to ask and look for Higher resources; and to discover, through our own *personal experience,* that these Superior resources exist and that they can provide *real and effective help.*
7. In conclusion, human suffering is an "alarm system" which tells us that we must **urgently** do something—seek for answers, look for solutions, use all of our resources, or ask the help of Heaven. It thus constitutes the "royal way" to evolve, to grow, to mature . . . until the *love of Beauty, "Truth", and "Goodness" will take its place!*

Can a human being ever receive "more suffering than he can bear"? Yes and no, this is a complex question that sends us back to our core insights and conclusions regarding suffering. Suffering is just as much created by people themselves as it is sent by God. But God never sends us more suffering, or trials, than we can face and bear. On the other hand, a human being can very well "put himself", through his own actions and by violating certain natural, human, or spiritual laws, in a situation that is "too much" for him. In a situation which is beyond his capacities to confront and, therefore, to "crash", physically as well as psychologically, to dissociate, break, and alienate his body, his personality, and his spirit. Helas, the world is filled with such people, psychiatric hospitals in particular!

If a person starts to drink, to take drugs, or to degenerate morally, that person is very likely to "crash". And if a person does not develop certain faculties and aptitudes, his inner equilibrium, or if that person becomes lazy and fails prey to lower states of consciousness (thoughts, emotions, desires, impulses, and perspectives), that person can very well be "unable to cope" with certain situations which, sooner or later, will manifest. Finally, if a person does not use her human resources, she will never be able to get "the help of Heaven" and thus could be "unable to cope" and crash.

What complicates matters is that human suffering, in addition to **antecedents,** also has an *objective* and a *subjective* side. The "objective" side is the problem, the situation, the difficulty which arises while the "subjective" side is the *attitude,* the state of consciousness, the answer that the human being gives to a given problem or crisis that presents itself. Under normal circumstances, a person who has established a *conscious and living contact with His Divine Spark* will be in a position to face *all human situations without "crashing".* Such a person will "bear his cross" to the very end and might even "die" physically but never **psychologically** or **spiritually.** History gives us marvelous examples of this type of person in Jesus, Moses, Mohammed, or the Saints and Martyrs of all religions.

The distinction between the "objective" and the "subjective" dimension of human experiences can help us to understand and explain great paradoxes and very complicated problems. For example: the reconciliation between divine **Justice** and **Compassion** as well as "the forgiveness of sins" and "absolution". If God is completely just (that is, if every *cause* always and inevitably brings about certain *effects* that correspond to it) how can He then be *compassionate* and *forgive?* How can a person make all kinds of mistakes, hurt or exploit others (that is, set in motion certain "effects" and "consequences") and then **repent** and have his "sins" and "mistakes" **forgiven** without destroying "justice" and the universe? The "esoteric" answer is very simple: *justice* operates on the *objective* level while *compassion* operates at the *subjective* level. All causes that we set in motion *inevitably* bring about *objective effects.* On the other hand, compassion *helps us to transform our subjective attitudes,* our state of consciousness and our perceptions and conceptions, to better cope with the "objective consequences". The same principle is also at work with the "forgiveness of sins" and "absolution": they change our state of consciousness and re-establish the connection and "broken harmony" between the human and the spiritual Self, the conscious and the superconscious. This transforms our perceptions, comprehension, and attitudes, helping us to make restitution where we committed injustices, not to make the same mistakes again, and to accept, understand, and learn the lessons coming from our mistakes and their consequences.

A person who uses all her resources, to the maximum of her capacities, (i.e. who really "does her best") is always helped by the Heavenly Powers . . . which enables her to "face" and to "overcome" the crisis she is faced with. Likewise, a person who lives a balanced, normal, and healthy life is, generally, capable of coping with whatever Life sends her and with the karmic trials she is compelled to face. But if this person violates certain laws, becomes lazy, or falls prey to despair or to lower states of consciousness, then it is quite possible that she may "crash" psychologically even with *very little "pressure" or when facing "easy tests".* Moreover, we should note two interesting points:

A. That, before incarnating, a soul *chooses* (more or less according to her level of consciousness and evolution) the kinds of *experiences* and, therefore, *sufferings* she will have to "face" in the life that is immediately before her (and the more evolved she is the greater is both the relative "freedom" and "the range of choice" and the difficulty of the experiences she will be facing). In this sense many sufferings are doubly *self-chosen:* first, determined by the consequences which we have "set in motion" in a far distant past and "chosen" in terms of the "form" and "speed" by which these consequences will be experienced. Here, we also find the great paradox of **determinism** vs. **free will**. . . which are a *function of our level of consciousness and being.* Determinism does exist at the level of the objective consequences, which we have chosen or set in motion in our past; while free will also exists but, always and essentially, at the subjective level of our perceptions, conceptions, and comprehension which, in turn, act on our behavior in respect to the objective consequences.

B. That, generally, the more a soul grows, matures, and makes decisive progress on the path of spiritual evolution, the more she has to confront and face adversities and sufferings that are becoming harder and harder. This is so true that the neophytes of authentic Mystery Schools are warned that they will receive a *Crown of Thorns* (that is, all kinds of tests, trials, persecutions, and difficulties) before receiving a *Crown of Light* (which symbolizes the activation and illumination of the Head psychospiritual center) which brings *conscious immortality* and genuine *self-mastery*. This principle was beautifully manifested in the life of Jesus Christ. . . Who received a "Crown of Thorns", just as real as symbolic, for all the good He did to humanity. Likewise, many Saints, Sages, and Knights of Christ know very well that the best "sign" of "divine Favor" and of the "Gifts of Heaven" are . . . all kinds of *sufferings and pains* that will befall them.

A rapid review of the history of religions will illustrate quite clearly this "contradiction"—so opposed to our instincts and the "ways of the world" which separates the "sacred" from the "profane", the "Christian" from the "Pagan", and the "Jew" from the "Gentile". The latter always saw suffering as being negative, as a form of "punishment", as something to be avoided at all costs; while the former perceived suffering, just as joy, and *everything in life,* as being a "Gift from God" and an opportunity to grow, to mature, to learn something important and valuable. This depends, therefore, from *our level of consciousness.* "Below, there is **duality** (Good and Evil) while "Above" there is **unity** the Supreme Good only . . . even if difficult and painful to accept and bear.

From the standpoint of spiritual consciousness, the world is perceived in a **holistic** fashion: everything comes from God and must, eventually, serve God's Plan and the glorification of His children, human beings. Thus, here, joy as well as suffering are **positive** and fulfill God's Purpose. All human experiences, therefore, as well as all the parts and facets of our being and consciousness, must be **accepted with gratitude!** What is "below", or "inferior", within and without ourselves, must not be "rejected", "cut", and "destroyed", but, rather, **spiritually integrated and transmuted** to, eventually, "serve the Inner God".

Seen through this perspective, the sufferings and persecutions of the great Martyrs, Saints, Sages, and spiritually awakened persons acquire a very logical and rational meaning and purpose . . . as do their attitude and acceptance of them. Seen in this light, sufferings and difficulties are truly a "Gift of God", a **privilege**, and a great opportunity of growth and of personal realization . . . which one must "deserve" as the ancient knights used to say!

One day, as I was travelling in the South of Italy to meet Padre Pio, I noticed that, as my car went faster, so did the "friction" and "air-resistance" also increase. In a flash, I finally got the "key" to understand the "paradox" of suffering in human experience on earth: the more one "accelerates" one's evolution and becomes **conscious,** the more sufferings and difficulties will increase. . . in spite of the fact that one does not seek them and even seeks to avoid them . . . until the day when they will completely disappear! But it is essential to distinguish between sufferings that are the natural "result and consequence" of the violation of natural laws and those which are "a special gift" to allow us to evolve more rapidly. This difference can, generally, be found at the level of the *attitude* of the person and in her knowledge of the manifestation of the "male" and "female" principles in her being and life.

Without spiritual consciousness and "Grace" (spiritual Energies and Light) one rejects suffering and becomes **depressed** when suffering arrives . . . which makes us even more "hardened", "cynical", and "bitter". . . and which leads to emotional and physical exhaustion. With spiritual consciousness and the "perspective from above", however, one can accept suffering with gratitude and use it in a creative and constructive fashion . . . without ever "breaking" under its yoke.

What should be our attitude towards suffering? In view of what we have just stated, it is quits clear what our attitude towards suffering should be: we must, first of all, *accept it with **gratitude,*** as a "Gift of God". We must exert ourselves to understand its causes and to learn and integrate its lessons . . . realizing that it repre*sents an opportunity to perfect ourselves—to* develop different aspects and faculties of our personality to bring us "face to face" with a much larger range of human experiences . . . and to help others who are living the same experiences.

We must understand that suffering comes, for the most part, from *ourselves:* from what we have done and from the causes we have set in motion. That we could also have "chosen it", before we incarnated in this world, so as to "settle certain accounts", to learn certain lessons, and to develop certain capacities. But that suffering could also be a special "Gift of God", a "grace", or a privilege, that we have earned through our efforts to enable us to evolve more rapidly and to "bring to light" new aspects and facets of our character. In all cases, we must realize that suffering, whether created by ourselves, self-chosen, or sent by God, is *ALWAYS AN OPPORTUNITY FOR GROWTH AND PERSONAL DEVELOPMENT.* This is why our attitude towards it should always be one *of grateful acceptance* . . . and to do all we can to learn as much as possible from it.

At the practical level, we must do all that is humanly possible to overcome the difficulty that suffering represents, using all of our resources and capacities, never stopping until *everything has been tried.* Above all, we must realize that ALL HUMAN SUFFERING ALWAYS HAS A MEANING AND A PURPOSE . . . WHICH CAN

BE DISCOVERED, AT ITS APPROPRIATE TIME. Then, it is very important to PRAY, often and with fervor, to fill our "Auras", or "Energy Bodies" with LIGHT, which will transform and raise our level of consciousness. For this is what will enable us to "understand" it, to "accept" it, and not to be "crushed" by the weight of this trial. Finally, we must accept it and "live with it", the best we can (the "female" Volarity), but only when we have *done everything possible to eliminate it (the* "masculine" polarity). We must also always ask for "Grace" and invoke the "spiritual Light" to fill our being and consciousness with the "light" that will give us the **comprehension** and the **strength** to accept it, the intuition to grasp its true purpose, and the **wisdom** to be grateful for it and to use it in a creative and constructive fashion.

Finally, we must also realize that suffering, like many other things, *will exist for us so long as it is necessary for us to learn something important;* that, like the "Devil", once we have learned its lessens, *it will disappear forever!*

Practical aspects: How to transform destructive suffering into creative suffering? This, in fact, was the central theme of the last work I wrote, *Apocalypse Now,* dealing with the awakening of spiritual consciousness. To summarize, as briefly and as practically as possible, this great transformation: the "metamorphosis" of destructive and negative suffering—which is the worst enemy of our physical and psychological health—into creative and positive suffering-which is our "best friend" and the motor of our human and spiritual growth, I would mention the following points:

A. First of all, to really realize that suffering, as many other things, is a FUNCTION OF OUR LEVEL OF CONSCIOUSNESS AND BEING. In few words, this means that "Below", in lower states of consciousness, suffering is, automatically and unavoidably, lived as *DESTRUCTIVE and EVIL.* This means that the first, and the most important thing to do in the "alchemy of the transformation of suffering" is TO EXPAND AND RAISE OUR LEVEL OF CONSCIOUSNESS (remember that Assagioli said: "Below" there are no solutions whereas "Above" there are no problems").

B. To act and transform whatever function of our psyche, or aspect of our consciousness, we must first understand the structure and the functions of our psyche and have mastered the psychological processes connected with each one of them-what I call the "Muscles of Consciousness".

C. These "Muscles of Human Consciousness" are:
CONCENTRATION connected with Willing.
MEDITATION connected with Thinking.

DEVOTION connected with Feeling.

VISUALIZATION connected with Imagination.

INVOCATION-EVOCATION connected with Intuition.

THE DIRECTION AND TRANSFORMATION OF BIOPSY-CHIC ENERGIES connected with Impulses.

OBSERVATION, EXTERNAL AND INTERNAL connected with Sensations.

D. Here, it is essential to know, to be able to identify *in oneself,* and to use practically what I call the "Consciousness Check-list".

E. Finally, one must realize that the work of self-knowledge and self-actualization always passes through the CROSS OF REALIZATION *(understand* with our Head, *feel* with our Heart, *will* with our Shoulders, *live* with our Body to BECOME this knowledge). And that there are no substitutes for a regular, conscious, and devoted PRACTICE!

　1. To carry out and realize this "great transformation", which corresponds to what our present "level of evolution" and "state of consciousness" demand of us . . . and which is also "the great challenge of our times", one must, first of all, *become aware of our sufferings,* enter into conscious contact with them, and RECOGNIZE THEM!

　2. If we are suffering, this means that we have SOME WORK TO DO ON OURSELVES, that an important "alarm signal" is telling us that we must direct our attention and give out time and energy to "CHANGE SOMETHING".

　3. This means that we must *understand what is going on, the nature and meaning of this suffering* to ACCEPT IT AND WORK UPON IT.

　4. Then, we must *act upon our emotions and transform them, to **emotionally** accept this suffering and direct its energies towards a constructive end.*

　5. Then, we must *act upon our will to transform our **behavior**—to act in a positive way.*

　6. This logically implies an EXPANSION AND TRANSFOR-MATION OF OUR CONSCIOUSNESS—*a connection between the conscious and the superconscious, between the human and the spiritual Self:* THE AWAKENING OF SPIRITUAL CONSCIOUSNESS.

　7. Finally, this implies the paradox to *do everything that is humanly possible, to use all of our capacities and resources to overcome the difficulty which engenders this suffering,* to then ask "the help of Heaven" either to *eliminate this*

suffering or to accept and learn to LIVE WITH IT. And this, in turn, also demands an intuitive knowledge of "God's Will" and of the proper use of the *"masculine" and "feminine" polarities in our own consciousness, being, and life.* But once, we have reached a genuine breakthrough and expression of our spiritual consciousness, we will also have achieved the *knowledge and understanding of what is GOING ON and of what we MUST DO, and have THE STRENGTH TO DO IT, to accomplish what must be done!* Then, the "Great Work", the "essential metamorphosis" will be realized by the Self, the Divine Spark, which lives IN SILENCE in the "heights and depths" of our consciousness and being!

Appendix G

MAN THE SKY-SCRAPER:
The vertical Axis of Human Consciousness as Essential "Key" to Holistic Understanding.

A truly primordial and essential intuition of all the sacred traditions of the past is that which I represent, today, with the modern concept of *Man the Sky-Scraper*. This concept, and the core intuition it embodies, are indispensable to properly grasp and understand, rationally, the incredible differences of perception, comprehension, and definitions of *reality* which characterize the "citizens of the Global Village". It is very easy to see, in fact it happens everyday, that *exactly the same situation event, or external condition* can be experienced and lived in a *very different way* by different persons . . . or even the *same person* at different times or in *different states of consciousness*. Obviously, all depends on how this person perceives, conceives, defines, and reacts—at the spiritual, mental, emotional, and physical level—to a given existential situation. And this, in turn, depends on *his/her level of consciousness and being!*

What this means, in other words, is that our way of perceiving, conceiving, and reacting to reality, or to a specific situation, is strictly a *function of our level of consciousness and being*. When we change our level of consciousness, we concomitantly change our perception, conception, and reaction to reality. This notion was well known by the old Sages and by the sacred traditions. This is why the quintessence of Greek Wisdom was expressed in the famous "Gnothi Seauton" (Man, know thyself!) which was inscribed on the most important Greek Temples. We find the same insight in the concept of the "magical mirror", of the sphere of sensation", and of the "alembic" of the magical, hermetic, and alchemical traditions.

This insight, and the concept which embodies it, are essential to properly understand the reactions of people who are located on different levels of this "vertical Axis of Consciousness" towards their various existential situations. Let us now explore it a little further and in a more concrete way: if we enter a sky-scraper and look outside from the 1st, 10th, 40th, 80th, or 100th floor, what we "see", our perception of reality, changes *dramatically*. Below, we have "myopic" vision and perception, limited to what is *immediately* in front of the sky-scraper at this level. But the more we rise, the more our vision, our physical perceptions, *change,* the more reality is apprehended as a "whole" with a vision that is far greater, more complete, and thus *real.* The same thing happens when we climb to the top of a mountain or when we climb in an airplane. To rise means to see, thus to *understand,* "wholes" that are greater and greater. To descend means not to see anymore, or to see only *parts,* "fragments" that become smaller and smaller.

The core point of this basic insight, which I represent today with the image of "Man the Sky-Scraper" is the following:

"Each human being can be represented by a "sky scraper" with 100 floors. That is, there exists within him an "axis of qualitatively different levels of consciousness". There also exists an "elevator", a means of making the "human self" and its "field of consciousness" go up and down this axis. . . as an elevator would climb to the 100th floor or go down to the 1st floor. Herein lies the true "key", or "substance" of human growth and spiritual awakening. . . of true progress. . . which consists in knowing this "elevator" and to be able to use the "buttons" that make it go up and down, to *rise to a superior level."*

What we see when we look out of the window on the 1st, 20th, or 100th floor is just as "real" and "true" but it is *not the same thing!* A proper grasp of this insight and its image can greatly help us to *understand,* and thus *to accept,* people who function on different levels of consciousness and being; that is to say, who are located on "different floors". And to do this without getting angry at them, blaming them, or seeking to convert them to our perceptions, conceptions, and values. To use another image, or analogy, we all go through the various "stages", in the life-cycle, of the "baby", the "adolescent", and the "adult". And what we expect of an "adult" is certainly not what we expect of a "baby"! Moreover, there is an "organic growth" that leads the "baby" to slowly become the "adult" . . . and the person who is on the 1st floor to, eventually, climb to the 100th floor. This process is first "unconscious", that is, which does not depend on our will and on our conscious cooperation but which then becomes more and more *conscious,* depending on our *willing* cooperation and commitment.

The "Axis of our level of consciousness and being" plays an absolutely *vital* role for all that we consider most "real" and "important-for our sense of identity, our perceptions, conceptions, and reactions to external reality, as well as for the expression of the 7 functions of our psyche—for willing, thinking, and feeling in particular. Hence, it also plays an essential role for our relationship to religion, politics, economics, morality, love, health, and the rest.

To better illustrate and render more concrete this fundamental insight and image, I would like to tell a story. Imagine a famous professor, with several degrees and an international reputation. He is working in his studio, located on the first floor of his house. His 9 year old son is playing in the garden where there are trees. They are waiting for the brother of the professor who is coming with his wife and their three children on the 3:40p train. And it takes about 20 minutes to go by foot from the house of the professor to the train station.

The son of the professor climbs on a tree about 30 feet from the ground. It is 3:20p. Looking around him, the son of the professor sees, on the road that leads to the house, two adults and two children who are approaching the house. Very happy, he yells "Daddy, Daddy, there they are, they are coming—my uncle, my aunt, and my nephews". The professor looks at his watch, shakes his head, and answer: "come on, it is only 3:22p, it is impossible, their train has not even arrived yet; they must be other people!" But, a few minutes later, the two adults and their children arrive and, indeed, it is the uncle, the aunt, and the nephews of the son of the professor. They had simply taken the previous train which arrived at 3:05p!

The reasoning and deductions of the illustrious professor were perfectly correct, in relation to what he knew. But, as he was located on a *lower level* than his son, who had climbed on a tree, in spite of all his knowledge and intelligence, he could not see what his son could see **directly.** In terms of the analogy of "Man the Sky Scraper", the son of the professor has climbed to a higher floor than the one on which stood his father. Therefore, he perceived reality in a different fashion!

This is an essential point: there exists a simultaneous growth and development of human consciousness (and of its faculties) *on the horizontal and on the vertical level*—on the vertical level in **quality**, going from one level to another, and on the horizontal level in quantity (*plus* or *minus*) but remaining on the same qualitative level. This can explain many paradoxes, antinomies, and contradictions, as well as the extraordinary diversity of viewpoints that human beings have. There are, in fact, human beings endowed with a great intelligence and sensibility, who perceive, conceive, and define reality in a certain way (which is underpinned by their present level of consciousness) and who react to given situations in conformity with their level of consciousness. We could cite, for example, Freud, Marx, and Voltaire. But, there are also other human beings, equally bright and sensitive, such as Plate, Bergson, and Assagioli, who perceive and define reality in the exact *opposed way* and who react very differently to the same specific situation. This is an historical and academic fact.

For me, it is clearly the notion of the "vertical and qualitative Axis of consciousness" of a person that can explain, *rationally,* the great diversity and complexity of conceptions of reality, of axiological and ethical values, of religious and political conceptions of human beings. Hence, it is this fundamental intuition which can help us to "reconcile opposites" such as Matter-Spirit (materialism-spiritualism), egoism-altruism, political right-left, pessimism-optimism, hope-despair, etc. It is also this image of "man the Sky Scraper" which can make sense of the "vertical" psychiatric paradox of people who fall sick, who have a nervous break-down, or a "burn-out" for very ordinary pressures and disappointments while other human beings will remain healthy and psychologically "integrated" even in the worse situations and under extreme pressures and sufferings. Finally, it is also here that we can find the answer to the great paradox that the very same religion can be interpreted and lived in one way by some people and in a different, if not *opposed way,* by others; that prayer accomplishes nothing for some while it can literally work out "miracles" for others; and that "going to Communion" can be a very normal and "unconscious" experience for some, while it is the most intense, profound, and life-giving experience for others. Lastly, I believe that it is also here that we find the "key" to understand the "opposition" between the "exoteric" (outer, revealed, for-all) and the "esoteric" (inner, hidden, and for-the-few) approach that can be so bewildering and confusing to so many people. And this would also explain why, with the passage of time, with human growth and the expansion of human consciousness, *things do change* and *transform themselves,* both inwardly, or subjectively, and outwardly, or objectively.

In the material world, we find, in fact, a phenomenon which is very rare in creation . . . and which affords us a *unique opportunity* for personal growth. The fact that human beings, "souls", of *very different levels of consciousness and being* meet, become aware of each other, and interact. This situation greatly facilitates and stimulates the growth, the opening of consciousness, and the self-actualization of all those who are thus involved. The sacred traditions have taught us, for a long time, that in the "inner, psychic and spiritual worlds", only *beings who are on the same "wave length" and who find themselves on the same level of consciousness and being, meet, become aware of each other, and can interact in a meaningful and real way.* This, by the way, has now been fully corroborated by people who have had NDE and OBE (near-death experiences and out-of-the-body experiences).

What this means, practically speaking, is that a person who *raises* or *lowers* her level of consciousness and being, in relation to other people, will see them "disappear to their vision" and no longer "be there". This is, precisely, what occurs at the death of a person, when the physical body is destroyed and when the "human self" and its "field of consciousness" move from the physical body to the soul.

In the invisible worlds, on the psychic and spiritual planes (etheric, astral, mental, and spiritual) there is a force that acts, as *gravitation* does on the physical plane, in such a way that everyone finds himself, "sees", and interacts on the same "wave length" and on the same "plane". Thus, those who are *above* or *below* a certain "wave length", who are on a "plane" or a "floor", higher or lower, *do not see* and *cannot meet or interact with each other*. There exists a true "separation, just as TV programs which are on different frequencies are "separated". This law, however, does not hold for the physical world, or the material plane. Here, we all have the great challenge and the marvelous "growth-opportunity" to meet and interact with beings who are on higher or lower "floors" than ours.

This is also the reason why Love, which transforms multiplicity into unity and which establishes *right relationships* between "parts" and "wholes" ever greater, is the *only force in the universe* which can reunite and reconcile opposites, connect the strong and the weak, the rich and the poor, the high and the low in a "bond of love". This is the force and energy which binds all "worlds" and "dimensions", all levels of consciousness and being. . . especially in the material world which presents such huge differences and varieties of beings.

It is also interesting to note how, in the material world, *union,* fusion, frees and generates energy while *separation* binds and consumes energy. On the human level, union brings joy, happiness, peace, and health (under "normal" circumstances. . . for there are always exceptions to every rule) while *separation* brings pain, suffering, anxiety, and illness. On the spiritual plane, union brings growth, harmony, and Life, opening the "gates of Paradise"—of our Communion and Reunion with God—while separation brings devolution, anxiety, Death, and opens the "doors of Hell—of "Communion with the Devil" which, etymologically, means precisely "separation" or "taking apart".

This brings us to the heart of our discussion on the image and analogy of "Man the Sky Scraper". For me, a human being can be represented by a sky-scraper of 100 floors, each of which represents *a different and separate state of consciousness and being.* At the center of this "sky scraper" we find an "elevator" with "buttons" that can make it go up or down. Here, the "elevator" represents the "human self" with the "field of consciousness" and its "7 functions and muscles". And, it is precisely these "Muscles of Human Consciousness" (representing the "buttons") which, when properly applied, make the elevator go up or down different "floors" of the "sky scraper". The "sky scraper" itself represents the "vertical and qualitative Axis of our consciousness". To a certain "level of being" corresponds always a certain "level", "frequency", or "state" of our consciousness and vice versa.

This is why when we change our level of being, automatically, we change our level of consciousness. . . and that when we change our "level", or "frequency" of consciousness, we can make our level of being rise or fall and *transform it*. It is also here that come into play *purification, consecration, and communion* with the spiritual Self as a major way of expanding our consciousness. . . and thus to grow and to raise our level of being.

Fasting and *Praying,* emptying and filling our being, are also ways in which we can make the "elevator" go up and down. And maybe the simplest, most direct and effective way to "make the elevator rise to the higher floors" is the proper use of FAITH, in its precise and technical meaning (that is, to open one's heart, mind, and soul and to direct all of one's attention, thoughts, and feelings on a chosen point "on top" of the sky scraper).

The 100 floors of the sky scraper represent, *symbolically:* the *unconscious* (the basements and the first 5 floors) what was once called "Hell"; the *subconscious* (from the 5th to the 20th floor) what was once called "Purgatory"; the *preconscious* and the *field of consciousness* (from the 20th to the 40th floor) what was once called the "Earth"; finally, the *superconscious* (from the 40th to the 100th floor) what was once called "Heaven". Thus, in learning how to make the "elevator" go up and down we get the "keys of Heaven and Hell" which we could call today the "opening of the superconscious and of the unconscious".

The central point of our discussion on "the vertical Axis of consciousness and being" is the following: What does it mean and what are the implications of going "up and down" this axis? The expansion and transformation of human consciousness can take place on two "axes" which must, ultimately, be integrated: on the *vertical* axis, it can go *up* or *down* and on the *horizontal axis,* it can *spread out.* Our modern scientific culture emphasizes quantity rather than quality, analysis rather than synthesis, and has focused its explorations and analyses almost exclusively on the *horizontal axis,* on having more or less, rather than on being and on *qualitative growth.*

Our educational system, our society, and our literature (with the exception of the sacred, spiritual, and religious traditions) lead us, either consciously or unconsciously, with an incredible force to seek and possess only *quantity*—to have more or less of this or of that. Today, we are witnessing an incredible paradox whereby people have always more and are always less happy. Maybe this is what Jesus foresaw when He stated: "What does it benefit a man if he owns the whole world but loses his soul?"; what Max Weber predicted when he told us that the "disenchantment of the world" would come; or what Ralph W. Emerson intuited in his fundamental question: "Modern civilization has built enormous buildings and powerful machines, but what has it done for the human being who live in these buildings and who drives these machines?"

Today, it is imperative that we make the transition from *having* to *being*, from quantity to quality, which means to rediscover "the vertical Axis of consciousness and being" . . . and to learn how to move consciously on this axis. To *go up or down* on this axis is a *vital question*. It is vital (in the true meaning of the word) because "above" we find Life, Consciousness, Love, Liberty, Joy, and Self and Being while "below" we have Death, Unconsciousness, Indifference, Hatred, Slavery, Suffering and Alienation—non-being. Moreover, going "up or down" has a direct and vital impact on the three "royal faculties" of the psyche, as well as upon a number of other functions.

It determines, in fact, *thinking, feeling, and willing*. That is, Consciousness-Knowledge, Love, and Self-expression or Creativity. Moving up, we understand what was, before, incomprehensible, we discover new meanings and thinking becomes clear and precise while moving down, we go towards non-comprehension, the lack of meaning. Going up, we become able to love, to feeling deeply and passionately, we discover the "taste of Life", of the World, and of Human Experience while going down, we move towards indifference, disgust, frustration, and we lose the "Joy of Living". Going up, we succeed in "being one self" and "expressing one self", to change one's personality and the world, to "create", to "make a difference", while going down, one falls into alienation, one becomes a stranger to one Self, to Life, to the World—we become a *thing* rather than a *person* and, therefore, a victim of circumstances instead of being the master of one self and of one's destiny.

When we move up, the images, the symbols, the myths, and the rituals of the sacred traditions "speak to us" and unveil their "Mysteries", their deeper implications and applications, while going down they cease to speak, they "veil" their "Mysteries" and become "superstitions" and "illusions". Going up, a human being becomes capable of accepting all the parts and aspects of himself, of the world, and of Life to integrate and reconcile them, while going down he accepts certain parts and aspects to reject others, thus entering into conflict with one self and with the world. Going up, one discovers Being, God, and, therefore, Faith, Hope, Charity, while going down one discovers the Devil, hence, separation, doubt, despair, and egoism.

It is only in moving up that one discovers true peace, serenity, and harmony, both inner and outer, while it is going down that one falls into conflict, disharmony, and strife, both inner and outer, and, therefore, that one becomes *ill.* It is "above" that one finds unity, the holistic or global vision of reality, while "below" we find multiplicity and a "myopic" and partial vision of reality. Because it is truly "above", in the superconscious and in the Self that one can find the Source and Essence of Life, of Love, and of Knowledge which must vivify Matter. "Above" we have the reconciliation of opposites, union, and true synthesis, while "below" we fall, *inevitably,* into paradoxes, antinomies, separation, and conflicts. This is why Roberto Assagioli used to say that: "Below, there are no real solutions to the most important human problems, while "above", there are no problems" . . . and that one of the basic injunctions of the Primordial Tradition has always been to "Seek first the Kingdom of God and His Justice"; that is, to rise to the higher levels of consciousness to awaken spiritual consciousness so that "all these things shall be given unto you"—the true solution to all our problems, the right measure and proportion for all things, and the awakening of the intuition.

On the physical plane, in fact, things work pretty much the same way: our perception, conception, and definition of reality change radically as we climb on a mountain or on the higher floors of a sky scraper. What we can see, hear, smell, taste, and touch on the 1st floor, on the 10th, 40th, or 100th is absolutely not the *same thing,* just as when we climb a mountain, reality change dramatically as we move from 300 feet to 1,000 feet, and to 3,000 feet. Seen from "above", we have a "global" view where "parts" blend to form a comprehensible "whole". While "below" we have a partial view of "parts" which, alone and unconnected, have no meaning, integration, or purpose. The perception of a given place is radically different for the butterfly than it is for the caterpillar! Also, as we climb higher, learning to "fly" like the birds, to rise above negative situations, one can avoid great many dangers, illnesses, and conflicts.

Finally, one finds also the same principle and the same "lesson" at work in human societies and social stratification. The more we rise on the social and professional scale, the more reality and the experiences one lives change. "Above" one is unique, irreplaceable, while "below" one is very replaceable . . . today even by machines! The sociocultural experience of a taxi driver in a one star hotel or in an inexpensive restaurant is dramatically different than a prime minister in a five star hotel or in a very expensive restaurant! One can even find, in the same society, the paradox and apparent "injustice", that "below" there are people who are dying of hunger while "above" there are people who can eat all they want, delicious meals in the best restaurants, that might even be too much for their good health!

To conclude, one can say that Life, Love, Creativity, Understanding, Peace, Justice, Freedom, Self-Expression, Health, Happiness, and the "Joie de Vivre" can only be found "above", in the higher states of consciousness, in "Paradise", and never "below", in the lower states of consciousness, in "Hell"! Hence, the *fundamental choice,* the most important thing in all situations, is always that of *knowing how and being able to* **climb higher,** towards Paradise where the Self and God can be found together with all that one could ever desire or dream of. Likewise, to avoid many dangers, difficult situations, and disasters, one must learn how to "fly like the birds" higher always higher! This is the true wisdom, the "key to the art of living in our times" when we are now discovering the "keys of Heaven and Hell", the opening of the unconscious and the superconscious.

It is also here that one shall find the authentic solution to all the great human problems-the problems of religion, science, philosophy, as well as those of morality, politics, economics, medicine, and education—of all that is truly fundamental and essential in the consciousness and life of a human being. For everything is, in ultimate analysis, a *function of our level of consciousness and of our level of being*. This is the reason that, in human life, we find so many paradoxes, contradictions, seeming injustices, and no real and effective "shortcuts". . . but a long journey inside of ourselves towards the top of our "Sky Scraper" where the Self, the Divine Spark, the Living Christ await us!

One of the great "Gifts of Heaven" and certainly the most important treasure, or "wealth" I have found in this world, has been to meet and to interact with a very wide number of human beings who "cover" most of the "human spectrum". Thus, I met "ordinary people" of various countries and cultures, but also criminals, idiots, and insane people at the "bottom of the scale" and Geniuses, Saints, and Spiritually-Awakened Persons at the "top of the scale". One thing that struck me in all these encounters, and which I noted several times in my diary, was the enormous diversity of their perceptions, conceptions, and definitions of reality, of the world, of human beings, and of the various human problems. I was so "impressed" that I wrote a book, *Spiritual Man in the Modern World,* to try to explain and make sense of this incredible diversity.

Even though we are all living on the same earth and world of matter, it is now quite clear to me that there are people who "come from and live in worlds" that are very, very *different* and who, therefore, have a very different system of values, priorities, desires and "points of reference". It is this realization that made me finally understand the famous Platonic analogy that there are human beings who have "gold", "silver", "bronze", and "iron" in their "hearts". That is, that there are people whose basic values and most important desires are quite different, if not **opposed.** Thus, some seek *knowledge* and the *love of God* above all (those who have "gold" in their "hearts"); some seek *power* (those who have "silver" in their "hearts"); and others seek *security* (those who have "bronze" in their "hearts") or *pleasures* (those who have "iron" in their hearts"). It is the insight and the image of "Man the Sky Scraper" which helped me to understand, **rationally,** these differences as well as to understand the paradoxes, antinomies, contradictions, and conflicts that, more and more, confront the citizens of the "Global Village". They are absolutely *essential* for a true understanding of human beings who find themselves on different levels of consciousness and being.

Another basic principle concerning this insight is the following: people who are on higher levels of consciousness and being can always "descend" and understand those who are on "lower levels" by making efforts and lowering their "lights", "vibrations", and "levels of consciousness". On the other hand, those who are on a "lower level of consciousness and being" *cannot* "rise" and "understand" those who are on a "higher level" (if not temporarily, for a brief moment, being "pulled up", as it were, by the presence and the "radiations" of people who are on "higher levels"). To illustrate this principle, I will tell you the story of a couple of real and concrete situations that I have personally lived.

Once I met a boy who was a "petty thief" who lived and helped his family by what he could "take" or "steal" from others. After some time, we developed a friendship and talked a great deal. Often he would ask me, in all confidence, why I never tried to "take things from him" or from others, and, especially, why I **gave** things away, made presents, and never expected anything in return. For him, this was totally *incomprehensible.* One day, he even told **me,** with an incredible archetypal and symbolic meaning, "it's as though I was an inhabitant of the earth and you of the sun"! Now the basic, most fundamental tendency of the "earth" is to *take* while that of the "sun" is to *give* and to *radiate.* The first is, also, the basic tendency of the personality while the second is the essential tendency of the "individuality" or of the "Soul". . . whence we have the great paradox and contradiction between "egoism" and "altruism"

. . . two basic and opposed tendencies that one finds, in different degrees, in all people.

The other story is the following. I met and became friends with a man and a woman who came from very prominent families and who had great wealth. Both were very drawn to, and interested by, spirituality and, therefore, spiritual teachings and the "esoteric" dimension. Moreover, both were at the level of consciousness and being that I call "that of the Disciple", of the "Great Turning Point", "Metamorphosis", or "Conversion". Both had travelled a great deal throughout the world. They had the means, the times, and the "social contacts" to meet all the people they were most interested in, including clairvoyants, healers, gurus, nobel prize winners, and internationally recognized "Saints". When we got to know each other better and had reached a certain level of intimacy and complicity, both of them asked me: Do truly "spiritually awakened persons", with exceptional powers, knowledge, goodness and creativity really exist? And if so, where are they and how can we meet them? For all the people we have met, who should have been in that category, really were not, and were, basically, "ordinary people" with a little more vitality, intelligence, courage, and ambition . . . or obsession! These two people who were so "cosmopolitan", with so much money, opportunities, and social contacts were, deep down, disillusioned, sad, and basically *skeptical*. Why and how can one explain this?

To me, in the light of the image of "Man the Sky Scraper", the answer is quite simple and logical: *they sought in the world that which they first had to discover and activate in **themselves**!* That is, they remained blocked on a certain level, or "floor" and perceived and interpreted EVERYTHING on the level of this "floor" . . . even people who could, indeed, have been "authentic" and "superior" . . . but who remained an undecipherable enigma, and who did not unveil, or manifest, their superior nature, knowledge, and capacities. And it is here that we find the deeper meaning of the biblical saying: "Do not throw pearls before swines"; that is, that we can only truly understand that which is on our level, or "floor", that which is "below", but not that which is "above", or on a "higher floor". Once we have really understood the great "discovery", or "conclusion", of modern physics: That everything, absolutely EVERYTHING, in our universe (that is, the entire reality knowable by human beings) is VIBRATION, ENERGY, and LIGHT vibrating on *different frequencies,* then we shall really grasp and understand this great "arcana" of the sacred traditions. In other words, that we can "perceive correctly" and "truly understand" *only that which is found on our level, or "floor" of human consciousness and being.*

Once we accept the new/old conception of human nature as being *four* and not *three* basic "ages", or levels of maturity, (the biological, emotional, mental, and *spiritual* age), then we shall realize and accept, logically and naturally, that there are human beings *on different levels of consciousness and being* . . . and that reality is something quite different for them, corresponding to their specific "level". And then we shall be able to develop a differential anthropology, psychology, and sociology of each "type", with characteristics that are peculiar to their level to "perceive, conceive, define, and react" to the *same situation* in their own specific ways. Taking as basic "point of reference" the three "royal functions of the psyche", *willing, thinking*, and *feeling*, and the 7 Chackras of the Eastern Spiritual Traditions, I have attempted to set up a tentative "hierarchy of human beings" on 7 different levels of consciousness and being.

In our personality, or "lower self", we find a certain activity and expression of these three functions as we find them again, but transformed, at the level of the "individuality", or "Higher Self". Between the personality and the individuality, we find the psychospiritual Center of the Heart. It is truly the "opening", "activation", and "awakening" of the "Heart Center" which constitutes the great "Passage", "Initiation", or "transformation" from being a "slave to the personality and its desires" to being the "master of ourselves and of our destiny", and from living in the "world of illusions" to living in the "world of eternal Reality". Likewise, when we look at the "Chackras" of the Eastern Traditions, we discover that the first three chackras govern our instincts and survival impulses at the physical, emotional, and mental levels; while the last three govern the expression of the Divine Wisdom, Love, and Will. And it is at the level of the fourth chackra, or Heart Center, that we find the great "passage" or "transformation" from the moral, human, and egoistical ("geotropic") dimension to the immortal, spiritual, and altruistic (heliotropic") one.

Starting from the bottom up, I would set up the following tentative "hierarchy" and set of correspondences:

1. First chackra: human will, instincts, impulsions—*primitive persons.*
2. Second chackra: human emotions, desires, egoism—*ordinary persons.*
3. Third chackra: human thoughts, egoism—*talented persons.*
4. Fourth chackra: Heart Center, Love Initiation, passage from the "rule of the personality" to the "rule of the individuality"—*true disciples* of the authentic spiritual schools and Masters.
5. Fifth chackra: spiritually illuminated thoughts—*Geniuses.*

6. Sixth chackra: spiritually illuminated emotions—*Saints*.
7. Seventh chackra: spiritually illuminated will—*true Masters*.

As all functions of the psyche and, in particular, the "three royal ones" are *functions of the level of consciousness and being* of the person who utilizes them, it follows, logically, that there are *seven types of human beings* who constitute the "natural hierarchy" of the world of matter. Each of these will, therefore, perceive, conceive, define, and react in a *qualitatively* different way to all human conditions and situations. In other words, this means that we will have, logically, *7 qualitatively different ways* of perceiving, conceiving, defining, and reacting to religion, politics, economics; to understand and express knowledge, love, and will; to perceive and react to illnesses, accidents, injustices, suffering, and the manyfold experiences of life on earth. Moreover, we will also have 7 qualitatively different hierarchies of values and moral principles. For example, on the level of the first chackra, there is an "iron rule" whereby everything, without exceptions, is immediately related to one's body, instincts, desires, and interests; while on the level of the seventh chackra there is also an "iron rule" whereby everything, without exceptions, is immediately related to the Self, to God, to the "Common Good". This because "below", we perceive and define ourselves as our "physical body", while "above", we perceive and define ourselves as the "Self" which manifests through the bodies and the souls of all human beings.

"Primitive, ordinary, and talented persons" correspond to the "Work of Nature", to the stage of the "infant, the child, and the adolescent" in the human life cycle, while "Geniuses, Saints, and Masters" correspond to the "Work of Art", to the stage of the "adult, the mature person, and the old person". To reach these levels, human cooperation, conscious evolution, serious work, where each person practices "personality" and "Soul" "sculpture", are necessary because, without the conscient and focused use of our will, thoughts, and feelings, it is impossible to reach the higher levels. As for the "Disciples", they represent the "Great Passage", the "Initiation of the Heart", where the "center of gravity" of the person passes from the personality to the individuality, and where instinctive and natural "egoism" becomes conscious and voluntary "altruism".

The "primitive person" is driven and ruled by its instincts or impulses. He has not acquired self-knowledge or self-mastery and is, therefore, always in conflict with his environment to satisfy his primary needs. Biological survival is the crucial "evolutionary task" for him. At his level is the "law of the jungle", "Might is Right" which predominates. Suffering, pain, and fear are his "masters" and govern his evolution. He learns by "trial and error" and he "pays" for his "mistakes" by *physical pain*. Here, "corporal punishment" plays a fundamental role at the level of "communication"—it is the only thing that these people truly understand.

The "ordinary person" is driven and ruled primarily by his emotions. He, too, does not have a true knowledge and mastery of himself to become the "captain of his own ship and destiny". He is manipulated by others through his own emotions. Here, it is *emotional survival* which is essential and connected with the second chackra. Here, it is passionate and egoistical love, the "falling in love" that is the most "real" and important experience. The "ordinary person": feels controlled and "shaped" by society, his superiors, and the institutions to which he belongs—his family, his church, his work, and his political party. The center of his aspirations and primary values are to satisfy his primary needs—eating, sleeping, having a family, affection, discretionary time, as well as material and emotional security.

The "talented person" is driven and ruled by his thoughts and by his ego. He also does not have a real self-knowledge and self-mastery, but he thinks he has them! By his reason and his will, he thinks he can "make his way in life", become an "important person", and actualize himself and his desires through competition. He always perceives life and society in dualistic terms: rich/poor, winners/losers, happy/unhappy persons. He is the person who has reached a certain "actualization and integration" of his personality. He "knows what he wants" and he knows "effective means to get what he wants". He possesses authentic talents and abilities . . . but he remains egoistical and egocentric—ruled by his personality and its three primordial instincts: biological survival linked with the first chackra, emotional survival linked with the second chackra, and social/egoic survival linked with the third chackra.

He is the person who has reached the maximum point of personal development, the culminating point of the personality wherein a person wants to "know" and to "dominate" society and the world to realize himself . . . and to live the "good life" on earth. It is the last stage before reaching the "Great Passage", the true "Conversion"—the "death of the ego" to reach the "birth of the Soul". It is in this category that we generally find the political, economic, industrial, and religious leaders. It is also here that we can find the scientists, the artists, the physicians, and the educators who have made a "name for themselves".

The authentic "Disciples" are those who have reached the "opening of the fourth chackra", the "opening of the Heart"; who have gone beyond the "center of attraction of the personality and of the "human self"—of the "earth"—to enter under the "center of attraction of the Soul" and of the "Spiritual Self"—of the "Sun". These are the people who have lived, or are living, the true "Initiation", the "death" and "resurrection", the total and radical transformation of their values, goals, and wills. And it is at this stage that every person will live the "to be or not to be" of Shakespeare where everything must be reevaluated and redefined—to live through and for the "human self" or through and for the "Spiritual Self".

It is also at this stage that one encounters the "Great Crisis", or "Metamorphosis of personal identity": Who am I? Where do I come from and where am I going? Why have I come on earth and what must I do here? Finally, it is also here that the true manifestation of God, "Revelation", or "Theophany" occurs. Up to this stage, human beings really create "gods in their own images". . . who change and transform themselves with the expansion of their consciousness-as they are a function of their level of consciousness and being. Up to this stage, therefore, we really have "idolatry", the "confusion of reality with its images", and the projection of one's own "ideas and phantasms" upon reality, but not reality *itself.* Up to this stage, religion is, and can only be, *exoteric:* God, Tradition, and Authority are apprehended and conceived as being *outside* rather than *inside* of oneself. Hence, up to this point, prayer remains intellectual, egoic, "dead", and "ineffective" . . . to become then, beyond this point, "spiritual", "coming from the Self", "living" and "effective". . . capable of producing "miracles". In other words, the "Disciple" dies to his own ego, to the phenomena, illusions, and "charm of the world". . . to be reborn to noumena, to reality, to the "Real World" . . . where we are all "brothers" and "sisters", connected one to the other, and "One" in the deepest sense of this word.

It is perhaps because many people, born at the end of W.W. II, were able to enter the stage of the "Disciple" that we reached what has been termed the "age of anxiety", at the "age of insecurity", the "age of the crisis of trust", of the almost total rejection of society and of the "establishment" on the part of many people who were struggling between the two basic influences-that of the personality and that of the individuality. They aspired to something better without, *yet,* being able to realize it. The "Hippies" were a good example of that.

"Geniuses" are persons who function at the level of the fifth chackra and who have become the "channels", or "instruments", to manifest and radiate the Light and the Wisdom of God in the world . . . or, at least, *in part.* Here, thinking, reason, and one's thoughts reflect now God's consciousness or, at least, the "Higher Consciousness" and no longer those of the "human self" with its limited and egoic perceptions of the world and of the Self.

"Saints" are persons who function on the level of the sixth chackra and who have become the "channels", or "instruments", to manifest and radiate Spiritual Fire and the Love of God in the world . . . or, at least, *in part*. Here, feelings, desires, and emotions now reflect God's consciousness or, at least, the "Higher Consciousness" and no longer those of the "human self" with its limited and egoic feelings and desires. The Love they express and radiate is a universal, impersonal, and "efficacious" love in the sense that it enables the loved ones to *grow*, to develop, to actualize their potentialities . . . and not to satisfy the "caprices of their ego" or to bring a temporary "well-being" based on gratified desires and wishes . . . which is, generally, the case with human, egoic, love.

"Saints" are true "generators" and "radiators" of "Love Vitamins" at their highest level, which manifest as an inexhaustible source of healing, generosity, elevation, encouragement, and "vivification" for human beings in a world where . . . true love is rarer and more precious than gold!

"True Masters", Who are extremely rare on our planet, are persons who function at the level of the seventh chackra and Who have become coordinated and perfected "Temples" to manifest God's Will, the true Will of the Self—His Creative Energies—on earth. They are the only persons, on earth, Who have succeeded in integrating perfectly Wisdom, Love, and Creative Energies in their own consciousness and being. It is in this way that they can act as the "representatives" and the "transformers" of the Divine Will, Energies, and Attributes in all the *Worlds of Creation* (or, at least, at the human level and on earth!).

They are the persons Who "know themselves" and Who have achieved the true "control and mastery of their consciousness and being", Who are, therefore, fully *reintegrated* and Who have succeeded in completing their growth and in fulfilling their destiny on earth. Now, it is the Christ Who thinks, feels, wills, speaks, and acts in Them and through Them. Liberated from the "chains of destiny" and of "necessity", They are free to accomplish, *consciously* and *fully*, the mission They have chosen in this world and what God has entrusted to Them. If They live for a certain period of times amongst us, it is because They have freely chosen and willed it . . . to accomplish a task that Divinity has conferred upon Them.

They can incarnate and operate everywhere, in all races, religions, countries, and civilizations . . . and live the "ordinary life" of an "ordinary person"; all the while being permanently aligned with the Light, the Fire, and the Creative Energies of the Spirit . . . which They manifest and radiate in the world. Like Jesus, Who is Their archetype and prototype in the world of matter, They represent and offer us a **LIVING MODEL** of the human being who has reached his perfection and the complete realization of his being. . . something which we shall **ALL BE,** one day, when we shall have completed our "Pilgrimage" in the world of matter.

Once we truly grasp and understand the fundamental insight and image of "Man the Sky Scrape", then we will have a great KEY, and ESSENTIAL KEY, to work upon and transform our *personality* and the *world*. That is, instead of seeking *outside of one's self,* in the world, in others, that which is truly **essential**; one can begin *right away,* to look for it *in one's self* by PURIFYING, CONSECRATING, and UNITING THE FIELD OF CONSCIOUSNESS WITH THE SUPERCONSCIOUS, THE HUMAN WITH THE SPIRITUAL SELF! Because this is the one and only way in which we shall ever find God, the Self, the Ultimate Reality, together with the true Masters, Teachers, or Superior Beings Who will then *manifest to our consciousness and perceptions!* For, should we not find Them first *within one's self,* we could never find Them in the world . . . where They exist but where They remain, fatally and ineluctably, "hidden", "invisible", "silent". . . OCCULT!

To better explain and illustrate this great insight and analogy of "Man the Sky Scraper", I would now like to cite a few personal examples that led me to "discover, experience, and appreciate" this profound truth. Perhaps the greatest "lesson" that I learned, concerning the "vertical Axis of consciousness" came to me during periods of great crises in my life when I never thought I could learn something so valuable! A little after my 20th birthday, I went through a terrible motorcycle accident which left me half paralyzed and with all kinds of physical problems (pains, tensions, limitations) and psychological problems (depression, confusion, self-blame, and frustration). Medical authorities, my family, and my friends all perceived and defined this situation as a "great catastrophe and tragedy" for me. Hence, I, too, perceived and defined my situation as "something dreadful" so that, in addition to my physical sufferings and limitations, I also suffered a great deal psychologically.

At a certain point, I even concluded that I had three basic choices: End my life, which then appeared to me as a "long series of sufferings and limitations" for me as well as a "heavy burden", economically and psychologically, for my family and my closest friends. Continue to "vegetate" and to seek to make my life as pleasant and secure as possible. Or, *climb unto a higher level of consciousness* which would hold the key to "why this accident occurred to me" and "how I should live it", or "what I should now do with my life". Unconsciously, at first, I set to use the perspective and the methods, I had already learned from several persons, to *climb to a higher level of consciousness of being—*to rise to a *higher level.* And it is particularly through the regular use of prayer, physical exercises, meditations and efforts, that I succeeded in "changing floors" and "climbing to a higher level". To a level which enabled me to "reframe my situation, to "accept it", and, later, to heal slowly and fulfill the "deep calling" I felt "swelling in the depths of my consciousness". This was the first time that I had lived a direct experience of the "existence and implications" of ascending or descending on the vertical Axis of consciousness with all of its implications.

In symbolic language, I had found myself "in Hell", that is, in a state in which I suffered, physically and psychologically; in which I was depressed and asked myself "why I had ended up in such a situation"? "What I had done to deserve this"? And, "what I should do about it"? At the time, I had very little hope to really heal and to have a better future. But, little by little, practicing prayer with great intensity, devotion, and concentration, my "state of being" and my "level of consciousness" *changed*. Without being truly able to understand my present situation, I succeeded in "accepting it", in "living with it", and in doing something valuable with my time, energies, and resources. Thus, I read a great deal, I meditated, and I reflected. I met different types of people, some of whom helped me to "reframe" my situation, to perceive it in a new light—I was living a *spiritual test,* a kind of "Initiation" and, specifically, the "Earth Initiation" where the body is broken, where one has to accept handicaps and limitations of a physical nature.

Little by little, through *prayer,* I became consciously aware of the Light and of the Spiritual Energies which, when they manifested to my consciousness and "filled my being", brought me an undescribable *energy* and *joy.* My pains were diminishing and my strength was rising. One fine day, I became aware of the fact that my accident had forced me to "look inside of myself", to "ask Heaven for help", and to learn "how to pray"—that is, to "draw down the Light" so that my consciousness could expand and rise. In fact, without this accident, I would never have learned how to pray and to, thus, discover the Light and the Spiritual Energies-and I would have remained on a "lower level of consciousness". Thus my accident was "transformed" into a "school" for self-learning, into a marvelous "opportunity" to discover things which, otherwise, I would never have even "dreamed of", and to acquire the most important skill of my life-conscious and living *prayer.*

From "hell", I moved, little by little, with various "ascents" and "descents" first to "Purgatory" and then, eventually, to "Heaven". What had been the worst catastrophe now became the "greatest opportunity"—an incredible "trial" and chance to learn and to live the greatest experience of my life to date. This experience helped me to "relativize" all human experiences and to understand that one can perceive and live them on very different levels and with very different meanings. Thus to realize that, in the end, maybe ALL HUMAN EXPERIENCE, even the hardest, the most difficult, and the most "unjust" might well be a "trial", or an "opportunity" to discover, learn, and live things that are very important, even **vital,** for one's own evolution and for the actualization of one's being. This way my first and great "Initiation". . . but not the last.

Having lived this experience, I included prayer in my daily life and I continued praying, whether my life was "easy" or "hard" . . . but, I admit, more when things were hard, when I was in difficulty, or in a "state of crisis". Without realizing this, or calling it by this name, I had discovered and *lived* my first encounter with the "vertical Axis of consciousness" and the possibility of *changing one's consciousness* by "ascending" or "descending" on this Axis.

Thus, I learned that one can perceive, define, and react to ANY HUMAN SITUATION in *very different ways which are a direct function of our level of consciousness and being.* Thus, by changing my level of consciousness, through appropriate techniques, (by climbing to a higher "floor" in terms of the analogy of "Man the Sky Scraper"), I could radically change my perceptions, conceptions, definitions, and reactions to this situation. I could, in other words, "move from Hell to Earth, to Purgatory, and, finally, to Heaven"— perceive this situation as a "terrible catastrophe, reject it, and feel sorry for myself, suffering a great deal emotionally from this, or perceive this same situation as a great "trial" or "spiritual Initiation", accept it, do the best I could under the circumstances, and . . . greatly diminish my psychological suffering.

I remember that, during the first days of another great "test", I had to constantly "guard and protect" my heart (emotions), my imagination, and my thoughts, and, especially, *pray, as often as possible, with the greatest fervor* lest I would easily "fall back" to "Hell", a "state of consciousness", or a "lower floor" where, again, I would greatly suffer. It even happened to me to pass from one state of mind to another, from "hell" to "heaven" within the space of half an hour! Moreover, I quickly learned, this time existentially and experimentally, that it was *prayer,* or a great concentration and projection of my *attention, thoughts,* and *feelings* towards the superconscious and the Divine Spark, which acted as "the buttons of an elevator" to change and raise my level of consciousness. In theory, I already knew this well, but now I was given a chance to personally *live and experience* this—which is something quite different! Not only, but this "imprinted upon my consciousness" the fact that one can always and, almost, **immediately**, change one's state of consciousness, "climb to a higher floor", through work upon oneself and an expression of Love.

Paradoxically, it is when I was "thrown into Hell" that I **experientially** discovered the "keys to Paradise" and that I learned how to operate the "inner elevator" of our "sky scraper, or vertical Axis of consciousness". And this is, perhaps, why it is said that "to go to Heaven" one must first "descend into Hell"! Once one discovers, personally and experientially, this great truth, then a whole universe of new possibilities and of a great "inner work" opens to our awareness and gives new meaning and purpose to our lives on earth. For it is at this point, and at this point only, that one finally understands the great truth, repeated by many people but seldom truly understood, that *the key to reality, to our being, to Life, Love, and Knowledge, as well as Health and Happiness, is to be found INSIDE OF OURSELVES! And* this *"key"*, at least for me, resides in the proper understanding and in the practical application of the insight contained in the "vertical Axis of consciousness".

Obviously, one can wait for a major crisis to "hit", or to hit a loved one, before one discovers this fundamental "key" and begins to pray. But it is well to remember that one can also live through very serious and even "fatal" crises without discovering this "key" and practicing prayer. The wisest and most prudent solution is, doubtlessly, to immediately "enter the school of prayer" and to subject oneself to a psychospiritual discipline, as well as to learn, theoretically and experientially, the great truth and principle that lay behind the analogy of "Man the Sky Scraper" and the insight of the "vertical Axis of consciousness". Because this is the only way to truly "open oneself fully to Life", with all of its joys and sorrows, trials and adventures; to say a big "YES" to Life, without accepting the part that we find pleasant and rejecting the part we find unpleasant; and to LIVE WITHOUT FEAR!

It is the discovery and use of the "Philosopher's Stone" which enables us to live WITHOUT FEAR and, at the very heart of this "Stone", it is the "vertical Axis of consciousness" that we find, expressed in words, symbols, and analogies that change and differ, but which always point to the same great truth. My hope and prayer is that you can make YOURS this truth and principle, through your own efforts and experiences, that they may bring Peace and Joy to you. And that they may "exorcize", once and forever, the greatest "Devil" of all times . . . **FEAR** (which results from the lack of FAITH which, in turn, is the consequence of a "low level of consciousness"). Once that you will have understood and lived this, the Earth, Life, and Joy, in all their complexity, diversity, grandeur, and glory **WILL BE YOURS!**

Health and Disease, Sin and Salvation in the Coming Age

In the coming Age, and already *today,* we are witnessing a closer and closer connection and relationship between *health* and *spirituality.* For the body is truly a "mirror of the psyche" as the psyche can be a mirror for the Soul. Thus, as we realize that nothing, absolutely *nothing,* happens by chance, or hazard, and that everything has a cause, a meaning, and a purpose, whatever happens to our body or to our psyche has a cause, a reason, and a meaning. The logic is inescapable: either the universe and life are ruled by chance and hazard, or by laws and harmony, and if they are ruled by law and harmony, then nothing can happen to us by simple "accident" . . . and certainly not a serious "disease" or "accident".

The first serious and genuine step towards spirituality involves *healing*—our holistic health—as the early Christians and all candidates to genuine spiritual Initiation well know. For "health" is inner "harmony", or "ease" with the laws of nature and of God (Nature being the *immanent,* or unconscious, *aspect of God and Humanity* being the *conscious* aspect), just as disease is "disharmony", or "lack of ease". But, true health is a lot more than "Mens sana in corpore sano", than a healthy mind in a healthy body, just as disease is a lot more than pain and dysfunctions in various physical organs, or in our psyche.

A great "paradigm shift", or transformation, is also in the process of taking place in medicine, and in our very conception of health, illness, and therapy. Thus far, we have taken a "piscean", or dualistic view, of health and disease: health is good and disease is bad, just as we defined joy as good and suffering as bad. And yet each has a place, a function, and a meaning that is, ultimately, for . . . our own good and evolution.

The first and perhaps greatest "breakthrough" and "new discovery" of this new "state of consciousness', or "paradigm shift", is that disease, like suffering, has *two faces:* a constructive and a destructive, a positive and a negative face and aspects. Thus, we can also (and will) live sickness as something positive, as another opportunity to grow, to learn, and to improve something. We will learn to "accept, live, and experience" illness as a "friend", as an "initiatory way"—as bringing to us an important message. The message that we must change something in our lives, that we cannot go on the way we are going. Sickness, in other words, functions as an "alarm system", requiring attention and action, as well as a form of "invitation" to move on to a higher and better level.

Today, the whole medical profession, just as the clergy, are presently going through a major crisis, a true redefinition of its very *identity* and distinctive *function*. Human consciousness is expanding, vibrations and energies are "rising" and the basic "rules" or health and disease are changing.

Until very recently, the official "allopathic" medicine of the West has been *scientific* (read, materialistic and rationalistic) rather than truly "empirical", i.e. based upon direct observation and personal experience), *analytical* (i.e. specializing more and more), *therapeutic* (removing problems once they occurred), *monopolistic* (driving out all other, competing "alternative" or "traditional" forms of medicine), and focused on *removing symptoms* rather than changing the *causes!* It has been essentially *passive* (i.e. having the patient "take the pills", undergo surgery, or follow a given therapy) rather than examine and change his dysfunctional attitudes, life, or relationships. And it has been, fundamentally, a medicine of the *physical body*.

The new, emerging medical paradigm is quite different! It is "scientific" in the sense of truly taking observation and experience as its final court of appeal, *"holistic"* in terms of "looking at the whole person within the context his *entire* life", "preventive" in the sense of educating people to understand the laws of life and health rather than curing the ill, "inclusive" in the sense of working together with many different but complementary approaches, and focused at getting at the level of the "causes" rather than merely suppressing the symptoms. It is also *active* in the sense of requiring the patient to examine his life, to change his dysfunctional attitudes, behaviors, and relationships, and to undergo a "reframing", or "conversion", which will deal with the true causes of the problem. And it is becoming, more and more, a *medicine of the "energy bodies"* rather than of the *physical body*.

The first major qualitative step was taken with the so-called "psychosomatic" medicine which saw, and dealt with, a very close connection and interrelationship between the body and the psyche, where negative thoughts, feelings, and energies would create psychological and physical illnesses. Now, we are almost coming around "full circle" and, again, looking for *spiritual causes* for the whole range of human illnesses—hence the rediscovered connection between health and spirituality.

272

Another "core insight" is that of the "repression of the sublime", namely that, if a person does not resolve the "enigma of the Sphinx", the problem of *identity,* and rejects his higher energies and inspirations, he will fall sick and lose his "ease". If people do not do what they have come to do in this world—if they repress the "voice of their Soul", of their Divine Spark, they will lose their "harmony" and develop various symptoms. Rather than "missing the boat altogether' and wasting the time, energies, and opportunities of the present incarnation, *energy is increased,* or withdrawn, and "pressure" is applied by the Soul to create *enough discomfort and tension,* that the person will pay attention and, perhaps, change direction and course of action—so that the fundamental purpose of this life can still be achieved.

While Freud saw religion as an "infantile neurosis" to be outgrown, Jung saw it as an indispensable element for one's own growth, health, and individuation. The old medicine was, basically, *a one-dimensional* medicine, while the new medicine is a *multidimensional* one. Here, an entirely new question which is now being raised is that of the "connection" and "flow through" between the various planes (e.g. from the spiritual to the mental, from the mental to the astral, from the astral to the etheric, and from the etheric to the physical plane, and vice versa). My basic intuition and position here is that the proper and healthy function of the higher vehicle has a *positive* and a *causal* effect on the workings of the lower ones, but not vice versa! That is, a healthy spiritual body, filled with life and harmony, can heal the mental, astral, etheric, and physical body (if the connections are made and the channels are "open"), but a healthy and vital physical body cannot heal and realign the etheric, astral, mental, and spiritual bodies.

As soon as we are truly considering a medicine of the "energy-bodies", then many of the old, traditional approaches, such as homeopathy, acupuncture, and laying-on-of-hands begin to make new and a lot more sense! So does prayer, ritual, and spiritual healing, which are, essentially, *vibrational* and *energy* medicines . . . and religion and spirituality reacquire their basic therapeutic nature and role. This new conception also assumes that health involves growth and evolution—*dynamism*—rather than homeostasis and equilibrium—maintaining the status quo. And that any basic threat or block to the growth and evolution of the person, as well as any major frustration of the will and "loss of meaning" would, in themselves, be pathogenic and causes for diseases.

Having defined our basic premises and established a general "theoretical framework" to look at "health and disease" at the end of the 20th century, I will now attempt to define these key terms, as well as the essential principles and means necessary to preserve or restore "health". Let us begin with "health" and ask ourselves what is "health"? Health is simply the proper "alignment", or "connection" between all of the "bodies" (the 7 vehicles of Life and Consciousness of a fully actualized human being) of a person and his or her spiritual Self. It is the ability to know, be and express one's full and greater Self on *all planes of being*—which implies the right functioning of each body and the right connection between all "bodies". In functional terms, it is what the Greeks called "Harmonia", and the early Christians "Peace". Moreover, this condition is not *static,* based on "homeostasis", but "dynamic" and based on growth, evolution, and self-actualization.

On the *physical level,* health involves *physical strength,* coordination, and the ability of our biological organism to do what we ask of it without pain or strain. On the *emotional level,* it involves *courage,* looking forward to the "day ahead" and all of its challenges; and actually being eager to live, to face challenges and adventures, and to express oneself, discovering and realizing one's true nature. On the *mental level,* it involves a *clear perception and understanding* of what is in the world and in oneself—to make sense of one's daily experience. It means to have a clear, perceptive, and effective mind, which is the opposite of confusion! On the *spiritual level,* it involves the proper functioning of our intuition, inspiration, and discernment. It means to "know" and to "want to do" God's Will, the Will of the Divine Spark, rather than that of the ego or the "human self". It also means FAITH, in the double, technical meaning of:

a. Having hope in a better future, the realization that everything has a meaning and a purpose which are, ultimately, "good" and "working for our own growth and self-actualization", and that God is aware of, and working through, the universe and ourselves.

b. Being able to focus and express our will (through concentration), our thinking (through meditation) and our feelings (through devotion). This means to be able to direct to a specific point (in ourselves or in the world) all of our attention and creative energies, all of our love and emotions, and all of our knowledge and ideas.

When we take all of these aspects and dimensions together, on all planes, "health" then means "la joie de vivre", the joy of being alive, the ability to be and express oneself fully and consciously, and to "consciously speed up" and complete our evolution and destiny. In one sentence, it simply means *being what we are meant to* be . . . which can only be fully realized when we have achieved "union with God", or the proper "alignment" and "integration" of the human with the spiritual Self!

What is "disease" or pathology? It is simply the opposite, or the lack of, "health" and of what we have defined as faith. It is first and foremost being a stranger to one's self, being cut off from the spiritual Self—being an "alien" . . . to one's self (which, interestingly enough, is the true *etymological* meaning of "disaster"). It is not knowing who we are, where we come from, where we are going, and why we are here; why certain things happen to us, what we should do, and what God and Life expect from us! It is to have lost our "Peace", our "Harmony", our very Self . . . and thus grace, or Light and Life! It is being separated from God and from our Divine Spark!

On the *physical* level, disease involves an "energy-weakness", a dysfunction, tension, or breakdown of one or more organs, or systems of organs, which may or may not involve pain. In any case, it implies that the biological organism is not functioning and thus cannot be utilized as it normally would. On the *emotional* level, it involves fear, anxiety, tension, suffering, and an emotional "roller-coaster" which has gotten out of control, conditioning adversely our consciousness and behavior. It also implies ceasing to "love ourselves", and ceasing to love life with its challenges and adventures—the desire to "run away", "fall asleep", and avoid daily experience. It may imply becoming ruled by, or addicted to, compulsive self-destructive behavior or patterns (alcohol, drugs, sex, gambling, eating, or destructive relationships). Behind all of these "symptoms", it may also involve a "short-circuit" within our "Heart Center", our astral body, and the inner flow of the life-forces.

On the *mental* level, it involves *confusion,* a blurred perception of reality and of our experiences in the world and within ourselves, and a lack of understanding what is happening, why this is happening, and what we should do about it. This "cognitive darkness" and confusion can lead us to make costly mistakes, perpetuating dysfunctional patterns, and becoming passive and demoralized—"lost" or "cut adrift on the sea of life". On the *spiritual* level, it means being cut off from our higher Self, from our inner Source of intuition and inspiration, from the very inner "Spring" of Life, Love, and Knowledge. It is truly being "disgraziato", as the Italians say—etymologically, "cut off from grace or the spiritual Light". It manifests as lack of faith, despair, imbalance, and separation.

Moreover, while the spiritual Self and the spiritual bodies cannot be "sick" in themselves, they can be "short-circuited", "separated from", or "disaligned", "cut off" from the other vehicles, or "bodies", of the personality. It is this "separation" or "short-circuit" which constitutes the essence of "'disease" or pathology. So long as

275

Grace, Light, or spiritual Energies can flow through our vehicle and reach the human self, or ego, we may, indeed, be limited, restricted, deprived of something important, or experience pain, but we will never fall into the emotional, mental, and spiritual "darkness" of not knowing what is happening and what we should do, and into the agony of despair and utter confusion.

Thus *healing,* true, holistic, and complete healing always involves "working down the planes" from the spiritual to the physical level. It involves re-establishing the "link" and proper alignment between the spiritual and the human self and between the Soul and the personality. This so that the Light and the spiritual Energies can flow freely between them in an "open circuit", recreating and harmonizing each body, on its own level and through its own laws. Hence, it does use conventional medicine (allopathy) as well as alternative therapies (naturopathy, homeopathy, acupuncture, etc.) and psychic and spiritual healing (laying-on-of hands, praying, and visiting Sanctuaries).

It is interesting to note that the Great Work, just as true Religion, has two essential aims: *to heal the sick and to enlighten those who are in darkness* so that, by degrees, human consciousness may be changed and exalted, and, through this expansion of consciousness, a person may first become aware of and then unite with the Spirit within. The most complete and effective series of *spiritual* exercises put together for that purpose is the Divine Liturgy, or Mass, and the older Healing Service in the Catholic Traditions.

Both the Mass and the Healing Service operate as an integrated series of *psychospiritual exercises and operations to* heal the sick, to enlighten the ignorant, and to bring more Light to us so as to cause a *change and an expansion in our consciousness.* But they do it in a different manner and with a different emphasis. The Mass focusing primarily on *spiritual enlightenment,* by Communing with Christ, and secondarily on healing our various sicknesses. The Healing Service focusing primarily on *healing,* through the operation of the spiritual Light, and secondarily on enlightenment. The first being a "preliminary step" for the second, and the second the true culmination of the first.

In terms of "sequence", we could say that the Healing Service precedes and is a "preparatory step" for the Mass, which is why the former is celebrated on *Saturdays* while the latter on *Sundays.* These two major rituals, however, should be seen as being inwardly related and complementary to each other. The first aiming at bringing the sick to the level where true spiritual enlightenment and growth can begin, and the second aiming at taking those who are "well" and "normal' to evolve and grow more rapidly to a higher or spiritual level. For those who are interested in the social sciences, there is a slight parallel between psychoanalysis and psychotherapy aiming at healing psychopathology, at reintegrating the individual's psyche, and at enabling that individual to adapt to, and cope with, his social milieu . . . and existential psychology and "height psychology" which aim at leading the individual to the fullest possible realization of his or her human potentialities.

Briefly put, the Healing Service aims at healing *all of our diseases and deficiencies, and at making us* **whole human beings.** This it does through PSYCHOSPIRITUAL OPERATIONS involving *our human efforts,* the theurgic work of the Officiant, and the Light, Consciousness, and Energy transformations of the Healing Angels that are present, the cosmo-telluric energies of the Sanctuary, and the *free outpouring of Divine Light*—which is the curative agent in this process. For, in ultimate analysis, the work of the Angels, of the Officiant, and of the individual, together with the energies of the Sanctuary, all aim at OPENING CHANNELS FOR, AND AMPLIFYING OUR SENSITIVITY TO, *THE DIVINE LIGHT* that is invoked and that flows from the Altar and from our own Tree of Life.

The operations of the Healing Service are neither a purely material nor a purely spiritual process but a *psychospiritual one;* they do not involve physiological exercises or transformations, but a *transformation of human consciousness.* For it is through such an alternation and expansion of human consciousness that these psychospiritual operations affect both the physical and the psychospiritual processes of our being, and that they are projected unto the psychic atmosphere of the place where we operate. The Healing Services of the Catholic Traditions do contain, in their operations, and make available to the individual, the famed PANACEA, the universal "medicine" capable of healing, by degrees and in time, ALL HUMAN DISEASES. Let us now continue our esoteric analysis and explanation by asking the following questions: What kind of diseases can human beings fall prey to? What is the Panacea and how does it operate? And who, and in what manner, do the Healing Services heal?

A. *What kind of diseases can human beings fall prey to?* Human diseases are almost as many and as varied as are human beings themselves. Yet they do fall into certain broad categories which can be easily classified. These are:

1. Physical diseases.
2. Emotional diseases.
3. Mental diseases.
4. Spiritual diseases.

5. Diseases that prevent us from coping with our normal tasks in life and with coping with "reality" as it is socially defined.
6. Malfunctioning, stresses, and tendencies that will eventually result in diseases that will make us unable to cope with our normal tasks in life.
7. Immaturity, incompleteness, and "blindness" that prevent our spiritual Self from manifesting Itself and our whole nature from being, on the material plane, what it is on the spiritual planes and what it could and will be.

At the core of all diseases, we find precisely what the very etymology of the word implies: a *dis-ease,* a "lack of harmony", a break and disruption in the alignment of our various vehicles and their faculties, and the divine Spark. To heal on all levels, therefore, implies *restoring that harmony, that proper alignment between the divine Spark and Its vehicles . . .* which is what true spiritual "harmony", or the "Peace that passeth human understanding" really is.

Let us take an example from the physical plane. Should a block, stress, or injury prevent the circulation of blood, of lymph, and of nervous energy, the organs and cells that remain "cut off" would begin to "fall sick", that is, to cease their proper operations and eventually to decay. In order to perform these functions, to remain vital and alive, they must remain *properly aligned with the rest of the organism,* or "in harmony with the body".

Let us now move onto the level of the emotions and of the mind. Here, again, we find the same principle at work. Psychopathology is, essentially, DISSOCIATION, dissociation of cognition and affect, of affect and conation, and of cognitive and conation; or it is the dissociation between the subjective and the objective levels of reality—between what one is and what one claims to be, between what one says and what one does, so that the lower elements end up by ruling the higher, thus breaking up the proper ¢hierarchy" or "linkage" of levels. And what is dissociation if not *disharmony, a* break or disruption in the integration of the psyche?

Let us now look at the *ethical* question. What is "evil" if not "unbalanced forces", misapplied energies? And what are these if not, again, a lack of harmony, or true "peace", and of proper "alignment"? Finally, on the spiritual level, we do not have diseases proper but, rather, *blindness,* or the inability for the Spirit to express Itself, to manifest Its attributes, and Its Life-giving force. And this, once again, can be seen as a lack of proper integration between man's various vehicles, between his various human faculties and his spiritual Self.

If disease is a "disharmony", a "break in the proper alignment" of man's vehicles and of their systems, then healing is, essentially, *the restoration of that harmony, the achievement of Peace, or the re-alignment and proper coordination of man's bodies, their faculties, and the divine Spark.* In that manner, and in that manner alone, can spiritual, mental, emotional, and physical diseases be truly HEALED; malfunctioning, stresses, and tendencies that would, eventually, result in disease be corrected in time; and immaturity, incompleteness, and blindness be made "whole".

B. *What is the Panacea and how does it operate?* The Panacea, or universal medicine, is the DIVINE WHITE LIGHT OF THE SPIRIT! Its basic modalities and expressions are the following:

1. It operates by flowing down the planes, from the spiritual to the physical, and by restoring harmony, proper alignment, true Peace, and real "psychosynthesis" between man's vehicles, their faculties, and the divine Spark.

2. In order for spiritual Light to flow through a person's being, there must be an *outpouring of Energy from above* answering a *call and longing of human effort from below.* There must be, in other words, an "opening" at the spiritual level an "opening" at the physical level, and a proper "set of channels" at the psychic levels.

3. The path that the spiritual Light follows, in its outpouring from the spiritual to the physical level is that of the Tree of Life where its various "receptors" and "transformers" are the psychic and spiritual Centers or "Sephiroth".

4. It is the Tree of Life in each of us (and its various Centers) that must be activated, "unclogged", balanced, and "lit up" in order for the Light and Life of the Spirit to truly flow through us and heal us at all levels.

5. Technically speaking, this is the *purpose of the Healing Service:* to light up, activate, and coordinate the various Centers on the Tree of Life so that true and lasting healing may ensue on the different planes.

6. Furthermore, this is what each of the prayers, petitions, and formulae of the Healing Service are designed to accomplish—most of the time without even the candidate being aware of what is transpiring on the inner planes!

7. This is why the Head Center (Kether: the point of "spiritual contact"), the Heart Center (Tipphereth: the central "prism" or distributor of Light), and the Feet Center (Malkuth: the point of "physical contact") are so important and why so many prayers and formulae of the Healing Service are designed to stimulate them into activity.

8. This shows us, beautifully, the importance of participating actively in a Healing Service and to "reproduce" the "Service of the Temple" in our own consciousness and Aura: Because the Light must first *flow within oneself* and help must always come first from *within oneself,* from one's divine Spark, before one can be receptive and "open" to the light and Healing which come from without. Should this not happen, the Light projected from the Altar and by the Officiant and the healing Angels, would simply flow *around us* without *penetrating inside of us,* where the alchemical operation, the transmutation and expansion of consciousness, must take place.

9. Finally, this is also why RELAXATION, WHETHER *PHYSICAL* (neuromuscular) or *psychological* (the release of worries, stress, and anxiety) is so important as a prerequisite for *truly effective spiritual work.* . . . For "relaxation" induces a partial expression of true harmony, peace, and of the correct alignment of the vehicles, their faculties, and the divine Spark.

C. *Who, and in what manner, does the Healing Services heal?* In the Temple, in the macrocosm following the lines of the Greater Mysteries, the Divine White Light originates in the Holy Trinity (the Infinite Ocean of Life and Light). Then, it flows through the *Celestial Hierarchies* all the way down to the *two healing Angels* that always minister at all duly "consecrated" Altars (and which are represented by the two icons on each side of the Cross on the Altar). Thus, through the healing Angels and the Officiant, the Light is projected through the Temple and the Tree of Life of all those who are present and participating in the Temple. This takes place on the *visible* and on the *invisible* planes, and is extended to the City, to Nature, and to the *whole world* as a stream of purifying, healing, and elevating energy which is "grounded" by the cosmo-telluric forces of the earth and of the place where the Temple happens to be.

In human consciousness, in the microcosm of our Aura, following the line of the Lesser Mysteries, the divine Light originates in the Head Center (Kether). Then, it flows to the Heart Center (Tipphereth) via Its transformation in the Cheek and Shoulder Centers (Chockmah and Binah, Chesed and Geburah). From there it flows to the Sexual Center (Yesod) via the Hip Centers (Netzach and Hod), and is "grounded" in the Feet Center (Malkuth). On its downward and outward path, the Light heals, vivifies, and reintegrates ALL THAT WHICH IT COMES IN CONTACT WITH—to the extent that receptivity and "openness" to It exists.

In the macrocosm, it reestablishes the "Great Chain of Being"— harmony with the Celestial and terrestrial Hierarchies. In the microcosm, it re-establishes true "psychosynthesis", or the proper alignment of man's vehicles, with their faculties, and the divine Spark. It also blazes open, both in the macrocosm and in the microcosm, a "path", a "ladder of Jacob", through which man and God, the conscious and the superconscious, can be reconnected and fused into ONE.

Each one of us, who is present and participating in the Healing Service, or whose name is mentioned at the Altar, receives JUST AS MUCH LIGHT and, therefore, JUST AS MUCH HEALING, as he or she is *asking for, ready to receive, and able to utilize properly*. Healing, to a greater or lesser extent, can then take place at the spiritual, mental, emotional and even *physical* levels; at the level of "prophylactic intervention", or even at the level of enhancing our *wholeness* and the *growth* and *actualization* of our being. It is not only *we* who are healed but also the City, Nature, and the whole world in which we live, and ALL THOSE WITH WHOM WE COME INTO CONTACT WITH *as our Aura has been filled with LIGHT which it now RADIATES in its turn!*

Sometimes, however, we may not get the specific healing we asked for when asked for it—for this depends on our faith, our destiny, and divine Purpose. Yet, if we pray and participate with all the faith we can muster, SOME HEALING AND HELP WILL ALWAYS COME—be it "no more" than *understanding* and *having the strength to accept our present "illness"* and to see a divine Purpose and valuable lessons to learn in it.

In summary and in conclusion, the Healing Services of the Catholic Traditions can be described as:

1. One of the two most complete, practical, and effective Rituals of the Christian Church, which central aim is HEALING ON ALL PLANES, leading to SPIRITUAL ENLIGHTENMENT.
2. Their operation involves a down-pouring of divine Light answering a "call" and effort from below, which produces a progressive transformation and expansion of human consciousness.
3. They provide:
   a. A complete and well-integrated series of formulae to practice and develop concentration, meditation, and contemplation, as well as a complete series of spiritual exercises.
   b. A practical, safe, and effective method of activating, cleansing, equilibrating, and lighting up the whole Tree of Life.
   c. Hence, they provide a practical, safe, and effective way of altering and expanding human consciousness.

d. A practical and effective way of communing with the spiritual Self, the Christ within.

e. A practical and effective way of obtaining balanced, safe, and integrated HEALING for oneself, for others, and for the world.

f. A practical, safe, and constructive way of coming in contact with the Inner Worlds, the Celestial Hierarchies, the Communion of Saints, and the Brotherhood of the Rosy-Cross.

g. A simple, effective, and safe way of *consciously speeding up* one's spiritual evolution and of actualizing, in an integrated fashion, our most important human and spiritual faculties.

h. A simple, effective, and safe way of applying the teachings of the Spiritual Traditions in one's daily life.

4. They function pretty much as a symphony or a radio set does. The invoked Light comes down through the planes, via the Celestial Hierarchies and the Officiant, in the macrocosm, and through the Tree of Life in the Microcosm, being then, in both cases, "grounded" by the cosmo-telluric energies of the earth and of the Sanctuary. Then, it blends into the collective atmosphere of the Temple and of our Aura (or "Sphere of Sensation"). From there, it is projected unto those whose names are invoked and into the atmosphere of the City, bringing healing and enlightenment to those who "seek it" and who are on the same wave-length". Therefore, it requires our TOTAL PARTICIPATION, which will lead each one of us to make his or her *unique contribution* by adding to the healing "stream" by the refraction of the Light in one's Tree of Life and by "playing his own unique instrument"—his own "Soul-note and frequency"!

One should not forget that Light and Energy also "flow up" from the earth, through the subtle network of cosmo-telluric currents which are channeled by rock and water. This is what explains why there are, indeed, *special places* where Sanctuaries are built (e.g. Chartres, Lourdes, Ste. Anne de Beaupres) sometimes on the very spot where earlier religions also built or had a special Sanctuary of "Holy Place". It is when we have the three-fold juncture of strong and "alive" cosmo-telluric energies, Angelic Presences and Energies, and the *right inner preparation and devotion* of the candidate. . . that the Tree of Life becomes an INCANDESCENT FILAMENT and the Aura filled with Light and Energies. It is then that true healings, conversions, ecstasies, visions, and out-of-the-body experiences take place. . . in the most *natural way!*

Having looked at and analyzed Health and Disease from a spiritual and esoteric viewpoint, let us now do the same with the basic symbols of "Sin" and "Salvation". It should be very clear, at this point, that there is a very deep and intimate connection between *sin and disease* as there is between *healing and salvation*. For it is "sin", or "transgression", both individual and collective, that brings about disease and sickness, just as it is salvation that brings about holistic health.

At the exoteric level, sin is, generally, connected with morality and is seen as "evil" or "bad" as it implies the "transgression" of a divine commandment. God is supposed to "get angry" at sinners and to consign them to hell. At the spiritual and esoteric levels, however, "sin" has little to do with morality, and with conventional morality in particular! It has to do with temporary imperfections which get people to violate universal laws, whether at the physical, at the human, or at the spiritual level . . . and to pay the price! Here, God is not "angry" (an absurdity) nor does He-She consign anyone to "hell" or to "eternal damnation". Being our Father and Source, as well as "unconditional Love", this would also be an absurdity.

When we transgress basic laws and principles (going "across" rather than "with" evolution) we "cut ourselves off" from our Source and our Self, and thus lose Light, Energy, Life. . . and Health! This means that we lose the ability to do "what we want". . . until we "change our ways", "plug back" into the flow of evolution and "pick up" where we "left off". . . or "die" to "start anew". Hence, there is a limit to both "sin" and "evil", as their ultimate consequence is death! But, from every mistake a lesson can be learned and from every failure a success can be born . . . as God can and does "redeem" all human mistakes and errors . . . in due time!

Salvation, therefore, means something very different, at the spiritual and esoteric level, than it does at the exoteric level. At the exoteric level, it generally means "belonging to a certain religion", or "Church", living by their moral code and precepts, "accepting Jesus as our personal Savior", etc. This should lead us, when we "die" to enter "heaven", "eternal happiness" and be reunited with God and with our true Self.

At the esoteric level, however, it means to be in a "state of grace", filled with Light and properly connected and aligned with all of our "bodies", their faculties, and the spiritual Self. This so that we can *consciously direct our attention, vital energies and resources, our thoughts, feelings, time, and faculties to further our growth and evolution.* Simple put, it means to cooperate **consciously** and direct our efforts, energies, and resources to further accelerate our growth and becoming. It means to "be and do" what

God, the divine Spark, wants us to "be and do", period! Within this state, which can be achieved at one point and time of our earthly lives, we shall know **intuitively** *what to do and what not to do,* how to be patient, and how to rejoice in the ineffable gift of Life . . . and in the unspeakable marvels that await us along the way and at the end of our journey!

Appendix I

The Art of Living at the End of the 20th Century

Of all the arts, and there are many, *The Art of Living*, is certainly the most important, the least known and practiced, and, today the most needed as it corresponds and answers emergent, vital, and imperative **needs** and **aspirations** of our times. It is clear to most people that, today, our life and problems are ever "complexifying;" that our consciousness is **expanding** towards both the depths and the heights; that we are experiencing, in an alternating and exacerbating cycle, devitalization and a chronic fatigue as well as an "implosion" of psychospiritual energies and a great intensification of our sensitivity. We are witnessing, at the same time, the greatest breakthroughs in modern Western Medicine and the appearance of entirely new and baffling diseases of which AIDS is but the best known and most tragic case. Economically, we are experiencing the fifth generation of computers and the first generation of "robotics" while, at the same time, we are on the brink of one of the major economic crises of this century which could greatly reduce our standards of living. In this situation, it is becoming increasingly clear that a **conscious** *Art of Living*, suited to our nature and emergent needs and aspirations, is becoming a vital necessity. With the demographic explosion and the appearance of *overchoice*, together with the distinguishing features and tendencies of our age (see *Apocalypse Now*, Llewellyn Publications, 1988), the only way that we will be able, not only to actualize our potential and faculties, but to literally **survive** at the *human* level, is to **develop and implement a comprehensive philosophy and an integral ART OF LIVING.**

Today, you and I are standing in the very midst of the Great Passage, of the transition between our adolescence and our adulthood, between the Piscean and the Aquarian Age, in which humanity will become more and more **conscious**, alive, and powerful . . . for Good as well as for Evil. Thus, a multidimensional, interdisciplinary, and **conscious** philosophy and art of living ARE, indeed, *the Great Challenge of our times*. In my trips to, and work in, many countries (The USA, Canada, France, Italy, Switzerland, and Spain in particular), in reading and meditating upon the literature of many disciplines (sociology, psychology, anthropology, psychotherapy, medicine, as well as the emergent parapsychology, esoterism, and spirituality), I have found some essential ideas, **fragments,** and germs leading towards the systematic unfoldment of such a philosophy and art of living—but not yet its final structure which, in any case must be a PERSONAL REALIZATION!

It is also clear that an **art of living** is not a **science** and must thus be adapted, refined, and personalized by **each person,** taking into account his or her level of consciousness, values, and personal experiences. And yet, there are basic "laws", "principles", and "core intuitions" that could form the "skeleton," or "substance" of this philosophy and art of living—reference points and points of departure which must then be adapted and personalized for each person at his or her particular situation, and "moment" of his or her life and development. It is these "laws," "principles," and "central intuitions" that I would now like to discuss with you and which will constitute the heart of this lecture. It is also these essential insights that, I believe, will constitute the foundation of the "integral," or "holistic" **education** of the future, the seeds of which have already been planted with some burgeons beginning to appear, here and there, in different disciplines and in various countries. In its essential structure, this philosophy and art of living rest upon the following essential points:

1. A general theory of human nature—what is a "human being?"
2. A specific model of the Psyche—what is "human consciousness" in its specific structure and functions?
3. The vital principles of holistic and preventive medicine which are now emerging.
4. A personal **autobiography** with its continuation in a **journal** of our personal life, work, and growth.
5. A theory and personal application of **the Love of God,** Worship, or *Prayer.*
6. A theory and personal application of the **love of our fellow humans,** of "good will in action," or of *Service.*
7. A psychospiritual discipline to be followed, alone and in a group-the formation of a "Love Vitamin Generator," of a "Circle of Light," of a "Living Church for the New Age" which I have called "the Noah's Ark of our Age" or the "Spiritual Family."

If you or I look at all the lectures and workshops I have given in the last 7 years, at all the books and articles I have written in the last 10 years, it will become quite clear that their "heart and core" deal precisely with this "philosophy and art of living" which constitutes the great personal and collective change of our times for education, religion, and medicine.

In the last 5,000 years and, especially, since the Renaissance in the West, human evolution has gone through an enormous transformation, a **qualitative metamorphosis.** In leaving *Nature to enter Society,* human beings have transformed their consciousness and their becoming—beginning with a slow and external *unconscious evolution* to now arrive at an internal and ever-accelerating *conscious evolution.* In simple words, this means that, today, if we want to acquire certain things or, especially, **become something,** realize certain objectives, we must **involve our** *whole selves to* realize and incarnate our dreams and visions. It is no longer God or Nature, or even *Society* and its institutions which will assume and insure our being and our becoming—it is **ourselves** who must do it, frightful and painful as this may seem to many, starting with the inside of our being and consciousness to arrive at an external materialization and objectification. This, perhaps, is the "occult" reason why all great social and cultural institutions and traditions, all traditional values, and all external reference points are beginning to dissolve and disappear. Why the Great Beings, Saints, Sages, and Masters are hiding, going into the background and are leaving public life! To enable us to change our basic attitude towards life and ourselves—to change the focus of our attention and of our efforts from *extraversion to introversion* and from *infraversion to supraversion.* And that the words "liberty," "responsibility," and "integrity," as well as "assume control over your being and your own life," are becoming the key notes of humanistic psychology and of the Human Potential movement with the New Age Consciousness. It is in the framework of these new emergent conditions and expansion of human consciousness that this philosophy and art of living, with an integration of new perceptions, intuitions, and realizations, are becoming an essential necessity. A necessity which will become all the more imperative as we pass from the "empire of the Head to that of the Heart," from Analysis to Synthesis, and from a reductionistic and alienating materialism to an integrating and vivifying spirituality.

The development and articulation of each of the "7 dimensions," or "core aspects" of this philosophy and art of living can be found in the many books, articles, and lectures I have written. For our purposes here, I will limit myself to do two basic things:

1. to get to the very "heart," or "quintessence" of each one of them; and,
2. to connect and integrate all of them into a larger framework which I call a "comprehensive philosophy of life"

and an "integral art of living" for our age. Please bear in mind that this **philosophy** and this **art,** in each of its 7 vital dimensions must go through the 5 stages of incarnated Wisdom, which are:

    a. be properly *intellectually* understood and synthesized to;

    b. descend from the "Head" into the "Heart" to be not only *intellectually* grasped and understood, but also *emotionally felt to* then be;

    c. be *wanted* by the will. . . which will bring them to;

    d. be *lived* in our consciousness, being, and daily life;

    e. so as to *BECOME THEM!*

A. *A general theory of human nature:* here the key insights are:

    1. that a human being is a true *Microcosm* of the Macrocosm—a synthesis of all of reality, a Child of God;

    2. that a human being is not yet a completed being, but a being-in-evolution, a being-in-becoming, who must now know himself, master himself, and integrate himself—assume himself—so as to *consciously complete himself;*

    3. that a human being is not yet a "unified and integrated being," that he remains a multidimensional being on his way to completion. As such, human beings have:

        a. a *biopsychic nature,* their physical body;

        b. a *human nature,* their Psyche, or Soul, composed of several subtle energy bodies which are still unfolding (their etheric, astral, mental, and spiritual bodies); and,

        c. their *spiritual nature,* the Divine Spark, the as yet unknown Self.

    4. The Great Work and Challenge of our Age, and of all times, has always been that of actualizing and realizing our *psychosocial nature,* our human consciousness, to harmonize it with the *physical body* and with the Divine Spark. To become, in this way, a **Temple of the Living God** which involves the Second Coming of Christ in our Heart, Soul, and Being.

B. *A specific Model of the Psyche,* the old Hindu science of the Antahkarana, the specific structure and functions of human consciousness:

        a. the structure of the Psyche, the "Egg of Psychosynthesis" with its 7 structural component parts: the human self, the spiritual Self, the field of consciousness, the preconscious, the subconscious, the unconscious, and the superconscious;

b. the functions of the Psyche, the "Star of Psychosynthesis": willing, thinking, feeling, intuition, imagination, biopsychic drives, and sensations; and,

c. the essential work of the individual consists in knowing, exploring, and mastering the *7 functions* of the Psyche with their energies as well as to make the whole "Egg," or Unconscious, Conscious.

C. To know and to be able to live by the *7 basic Principles of Holistic and Preventive Medicine,* that is:

1. *Nutrition*—knowing how to feed oneself;
2. *Sleep-getting* good quality and the right quantity of sleep;
3. *Physical Exercise*—getting the right kind and enough of it;
4. *Sexual and Love Life*—to know and be able to direct one's sexual and emotional life;
5. *Emotional and Intellectual Life*—to know, feed and manage them properly;
6. *Social Life*—understand it and be able to organize it properly (Love Vitamin Generator, Circle of Light, Spiritual Family); and,
7. *Spiritual Life*—to know and be able to feed one's Soul: Worship and Prayer.

D. *Write an Autobiography and then continue it with a Journal.* Meditate upon and then write your own autobiography, organizing your materials around the following 7 basic points:

1. What has happened to us (female polarity)?
2. What have we caused to happen by our own acts and words (male polarity)?
3. The events that we have lived (external, objective polarity).
4. Our way of perceiving, defining, and reacting to the events we have lived (internal, subjective polarity, the true axis of human and spiritual growth).
5. Our human relationships with the persons who are most important to us (psychosocial network).
6. The unfoldment of the events we consider crucial for us in their psychological order.
7. What we have learned, understood, felt, loved, wanted, and created.

Then, we continue this autobiography into the future by keeping a *journal* organized in the same fashion, together with a *workbook* describing the work or exercises we have done, when and with what results.

E. *A theory and personal application of the Love of God, Worship, or Prayer:*
   a. *Choice of the appropriate techniques:* Using Images, Symbols, and Rituals as consciousness and energy transformers. Nature and Use of Divine Names, of the Sign of the Cross, the Our Father, the Ave Maria, or the Ten Commandments.
   b. *Knowing and having developed the "Muscles of Human Consciousness"* and the techniques necessary to make Prayer "hot" and "alive"—an agent of psychospiritual transformation: Concentration, Meditation, Devotion, Visualization, Invocation-Evocation; developing Faith and activating the psychospiritual Centers.
   c. *Integrating the timing and sequence of Prayer with other activities.*
F. *A theory and personal application of the love of our fellow humans, of "good will in action"; or of Service:*
   a. Choice of a *vocation* and *avocation to* utilize one's energies, train one's faculties, and express one's self in work that is useful to others-studies, professions, contributions.
   b. Expression of good will, hobbies and volunteer work to enrich others and oneself. To feel and live the fact that to "serve others is to serve God and one's self"—to *express love.*
   c. Integrating the timing and sequence of Service with other activities (Work, Prayer, and Relaxation).
G. *A psychospiritual discipline to be followed alone and in a group:*
   a. Here, one must make the right kind of choice of a discipline or "Path" to be followed daily. Create one's "growth and life project" that corresponds to one's nature and to the present period of one's life.
   b. Alternating, in a harmonious fashion, between personal work and group work, spiritual and physical, emotional and mental work; work and play; desire and duty.
   c. Create or join a "work group" or a "Spiritual Family."

The very heart and essence of a philosophy and of an art of living consist in:

1. knowing oneself, accepting oneself, integrating oneself, and perfecting oneself *in all the parts and aspects of one's being and consciousness,* in the heights as well as the depths, in the Light as well as in the Shadow, *without exceptions.*

2. Hence, to be able to know, accept, integrate, and perfect *all the parts* and aspects of the Universe and of Life, both high and low, without exceptions.
3. This will bring the true "Philosopher" and "Artist of the Art of Living" to be able to live without fears, worries, anxieties, remorse, guilt, or cravings, in full appreciation of oneself, of Life and its trials, with gratitude towards God for the Gift of Life and the Joie de Vivre which, for me, is the true meaning of a full, conscious, and adult life!

In our Age, the development of a comprehensive philosophy of life and of an integral art of living is one way of **consciously** finding Peace, Harmony, and the *right relation* between all the parts of one's being and all the parts of creation. This with the proper **discernment** of the right measure, the right proportion, the right distance, and the right timing . . . which I wish to all of you or, should I say, "to all of us!" This is not easy to achieve and can probably not be realized in just one life on earth. Yet, this is our destiny, such as I can conceive it at this point, and the goal towards which all my efforts and aspirations are directed. For it is, indeed, in this "Art of Living" that one can find the *Philosopher's Stone* (the key to true knowledge), the *Elixir Vitae* (the key to **conscious** immortality), and the *Panacea* (the universal medicine) which is authentic **Holiness** manifesting itself by an explosion of new and vivifying energies culminating in the *Joie de Vivre!*

Appendix J

To Know and Do One's Duty:
The Essential Key for Health, Peace, and Happiness

In most, if not all, the lectures I have been giving, here at the UN in NYC, I mentioned the crucial importance of "knowing and doing one's duty", of discovering what one has come to do in the world, what is one's special and unique "calling", "work", "mission", what the Hindus would call "dharma" and the Ancient's "God's Will." There are many names and labels one can give to this all-important realization, but there is *one fundamental reality* behind them, and to "do" or "not to do" this can have very important and ever-intensifying **consequences**, at many levels, for a person, a group, and a society. This is the reason why I decided to dedicate a complete lecture/workshop to this subject, its nature, its dynamics, its realization, and its multiple consequences. I offer these to you with my mind and my heart in the hope that they will help you realize something that is becoming evermore important and that could have crucial consequences in your life and in the lives of those you live and interact with. Unquestionably, this is one of the "truly crucial questions. . . and **challenges** of our times". But, it is not only a question of *knowing* and *feeling* this, but also and especially of being able to **do it,** to **realize it in your life and being!**

When I began studying and experimenting in a *living way* with the teachings of the sacred traditions and of the great universal "Primordial Tradition", I meditated and reflected at length upon a real "kuan", "mind-twister", or "paradox" which is clearly stated in the Judeo-Christian Scriptures, "the wisdom of men is foolishness in the eyes of God" and the "Wisdom of God is foolishness in the eyes of men". . . What could this possibly mean? What is the "wisdom of men" which is "foolishness" in the eyes of God and the "Wisdom of God" which is "foolishness" in the eyes of men? Studying and reflecting upon the development and course of Western civilization from the Renaissance (the real, actual birth of the "modern era") to our days, I was stuck by the fundamental axiom and program of Science and of the "scientific method" which constitutes one of the most important foundations of the modern period: "voir pour savoir, savoir pour prévoir, prévoir pour pourvoir" (to see in order to know, to know in order to predict, and to predict in order to control, to obtain **power**). What has Western civilization and the modern world done with Science and with the scientific method? How have we applied this new "paradigm" that substituted *tradition* and *authority* with *direct observation* and *personal experience* that can be *reproduced* and *repeated* by others who observe the same *rules* and operate under the same *conditions?*

Clearly and unquestionably, we have applied it to *raise our material and social standards of living*, to *make life easier, more secure, predictable, and* **comfortable** *for every one* (or, at least for the upper, middle, and working classes!). And what is it that the whole world, socialist or capitalist, North and South, developed or developing nations, want more than anything? An *easier, more secure, predictable, and comfortable life!* In other words, to have the *consumer goods* that industrial and developed nations have acquired. So this, perhaps, is the "wisdom of men" As Freud once stated it in his "reality principle", *to seek pleasure and avoid pain!* To ensure the fundamental human rights of freedom of speech of religion, of employment, and of economic, social, and political security; to maximize health, wealth, communication, and self-expression and thus to free oneself from fear, anxiety, frustration, injustice, and pain! Have we achieved this and with what results? To a certain extent, especially at the technological and material level (as shown by our more efficient and powerful machines and gadgets, by our raising income and extending life-span) we have achieved a good measure of this, but with a strange and ominous paradox: As we get more and more of the "material good things of life" they mean less and less psychologically, not to mention **morally** and **spiritually,** and they also bring disastrous "side effects" such as pollution, the destruction of ecosystem, and a radical (and in my opinion **negative**) change in our *value system* and in our *relationships* as evidenced particularly in the eroding *family system.* At the level of the individual (the microcosm), they also brought a progressive weakening of our character, integrity, and vitality; a clouding of the mind, a poisoning of the heart, and an impotence of the will. And all of these, together, are culminating in a slow decrease of our sense of *reverence for life*, of *appreciation for what we have and live*, and a *twilight, or even* **eclipse**, *of our joie do vivre!* What a contradiction! When we got what we wanted and worked so hard, for over such a long period of time, it did not bring half the fulfillment and satisfaction our ancestors, who worked so hard to make it happen, thought it would bring. Yes, this is, indeed, the *wisdom of men* which is *foolishness* in the eyes of God!

At this point, we could well ask then, "what is the "Wisdom of God" which is "foolishness" in the eyes of men"? After much thinking and experimentation, and many personal experiences, I am quite convinced that the "Wisdom of God" is. . . **growth**, *becoming more than what we were when we arrived on this planet, actualizing our many potentialities and faculties*, and *realizing our destiny!* In other words: answering the "riddle of the Sphinx", the problem of identity: Who am I (the problem of human nature)? Where do I come from (the problem of origins)? Where am I going (the problem of destiny)? And, most important, *what have I come here to accomplish?* What is my "dharma", my "calling" or "vocation in life", what is "God's Will for me"? In simple words: *What is my duty!* This I feel, is the true reason for incarnation on planet earth, the underlying "spiritual" reason for which we find ourselves in a physical body on a material planet, and not to be "secure", to "enjoy the good things of life", and to satisfy all the demands of our ego, justified or unjustified! What is even "stranger" and more paradoxical is that when we do this, when we fulfill our "duty", and "forget ourselves", then we also receive all that which is most important for us: the sense of wonder, magic, mystery, and appreciation for life and its countless adventures, the sense of reverence for Life, and the true *joie de vivre,* the" peace profound that passeth human understanding", and the inner realization of self-worth, personal dignity, and the meaning, purpose, and **value of Life!** Truly, this must be the "Wisdom of God" which we may now no longer regard as "foolishness" but rather as true wisdom, what is most important for us!

Many of the great minds of our century, scientists, researchers, thinkers, philosophers, and mystics of our times have, in one way or another, warned us about this and told this story through the prism of their own personal experiences and understanding. Emile Durkheim, at the turn of the century, in his study of suicide, seriously questioned one of the most "sacred" beliefs of the 18th and 19th centuries: that **progress,** at the material and human levels, was inevitable and would continue for as long as human beings would apply **reason,** the highest human faculty, to the study of the material and human dimensions of our lives. The data he gathered on suicides clearly showed him that suicide rates **increase** with the passage of time, as well as rates of psychopathology and antisocial behavior. Now if there were genuine **progress** these should *diminish* rather than *increase!* Max Weber spoke of "der Entzauberung der Welt", of the disenchantment with the world, that would occur, more and more, as people put all their psychic energy and attention into gathering **knowledge** and **power. . .** at the expense of **emotions** and **intuition**. This, he stated, would lead them to *rationalize* and *program their lives* so that they could obtain, more and more, all the things they wanted (money, security, machines, and gadgets) but which would *mean less and less* and leaved them without any true joy, appreciation, wonder, and excitement which are *emotional qualities* that only *feeling* can bring about. André Malraux is reputed to have gone as far as stating that "the 21st century will either be **spiritual** or **not be at all**". Albert Meglin, a noted French industrialist who created the **Université Populaire**" in Paris wrote a book called *Le Monde à l'envers* (the world turned upside down). Pitirim Sorokin, in his diary, stated quite clearly that there were three things that never disillusioned him and always brought a great deal of peace, strength, and joy in his life, even *under the most difficult of circumstances*. Namely, the realization that an Infinite and Loving Intelligence is present and behind all things, that love begets love and violence and hatred more violence and hatred, and finally that the most genuine and profound source of true peace, fulfillment, and joy is *doing one's duty!* Other major thinkers came to somewhat the same conclusions but in other words and in other ways. This small sample, however, can both focus our mind on our subject and better enable us to grasp what is truly **essential** in our lives and in our world.

In this physical world, not everyone can obtain real knowledge, power, love, understanding or even **health!** But, every person can, to a certain extent, succeed in realizing a sense of genuine and profound **peace,** personal, **fulfillment,** and human **happiness!** On the surface, this may seem a paradox, an enigma, and a contradiction, but it is a profound truth which I have *personally verified and lived* and which we can all "verify and live", but on one essential condition: to be able to *know* and to *accomplish one's duty,* which is a simple but not an easy thing to do'

In this life, I have traveled a great deal, both in the outer and inner worlds; I have reflected and meditated at length upon the "Fundamental Questions" of the "Human Condition" which I have explored in depth; above all, however, I have met unusual and extraordinary persons, thinkers, scientists, researchers, philosophers, and spiritually awakened persons, Saints, Sages, and Seers. One thing that the latter never ceased to repeat to me and to point to as being extremely important was simply that: *to know and to be able to accomplish one's "duty"* is a truly fundamental "key" of Life. Intellectually, at first, I accepted this but failed to perceive its depths and implications. But then, as I set out to "verify" and "live" this truth in my own life, it slowly began to unveil its incredible implications and to reveal its fabulous treasures. . . which, today, I would like to share with all of you. Like all "essential truths" of life, this is deceptively simple and straightforward, but it really has no substitute and is an indispensable component of any authentic and effective "philosophy and art of living".

Generally, but today in particular, people run here and there, make a lot of efforts and sacrifices, giving their time, energy, and attention to *earn money*, to *keep one's health*, to *find a mate or companion*, and to *learn or to affirm themselves in the world*. On an inner and higher level, one may make a lot of efforts and sacrifices to *become and live more consciously;* hence, to *know more*, to *feel more passionately* and *to love more intensely*, and to *better express one's self!* Yet few people really seek, consciously or unconsciously, to *know* and to *accomplish their "duty"!* How can we explain this paradox and "puzzle" when this knowledge and realization are so important for our overall well-being, health, integrity, fulfillment, and happiness?

To begin with, I think that few people are aware and realize that we *all have a "duty", a "calling", or a "mission" to accomplish in this world!* But then, there are people who, intellectually, *know this truth* and are *aware of some of its implications*, but who have no idea as to how to *access, verify, and live this "knowledge"*. Together, therefore, we shall begin by defining what we mean by one's "duty", "work", "calling" or "mission". Then, we will reflect and experiment on the best ways to *discover* and to *personally verify* this important knowledge. Finally, we shall see how we can best *realise this duty in our daily life*.

1. What constitutes our "duty", "dharma" "work", "calling", or "mission" in this world?

   Our "duty" or "dharma" (as it is called and well-known in the East) is simply *God's Will*, the Will of our spiritual Self or Divine Spark, in regards to what we have come to do and accomplish in this world. This is what Plato had in mind when he told his students that the "highest learning" was none other than **remembering**, remembering what they had come to learn and do in this world, and which their higher Self had, in fact, *chosen* before they incarnated in their physical body. In this sense, *every human being who comes in this world is a "missionary"*, but few realize this consciously and succeed in doing it, at least at the *conscious level!* All human beings, and that means *all of us*, have come in this material world to learn certain lessons, to actualize certain potentialities and faculties, and to live through certain "tests" and "trials"—this in order to **grow** and to *become more than what we were when we "arrived" when we were born!* It is, therefore, in this sense that we all have a "duty" to "accomplish", a specific task and a series of tasks to accomplish throughout our lives as well as in each specific cycle, subcycle, and supercycle of our lives—certains things that we must do each day, each week, each month, each year, and throughout our entire life. To become aware of this "duty", of the work and tasks that we must accomplish, means to "unify our whole being and consciousness (conscious, unconscious, and superconscious; our attention, energies, and resources) with the universe, *and to put them into harmony with what we are doing*. This may, at first, be far from easy and it may well elicit a certain "resistance" or "antagonism" on the part of certain aspects of our own being and consciousness (of our lower self) as well as from other persons. . . whom we may care a great deal about or who might be our organizational superiors!

Yet, I can tell you by direct personal experience, that the "rewards" and "consequences" are more than worth all the efforts, energies, and sacrifices that we may put into this. For, to truly accomplish these tasks and to *do our duty,* inevitably and unfailingly bring with them a *peace profound,* a sense of *fulness, self-worth* and *integrity,* and a *joie de vivre* (wherein one forgets time, oneself, and everything else becoming *fully absorbed and vivified by what one is doing*) that *nothing else in the world can possibly confer*. This, therefore, is one of the "great secrets" of Life which is so "simple" that most people do not even pay attention to it and fail to realize it. . . with all of its consequences. The only final and definitive "proof" of this consists in *personally and living* this profound truth: to *know* and *do* our *duty* for a certain period of time (at least for a few days) and then to see what transpires in our consciousness, in our being, and in our lives. But, to do this one must, necessarily, first *know* and *be able to identify* what is our "duty"?

2. *How can we determine and verify what constitutes our "duty"?*

According to the Western spiritual tradition, which has very precise and specific teachings concerning this subject, every human being who is born in this world has a "duty", some "work", a given "calling" or "mission": *a series of specific tasks to accomplish*. Our "duty", therefore, contains the set of lessons, trials, tests, work, and tasks which we have chosen to accomplish in the physical world, to further our evolution and development, before we actually incarnated. We choose "in part" the "duty" and the tasks that we will be called to "go through" and "live" in this world. The "other part" comes from the spiritual Beings Who govern the destiny and becoming of human beings in this world; the Beings that in the East are called the "Lords of Karma". The more we evolve and become conscious, however, the greater the amplitude of our choices and "free will" becomes. Moreover, the spiritual tradition is also

298

quite explicit in stating that there is a *direct relationship* between the growth of a person and the trials and difficulties that this person will be called to face in her life. The price of **growth, transformation,** and **rising to a higher level of consciousness and being** is always and inevitably more **pressure,** difficulties, efforts, sacrifices, and **suffering. . .** unless one truly learns how to **love in a living and authentic way!**

From the "spiritual perspective, therefore, it is quite clear that it is *we, ourselves,* who have chosen to live many (but not all!) of the experiences, tests, trials, and lessons that we will encounter in our lives. It is also manifest that the harder and the more challenging our life is, the more we will get *real* and *rapid* "opportunities for growth and Self-realization". And this is the basic reason why Sages never complain about what happens to them, even in the worst and most difficult of cases, and, somehow, manage to "Thank God" for *all they have to brave and live in this world.*

Our "duty", "calling", or "mission in this world can be subdivided into two distinct perspectives:

a. *The global perspective,* the essential "tasks" and "lessons" for which we have come in this world—*our essential duty.* The "Peace profound, that passeth human understanding" of which religion speaks, a sense of fullness and plenitude, of self-worth and personal integrity, and our very **joie de vivre** depend, essentially, upon our ability to *know* and to *accomplish* this "essential duty". When we actually do it, especially **consciously,** but even **unconsciously,** we seem to "forget time" and "ourselves", we become fully and completely absorbed in what we are doing, we seem to "lose weight" and to be inspired, vivified, and carried along by then the very forces of the universe. Whether we still have 40 years or more to live or just a few months or days, whether we are sick or well, poor or rich, alone or in an intimate relationship, nothing seem to matter except what we are doing and to do it as consciously and as **impeccably** as possible. Likewise, when our time will come to leave the physical world to return to our *spiritual home,* it will be *whether, and to what extent, we have accomplished this duty* that will constitute the fundamental criterion by which to evaluate the "success" or "failure" of this life.

In most cases, it is a question of "percentage" and not of "total" success or failure for even under the worst of circumstances, there is always something positive and of value that we gain for our growth and Self-actualization from any incarnation. Using a very "human optic and yard-stick, I would say that if we succeed in doing *50% or more* of our "essential duty", this life has been "worth-while" and we have passed the "incarnational exam". If we succeed in doing *75% or more,* this life is a "great success" while if we cannot reach the 50% mark, it is a "qualified" failure". In my personal case, today, I esteem that I have already accomplished around 70% of my "duty" (which I have known, with an incredible degree of *clarity* and *certainty* since the age of 15!), which already makes it a "success". On the other hand, I also realize that the next *9–16 years* will be the "crucial and decisive years" of this life-time. This, on the one hand, because they will be the last truly *productive years* and, on the other hand, because *never before in my life,* I have had as many resources, skills, and overall means to complete my work and mission.

b. *The partial perspective,* cycles, and various manor "steps" and "lessons"—our *relative duty.*

Each cycle, supercycle, and subcycle in life (for me personally: *1 year, 8 years,* and *3 months*) contains one or more "lessons", "tasks", or "duties" which we can *know* and *accomplish.* . . or not! The "fruits" or "consequences" of this are basically the same: obtaining that peace profound, that sense of fullness and plenitude, of personal worth and integrity, and of **joie de vivre.** . . or the opposite!

Here, moreover, we find two basic factors, or dimensions, that must be taken into consideration:

1. *The external objective events:* that takes place in the world and which we undergo.
2. *Our subjective or "psychological" perceptions, conceptions, definitions, and reactions to these events* which constitutes our "lived experience".

Basically, this means, therefore, that we can understand, realize, and incarnate our "duty" in two basic ways: through our *consciousness perceptions and attitudes*—the "psychological" or subjective dimension—and through our *basic choices and actions*—the "material" or objective dimension.

How can a person discover and verify his/her essential and relative "duty"? This is the fundamental question that we find at the very heart of the present lecture workshop. The essential key is quite simple. . . but one must both *find it* and *activate it!* This key is none other than our *intuition* and our *spiritual consciousness;* that is, the capacity to

consciously contact the superconscious and the spiritual Self!
And this, obviously, implies a *transformation and expansion
of our consciousness, energies and vibrations!* The spiritual
Self, the Divine Spark or "essential Self" well knows the
reason for which It has incarnated in this world just as our
"Soul", our superconscious, knows and can thus "remember" (as Plato would say) the basic incarnational "tasks",
"lessons", and "work" it has chosen. With these insights,
the answer to our "fundamental question"—how can we
know our "duty" and "remember" what we have chosen to
accomplish in the world during the present life-time is quite
simple: it involves *building a "channel", or a "bridge" that
will connect our field of consciousness with our superconscious and our human with our spiritual Self!*

Another very important question, which logically follows
the foregoing one is: *How can we distinguish and discern
our authentic "duty" and the genuine "tasks" and "lessons"
which have come to carry out and learn in this world* from
our personal and subjective desires, fantasies, projections,
phantasms, and imagination? It is not as simple as it may
look, at first glance, and it is *easy* and *human* to make
mistakes. And, again, the answer is, basically, the same: we
must raise our consciousness, activate our intuition, and
awaken our spiritual consciousness to acquire the *spiritual
discernment* which can truly enable us to make that
distinction. In addition, however, there are two simple and
basic criteria which can greatly help us *distinguish* and
verify our authentic "duty" and "essential tasks" from
possible fantasies and projections. These are:

1. *A subjective criterion:* the "peace profound" the sense
   of fullness and plenitude, of personal worth and
   satisfaction, the *joie de vivre* and feeling that one is
   lighter and more inspired and energized, and the
   ability to "forget time" which one, inevitably, acquires
   and experiences as one genuinely accomplishes one's
   "duty" and the "work" that one has come to do in this
   world.
2. *An objective criterion:* sooner or later one will find
   other persons who will *appreciate* what one does and
   who will encourage one to continue along these lines.
   In other words, this means not only "loving and
   enjoying" what one is doing, but also doing it well,
   doing it in an impeccable fashion and thus being quite
   successful in doing it.

3. *How to realise and accomplish our "duty" and "essential tasks".*
Here, we find ourselves confronted by a major *paradox* because
doing our duty is, at the same time, the easiest and the most
natural thing one can (if one knows what it is, which is the
perspective of the Self) and the most difficult thing one can do
and which requires a great deal of vigilance and an "ongoing
inner struggle" (if one does not "really know" what it is, which
is the position of the human self). If we have acquired the
understanding of our "duty", "work", and of the tasks we have
come to accomplish in this world (which can only come from
"above, from the Self in the form of "energies and impulses"
and from the superconscious, in the form of conscious
awareness) then nothing is easier, more natural and
spontaneous. . . even if other *important persons* do not
understand this and if the world and our "lower self" oppose
this. On the other hand, if we have not acquired this most
important knowledge and understanding (of who we are, where
we come from, whither we are going, and of *what we have come
in this world to accomplish*) then nothing is more difficult,
obscure, ambiguous, and impenetrable!

Without this essential "knowledge and understanding", we
try one thing and then another, we look at our economic, social,
professional and egoic *interests*, and we seek the "advice of
experts", but we remain perpetually confused, lost, frustrated,
and "cut adrift on the Ocean of Life".

It is, however, also possible to **progressively discover** our
"duty", "work", and the various "tasks" and "lessons" we have
come to learn in this world. We can do this by "trial and error",
trying out various occupations and activities to see which ones
bring us the greatest personal satisfaction while, at the same
time, enabling us to do a "good job" which is recognized by
others. We can personally experiment with different situations
and creative activities, letting things grow and unfold until we
can "see more clearly" as to how we can handle them. If we
apply our "subjective" and "objective" criteria to various
occupations and productive activities, it is quite possible to,
little by little, discover our "duty", our "calling", and our
"mission" in this world. When we actually "find and live these"
they will, inevitably bring in their wake the peace profound, the
inner satisfaction, and the sheer joy that are their unmistakable
"signature." We should also link with the former the external
recognition and "success" which are their "objective
corollaries". If we *love what we do* and *do what we love* we will,
generally, be "right on target"! We can also consult competent
persons, psychologists, counselors, astrologers, etc. who could

offer very valuable help and insight. . . not to make our basic decisions for us but to clarify our own mind and intuition regarding this very fundamental question. As we shall always have to live with its consequences, it is, in ultimate analysis, always **we** who must make the final decision.

Finding our "duty", our various "incarnational tasks and work", our "essential and relative calling" in this world can occur at *any* and *all* ages. . . but with different consequences! It really is never **too late** to achieve this. Sometimes, an entire lifetime is necessary only to discover this, to truly find out *who we are* and *what we have come to do in this world:* what is our *authentic duty,* but without being able to actually *live it and realize it.* Finding our "duty", the various "tasks" we have come to do in this world, and our "mission", here is an intrinsic and fundamental part of answering the "riddle of our own Sphinx", the problem of our identity, and the enigma of our own nature, origins, and destiny. . . which is just one more reason why of all knowledge **self-knowledge** is the most important. . . and why being able to **express oneself** and **accomplish one's duty** may well be one of the most powerful "medicines" of the future. It fact, it has long been known that "doing one's duty" and "carrying out one's mission" was possible even when a person was very ill or grieviously wounded. Somehow, that person found the almost "superhuman strength" to "get that work done" and then, but only then, "drop dead". I think that this, better than anything else, shows us the **power** and **importance** of "doing one's duty", "being faithful to ourselves", and "carrying out our work or mission" right to the very end!

Practical work: Workshop program

The fundamental questions we shall seek to answer in this workshop and the *basic work* I suggest to you— the core *tools* and *skills* we shall seek to define and refine together are the following:

1. How can we know and realize, through *direct personal experience*, that "knowing and doing one's duty" is *one of the fundamental "keys" to find peace, happiness, and creativity?*
2. How can we *look for, find,* and *verify* what our "duty" and the global and specific "lessons" and "tasks" we have come to learn and accomplish in this world are?
3. How can we realize and incarnate this "duty", these "tasks" and "lessons", once we have discovered them?
4. What is the "structure", or the "anatomy" of human consciousness?

5. What are the "functions", or the "physiology", of human consciousness.
6. How can we know and activate our *intuition* and thus create a "bridge" or "channel" between the field of consciousness and the superconscious?
7. How can we personally awaken, test, and utilize *spiritual consciousness?*

Core methods and specific practical exercises

a. Disidentification and Identification with the Self (core exercise of Psychosynthesis).
b. Mental Imagery and the Guided Day Dream.
c. Prayer: Silence and Theurgy.
d. Deep Relaxation.
e. Spiritual Fire: Passion and Vital Energy.
f. The Silent Witness and Listening to the Self.
g. The "Holy or Inner War".
h. Writing one's autobiography.
i. Writing Letters to the Self (Vertical Telepathy).

Core Image: Visualize a person radiant with Light, Life, and Joy doing his/her work and forgetting everything else— time, self, others, and money. Then, introject this image and fuse with it, **become it.** For a brief moment, see, feel, and experience what this is like.

Life as a Triple School:
The "School of Knowledge",
the "School of Love", and
the "School of the Will"

One of the most fundamental queries and quests of human beings, as long as they have been in this world, has been and is: **What is Life**? Some have sought to answer this question and search by providing one or more fundamental **image** to describe how Life appeared to them. Others sought to carry out long scientific investigations to answer them in mathematical equations and analytical statements. Already at a very young age, as soon as I was able to think in coherent fashion and to ask basic questions, I have asked the same questions. From the very onset, however, I was far more "moved" and "touched" by live and evocatory **images** than I was by cognitive or philosophical statements. The very first image, that came always spontaneously from the inner recesses of my consciousness and from my early observations and experiences, was that Life in this world as "hell", a "fall" from a higher state of being and consciousness, to lower, darker, and more painful ones.

As a child, I lived for a while (roughly from the age of three to six) **simultaneously** in *two distinct worlds:* that sensory, material one of my body and the spiritual, visionary one that I was still, for some inexplicable reason, able to contact in higher states of consciousness. I would slip, back and forth, between these two worlds and muse over their significance and "reason for being". Thus, I lived, directly and experientially, in my own being both the myth of the "Fall" and the myth of "original sin" which one can find in all religions. I did not for a moment even "doubt" that a "paradise" did exist and that we came from it, for I could still "access" this "paradise lost", but I could not understand why I had to come into a "tiny body" in a dark, dangerous, and painful "lower physical world" where confusion, suffering, violence, and lies were prevalent. I naturally assumed that I must have committed some strange and terrible "sin" which I had to expiate by incarnating in this "lower world". Later, however, I slowly developed and articulated three *essential images* to represent what life in this world is all about. And it is these "basic images" that I would now like to share and analyze with you in that I feel that they explain much and make life far more meaningful and understandable that it would be otherwise. The same "service" or "explanatory power" that they gave to me, I feel they can also provide for you. These images were that of Life as a "triple school", the *school of knowledge,* the *school of love*, and the *school of the will.*

One of the most fundamental teachings of contemporary sociology, a cardinal axiom of sociology 101, as it were, is that our *behavior* (what we say and what we do) are the result of a triple process: *thinking, feeling*, and *willing.* Some people think first, then make a decision, and finally they act on that decision and this constitutes what we call *rational action.* Others are driven by their impulses, their emotions, fears or desires, to make certain decisions that they will then act upon, and this is what sociologists call *irrational action.* When I began, in earnest, my career as a lecturer, writer, and teacher, I also noted that if one wanted to truly "reach a person", in a "holistic" way (as some would say today) and in an *effective fashion,* one had to provide *ideas to feed the mind, images to activate the heart,* and *practical exercises to dynamize the will . . .* and *realize the idea and the image.* The ideas touch the *conscious mind,* but the images touch the *unconscious* which is far older and more powerful than the conscious. This is, perhaps, the reason why the Chinese have a very old proverb that "one image is worth a thousand words"! Be that as it may, the central point is that it is *images* that really touch the *core of our being* and that provide an almost inexhaustible "source" of inspirations, analogies and correspondences.

The "vision", "image", or "conception" we have of the world and of reality play a most important and primordial role in our everyday life. The impact of images, symbols words, myths, and rites upon human consciousness and, therefore, upon our *behavior* is well-known today. The sacred traditions, the esoteric side of religion, and the Philosophia Perennis have always taught this and embodied it as a fundamental **arcana** of their philosophy. Modern pioneers and major intellectual thinkers such as Carl Jung, Roberto Assagioli, Mircea Eliade, Pitira Sorokin, and Joseph Campbell have called our attention to this fundamental teaching, sensitized us to it, and re-introduced it in our modern social sciences—psychology, anthropology, comparative religion, psychotherapy, and sociology. The esoteric perspective (Hermetism, Astrology, Alchemy, Quabbalah, and the mystical side of religion) always stated that, "it is by *words* and *images* that all inner Powers are awakened and re-awakened". Carl Jung went as far as stating that the symbol and the image constitute the very "machinery." by which human consciousness and our vital energies are transformed. In other words, our basic "vision", "image" or "conception" of the world play an extremely important—

conscious and unconscious—role for our behavior, our health, our creativity, and our happiness in this world!

It is interesting to note that the first book I ever wrote, and which was inspired and "guided" by Pitirim Sorokin was called: *Spiritual Man in the Modern world* (The University Press of America, 1976). It dealt, essentially, with an exploratory study of one's "conception" or "image" of the world and of one's image of oneself. In this study, I sought to demonstrate, in a systematic and scientific way, that our conception of the world is, in fact, a *mirror,* or *reflection,* of the image that one has of oneself. Moreover, that these two images play an absolutely **essential** role for our psychological and physical health, for our creativity and productivity and, especially, for our **happiness**—for what we do and what we shall become in this world. I went as far as claiming that our conception of ourselves and of the world act as an "electromagnetic field" to determine, subliminally, what we will do and what we will become!

Many years have passed since then, but eventually, out of my many studies, researches, experimentations, and personal experiences, emerged a *trinitarian conception* of human nature, as much at the *structural* than at the *functional* levels. A human being is, indeed, a *living trinity*: body (biological organism), soul (psyche, human consciousness), and spirit (Self, Divine Spark, or spiritual nature). This trinitarian being also expresses and manifests himself/herself by the "functional trinity" of the "head", of the "heart", and of the "shoulders"; that is, through his *thoughts* (thinking), his *emotions* (feeling), and through his *choices* (willing) manifested by his actions.

It is from this fundamental vision of a person as a "living trinity" that emanates a triple *image,* or vision, of the world which is directly connected with the three "core" psychospiritual Centers and to the three "key" functions of the psyche, which are connected with these three Centers (Head: thinking; Heart: feeling; Shoulders: willing). These three images, or basic conceptions, of life on earth are the following:

- *The world is a school* where we are both *students* and *teachers.* This "school", moreover, has a triple manifestation: that of *consciousness* and *knowledge,* that of *love* and *sensibility,* and that of *willing* and *creative self-expression.* The world, in other words, is a "triple school" wherein one learns to ever better know oneself, the world, and life in that world; wherein one learns to feel and love ever better; and finally wherein one learns to express oneself and to create in an evermore conscious and full way.

What is interesting here is that, if we continue developing our metaphor of "life as a school", things do not become "easier" when we go through a school but ever harder! The more progress we make and as we move from one class to another, the harder the exams become. The same thing is true for the "school of Life", as we mature and grow, the tests and trials of life become ever more sophisticated and complex. The exams given to a senior are far more advanced and difficult than those given to a freshman. The same thing is true in the "school of Life". We have come in this world to grow, to learn, to actualize our potential—to become "more" than what we were when we "arrived" or were born. Now to grow, to expand our consciousness and to transcend our present state we must, necessarily, take risks, accept painful limitations, and suffer. In this world, it seems that all "births" and all "growth" bring with them the proverbial "pains of growth". There is no other way, except that of an "authentic altruistic love", which we do not yet understand very well and are even less able to truly practice!

In this triple school we are both *students* and *teachers*. At first, when we are young, or in a receptive, feminine polarity, we are students and can remain such for the rest of our lives. Later, when we grow up, or when we are emissive and in a masculine polarity, we can also become teachers and remain such for the rest of our lives. In this world, we must, in other words, both *learn* and *teach,* receive and give, and, above all, *make exchanges with all kinds of persons,* both those who are on our level of consciousness and evolution and with those who are on a higher and a lower level.

• *The world as a psychiatric ward* where we are both *patient* and *therapist,* ill and healer. . . because it is truly in healing *others* that we heal *ourselves*. . . and in healing ourselves that we heal others. . .

Why are the world and Life a "psychiatric ward" . . . especially at the level of the heart, of love and feelings? Simply because, of all things, we understand least well and make "a mess" of those which are most important! Because, instead of doing "good", to others and to ourselves, we do "evil". Because, instead of building, creating, and giving our attention, time, and energy to *positive* things, we destroy and give attention, time and energy to that which is *negative*.

All living beings, and in particular human beings, seek, consciously or unconsciously, **happiness, harmony, fullness, and peace. . . but they seek them utilizing** the **wrong** *means* which do not bring what they are seeking. Most people give priority to *power* (money above all) and *knowledge* (which is a means to control or to obtain power) rather than to *love*. . . which is the only "force" that can truly bring joy, plenitude, and peace! Not everyone can really obtain great power or great knowledge in this world. Only a small elite can realize these two objectives for a number of complex reasons. Not only that, but even the few who obtain power and knowledge do not, necessarily, obtain joy, peace, and fullness with them. . . as the classical story of Goethe's *Faust* beautifully illustrated.

On the other hand, *every person*, even the least evolved, the lowest, and those who are afflicted with the greatest handicaps can achieve true happiness, peace profound, and a deep sense of harmony and integrity on the path of *love*! Provided, that is, that they learn how to really love in an altruistic and full way. This is, perhaps, the greatest "secret", as well as the greatest "paradox" of life on earth. A secret and a paradox that all great religions, and Christianity in particular, have tried, and are trying, to "reveal" to the world. Naturally, the "love" we are talking about here is the *altruistic* and *universal* love and not romantic or sexual love (which is always egoistical and blind!). The true solution to the "great problem and challenge" of "life on earth" is extremely clear and simple (at the cognitive level!): it simply consists in *learning how to love,* to become a "student at the great school of love", and to exchange *suffering* for *love* as the main "evolutionary motor or teacher".

Unfortunately, most people, all over the world, continue to evolve through suffering and conflict, to destroy rather than to build, and to fight rather than to cooperate and to mutually help each other. What we do, or do not do, is strictly a matter of *personal decision,* which can change or be made at any point in a person's life. Yet it also depends *directly* on one's *level of consciousness and being,* which is why it is so important to learn how to **consciously** be able to *transform our level of consciousness* and *raise* our *vibrational rate*! The "true solution", the "real remedy" to the essential problems and sufferings of life, *exist in each human* being, in each one of you, and that is the only place where they really be found! What is truly **essential** is always extremely **simple. . .** But, one must look for it "above", on the vertical dimension, and in the higher levels of consciousness, and not "below" in the lower levels where we usually function. Each "patient" can thus become a "doctor", or "therapist"; first, of *himself* or *herself,* but then also of others. . . by his **living example** and **higher energies** as well as by his knowledge and experience.

- *The world is also a battlefield* where we are both *aggressors* and *aggressed,* "oppressors" and "oppressed". In the physical world, a person must fight, with great courage and much strength, to remain "free" and to be able to *be* and *express* himself/herself. This is extremely simple, but it is also absolutely fundamental. What most "strikes" a sensitive and evolved soul when it incarnates in the physical world, is that it is immediately confronted with the *problem of evil* (whence the universal notion of a "Fall", of "original sin", of "suffering", and of "conversion"). Now "evil" just like "good", God, Man, and the Devil, or any other fundamental reality, is an ontological and existential *trinity*. In the physical world, "evil" manifests itself as a *lie,* or a "distortion of reality", as *aggression,* or violence (a dismemberment or "sacrifice" of one's self) which leads to becoming *a stranger to one's self.*

  What this means is that we cannot live in this world without being "aggressed" or "attacked", in our being and in our sensibility, in one way or another, at an emotional, mental or even physical level. Here, what is at stake is very simple: either we define and we create our own reality. . . or others, the "world", will impose theirs on us! The essential choice is, once again, very simple: either we express and realize our ideals or we shall find ourselves "blocked" and "alienated"; either one remains faithful to oneself and to one's mission or one "loses" one's self!

  This is the reason why the world is truly a "battlefield", external and internal, in the microcosm as well as in the macrocosm. At this level and seen through this perspective, the development of the will, of courage, of strength, of the "martial arts" play a primordial role to realize the Great Work, one's individuation or the completion of one's being. Here, the choice is to be a **warrior**, the "captain of one's own ship and destiny" . . . or a **slave**, in prey to external forces and beings.

Many well-meaning persons, particularly those who seek and privilege goodness, love, kindness, charity, and sensibility— what one could call the "venusian qualities"—think that compromise and weakness are virtues. That is wrong! One must, in fact, be able to cultivate and utilize both: the marsian qualities" (the male polarity) and the "venusian qualities" (the female polarity). One of the fundamental qualities and attributes of God, of the Ultimate Reality is, precisely, Life, Force, Strength (Creative Energy) together with Love and Goodness, Knowledge and Wisdom. These qualities and attributes are, in fact, but the different "facets" of the *same diamond,* the Self, the Divine Spark within each one of us. Without Life,

310

Force, Strength, or *Creative Energy*, it is impossible to *know, become, and express one's self!* Without this "energy" and "quality" one would "lose one's self", become a "stranger to one's self, and thus *fail in the great Adventure of Life!*

From time immemorial, the sacred traditions, particularly the Western ones, have claimed that there are three "royal paths" to unite with God, with inner and outer Reality. These are:

- *The Mystical Path,* the way of the Heart, of Love, and of receptivity and submission to the Self. This is, basically, a "feminine" and "passive" Path which leads to union with God through desire, love, and grace. In the Orient, the Path is known as Bhakti Yoga.

- *The Heroic Path,* the way of will and action, the way of organization and creation in spite of all possible obstacles. This is, basically, a "masculine" and "dynamic" Path which leads to union with God through action, creation, realization, and the incarnation of the highest values and ideals. In the Orient, this Path is known as **Raja** and **Karma Yoga.**

- *The Gnostic Path,* the way of knowledge, of the "head", of the comprehension of one's inner and outer experiences. This Path has two basic approaches, the masculine and the feminine, which leads to union with God through knowledge and understanding. In the Orient, this Path is known as Gnani Yoga.

When one thinks about it in an impartial and objective way, it becomes obvious that the expansion and transformation of our consciousness, the true "Metamorphosis" or "metanoia", require a growth, expansion, and **synthesis** of these three paths: of the psychospiritual Centers of the "Head" (Kether), of the "Heart" (Tipphereth), and of the "Shoulders" (Chesed and Geburah), which vehicle and convey thinking, feeling, and willing. And it is here, from this intuition and realization, that come my three basic "images", or "conceptions" of the world: that of the *school,* of the *psychiatric ward,* and that of the *battlefield.*

In the Greatest and Truest "School", which is life in this world, we must, necessarily, develop, grow, and express ourselves, and thus "walk", on *each one* of these three essential "Paths". And, at least for me, the most profound and authentic "image", "conception" or "vision" of these three Paths is that given by *the school,* the *psychiatric ward,* and the *battlefield.*

Practical aspects

In the first and theoretical part of this article, I have shared and analyzed with you the three great "images", or "conceptions" of the world which correspond, respectively, to the Head psychospiritual Center (thoughts and knowledge), to the Heart psychospiritual Center (emotions and love), and to the Shoulder psychospiritual Centers (will and creative energies). Later on, I suggested to you that what we call the three "royal paths" to God, the "Gnostic Path" (Knowledge), the "Mystical Path" (Love), and the "Heroic Path" (Will and Action) are, in fact, deeply related to each of my three basic images. I have also sought to define and describe the nature and essential characteristics of these three "conceptions" of the world for the individual, for his health, his creativity, and his happiness. But, I have not yet explored and developed the *practical* implications and applications of these three images. So, this is what I propose to do now.

Let us begin with the first one, the world being perceived or defined as a *school* in which we are both *student* and *teacher*. If the world, and thus our lives in this world, are a "school", this means that the fundamental "object", or "purpose" of Life and of all our experiences in the world is none other than *learning something* and being better able to *understand something*. This "something" is, first of all, *ourselves,* our very own nature and consciousness, our reactions, limitations, and potentialities. Then, it is also the *world,* in its enormous diversity and infinite wealth, with all of its experiences, adventures, and misadventures. This means that when we are living something difficult, painful, or incomprehensible, we should ask ourselves the following questions, meditate upon them, and properly integrate them in our consciousness and being:

1. Why am I going through this particular type of experience?
2. What can this experience bring to me that will be useful for my personal growth?
3. What is the fundamental lesson I can learn from what I am presently going through?
4. I am presently "living", or "going through" a major "exam", or "spiritual test", which could force me to develop certain aspects and qualities of my being and consciousness? If I conclude that this is so, then in what consists this "exam" or this "spiritual test" and what are the aspects or qualities I should cultivate?
5. In the experience that I am now living, what is *my duty* to myself, to others, and to God? In other words, what is "being asked" so that I can "pass the exam" and learn the lessons it contains?
6. What is the "deeper meaning" of what I am now going through, not only at a personal but also at a universal and didactic level?

7. What constitutes the "right response" to what I am presently going through at *mental* and *emotional* levels (attitudes) and at the level of my *behavior* (actions)?

Then, we can move unto the next image, that of the world being perceived as a *psychiatric ward* wherein we are both *patient* and *therapist*. At the level of the heart, of the emotions, of our affective life, the present world is, unquestionably, a *psychiatric asylum*. Why? Because what is most important is also what is most neglected. Rather than using our energies and faculties in a positive, constructive way, we use them in a negative destructive way. Rather than building, we destroy; rather than healing, we wound, and rather than helping each other, we fight and compete with each other.

For someone who is more objective and detached, who would look upon our world from "on high", from a higher and larger perspective, it is obvious that our present world would then appear as a "psychiatric ward", as the "Kingdom of the Devil", wherein human beings appear as the most perverted and destructive beings who have ever existed! In a more "modern" and "diplomatic" language, we can well say that the world appears as a *psychiatric asylum* wherein we are the "patients", "sick persons who live in a "sick world". And yet, we can also become the "therapists" of ourselves and of the world, discover the great "universal medicine", **love** and **goodness**, which can heal both *ourselves* and *others*!

To heal from our "essential wound": the *loss of our identity*, of grace, or spiritual energy—hence, of *ourselves*—and the "atrophy of the heart" (of our intuition, hence of the Self and of the higher states of consciousness) we must meditate and carefully reflect upon the following questions to integrate them in our daily lives and personality:

1. What does "holistic health" and "psychosocial health" represent to me?
2. What is, for me, the most important and diffused type of "madness" and "craziness" of our times?
3. How can I remain "healthy" in a "sick" world?
4. What are the theories and the practical means that will enable me to *re-equilibrate*, *relax*, and *recharge* myself—to reconnect myself with the spiritual Energies, the divine Light and Fire?
5. How can I "rediscover" my "center" and my "integrity" when these have been (temporarily) lost or fragmented?
6. How can I find, once again, objectivity, clarity, and a real connection with the world and with things as they really are?
7. Who are the true "doctors" and "therapists" for the ills that afflict us today? How can I recognize them and what are their distinctive characteristics?

Finally, we have the image and metaphor of the world perceived as a *battlefield* in which we are both *aggressors* and *aggressed*. Now, if the world is truly a "battlefield", then one must fight to remain free and to keep one's integrity. . . or die and lose one's integrity! This is a logical and unavoidable "consequence" of this "vision". . . which asks that we become "warriors" or "Knights of God".

In the world and during our lives on earth, we are thus all called to "face evil" and to "wage war", but a "jihad", or "holy, inner war", not so much against the "infidels" or those who are evil in the world as against our very own "lower self", against our "ego", or negative tendencies! And this war, as St. Paul had already warned us, is an *inner war,* a psychospiritual and not a physical war!

Paradoxically, one must learn "harmlessness", or "ahimsa"; that is, not to attack, harm, or wound others or oneself. In other words, here one must learn the *alchemy of the transmutation of negative into positive elements* (thoughts, emotions, impulses, desires, words, and deeds, as well as energies and vibrations). As aggression and violence, both at the quantitative and at the qualitative level, are now greatly increasing in the world and in our historical period (being an integral part of the "exam" of the end of the century), this aspect and dimension play an essential role in any "art of living" adapted to our times.

To come out victorious from this "inner war", but which also includes an "outer aspect", it is very important to meditate and reflect upon the following questions to be able to integrate them in our daily life as well as in our personality:

1. What is "attacking" or "aggressing" me at the present moment . . . or that I might "attack" or "wound"? And why is this happening to me and why I am doing this to others?
2. What is the deeper meaning of this aggression and violence? What is really "at stake" here?
3. What can this aggression and violence teach me?
4. What is my "duty" towards myself, towards others, and towards God in this situation?
5. What is the *right response,* or *reaction,* to what I am presently going through at the spiritual, mental, emotional, and physical level?
6. What are the *weapons* and the *resources* that I have in order to confront this aggression and violence?
7. What is the best way in which I can use the weapons and the resources I have? What depends on me (masculine polarity) and what is the help I must ask Heaven (feminine polarity)?

Finally, one must also be able to meditate upon and integrate, in one's being and in one's daily life, the last questions that follow:

- How can I be able to find and preserve balance, justice, and a living connection with Reality, at the physical, emotional, mental, and spiritual level?
- How can I better know, connect with, heal, and feed my heart, my body, and my spirit?

Last, but not least, it is most important to always remember, as Roberto Assagioli stated so many times, that "below" (in the lower states of consciousness and being) there are no solutions; while "above" (in the higher states of consciousness and being) there are no problems"! We must realize, in other words, that true "holistic health" (physical, psychosocial, and spiritual) can only be realized "above", in the higher states of consciousness wherein one is in communion with the Self, with the Christ-within!

The New Frontiers and the Greatest Discoveries of Our Times

One of the most fundamental principles taught by all spiritual traditions and, today, on the way of being "rediscovered" by the latest findings of modern science is simply that: All that which exists in the cosmos, in creation, is endowed with Life and Consciousness and, therefore, with meaning and an **ultimate purpose.** All that **lives** is *dynamic*, in evolution, and thus it *changes* and must *change!* The great law of Life is the law of change. Heraclitus, the great classic Greek philosopher, had become aware of this fundamental truth and expressed it in his famous sayings: "all changes and is transformed" and "one can never swim twice in the same river". Parmenedes, another great Greek philosopher, enunciated and taught the equally famous but opposite principle that "truth and all that is **real** does not change and is eternal". One can explain this apparent paradox and "reconcile the two opposites" by realizing that Parmenedes was speaking of God, of the ontological dimension while Heraclitus of creation, of the universe, and of the **existential** dimension. It is only with Death or with spiritual Initiation (which entails a certain "death") that one can enter into the ontological and spiritual dimension where things do not change and are eternal.

The universe, the whole of creation, is in full evolution and expansion. From the "Doppler shift", we know that galaxies are moving away from each other at inconceivable speed and that the universe "grows", "evolves", becomes ever greater, more "alive" and conscious. In the microcosm, in Man, we find the same thing. . . which reminds us of the great hermetic principle that "below, things are as above, and that above things are as below". In Man, however, it is not the body but rather *consciousness* which is in full expansion! This "expansion", or "transformation" actually implies three very simple, concrete, and specific things: *to know more, to feel more, and to express oneself and create better;* that is, to *amplify one's capacity to know, to love, and to create.* Thus, it is logical to expect that human cultures and civilizations are also growing, changing, evolving. What are the "new frontiers" and the "greatest discoveries" of our times? What lies at the very "cutting edge" and "forefront" of present research and discoveries? This is what I propose to analyze together today.

Up to now, in my studies and investigations of our society and epoch, I have focused largely upon the "great crisis", "passage", or "Apocalypse", which we are all living, both as spectators and as actors; that is, I have privileged and emphasized primarily the "negative", "destructive" and "shadow-side" of the *great transformation* which runs, globally, from 1950 to 2050, more specifically from 1980 to 2020, and which epicenter is 1992–1996. As I have described it and analyzed it in several of my books and in many lectures, this great quantitative and qualitative crisis has three fundamental dimensions:

> *The physical dimension:* a profound and global **economic crisis.**
>
> *The human dimension:* an explosion of **aggressiveness** and **violence.**
>
> *The psychospiritual dimension:* a great increase in **madness,** in **psychological imbalance.**

Our times can best be characterized by 5 great hermaneutic or "explanatory" principles which enable to better grasp and understand what is happening in the **world** and in **ourselves.** These are briefly:

1. *The principle of polarization:* one can no longer remain "neutral" or "indifferent", one must make a **choice** and take a position, right or wrong as it might be.
2. *The principle of intensification:* everything is becoming ever more intense, violent, "conscious". Thus it becomes ever harder to "remain asleep", and to continue on one's way without assuming responsibility for the **consequences** of one's attitudes, words, and deeds.
3. *The principle of acceleration:* Everything is happening at an ever-increasing speed. What used to take years or months is now occurring in days, hours, and even seconds or microseconds!
4. *The principle of "psychologization" or "etherialization" of reality:* "reality" and our **experience of reality** appear evermore as "psychological" or "mental" entities and ever less as "material" ones.
5. *The principle of the expansion and transformation of our consciousness:* the entire range of our "knowledge" and of our "human experience", of **reality,** are changing and transforming themselves, both at the qualitative and at the quantitative level, leading us to making "incredible and fabulous discoveries", to the famous "coincidentia oppositorum", to the integration of opposites.

Probably the distinctive characteristic of our times and of its "crisis" is precisely that: the best and the worst, *the most horrible and the most wonderful things,* Heaven and Hell, the unconscious and the superconscious, are opening up, and are becoming *evermore accessible to an ever-increasing number of persons.* Never as today, can we see so many persons going towards "life" or towards "death", towards regeneration or towards degeneration, towards the realization or the destruction of their being and identity at such a high speed! What this means, basically, is that we must, necessarily, live in a more conscious: responsible, autonomous, productive, and joyful way. This because if we make the "right choices" the "rewards", or consequences, are ever greater and stronger just as if we make the "wrong choices", the "punishments", or consequences, are ever-more disastrous and painful.

For the last 20 or so years, I have always been a "pessimist in the short-term" and an "optimist in the long-term". Our civilization and societies, both global and local, are still moving towards "greater entropy", degrading themselves and advancing, at ever-increasing speed, towards catastrophes and great sufferings. Yet, at the same time, there also exist the opposite tendency and phenomena: there are everywhere individuals, that are become ever-more numerous, who are doing incredible and marvellous things; who are rapidly moving towards self-realization and the fulfillment of their destiny and duty; who are moving towards ever greater Light, Consciousness, Life and Joy. Nature gives us a "speaking image" of this contradiction in that of a river. While the current takes most of the water downwards towards the sea, on both sides of the river there are always "small countercurrents" when water moves up the river towards its source! In this lecture/workshop, I would like to focus upon these "countercurrents", upon the fabulous things that are taking place in so many countries, right before our very eyes— upon the "new frontiers" and the "greatest discoveries" of our age, which have already been realized or which are in the process of being accomplished. Thus, the fundamental question to which I will seek to answer today is: today, in the 90s and at the end of the second millennium, what are the specific "new frontiers", "perspectives", and the most important "discoveries" of our times? Fundamentally and schematically speaking these are 7 (even though there are and there will always be other ones):

1. The discovery that our physical body is like a "chemical factory" which contains all of the resources and ingredients necessary to *heal itself from all known and as yet unknown diseases.*
2. The realization that the "mystery of Mysteries", the Self, the Divine Spark, resides in the depths and the heights of our *own*

consciousness! What this means is that *Ultimate Reality,* what is *most important,* and which we all, consciously or unconsciously seek, *dwells in our very self,* in the heights and depths of our consciousness and being.

3. The progressive realization that **everything,** absolutely everything that *occurs in the world* and that *happens to us,* has **meaning, purpose,** and **value. . .** which we can and should discover When we discover the "meaning", "purpose" and "value" of what we are living and of what is taking place in the world, then Life truly becomes **marvelous**, a great "school" or "laboratory" for our being and becoming. But, if we do not discover this "meaning", "purpose", and "value", then Life becomes absurd, meaningless, and a true "hell".

4. The discovery that "death" does not exist because only Life exists! That "death" is but a "passage", a "change" of dimension, frequency, and level of consciousness and being.

5. The direct and personal realization that the *purpose of our life on earth is not to be happy, have security, and gratify the wishes of our ego.* Rather, it is to *grow, to become more than what we are, to actualize our faculties and potentialities, and to realize our Self!* From the "human viewpoint", unfortunately, this entails taking risks, sufferings, sacrifices, and suffering.

6. The profound and progressive realization that all human being come in the physical world to "do something", to realize a certain "work" or "mission" (what used to be called "our duty" or "God's Will for us"). If we discover what we have come to do in this world and *if we do it,* if we fulfill our calling, then we are happy. But, if we do not do "our duty" and do not realize what we had come here to do, then we end up unhappy, miserable, tormented, even if we have *all that this world can offer!*

7. The direct and experimental discovery that *changing our consciousness* (that is, the "essential trinity" of *thinking, feeling,* and *willing*: of our understanding of what we are living, of our feelings and emotions, and of our choices and ways of acting) *we can change both our being and our lives.*

    Einstein once said: "if we change our way of **thinking** we can change our lives". This is unquestionably the *first step,* but others must follow in order to bring us to truly change; and these are our ways of feeling, our emotions, and our choices and decisions.

These "new frontiers" and "great discoveries" (which are not really so "new" in that they were "evident" to all persons who had *reached a certain level of consciousness and being,* in all races, religions, and countries) are really a *function of our level of consciousness and being.* In other words, they depend on an "exploration" and "articulation" of certain *levels of our psyche.* The truly "new frontier" of our times is that of the exploration and organization of our inner worlds and potentials. In other words, this means that from pioneers of new territories and from astronauts of new spaces and planets, we must now become endonauts and psychonauts of the inner spaces and potentialities of the human psyche. It also means to shift from a state of *extraversion, infraversion,* and the *dominance of the male polarity* to a state of *introversion,* of *supraversion,* and of the proper balance and equilibrium between the *male and the female polarities.*

These 7 "discoveries" and new "frontiers", and "transformations" (and there are many others, that have already happened and that have yet to happen) involve many theoretical implications and practical applications. The most important for each one of them that we will now analyze in greater details are the following:

1. *That our biological organism can heal itself of all illnesses,* both *known* and as yet *unknown.*

    If this assertion is correct, then it really behooves us to focus our attention, knowledge, and energies upon *natural, psychosomatic,* and *psychospritual medicine.* This so that we can discover the "springs", "mechanisms", or "triggers" that well activate the inner resources that will heal us far more effectively, at a much *lower cost* and *risk* (of side effects), than the ever-more sophisticated machines and allopathic remedies!

    This realization gives us, at the same time, **new hope** and a **new task:** The hope that no human situation and illness is ever "irreversible", totally certain and determined; and the task of looking *in ourselves,* in our own consciousness and being (and its *higher levels*) for the "solution" and "healing" that, before, we were desperately looking for in the *external world,* in doctors and modern medicines! (See the story of my own accident).

2. *The realization that the "mystery of Mysteries the Self, lies in the psyche, in the depths and heights of our own consciousness!*

    For thousands of years, human beings have sought, in all possible and imaginable ways, God, the Self, the "mystery of Mysteries", Ultimate Reality and the Source and Essence of Life, Love, and Wisdom in the *external physical world:* in mountains or caves, in sanctuaries and temples, in churches and cathedrals, and in Saints, Sages, and Seers. This without ever realizing that what they were seeking could be first and effectively found only *in themselves* (this because to contact something in the universe, one must first **vibratorily** "reawaken" it and "reactivate" it within oneself), in the heights and depths of one's own psyche. . . and then in the world and in others! (Indian Legend)

321

The external world with all of its dimensions, beings, and events (the physical, emotional, mental, and spiritual planes; the Angels, the Saints, Sages, and Masters; human beings and animals; as all human experiences without exceptions) are no other than an enormous "magical mirror" of our own nature as they are also an enormous "laboratory" for our own evolution, becoming, and the actualization of all of our faculties and potentialities. The external world, with its varied situations and events, offers us the true "labyrinth" and a way to get to the very *center of our being*, where resides the Self, the Divine Spark, with all of its treasures. When a person has truly properly understood this "perspective", then *all human experience*, without exceptions, manifest a deep *meaning*, *purpose*, and *value*. . . as "triggers" or "catalysts" for the discovery of the Self and the *conscious union* with the Self, the part of God in us!

3. The second "discovery", or "realization" leads directly to the third: that is, *that absolutely everything that occurs in the world, or happens to us, has a meaning, a purpose, and a value. . .* for our own *growth, evolution, and realization. . .* which we *can and must discover!*

Rightly so, Nietzsche stated one day: "So long as man has a "why" he can accept any "how". Viktor Frankl added: "All human situations are acceptable and bearable so long as they have a *concrete and real meaning* for the person who is living it". It is this paradox that can explain to us why people who live in extremely difficult and painful situations did not "crack up" or even die while other persons did "crack" or die in far less difficult and painful situations. For as long as a person can perceive meaning, purpose, and value in what she is living, she can "die physically" but safeguard her own conscience and integrity. And the opposite is equally true: one can very well survive physically while losing one's integrity and control over one's consciousness and being!

The fundamental question and "discovery" is therefore: *how can one unveil the meaning, purpose, and value of all human situations. . .* and on what is based this affirmation and "discovery"? The answer is extremely simple even though its **realization** is far more complex and difficult to obtain. In simple words, it is based on: *the expansion, deepening and heightening of one's own consciousness!*

Every human being can be symbolically represented by a **skyscraper.** Thus, what we "perceive", or "reality", change noticeably as one moves from one to other floors of the skyscraper. What we see from the 1st, the 10th, the 40th, or the

100th floor is absolutely not *the same thing*. Likewise, the *expansion* or *constriction* of human consciousness, symbolically the "moving up or down the sky-scraper", has a direct and unmistakable impact upon the three essential functions of the psyche: *consciousness-knowledge, love-feeling,* and *will-creative energies.* With the expansion and elevation of consciousness come the meaning, purpose, and value of all that which we are living through; while with the contraction and lowering of human consciousness the same meaning, purpose, and value **disappear** leaving us confused, lost, and in prey to anxiety!

Hence, to "find" or "increase" the clarity and force of the meaning, purpose, and value of our personal experiences, one must be able to *change and expand one's level of consciousness,* no other valid method really exists! We have come to make this "discovery" and "realization" at the societal level because scientists and thinkers (culturally and intellectually prepared persons who are recognized as such by society) have succeeded in expanding and raising their level of consciousness!

When this "discovery" and "realization" will be fully accepted and understood, in their multiple theoretical implications and practical applications, then much suffering, frustration, and existential anguish will disappear with their corresponding illnesses. Why? Because then people will understand **why** they are living certain experiences and the beneficial and real value these have for their own growth and for the actualization of their faculties and potentialities.

4. *The discovery that "Death" does not exist because only Life exists, and that what we call "death" is but a passage to another dimension and vibrational frequency.*

Perhaps one of the most profound and emotionally charged question that human beings of all times and cultures have ever asked is simply: *what is there after death?* Still today, we are asking ourselves the same question, but with a different perspective. We are now fully aware that **no one** and no religious, metaphysical, or philosophical tradition can ever **demonstrate,** in a meaningful and convincing way, that *death does not exist!* This answer, in other words, can only come from our own *personal observation and experience. . .* which are a function of our level of consciousness and being!

Yet, it is also true that more and more scientists and persons who are psychologically balanced and intellectually educated have lived, or are living, **direct personal experiences** concerning "Life after death". This concensus and convergence suggest that we are *multidimensional beings who live in a multidimensional universe* and that "birth" and "death" are but *a passage from one frequency to another, from one dimension to another.* Moreover, soon more and more people will be able to *consciously change their level of consciousness* or "frequency", and thus be able to *communicate with the so called "dead"*. By the way, this is what the Christian tradition has always called the "Communion of Saints". (Four theories: materialistic, exoteric, agnostic, and reincarnation with explanation, each one corresponding to a given *function of our level of consciousness and being* and thus to a given *spiritual age*).

What is the reasoning, the evidence, and "lived experiences" upon which rests this fundamental assertion? According to Raymond Moody, there are no **scientific** and **incontrovertible "proofs"** that there is "life after death" or reincarnation. There are only **subjective** "proofs" of a personal experience, which come from *inner visions* or *personal realizations,* but which are very "powerful" and "convincing" for the person who has lived them while obviously remaining essentially **subjective.** At the logical and rational level, there are only *two positions* that are internally complete and coherent, and thus logical and "valid": the *materialistic* theory which claims that we are our body and thus that we come from "nothing" to return to "nothing"!

Then, there is the *spiritual position* which argues that we are our "Soul", our spiritual principle, and that we "come from God to return to God", to an ever-greater Life and Consciousness.

For spiritually awakened persons who have activated their *spiritual consciousness,* the spiritual theory and position are **self-evident** and **obvious**. They are as incontrovertible as are sounds and colors for normal persons. For "normal" persons who function only at the sensory, emotional, and mental levels, and who have not yet awakened their spiritual consciousness, today we have the following evidence and testimony for "Life after death":

a. The teachings of all great religions and metaphysical/ esoteric traditions; oriental and "primitive" ones with **reincarnation** and the Western and Christian one with **resurrection.** Moreover, both of these are "backed-up" or "corroborated" by the personal visions and realizations of its saints, sages, and seers.

b. Near-death experiences (NDE) told by thousands of persons and popularized by Elizabeth Kubler-Ross and Raymond Moody.

c. The "stories" and "memories" of "past lives", spontaneous or provoked, told by ever-more persons of all races, religions, and cultural and intellectual levels.

d. The growing literature and experiences of mediums, sensitives, "channels" who claim to have received messages and information, more or less well documented, from the "other side".

e. Since 1993, we have the experiences and research of Dr. Moody who claims to have discovered in Greece an ancient but well-documented tradition, tested by many persons, to "enter into contact" and "communicate with" the "dead" (The *Oracle of the Dead*). What struck me about Moody contentions is the fact that all the persons who have lived that "contact" and "communication" with the "dead" have had their *lives transformed!* They gave more importance to love and to "relationships" and live their lives with more appreciation and joy than they did before having this kind of experience.

But, the true "mystery of death" and the fundamental "key" which gives us a new perception and comprehension of death has little to do with death itself and much to do with Life, with an "art of living". That is, to be able to live in the present with less fear, anxiety, and insecurity than before, and not to be too "preoccupied" or worried about what will follow our material lives on earth. At the heart of these we have the ability to live with new "values" and "priorities", with more wisdom and joy, being better able to understand *what we have come to do in this world* and to be able to *actually do it!*

5. *To realize that the purpose of life on earth is not to be "happy", to have security, or to be able to gratify our ego. . . but rather to grow, become more than what are, to actualize our faculties and potentialities, to **realize our Self!***

The great majority of people still live unconsciously and hence in an "irresponsible", dependent, and non-productive way with much pain and suffering. The basic reason for this is that these people are still "controlled" and "driven" by their impulses and instincts. At this level, the great law of Life is, simply, to *seek pleasure* and to *avoid pain!* It is what Freud has aptly called the "reality principle". Unfortunately, in our world of fundamental **duality,** joy and sorrow, life and death, and **change,** which involves *risks and insecurities*, are an ineluctable reality which human beings cannot abolish. What they can do, instead, is to learn how to "live with duality" and to "perceive what lies behind them", to grasp their deeper meaning and purpose. For, after all, we have not come in this world to find "paradise" here, happiness, security, love, health, and the satisfaction of the wishes of our ego! Rather, we have come to **grow,** to become more than what we are, to actualize our potentials and realize our true Self, the Divine Spark, which dwells in the depths of our psyche. These two perspectives are, in fact, *quite different* and with consequences that are *opposed*. The first is, essentially, the perspective of the human self or "ego". Therefore, today, it is still the most "normal" one, the one that is most diffused. The second, is the perspective of the Self, of the Divine Spark, which is still very rare in that a minimum of spiritual consciousness is necessary to develop it. But, it is also the only perspective which can truly lead one to the "peace profound", to the "reconciliation of opposites", and to be able to truly accept *all aspects of one's life,* integrating all contradictions, paradoxes, injustices, and vicissitudes of life on earth. When a person finally achieves that perspective, he will realize that in *all human situations and conditions,* without exceptions, *he can always learn something valid and useful, unfold his own character and integrity and thus grow!* Moreover, it is at this point, and perhaps only at this point, that true "life" and "maturity" can begin for a person. . . when that person realizes the true meaning, purpose, and final aim of Life on earth.

6. *The realization that all human beings come in this world to "do something", to fulfill a certain calling and that when they do it, they are happy, while if they do not do it, they remain unhappy.*

This principle follows logically and completes "organically" the preceding one. After one has discovered and lived the larger and more generic meaning of life in the physical world—which is to **grow,** to become more than what we are, even at the risk of suffering and to have to make efforts—Then comes the concrete and specific "discovery" and "experience" that we have all come in this world to do *certain specific things;* and, that it is only when we, consciously or unconsciously, do these things that we can truly be happy. More and more persons, today, are realizing that one of the great "keys" to peace, true security, self-worth, and joy consists not so much in *having things* as in *doing one's duty!*

This fundamental intuition and truth becomes "manifest" in the great paradox and contradiction that some people have a great deal at the financial/material level and are not *happy and fulfilled* while others persons who have very little may be very fulfilled and happy! The same paradox also exists at the level of one's health and vitality: some people, in very difficult and precarious situations, have a "glowing health": and an "enormous vitality" while other persons, in far easier and more privileged situations, have a precarious health and a low vitality! How can one explain this contradiction?

While, obviously, many factors are involved, the single most important variable here is that the first have *discovered and do their duty,* that is, they carry out what they have come to do on this earth, while the second *do not.* You can yourselves "experiment" with this affirmation in a very small but simple way. Take some time to reflect upon, to meditate, and to pray to understand better what is your true "purpose" on earth, what you can come here to do. Then, take a few hours, or maybe a few days, to truly do this in a serious, disinterested, and determined way. Then, give your whole self to doing it, studying the psychological consequences, upon yourself and others, as well as the objective consequences in the world and upon others and how they react to what you are doing. You will be "surprised" at what will happen and how happy, fulfilled, and joyful you will feel, as well as how others will also appreciate what you are doing. Once you will have a "small personal experience" of this principle, then you will be able to generalize it and incorporate it permanently in your character and in your life.

In the new approach to medicine and psychotherapy, there is an ever-growing number of researchers and psychotherapists who are becoming away of the crucial importance, for one's physical, psychological, and spiritual health, of *doing their duty* and of *having good relationships with other persons*— to be able to **create**, to **love**, and to make exchanges! At the cognitive level, therefore, there is a growing consensus that: *knowing one's duty and being able to do it* is one of the great "keys" to preserve and increase one's health, vital energy, creativity, and true happiness!

7. *The discovery that changing our level of consciousness* (that is, our knowledge and way of thinking, our capacity to love and to feel, and our will or way of making decisions) *we can change our being and our lives.*

In the last analysis, this is the most important principle or "discovery" in that it is upon it that, directly or indirectly, are based the other six, just as much at the cognitive level than at the affective and volitional levels. Hence, we can truly say that this is the greatest "realization" and "discovery" of our times. Basically, this assumption implies that it is truly in *changing one's self* (our ways of thinking, feeling, and willing) that *we can change the world!* And, moreover, it shows us the way in which we can become **creator** and **creature**, the "artist" and the "work of art" of our own being and of our own destiny. This also explains and reinforces the perennial teaching of the sacred traditions that "God and Nature have launched us on the great adventure of life", but that it is **we** who must collaborate with them to complete the **Great Work**—to become the complete and realized being we are meant to be!

This "principle" and "realization" also constitute the "last frontier" and the "greatest challenge" for humanity in our times: that of the exploration of the inner psychic and spiritual worlds, of the fullest actualization of our potentialities and development of our faculties. Few people, today, would deny this, but the fundamental question remains: *how can one transform one's consciousness,* how can one travel up and down the "vertical axis of our consciousness" (see the analogy of Man, the sky-scraper). What are the most effective means we can use to achieve a quantitative and qualitative transformation of our consciousness? Obviously, these are many and involve the three basic dimensions of our being (the physical, psychosocial, and psychospiritual part) as well as all the functions of our psyche, willing, thinking, feeling, and imagination in particular.

The fundamental point of this "discovery" and "realization" is not so much an intellectual or philosophical question as one's ability to have a *direct, personal, experience* of this, however small it may be! Today, with the many teachings and techniques pertaining to human and spiritual growth which are made available to more and more persons, it is relatively easy to have such a "personal experience" which can, literally, *change one's life!* All we need is the right motivation, the proper discipline, and much work!

The operational and practical means to reach this *transformation of our level of consciousness* are diverse and multiple, but the most practical and effective traditional means are few. Amongst these we have: Prayer and meditation (which is one of the five dimensions of prayer), true service to others, conscious efforts (at the physical, emotional, mental, and spiritual level) which are properly integrated in a spiritual discipline, and finally altruistic love, which is the essential "spring" and "driving-force" of life and evolution.

Practical aspects

To understand and integrate properly in one's life, so as really and personally benefit from these "new frontiers" and seven great "discoveries" of our times, here are the basic practical steps I can suggest to you:

1. Seek to grasp properly the meaning and implications of these "discoveries": reflect and meditate carefully upon each of them. What do they really mean *for you?* What theoretical implications and practical applications can they have in your life and for your becoming?

2. Find a group of persons with, more or less, the same values and interests you have with whom to discuss these principles and to use some exercises and techniques which are connected with them— with whom to set up a "Work-group".

3. Keep well-informed and up-to-date as to what is happening in the world, particularly in regards to the new "discoveries" and "possibilities" for humanity in the field of medicine, science and knowledge, human relationships, and of spirituality and parapsychology. This means practising **"networking"** (highly recommended by Robert Muller), going to various conferences and symposia, and to read quality journals which deal with the changes and discoveries occurring in the world (e.g. *The Futurist*).

4. Learn to manage properly your time, energies, and opportunities. Discover the great wealth, diversity, and "dance" of Life in your own individual life. Then, ask yourself: "what do I truly want from Life?" "What would I like to achieve before leaving this world"? "Who am I? Where do I come from and where do I going?" "What is my "purpose" and "duty" in this life?" "What do I want to become. . . and what can help me most and hinder me most in becoming what I want to become?"

5. Now take seven pieces of paper. On each sheet write one of the seven great "discoveries" of our time. Then reflect and meditate upon what this "discovery" means to you? What is its true "message" and what can you learn from this "discovery" which will enable you to better understand yourself, the world in which you live, and your life in this world. How can this "discovery" help you to live better—in a more conscious, responsible, productive and joyful way?

6. Continue the preceding meditation asking yourself whether there might be *other* "discoveries" or "realizations" which might be even *more important* for you. Why are they more important for you, and what are their implications and applications for your daily life? Maybe you might make some "discovery" or "realization" which could help both yourself and other. Are you willing to give time, energy, and attention to this enterprise? What is necessary to be successful at that?

7. Now, *change your state of consciousness* (with prayer or another psychospiritual exercise that has already worked for you). Then, in this higher state of consciousness, consider all that you have

done and thought up to now and see what new comprehension or "creations" can come from this.

Bear in mind and repeat to yourself that what life and our era demands of *all of us* is to *become more conscious,* to deepen and heighten our consciousness by energizing our thought-knowledge, love-feeling, and will-creative energies. Now to achieve this it is indispensable to take note and become aware of both **positive** and **negative** conditions and developments. Thus, reviewing mentally the great crisis of our time with its material dimension (economic crisis), human dimension (increase of aggressiveness), and psychospiritual dimension (increase in madness), it is very important to "balance" and "re-equilibrate" the *negative aspects* with the *positive aspects* (the new "frontiers" and great "discoveries" of our times). . . and to personally relate to these "two faces". For it is in this way that you will be able to come into deeper contact with yourself, with all your latent faculties and potentialities. . . and with all the "challenges" that today's world and society bring to us. In conclusion: remember that to each "danger" corresponds an "opportunity", to each "pain" a "joy", and to each "difficulty" a great goal to reach. . . to become more than what you now are!